Books by George Santayana

THE LETTERS OF GEORGE SANTAYANA
THE LIFE OF REASON (One-volume edition)
THE POET'S TESTAMENT: Poems and Two Plays
THE BACKGROUND OF MY LIFE: Vol. I of Persons and Places
THE MIDDLE SPAN: Vol. II of Persons and Places
MY HOST THE WORLD: Vol. III of Persons and Places
DOMINATIONS AND POWERS: Reflections on Liberty, Society and Government
THE IDEA OF CHRIST IN THE GOSPELS, OR GOD IN MAN
REALMS OF BEING
THE REALM OF SPIRIT
THE REALM OF TRUTH
THE PHILOSOPHY OF SANTAYANA: Selections from the Complete Works of George Santayana
OBITER SCRIPTA: Lectures, Essays and Reviews
THE LAST PURITAN: A Memoir in the Form of a Novel
SOME TURNS OF THOUGHT IN MODERN PHILOSOPHY
THE GENTEEL TRADITION AT BAY
THE REALM OF ESSENCE
THE REALM OF MATTER
PLATONISM AND THE SPIRITUAL LIFE
DIALOGUES IN LIMBO
POEMS
SCEPTICISM AND ANIMAL FAITH
EGOTISM IN GERMAN PHILOSOPHY
SOLILOQUIES IN ENGLAND AND LATER SOLILOQUIES
CHARACTER AND OPINION IN THE UNITED STATES
THE SENSE OF BEAUTY
INTERPRETATIONS OF POETRY AND RELIGION
THE HERMIT OF CARMEL AND OTHER POEMS
WINDS OF DOCTRINE
THE LIFE OF REASON: or The Phases of Human Progress
    I. INTRODUCTION AND REASON IN COMMON SENSE
    II. REASON IN SOCIETY
    III. REASON IN RELIGION
    IV. REASON IN ART
    V. REASON IN SCIENCE
LITTLE ESSAYS DRAWN FROM THE WORKS
OF GEORGE SANTAYANA
    BY LOGAN PEARSALL SMITH, with the collaboration of the author

CHARLES SCRIBNER'S SONS

THE
LETTERS
OF
GEORGE SANTAYANA

THE LETTERS
OF GEORGE
SANTAYANA

Edited, WITH AN INTRODUCTION AND COMMENTARY,

BY *Daniel Cory*

CHARLES SCRIBNER'S SONS NEW YORK *1955*

PRINTED IN THE UNITED STATES OF AMERICA
LIBRARY OF CONGRESS CATALOG CARD NUMBER 55-9677

Acknowledgment is made to *The Atlantic Monthly*
where some of these Letters were first published.

Foreword and Acknowledgments

When I undertook the task of assembling the letters of George Santayana, I was a prey to certain misgivings. In the first place, he had lived to the ripe age of eighty-eight, and had been an established writer for over sixty years, so that it was obvious the volume of correspondence to be investigated must be considerable. Secondly, Santayana was such an accomplished artist in so many fields—he was a philosopher, a poet, an essayist, a novelist, and an autobiographer—that I wondered if in the more spontaneous rôle of correspondent he might fall short of the very high standard he had always set himself. I knew that he had never sent anything to his publisher in an untidy condition, but always dressed for a public appearance. Above all, I did not want his friends or critics or general audience to say of him what has unfortunately been said of other distinguished writers: What a pity his letters were ever published!

With the arrival of the first batch of letters, however, most of my anxieties were set at rest. The volume of correspondence might prove formidable, and the business of eliminating merely "polite" or trivial letters a bit tricky; but on the other issues—the depth of observation, the quality of writing and therefore literary reputation—there was no occasion for alarm. Although I was Santayana's closest friend for the last twenty-five years of his life, and have read everything he ever wrote, the investigation of this large collection of letters soon proved a fresh and exciting adventure. They are essential as a revelation of his life and mind, and a further confirmation of his literary power.

It is impossible for me to thank all those who by their kindly cooperation have rendered my task so much more congenial. But in England I would like to thank Sir Edward Bridges, son of the late poet-laureate Robert Bridges, and Mr. J. Middleton Murry, for their promptness in sending me letters with the necessary explanatory notes. And Mr. Michael Sadleir of Constable for procuring the few surviving letters written by Santayana to his friend—the 2nd Earl Russell.

In America I am indebted to the Librarians of the Widener and Houghton Libraries at Harvard, Mr. Metcalfe and Mr. Elkins of the former, and Mr. Jackson and Mr. Bond of the latter, for having aided me in every way in my research work.

I want to thank Mr. Hugh Gray for having sent me (after considerable trouble to himself) the Conrad Slade letters. Professor John W. Yolton of Princeton, and my friend Mr. Corliss Lamont, were both very diligent in supplying me with the essential background for their letters. Another friend, Mr. John Hall Wheelock of Scribner's, has helped me in innumerable little ways. Then my fellow lodger at the Brattle Inn in Cambridge, Professor F. Stuart Crawford, has been very gracious in supplementing my glaring deficiencies in the matter of translations from Greek and Latin quotations.

And last but not least, I would never have completed my task so soon without the unfailing help and devotion of my wife. She has personally typed the majority of letters from both holographs and photostats.

DANIEL CORY

Cambridge
Massachusetts, 1955

Contents

CONTENTS

CONTENTS   xix

CONTENTS

Introduction

THE LETTERS open in the late summer of 1886, when Santayana had graduated from Harvard, visited his father in the old Spanish town of Avila, and then gone to Germany to share the Walker Fellowship with his life-long friend—C. A. Strong. The reader is aware at once of a young man of astonishing intellectual sophistication and refinement of aesthetic feeling, but—from a more worldly angle—Santayana strikes us as being rather innocent. He has been lost for too long in his books: tales of travel and adventure in his boyhood, then the more complicated tales of religion and philosophy at college. The opportunity has arrived, however, to "find himself" in and explore a world somewhat larger and older than Boston and the Harvard Yard. He is a dreamer, but would like to transgress the private frontiers of his dream for at least a season. And a glimpse into the boyhood and youth of Santayana is imperative if we wish to understand the psychological climate of his early letters.

When he was eight years old, his father had brought him from Avila to Boston to rejoin his mother and much older half-sisters and half-brother. (For his Spanish mother had first married an American—George Sturgis—and had promised him that their three children should be educated in Boston). Santayana was a typical little Spanish boy, and no doubt felt very strange in his new surroundings. His inability at first to speak English must have only intensified his loneliness: the other boys might laugh at him in school, and when he walked back to 302 Beacon Street, there was this additional difficulty of getting to know again his own mother. His bewildered young mind turned inwards, and shut out a recalcitrant world of incorrigible people and things. With the exception of his adored sister Susana, who was patiently teaching him his first English sentences (he who was to become such a master of the language!), there was no one to whom he could unbosom his manifold misgivings.

In a few years things got better, however, and although he continued to stay too much at home, he was a bright pupil at the Boston Latin School, composed verses very early in life, and even made quite a reputation declaiming in English. At least one of his school-mates—Edward Bayley—discovered that a dark-eyed young Spanish lad was not after all just another immigrant from Europe, with strange Catholic sympathies, but in this case a rather polite detached foreigner. Once the provincial crust of a New England reticence had been broken, and his foreigness forgotten in the flush of some shared enthusiasm, Santayana's response was whole-hearted and touching.

By the time he entered Harvard he was ready (at least intellectually) to hold his own as a freshman. He could certainly manipulate "ideas" in an astonishing manner, and express them in persuasive language. The truth or falsity of religion were important issues: the absence of beauty in his surroundings deplorable. I suppose he was what the tough-minded young men of my day called a "sissy." If you were primarily interested in "things of the mind" and showed no aptitude for sports, or an interest in "night-life", you ran the risk of such an accusation. Perhaps he was wiser than some of us in not trying to explore too many realms of being in his youth. All in all, he seems to have enjoyed a fairly full four years at Harvard: he contributed articles and poems to the *Monthly,* cartoons to the *Lampoon,* and acted "the leading lady" in some of the Hasty Pudding plays.

The fact remains, however, that Santayana was never overwhelmed by what Dean Inge once called "the current valuations of the worldling". No doubt he would have liked more spending-money as an undergraduate, but he would never have bartered the rewards of a serious student for the more glittering allurements of college life. His plans for the future did not include the possibility of amassing a fortune. Prosperity was not the only ideal to be envisaged in a life of reason. I am not suggesting that Santayana avoided the man of the world, or even the minion of fashion; on the contrary, he seems to have found considerable entertainment

in their company. But what was a "good" for other men was not
necessarily a "good" for him.

Perhaps his occasional digressions from philosophy have led
an old Bostonian lady to inform me that "Santayana was socially
ambitious and traded too much on his Sturgis relations." If we
adopt her hypothesis as a possible key of explanation, it must have
been a feather in Santayana's cap when, in the spring of 1886, he
was first introduced at Harvard to that remarkable Englishman,
the 2nd Earl Russell, and a warm friendship at once sprang up between them. How reassuring to know in Boston that a questionable
young Spanish aesthete was quite acceptable to an established
member of the English aristocracy! But this hypothesis of social
ambition is too easily assumed in certain circles: it was more a
question of counterbalance of interests, of spontaneous sympathy
—of the flame of friendship answering to a kindred flame.

It is in the light of such considerations that we can understand
the intensity of affection and loyalty that Santayana reveals in some
letters for his chosen friends. That is why I have tried to give the
friendly reader a glimpse into his early background. Boston and
Harvard were a severe test, before the turn of the century, for a
young man not born in New England, nor sharing its Puritan
idiosyncrasies nor "cultural" presuppositions. But a ray of Mediterranean sunlight might occasionally melt the icy margins of the
Charles. I still feel he remained to a certain extent "the Child in
the House," even after his graduation from Harvard. But such an
assertion needs to be qualified. The ideal of a fully-rounded adult
is only an essence, like the perfect circle, and never exemplified
in a human creature. All is a matter of degree and approximation.
If I find in Santayana a certain innocence or unworldliness, it was
nevertheless combined with a congenital common sense (call it a
native Spanish shrewdness) that was quite conspicuous. And I think
this collection of letters will bear me out. He was certainly less
one-sided and more reliable than some psychiatrists I have known.
It was only an ingrained tendency to return, after a brief holiday
in the busy public world, to the House within the frontiers of
consciousness, that I wish to emphasise. If Santayana has accused
William James of making "raids on philosophy," rather than feel-

ing at home in the realm of high abstraction, one might say that Santayana made occasional raids on the world of crude experience, or even "high society," in order to be better informed—more entertained in his Ivory Tower. And in his early letters to James one finds a fascinating interplay of conflicting temperaments. James is as irresistible as ever, full of kindly, almost fatherly advice and encouragement, with an eye to the pragmatic consequences of too much dreaming—too much imbibing of mere "culture" abroad. A Walker Fellowship involves certain responsibilities. Santayana is rather recalcitrant, with the stubbornness of a young man who will dream his own dream in his own way, and somehow or other his unworldliness must be accepted in Emerson Hall, or he will give up philosophy as a career.

When he finally did become an instructor at Harvard, Santayana was hardly an unqualified success. And when the question of his reappointment arose in 1893, we find George Herbert Palmer writing to his colleague James in the following vein:

Santayana is a good way from satisfactory. His subtle and beautiful mind has a strange lack of reality. The man is merely an amused observer, without stakes in the world he inhabits. I doubt if he will ever wield an invigorating influence among our students. Yet I should retain him. His damaging peculiarities grow a little less each year. He is a scholar, has lines of his own, and in Esthetics and Scholastic Philosophy we could not replace him. Unless you have a decided opinion to the contrary, Royce and I shall recommend his re-election.

In other words—as Ralph Barton Perry has put it—the Department of Philosophy wondered if it might have "hatched a duckling." But what a duckling! I think Harvard must admit even today that there was only one Santayana. Nowadays there is a host of small fry in philosophy—busy journeymen with their banners (duly embroidered with a Ph. D.) flapping in the very latest wind of doctrine. But where are the broad "lovers of wisdom" of yesteryear? At least James and Royce and Santayana were not nervous about "introducing a noun into the discussion"—as I heard a young Oxonian confess the other day. Perhaps they just assumed that the "introduction of a noun" *usually* indicated the presence of some object—say, a fellow-creature or a chair. They were not solely interested in talking about talk. If Santayana was out of sympathy with his famous colleagues at Harvard, it was not because he felt that they were not struggling with genuine issues: I can hear him reminding me now: "How much we all learned from William James!" But he did feel that the latter had encouraged a certain vulgarisation of traditional philosophical topics; notably, the concept of Truth. And he deemed it no shame to continue to spell the word with a capital T. James was by nature a forward-looking pioneer in the fields of psychology and philosophy; he had some remarkable insights: but it never occurred to him (or he was too impatient) that sometimes our most compelling ideas are more or less echoes from the work of our predecessors. *Leurs écrits,* said Piron, *sont des vols qu'ils nous ont faits d'avance.* But if the reader is inclined to doubt the esteem that Santayana felt for James *as a man,* I can only refer him to the letter written from Paris on December 6, 1905.

That Santayana disliked teaching, that his sympathies were more on the side of the student than in the administrative work of a Department of Philosophy, there is no denying. And yet he did his job so well that this attitude is rather puzzling. As another older Harvard professor—C. I. Lewis—has written:

. . . . I have never understood how one who taught so well and easily and seemed so perfectly oriented to those occasions when I sat before him, and who chatted so engagingly and graciously with a young and novice assistant, could have failed to enjoy teaching and the contacts which go with it. But such was the case. I still feel sure that there was something of satisfaction for him in it—else he would have been a more consummate actor than seems credible. But he found it insufficient.

"Insufficient" is not quite the right word. The business of teaching *interfered* with the free life of a man who remained a student at heart: it was imposed upon Santayana by the necessity of earning a living. There is nothing unusual about such a predicament; but some teachers fall in love with their work and are miserable when they have to retire. Not so with Santayana. Some-

where between the Child in the House and the old Sage in the
Ivory Tower, there is a Professor of Philosophy who hated to
graduate from the Harvard Yard—to be no longer one of a body
of undergraduates living within its sheltered precincts and sharing
its inimitable life. In short, he resented growing older and felt like
an outsider in his rooms at 60 Brattle Street. He had yet to experience that *metanoia*—that "change of heart" he has described so
movingly in his autobiography.

The rest of the story is well-known. He saved his money carefully, retired from Harvard in 1912, and "went home" to Europe.
Then, two years later, the war broke out and he was stranded in
England. I think his letters of this period will show what a profound effect the first great war had on Santayana's whole philosophy, and this fact is not generally recognised. He became convinced
that the possibility of establishing a "life of reason" in any quarter
was extremely remote: no longer do we find him talking about
"ideals," and his writings soon acquired a more sombre hue. When
the war was finally over he settled in Rome, and entered upon the
most satisfactory period of his life. For more than thirty years he
lived in comparative seclusion, composing the *Realms of Being,*
and meditating upon the ultimate themes of a disillusioned spiritual life.

These letters will also serve to dispel some current misconcep-
tions about Santayana. What was his precise position in relation to
the Catholic Church? His letter (August 10, 1939) to Father Hoehn
is the official answer. What did he really think of Mussolini, and
was he in any sense a neo-Fascist? The letter (December 8, 1950)
to Corliss Lamont should settle that issue. Let us hope it is still
possible (even in America) to be a conservative without being
branded a Fascist, or a liberal without being labelled a Communist.
Lastly, is the rumour that Santayana was more or less of a "cold
fish" well-founded? The beautiful and moving letters to Lawrence
Smith Butler (November 13, 1915) and to the Marchesa Origo
(May, 1933) would seem to belie such a notion. His solicitude for
others was not confined to writing sympathetic letters on sad occasions: I could speak of many unostentatious (often anonymous)
acts of charity. But as Hamlet says, "something too much of this."

Any philosopher who strives to see all events "under the form of eternity" is apt to be charged with "indifference"; because absolute impartiality is not a normal point of view for a human creature, but has something of almost divine origin about it.

It was not my intention, however, to guide the reader through this whole museum of letters: I have pointed out a few features in the background before leaving him to roam at leisure in the richly-hung rooms and echoing corridors that house this collection. There is something here for everybody: for the poet, for the metaphysician, for the literary critic, for the historian of culture who is interested in every wind of doctrine. And there is enough gossip to start many a hare of rumour behind the purple-glass windows of Louisburg Square, or in the remaining select circles of the Old World. There are trenchant comments on intellectual giants of the past, on Plato and Shakespeare, on Balzac and Dickens. And outstanding contemporary figures are not disregarded: Whitehead and Russell, Proust and Faulkner, all appear under the searchlight of Santayana's criticism.

Finally, there are in this collection at least a dozen letters of a very high literary order. Our attention is arrested by a *beauty of expression welling from a profundity of observation*. The touchstone of great art is always an inseparable marriage of form and matter. If some of these letters [1] are not considered as among the most remarkable written in the English language, I, for one, shall despair of contemporary canons of appreciation.

DANIEL CORY

Cambridge
Massachusetts, 1955.

---

[1] I will cite five examples: the *Letters* of April 29, 1922 (Lawton); August 17, 1930 (Murry); April 12, 1933 (Pearsall Smith); May, 1933 (Iris Origo); and November 15, 1945 (Merriam).

THE
LETTERS
OF
GEORGE SANTAYANA

To HENRY WARD ABBOT

GÖTTINGEN, AUG 16TH 1886.
P. ADR. FRÄULEIN SCHLOTE.
16 D OBERE KARSPÜLE.

Dear Abbot,

I had some hopes of getting a letter from you while I was yet in Spain, but I do not wonder at all at your not having written, for I know by experience what a bother letter writing often is. I am now comparatively comfortable and quiet, waiting for my land-lady's toothache to allow her to give me German lessons. My trunk and I arrived here without injury some five days ago. We had had rather a hard time on the way from Spain, getting shaken up a good deal and very dirty; but at Paris we managed to get put to rights again, and we started in very good trim for Cologne. I stopped there a day, admiring the cathedral and the yellow-haired barbarians. The women are ugly, but the men before they grow fat are lusty and fine looking after their species. I think, however, that you Americans are all the better for being a mixture of several nationalities, just as the English are in a great measure. These purer races seem to pay for the distinctness of the type which they preserve by missing some of the ordinary attributes of humanity. For example, the Germans as far as I know have no capacity for being bored. Else I think the race would have become extinct long ago through self-torture.

I hope to hear that you remain in Europe for the present. As I have told you I think more than once, it would be a pity, from my point of view, if you should go into business in Boston and make up your mind not to live for anything but what most men live for, namely, their business and their family. Now I have no quarrel with this state of things as far as the world at large is concerned; I don't want the community to spend its time medi-tating on poetry and religion. But there are always a few men whose main interest is to note the aspects of things in an artistic or philosophical way. They are rather useless individuals, but as I happen to belong to the class, I think them much superior to the rest of mankind. Now it seems to me that you ought to belong to the brotherhood theoretical also. Perhaps you would not be willing to go the length I am going, and start out avowedly with no other purpose but that of living in order to observe life. In that case it would not be well for you to study art and insist on Bohemianizing as I suggested to you that you might do. But still, without going to that extreme, why couldn't you keep as near as possible to the theoretical field? Why couldn't you study law? That is what your brother-in-law Stimson [1] has done, and you see how it has not at all interfered with his artistic work. But what I should be sorry to hear is that you are going to let your interest in painting and philosophy drop out gradually, just as a man drops his school friends and his classics. One is glad to come across them afterwards, but it is always a sort of surprise when one does. But the beauty of the thing is to be at home in the world of ideas and to remain subject to the fascination of studying the aspects of things. In one way a lawyer or political man has a better chance of doing this than a professor or artist, because in the case of the latter love of theory often degenerates into marriage. And when a man has the right of property over a thing it sinks for him into the world of practical business reality, while conceptions, whether artistic or philosophical, have no reality except in the world of imagination. So that the artist or professor is apt to be a ridiculous person—a sort of lunatic; for to treat an idea like a thing is like seeing ghosts—the result of mistaking a fact of imagination for a fact of experience. Therefore it may be quite as desirable, even from my point of view, that you should not study art; although if you feel that you can do something in that direction, why on earth don't you try? But it astonishes me that you Bostonians resist so much anything that takes you out of your town, when that is precisely what does you most good. I am wrestling with Herbert Lyman on this point and find it very hard to convince him. But I take for granted that you perceive the necessity of having heard something besides the Unitarian insipidities. Although I have preached you so long a sermon, my real object in beginning to write was to get a letter from you in reply, so as to know what you propose to do and how you are enjoying the season. I myself have spent a moderately agreeable month in Avila, and expect to spend a couple more here struggling against the

1 Frederic Jesup Stimson.

confusion of tongues. Then I go to Berlin, where Strong [1] is already settled. Houghton [2] is here now, rolling in luxury and waxing strong in pessimism. My room is also very comfortable, but the house is a tower of Babel, inhabited by about a dozen females of different nationalities, each more anxious to teach her own language than to learn that of the others.

Write soon and believe me

Very sincerely yours

To WARD THORON

GÖTTINGEN, AUGUST 16TH 1886

Dear Ward

My further sentiments may be expressed in

A PSALM OF TRAVEL

(or what the soul of the young man said to his grandmother)

I like to leave my house and home
And spew my insides in the sea,
With just one trunk on earth to roam,
That is the height of bliss for me;
To roam alone without my trunk—
That is the depth of misery.

I cannot part from what I prize
For all I prize is in my head;
My fancies are the fields and skies
I will not change till I am dead,
Unless indeed I lose my wits
Or (what is much the same thing) wed.

[1] C. A. Strong, with whom Santayana was sharing the Walker Fellowship in Germany. See *Persons and Places,* Vol. 1, Chapter XVI "College Studies," pp. 249–252.

[2] A. B. Houghton, who later became Ambassador to Berlin and London.

That freedom cheats us with a word
Which sets up knaves and murders kings,
We are not free till we have stirred,
So cut your mother's apron strings
And putting money in your purse
Fly off on the express train's wings.

I'll stay at home when I am lame
And coppers give when I have gold,
I'll modest be when known to fame,
I will be chaste when I am old.
Then all the angels will rejoice
To bring a lost sheep to the fold.

This is my only chance to taste
The sweet and bitter fruit of earth,
And in the struggle and the haste
I needn't ask what all is worth.
It isn't wasting very much
To waste the time 'twixt death and birth.

"Lie down as if to pleasant dreams
When you lie down among the dead."
So says a poet: but it seems
That it were better to have said:
As if to pleasant dreams arise
Before the time to dream is fled.

So let us dream of changing skies
Of rushing streams and windy weather:
Though we are bound by fortune's ties
We'll to the outmost stretch the tether,
And be it gay or be it sad,
We'll dream our little dream together.

In the course of which, by the way, an occasional letter from you would be a pleasant incident.

Affectionately yours,

To HENRY WARD ABBOT

AUGUST 27TH 1886
CARE OF FRAU STURM.
WERDER STRASSE 6
DRESDEN

Dear Abbot,

I must thank you at once for your letter. Of course I take an interest in you; what else should I take an interest in except in the doings and thinkings of people who have more or less my own point of view and my own interests, and especially of those among them whom I happen to have met and liked? As you say, we haven't been great friends in college; but that has an easy explanation. At first I had no friends at all, and after a while, when I could have made many acquaintances, I found the damnable wordliness and snobbishness prevalent at Harvard relegated me to a sort of limbo, the sphere of those who, though they might have committed no actual sin, had not been baptized in the only true Church. Of course such a limbo contained a good many souls; and among them I found some very good friends indeed, whom I by no means would change for others. At the same time, if college society were a little more simple and disinterested, I could have made friends not only in limbo, but also in heaven and hell. In hell I did make some friends, because that, of course, is always possible; but in heaven—unless Herbert Lyman be a cherub—I made no friends at all till the very last; for Ward Thoron must be counted among the fallen angels. You mustn't think that I am a sorehead, or that I think any fellows intentionally turned me the cold shoulder, because I had little cash and wasn't in a fashionable set: I know very well that I have a great many tricks that can make people dislike me, and that I lack all the qualities that go to make a popular fellow. I have never had any ambition to be a popular fellow: what I complain of is that a certain artificial state of things at Harvard makes it impossible for a man who is not a popular fellow to have those fellows for his friends who would have been his friends at school, and would be his friends in the world. So that the fact that there has been no "ease of fellowship" as you say, between us at college, is no reason whatever for my not taking an interest in you or for concluding that we really belong to different spheres. Certainly, after reading your letter, I am sure that you are just the man with whom I should like to talk things over. You have, whatever you may say, the contemplative disease; and what is more, you are able to escape the conclusions which people agree to be the proper one's to arrive at, although I fancy you feel a little wicked for doing so. For instance, what you say of your family, although the effort you make to say it perhaps leads you to exagerate, shows that you can open your eyes to look at those truths which it is considered wrong to see. It is wrong to see that right and truth may be subjective, imaginary things, or that one's family may be very much in one's way; yet you are willing to consider these heresies. But although your letter confirms my belief that you ought to go into the idea business rather than into any other, I see that you can't do so now. Of course a man shouldn't quarrel with his bread and butter, nor with his family even if he had his own bread and butter already. But if you go into business to please your mother or your grandfather, it is a great deal better than if you went into business to please yourself; you will in all probability not lose your taste for intellectual things, nor get very much absorbed in your employment. I myself would not hesitate to go into business if circumstances made it necessary for me to do so; nor would I think I was selling my birthright for my mess of potage. For after all our birthright is our love of observing; and a man can study the world in one place as well as in another. If you have an ambition to write novels, you lose nothing by going to an office every morning, where the values of men can be learned as well as the values of cotton and sugar.

So, although I am awfully sorry you can't be within reach of me this winter, I see no reason why you should regret your situation. Of course it is not ideal, since you are not as free as one likes to be—not as free, perhaps, as I am; because my family, having nothing to bribe me with, are very willing that I should follow my inclinations, and even help me as much as they are able. But your mother was not mistaken when she thought me an ungrateful son: I am ungrateful; because the amount of space occupied in my mind by my family and my obligations to them is infinitesimal compared with the amount occupied by my own ambitions. My father, who is very shrewd and cynical, and my mother who is determined and unselfish, and always ready to face fortune, both perceive this, and acquiesce in it. They know perfectly well that I like to be away from home, because I tell them so; but of course they also see that it is good for me. I am not the most comforting and loving of sons—but naturally they can't blame me for existing or being more or less as I am.—But although you are not as free as one likes to be, you probably will have leisure enough to read a little, and a good opportunity of seeing the world. Besides, as some old Roman said, to know well the ways of men, one house is enough. So I shall be expecting your first novel, as well as the news of your engagement to that divine creature which you so generously assign to me. By the way, I do not expect that either you or I can do as much as Stimson, whom I admire very much; but we can help make that atmosphere in which Stimsons bloom, and perhaps even greater men. We can't expect to be geniuses (and I believe Stimson has the quality, in what degree we cannot yet tell) but we can be lovers of the things of which geniuses are masters; we can be, like Norton,[1] maggots in the big man's cheese. And for myself, being a supercilious and Epicurean maggot, I like cheese better than Philistine potatoes.

In a week I leave Göttingen and go to Dresden, to be with Herbert Lyman. We are to have a room together, and I expect to have a delightful time, with the pictures and music, and the German books I expect to read. Herbert is a man whom I think as much of as my theory of human nature allows me to think of anyone. I am looking forward to being with him with real pleasure, but I am afraid he is going home for the winter. I shall be reduced to such men as Strong and Houghton, who to be sure, have a great deal to say that is interesting, but who are not wholly satisfactory. Nevertheless, I hope to pass the winter pleasantly, occupied with some new aspects of the same old questions. I am not insensible to the sincere compliment you pay me by giving me your confidence to the extent you do; but for God's sake, no compliments of any other kind. I don't know how much water there may be in my stream; but I am sure that many a sluggish river has more. I have not had the chance to stagnate: I have been shut in and forced down in one single direction, and much of my force comes from

[1] Professor Charles Eliot Norton.

my limitations. I have as much to admire in you or anyone (for I am not flattering) as you or anyone can have to admire in me. I am a slightly different specimen—more or less curious—a little rare, perhaps, because an imported article. But if you think it worth while to write to me, why, I shall be very glad, very glad indeed, to write to you, and preach your patience out. You may be able to be a little franker with me than with most people, because being an antimoralist in sympathies as well as in theory, I will not think any the worse of you for telling me what is psychologically true of you. . . . It will also be a great pleasure for me to hear through you about other fellows, and when the time comes, about the woman to be deeply and sincerely loved—by you.

Very sincerely yours

To HENRY WARD ABBOT

BERLIN, DEC 12TH 1886.

Dear Abbot,

Thank you very much for your letter and the accompanying copy of the Sentimental Calendar.[1] I have read the stories with great pleasure, and lent the book to Houghton. I think I like "In a Garret" best of all. "Mrs. Knollys" and "the Bells of Avalon" are also very touching. The play is good, but I think Stimson is at his best in the pathetic. His pathos is true—not false, moralizing pathos like Dickens'—but the simple feeling of the pity of it all —of the helplessness and failure of our plans. You notice in "In a Garret" the ultimate lesson of experience and philosophy, namely Fate, or the feeling that the world isn't run in our interest or with any reference to our needs—you notice this, I say, used as a *motif*. It is interesting to see how what made the best old tragedies also makes the best modern stories. I think Stimson has a wonderful faculty of idealizing—of giving the essence of a situation. Take as

1 *The Sentimental Calendar, being twelve funny stories*, by J. S. of Dale. [Frederic Jesup Stimson] C. Scribners Sons, 1886.

an example the description of the old lady's world at the North-West End in "In a Garret" or the friendship of the two fellows in "Two Passions and a Cardinal Virtue." But in Stimson's fantastic writing there is for me something unaccountable and wilful. I don't see the point, for instance, of all the incantations of the necromancer, although the story is interesting. This is probably owing to a defect in me, for I confess aimless fancy doesn't appeal to me in any shape, from "Midsummer Night's Dream" to "Alice in Wonderland". Art, it seems to me, must be more real than nature, or it loses its raison d'être. By more real, I mean more primitive, simple, and clear. A passion, feeling, or character must be presented more according to its inner essence and tendency than it can appear in the world owing to disturbing accidents. A composition which is nothing but a mass of accidents is worse than the truth, uglier than the reality. Why should one take the trouble of producing such a thing? Nature does it all too frequently; but she seldom succeeds in bringing a single seed or tendency to full development without distorting it and crippling it by some foreign influence. That is why she leaves room for art.

I go almost daily to the Museum here where there is a beautiful collection of Greek marbles and also a lot of early German and Italian paintings. I cannot pass from those statues to those pictures without feeling that I am passing from art to caricature. And nothing could be plainer than that the ancients conceived art as simplification—elimination of accidents, and expression of the soul as it would express itself in the most favorable possible environment. The Christians, on the contrary, in the service of religion, express the thwarting of the natural tendency of the soul, the crushing of spontaneous life by the pressure of overwhelming external power. This early Christian art is hideous—poor starved, crooked, cowed creatures, in which the attempt at humanity seems to be about given up. And it is interesting to trace the gradual recovery of the human type in the pictures of the renaissance. I notice the same thing in the streets. Among the Germans there are Mediaeval types and types almost classical. Among the peasants and mechanics one sees frequently the bandy legged, big headed, heavy nosed figures of the early paintings, and among the better class one sees the tall, stolid, robust, καλὸς καὶ Μέγας [handsome and tall] type of the ancients. Of course the fine Germans are coarser and sleepier than the fine Greeks; but the resemblance is noticeable and shows, as it seems to me, how the soul, such as it was or is, succeeds in expressing itself under favorable circumstances. The English aristocracy and the American too, are further examples of the same thing.

Excuse my delivering a treatise after this fashion, but whereof the heart is full the pen writeth. I am of course wrong and anti-Nortonian,[1] but I hate sentimentalism and pre-Raphaelitism with all my soul. It is not true that deformity expresses the spirit—it only expresses the sad plight of the spirit that can't express itself.

I am amused at the fun you poke at me, and at the advice Barrett Wendell gives me. I respect Scott for thinking me an ass, because it shows a certain robust healthiness of judgment. He doubtless sees the good and bad in me with tolerable impartiality, for Scott is a sensible fellow, and usually hits the mark in what he says. I do not pretend that he has much delicacy of judgment, but he is sound, and naturally values soundness above other things. Droppers, however, if I understand him, comes to the same conclusion in an other way. With him it isn't a spontaneous judgment of one man meeting another; he is biased by his crude dogmas and vulgar standards. I submit that his tribunal has no jurisdiction in my case. But every unsophisticated man is competent to judge any other, *as a man;* that your table should think me a poor sort of creature is perfectly natural and perfectly right. As far as I am a student, of course they have nothing to say in the matter. Ward's [2] case is less easily explained. And here let me once for all say that what I write about other people, I am perfectly willing they should see or hear. If not, I shouldn't say it. If they are foolish enough to get mad, it is they who are concerned. What I said about Ward's being a fallen angel was perfectly harmless and true, although perhaps not clear. But the unjust way in which the fellows at college treat Ward is to be regretted. It is owing to the prodigious social intolerance and narrow-mindedness which prevails in those parts; because Ward, if one takes him for what he is, and not for what Boston infallibility decrees every one should pretend to be, is a delightful fellow. He has more virtues, too, than people give him credit for. But Harvard society judges people on a utilitarian standard; on the use they are to Harvard society as swipes or circus riders.

[1] I.e., against the aesthetic preferences of Professor Charles Eliot Norton of Harvard.

[2] Ward Thoron.

I proposed not to bore you with any more of my metaphysics or ethics, but I will say a word by way of conclusion. If you want any more, go to Spinoza and Schopenhauer, where I get mine. I don't think Royce's [1] argument against absolute relativity is a mere quibble. But it is not what he makes it, a proof of the existence of one absolute, either in truth or right conduct. Truly the assertion of anything implies the absolute truth of something—viz. of itself. Likewise when we desire something we imply the absolute value of something—viz. of the thing desired. Further, thinking means the taking of some idea for true, and acting the taking of some aim for choiceworthy. There is then an evident contradiction in saying that you take nothing for true or in acting and saying that you think nothing worth having. Because to take something to be true is but a definition of thinking, and to think something worth having is but a definition of desire (or the tendency to act). But it doesn't follow that what is taken for granted is always the same truth, or the same aim: on the contrary history and memory report that the standards in both cases are variable. Royce's conclusion rests in fact on the idealistic dogma that knowledge of objects is but modification of the subject and therefore that truth cannot be a relation of similarity between the thought and the object, but must be a relation of congruity within a single thought (whatever such a thing may mean). Put this together with the observation that a truth must always be assumed in thinking, and you get his conclusion that a single thought—the same and not the same as mine—is always assumed. All this mystification arises from the impossibility of being a thoroughgoing idealist, because just as all thought implies a truth, and all desire a value, so all consciousness of any kind implies the existence of something not itself outside of itself. If I started as Royce does with the doctrine that there is but one real thought and one real aim, I should of course believe that there was an absolute true and good; but Royce himself would grant that if there were many separate thoughts and aims, there would be just as many separate absolute truths and goods. He too is an enemy of dogmatism, until he formulates his own dogma.

Your sincere friend

[1] Josiah Royce, the leading American philosopher of Idealism. This whole paragraph reveals that even at this early date, 1886, Santayana was condemning the logic of Idealism—the prevailing official philosophy of the time.

To *WILLIAM JAMES*

Dear Prof. James—

I was delighted to get your letter [1] this morning, and hope you will forgive my not having written. The truth is I was ashamed to do so, because I have done those things which I ought not to have done, and I have not done those things which I ought to have done, and there is no science in me. But I have been having a good quiet time, picking up some German, and finding out which way the philosophical wind blows in these parts. On the whole, I think this semester has done me good, although I have not carried out the plan about doing laboratory work. Strong, to whom I have handed your letter, has probably told you that we have taken Prof. Ebbinghaus' psychology and Prof. Paulsen's ethics. These with some public courses I hear go over the ground covered in the philosophical courses at Harvard; and they have served to get my notions in shape and to convince me that it is high time to turn to something less general.

We have been several times to see Prof. Gizycki,[2] who has been very kind and hospitable, lent us books and invited us to tea. We have not yet taken any courses with him, but I like his method and point of view very much, and admire his penetration. Prof. Ebbinghaus has also asked me to dinner (Strong was away) and made it very pleasant for me. He has a very pretty wife and a fat baby one year old, and seems to entertain students a great deal. He asks me to give you his regards, and says that he owes you a letter.

I find it pretty hard to make friends among the Germans, although they are good, simple-hearted people. The Americans are so much more lively that I always find myself going with them. There are a great many here, studying everything and nothing. I have been to some American dinners and kneipes, but otherwise

---

[1] James had written from Harvard and mildly scolded Santayana for not having written and told him about his impressions and work in Germany. In his letter James remarks: "I can imagine no happier phase in an intellectual man's life than to be, at your age, turned loose into Germany to absorb all he can. And I doubt not you'll make the most of it. 'To thine own self be true'."

[2] Georg Gizycki, professor of philosophy at the University of Berlin.

I have poked comfortably at home, reading Goethe, with whom I am in love. I find no difficulty in reading and understanding lectures, but I am helpless when it comes to talk.

We still propose to take up physiology, but I am afraid as far as I am concerned I shall do little in that direction. I do not know how to work. I think, apart from the spelling book and the Greek grammar, I have never studied anything except for pleasure and with enthusiasm; and I find it terribly hard to peg at things that I don't seem to grasp. I recognize that all this is an additional reason for trying to get a feeling for the severe, minute way of handling things, and I shall try to do something in that direction. But my vocation is towards the human, political problems. Even the metaphysical and ethical puzzles appear to me rather as obstacles to be cleared than as truths to be attained. I feel now as if I could pass beyond them into the real world. And as far as the world we live in—I mean the social world—is to be got at by study, it strikes me it is to be found in history and political economy (not counting literature). It is in this direction that I am drawn. Of course, if one could study everything, it would be very nice to understand the physical world too: but isn't it a fact that popular and second hand science, bad as it is, is less treacherous than popular Pol. Econ. and history? I can better afford to be misled about chemistry or physiology than about trade or the Reformation. That is why I am anxious to look into these subjects for myself.

Strong is looking well, and seems to feel up to things once more. He is very reticent about all personal matters, so that I know less about what has been troubling him than you probably do. I am afraid that I am not a sympathetic fellow for him to be with. Houghton is now in this house, and we have very lively discussion on all sorts of things.

I am awfully sorry about your wakefulness. Perhaps your having less to attend to this year is a good thing for it. Loeser [1] writes me that the philosophical club is much less active now, which I suppose means that '87 has few philosophers in it. I look back on our discussions there with great pleasure. Indeed, Cambridge stands in my mind for everything thats cosy and homelike.

With best regards to Mrs. James, I am,

Most sincerely yours

1 Charles A. Loeser, a classmate, and later collector and writer on art.

To HENRY WARD ABBOT

BERLIN, JAN 16TH 1887.

Dear Abbot,

I can hardly tell you how much you amuse me. If you must guard against my influence, why do you answer my letters immediately? Then you talk about yourself as inspecting the universal joke of things from the point of view of the grave, and wondering what is the use of taking life in the unsophisticated and primitive way you attribute to me. At the same time you blame yourself for lack of energy, and give me your paternal blessing, trusting my illusions may not be shaken too rudely. But I should like to know how the path of least resistance has led you to the point of view of the grave, (pun apart) which according to my naive notion of things lies decidedly in the direction of the greatest resistance. What you call the point of view of the grave is what I should call the point of view of the easy chair. From that the universal joke is indeed very funny. But a man in his grave is not only apathetic, but also invulnerable. That is what you forget. Your dead man is not merely amused, he is also brave, and if his having nothing to gain makes him impartial his having nothing to lose makes him free. "Is it worth while after all?" you ask. What a simple-hearted question. Of course it isn't worth while. Do you suppose when God made up his mind to create this world after his own image, he thought it was worth while? I wouldn't make such an imputation on his intelligence. Do you suppose he existed there in his uncaused loneliness because it was worth while? Did Nothing ask God before God existed, whether he thought it would be worth while to try life for a while? or did Nothing have to decide the question? Do you suppose the slow, painful, nasty, bloody process, by which things in this world grow, is worth having for the sake of the perfection of a moment? Did you come into this world because you thought it worth while? No more do you stay in it because you do. The idea of demanding that things should be worth doing is a human impertinence. That things are to be done is settled first: when things are all full grown, it comes into the foolish head of a little insect buzzing about among the flowers, to ask if things were worth having, and he settles the question according to the quantity of honey he finds. That is to say he decides whether it is worth while to live and buzz on the assumption that it is worth while to get honey—and the more convinced he is of the unalterable worth of honey the more forward will he be to proclaim the worthlessness of life. When he stops buzzing and worshiping honey —when he takes the point of view of the grave—he will stop asking for the worth of things.

The point of view of the grave is not to be attained by you or me everytime we happen not to want anything in particular. It is not gained except by renunciation. Pleasure must first cease to attract and pain to repel, and this, you will confess, is no easy matter. But meantime, I beg of you, let us remember that the joke of things is one at our expense. It is very funny, but it is exceedingly unpleasant.

You have decidedly the best of the argument about art, and yet I think I meant something by what I said. Greek statues say so much more to me than any other form of art, and the Greek view of life and nature appeals to me so strongly, that I am unjust to other forms. The hapless word essence—bastard in its birth, overburdened during its life, and dishonoured in its grave—seems to have made my sayings still more objectionable. I will venture on another formula, and say that all art should be characterization, not accumulation. Ancient art characterized natural tendencies, while modern art characterizes situations. But selection and the elimination of what doesn't help the characterization is as necessary in one case as in the other. I offer the humblest apologies for my rashness in regard to Stimson's story—I never looked for the moral! I see now what it means, but the way of expressing it still strikes me as a little wild. As I told you before, I am not a competent critic of the fantastic, being, so to speak, ghost-and-faery-blind.

You say you are a hero-worshiper—I have always felt an unsatisfied longing to be one—but I could find no hero. Tell me what is necessary to bring a man into the category of heroes—of course I don't mean what qualities in him, but what effects on the worshiper. I always have found a great difficulty in feeling the glow of admiration and the glow of loyalty towards the same persons. Admiration comes from qualities, and loyalty from obligations.

What one admires are abstractions and sides of character, but one is loyal to the whole man, as to one who is knit into one's own life. Perhaps I ought to confess that I worship one hero, although as a man out of history he oughtn't to count. I mean Byron. Toward Byron, I do feel a combination of admiration and loyalty; I admire what he is in himself, and I am full of recognition for what he has been to me. For you must know, Byron is my first friend among the poets, and my favorite.

I don't propose to return to the metaphysics of my last letter. Still, I must accept your challenge for a definition of the terms. By absolute I understand that which is self-existent—that which might exist if everything else disappeared. Now, I didn't pretend to say that each man is an absolute being: I conceive that only the universe is an absolute being. But I meant that each man's standard of truth and worth was absolute—i.e. that it could exist without the existence of the other standards. Of course, if the man is not absolute, his standard could not have existed unless the whole world related to the man had existed; and so the standard, *as a psychological fact,* is relative to everything else in the world. But as a standard, it is absolute. We could not have the metric system unless the whole world was what it is: but as a standard the meter is absolute, and does not derive its value from its relation to the yard.

As you say, before claiming to understand and much more to condemn a man, one must know what sense he gives to his words. His definitions are often harder to understand than all the rest of his system—as, e.g. in Spinoza. The book is here the definition of the meaning of the words. As a general thing I find it works pretty well to begin by accepting a man's conclusions, and taking for granted they express the well-known facts, to work back from them to his premises. Thus one can often get at an author's starting point and be better prepared to judge his logic. For instance, you hear a man declare that all men do and must act in the pursuit of pleasure. Accept the conclusion and see to what a definition of pleasure it will lead. You will have to grant that the pursuit may take place before the pleasure has ever been experienced. The pleasure therefore is not an image, not a memory, but a result. You will also have to grant that the pleasure pursued is not always attained. Thus you will arrive at the moderately true description of the facts which consists in saying that men must act in the pursuit of something of which they may have no idea and which they may never attain. Whether this uncertain something is a sensation or an action will be of no consequence. The difference between the hedonists and the naturalists will thus be reduced to an original difference in their observations. If a man believes that men usually know what they are about, he will like the hedonists: if he thinks men usually don't, he will like the naturalists. I like the naturalists.

Hartmann [1] is thought very little of in these parts. He seems to belong to the dreaming rather than to the talking school of philosophers. I have hardly read him; what I have read has seemed to me rather futile. I think the talking philosophers alone are worth hearing: they come to you as one man to another, on the basis of everyday facts and life. That is what makes Aristotle so much the safest and wisest of men. The dreaming philosophers should be read as one reads the confessions of converts and the plaints of lyric poets. It may be very beautiful and very profound, but it has only the interest of autobiography. To find out what may be known about the world common to us all, we must go to those who have thought it worth their while to talk about it.

Strong is back, and says he is all right. It is evident, however, that he is still rather restless and unsatisfied. Tantum religio potuit suadere malorum. By the way, do you ever read Lucretius? If you don't, I should advise you to try him. He fills me with the greatest enthusiasm and delight. The arguments are often childish, but the energy, the flow, the magnificence and solidity are above every-thing. I am now reading St. Augustine's De Civitate Dei, another splendid book. It is historico-lyrical, like the Bible, full of curious knowledge and broad lights thrown on the nature of the forces that made Christianity. It is not technical, except here and there, and so full of soul and divine madness that even the theology is never dull. And then the glory of the Latin, so majestic, so clear, so sonorous! I tell you our modern languages are mean and cramped in comparison.

Have you not seen Herbert Lyman? Tell me something about Ward,[2] not what he says of me.

Your dangerous friend

[1] Ed. v. Hartmann.

[2] Ward Thoron.

To HENRY WARD ABBOT

[The following letter is of interest in showing the flowering of philosophical ideas in the soil of Santayana's mind. But I must warn the reader that it makes rather heavy weather for the uninitiated, and he can hardly be blamed for skipping it.]

BERLIN, FEB. 5TH 1887.

Dear Abbot,

I am afraid I can't save you from solipsism [1] by argument, but I don't regret it much, since it is easy for you to save yourself from it by action. Philosophy, after all, is not the foundation of things, but a late and rather ineffective activity of reflecting men. It is not the business of philosophy to show that things exist. You must bring your bullion to the mint, then reason can put its stamp upon it and make it legal tender. But if you don't bring your material, if you don't give reason your rough and precious experience, you can get nothing from her but counterfeit bills —nostrums and formulas and revelations. Now a man's stock of experience, his inalienable ideas, are given facts. His reason for holding on to them is that he can't get rid of them. Why do we think at all, why do we talk about world, and ideas, and self, and memory, and will, except because we must? You say that you are will, and that your existence as such is given by immediate intuition. That is a rather complicated fact to be foundation of knowledge. If however it is a fact which you cannot doubt, it is a perfectly good foundation. Any fact you cannot doubt is—any inevitable idea is true. Now, if you imagine a being whose stock consists of this intuition of itself as will and of a world as ideas,[2] I think you will be unable to make that being believe in other wills. That being would not rebel against solipsism; anything else would be

---

[1] The doctrine (roughly) that "I alone exist." Santayana has always played with the possibility of Solipsism. See his early poem on it in *The Hermit of Carmel* (1901) p. 87; and his more lengthy treatment of the subject in *Scepticism and Animal Faith.*

[2] The influence of Schopenhauer is apparent here. See *Persons and Places*, Vol. I. Chap. XVI, "College Studies," pp. 248–249.

impossible for it. It happens that we are not such beings; our inevitable ideas are not a self as will and as a reservoir of images. This notion is at best a possible one for us—possible together with innumerable other notions. If you find, however, that you can actually get rid of all other ideas and live merely on this stock, nothing can prevent your trying the experiment. Be a solipsist. Say "My own existence as will and the existence of a world of ideas in my mind—these I cannot doubt. But this is all that I find it necessary to believe. With this faith I can do my business, make love to my sweetheart, write to my friends, and sing in tune with the spheres." If you can do that, what possible objection is there to your solipsism? Surely none coming from a sincere and disinterested philosophy. But *can* you do it? That is the question. I suspect that your business and letter writing, your love and the music of the spheres, would fill your mind with other notions besides those first inevitable ones, and make these other notions no less inevitable. They would increase your inalienable stock of ideas and make your philosophy unsatisfactory, not because it had not accounted for the ideas you brought originally, but because you had more ideas now which it would need a different philosophy to account for. You must keep one thing always in mind if you want to avoid hopeless entanglements: we do not act on the ideas we previously have, but we acquire ideas as the consequence of action and experience. If you habitually treat these visions of other men as if they were your equals, you will *therefore* believe that they have will and intelligence like yourself. Now, your own survival in the world depends on your social relations, so that solipsism is a practically impossible doctrine. It could not flourish except among isolated beings, and man is gregarious.

So much for the practical difficulties of solipsism. Abstractly the theory cannot be disproved—what theory can?—yet I think it is not without its arbitrariness. Not that it is more arbitrary than any other which does not express our normal mental habits; all I mean is that it has no more reasonableness than any other imagined, artificial system. For what do you mean by *self?* What do you mean by existence *in the mind?* So long as you believe in a self-existent world of objects in space, you know what you mean by the objects in the mind. You mean those objects which are not self-existent in space. If, however, you abandon (or think you abandon, for I think the argument proves you have not really done so) the notion of objects self-existent in space, your phrase "objects in the mind" loses its meaning, since there is no longer any contrast between two modes or places of existence, one the mind and the other external space. Objects now do not come into the mind, they merely come into existence. Ideas, if they have no real objects, are real objects themselves. The quality of independence, unaccountableness, imperiousness which belonged to the things now belongs to the ideas. They are yours—they are in you—no more than the objective world was before. This is what makes idealists invent a universal consciousness in which the ideas eternally lie: if this world is to be an idea it has to be an independent, objective one. For see what the alternative is: There shall be only my own personal ideas—but how far do I reach? Did the world begin with the first sensation I had in my mother's womb? Evidently my foetus is an idea in my mind quite as foreign to me as you are. Did the world begin with the first idea I can remember I had? But in that case the world has begun at different points, since sometimes I can remember an event which happened when I was four, but then I could remember what happened when I was three. Or shall the ideas in existance be only those I have at this moment? But this moment is nothing—it is a limit, it contains no ideas at all. Ideas are alive, they grow and change, they are not flashed ready made into the darkness. My ideas are therefore indeterminate in quantity and duration. As impossible as it is to say where one of them stops and another begins, so impossible is it to say where my consciousness becomes different from that of my mother, or wherein it is different from that of other men now. When in a crowd, in a contagion of excitement, we do not think in ourselves only but in other people at the same time. The bodies are separate but the consciousness is not. The result is that I have more ideas than I know; I can't trace them downward to their depth and full content, nor outward to their limits. In what sense, then, are my ideas mine? Only as the left side of a street is to the left; I only can talk of myself because I think of you, of my ideas because I postulate yours. If I existed alone, I should have no self, as the theologians very well saw when to save the personality of God they made him three persons. That is about all I have thought about solipsism. You say, or hint, that you are resigned to being an egotist and egoist but not to be a solipsist. The things are but two sides of the same; it is harder to deny the existance of other men in thinking than in willing, because in thinking we depend so much on words, and books, and education—all social things, while in willing we are more independent, at least we feel more independent, for in reality we are perhaps less so. The more fundamental part of us is where we have more in common, and where influences are more easily exercised. It is more easy to influence than to persuade.

Strong and I propose to go to England about the first of March, so that when you write again you had better address care of Brown, Shipley & Co.[1] It is possible I may stay in England the rest of this year, but I cannot tell until I have seen the place. I naturally have to go with Strong, as our partnership is of mind and pocket;[2] he is rather sick of this place because one is so isolated in it. Bad thing for a would be philosopher to complain of isolation. Poor Strong! he is like a man up to his middle in cold water who hasn't the courage to duck. The cold water is the antitheological stream. Hoping all this is nothing but your idea

I am sincerely your friend

To WILLIAM JAMES

BERLIN, FEB 21ST 1887

Dear Professor James—

I am very much obliged to you for your articles on Habit and on the Perception of Space. I have read them with great interest —all the more because they go over some of the points you brought out in Phil. 2 and 9.[3] I remember how much the idea of the nervous system as a sort of recording angel struck me at that time. It touches one of my pet questions, the sanction of Ethics, the supposed disappearance of which alarms Mr. Lilly[4] and his school. I

1 The London banking-house.

2 Santayana was sharing with Strong the Walker Fellowship.

3 Courses in Philosophy that James was giving at Harvard.

4 William Samuel Lilly.

can't help feeling that if people were more inclined to look for the sanction of morals in the facts, they would stop worrying about the future of morality.

The tone of the philosophers here is good-humoredly positivistic. Christianity and Hegelianism are mildly spoken of, and accounted for as historical movements. Some of the professors are transcendentalists, it is true, but hardly in the interests of theology. Dr. Denssen, for instance, is a thoroughgoing Schopenhauerian while Prof. Paulsen is a Spinosist, with tendencies toward state socialism. Prof. Ebbinghaus calls himself a materialist *im besseren Sinne*. But everybody (with the possible exception of Dr. Denssen, who will not hear of disbelief in the τὸ ὄντως ὀύ [that which really is]) is calm and benevolent, and thinks philosophy was made for man and not man for philosophy.

Strong and I intend to spend the coming vacation in England, where we find we can go very cheaply by way of Hamburg. My address will therefore be care of Brown, Shipley & Co. and anything sent to me for Strong will reach him. He is looking well and says he feels very much better. He has been working two hours a day over Lotze's [1] psychology and hearing lectures with me. He seems to be a little afraid of himself in view of the probability of his getting a chance to teach at Cornell next winter. I tell him he is well prepared enough and should thank his stars that he can begin to learn in a practical way by teaching. Still, considering what good friends we are, Strong tells me astonishingly little about himself, perhaps because he thinks I don't understand how he feels about things, or perhaps because he is naturally reserved. But the fact is I have no idea what has been the matter with him this winter, except that evidently he has not been at ease.

I myself have done very little tangible work, although I have been reading all sorts of things, especially Goethe. I don't think my time has been wholly wasted, as I have gathered a good many impressions besides a working knowledge of German—enough, that is, to read and understand, but not enough to talk connectedly. I ought to have got along much better with the language, but I have really had very little occasion to speak it, and the pronunciation is so abominably hard that I hardly trust myself with more than a syllable at a time. I enjoy hearing it, however, especially in the hearty, honest native way. On the whole I am very glad I came to

---

[1] Hermann Lotze, an influential metaphysician of the time.

Germany, although the superiority of the place from the student's
point of view is not so great as I had imagined. In health, too, I am
feeling well, better a great deal than last year when, as you may remember, I was a little under the weather. In Spain, too, during the
summer my stomach became refractory, but this cooler and moister
climate made everything all right again. For a while I had some
trouble with the complicated cooking here in vogue—but custom
can make one swallow any dish, even if it contains thirty nine articles.

    In England I expect to have a very good time, as I have never
been there for any length of time. In London, too, there are several
members of our—i.e. the Sturgis—family, whom I shall enjoy
meeting. Socially I have had a dull time here, as the Germans are
rather impossible to get at, and when gotten at not very entertaining, while the Americans are often far from pleasant. I have missed
my college friends very much, although they have been very good
in writing to me. In fact, I find myself with a rather formidable
correspondence to carry on, with my family in Spain, and my family in America, and my friends at present scattered in the four
quarters of the globe. The fellows that have just graduated seem
for the most part to be very much exercised on the subject of themselves and their future, as is natural enough. What I enjoy most
here is the Museum, where I go almost daily. The ancient statues
are the most beautiful things I have ever seen.

    Hoping you will find time to write to me again, I am

                              Most sincerely yours

To WARD THORON

OXFORD
APRIL 24TH '87

At last, dear Ward, I take a rhyming quill:
From its cleft point there springs an inky rill
Whose twisted stream, with intersecting flow,

Shall trace the ways my feet and fancies go.
They do not go together, for my feet
Wear the gray flagstones of an Oxford street
And wake the ivy-muffled echoes thrown
From great walls' crumbling honeycomb of stone;
Or press the rich moist fields that sweep between
Long hedgerows budding into joyous green.
But what can Oxford's halls or hedgerows be,
Or outraged lingering sanctities, to me?
Not of another springtime have I need
Nor of this cradle of a still-born creed,
But of bold spirit kindred to the powers
That reared these cloisters and that piled these towers.
Of some wide vision and determined will
With charm to captivate and strength to kill—
The world is wide: it is not flesh and bone
And sun and moon, and thunderbolt alone:
It is imagination swift and high
Creating in a dream its earth and sky.
Why then gape idly at external laws
When we ourselves have faculty to cause?
Build rather on your nature, when you can,
And bid the human spirit rule the man,—
Nay, not the man, but all the world as well,
Till man be god of heaven and of hell.
Come, mad ambition, come, divine conceit,
That bringest nature down at fancy's feet,
Alone creative, capable alone
Of giving mind the sceptre, man the throne,
Build us more pyramids and minsters still
On thine own regal cornerstone: *I will!* [1]

---

[1] If I am not mistaken, this youthful poetical epistle may be taken as a kind of skit on the prevailing German philosophy of the day—especially as exemplified in Schopenhauer's great work, *The World as Will and Idea.*

To WILLIAM JAMES

Dear Prof. James—

It's some time since I got your kind letter, including a card for Mr. Hodgson,[1] and a few days ago I received the second part of your essay on space perception, for which I am very much obliged. Mr. Hodgson has been very kind in asking me to all the meetings of the Aristotelian Society. I have been to three and found them truly interesting, not so much perhaps because the discussions were brilliant as because they gave me such a good chance to observe the state of the English mind. I find that the empiricists are decidedly on the offensive at present, and that the Hegelians are anxious to minimise their claims. Mr. Alexander [2] read a most interesting paper on Hegel's "Rechtsphilosophie" in which he maintained that Hegelianism rightly understood was and intended to be nothing but a description, a method of treating and classifying the facts of experience, and by no means an organon of discovery.

Here in Oxford I have not met many professors or fellows as yet, but I have seen a great many students who are far more intelligent and well-informed than we at Harvard. On coming to England I looked up our friend the young Earl Russell [3] who has been overwhelmingly kind to me; it is through him that I have come to meet all these men. I find them charming, with a gentle seriousness and self-possession I have seen nowhere else. Russell himself is not here but is studying engineering and navigation, and getting a yacht ready for the summer cruise. He is exceedingly clever and versatile, and hardly to be blamed (being an Irish landlord) for being at present disgusted with politics.

Strong who has naturally come in for a share of my gaiety seems nevertheless to be bored here in Oxford, and is going off to

[1] Shadworth Hodgson.

[2] Samuel Alexander, who later became the distinguished philosopher and author of *Space, Time and Deity*.

[3] The elder brother of Bertrand Russell.

Paris to meet his friend McDonnald, taking Cambridge and London on the way. He has been working steadily on Mill's [1] Logic, etc. in preparation for his next year's work. I have no doubt that when he has a definite and inevitable task before him he will find it easy and pleasant; but he seems to lack the faculty of intellectual delight, so that study is hard for him if it has no definite purpose. This is rather an American trait, isn't it? I've often noticed that my friends wanted to have an objective point, in their walks as well as in their work, and I wondered how on that principle they reconciled themselves either with life or philosophy.

I myself have been reading a good deal, but I don't find the lectures here interesting, with a few exceptions. The inferiority to Germany is very marked in this respect. I shall therefore leave Oxford somewhat before the end of the term, and go directly to Avila where I shall have complete seclusion and independence. I hope to put some unfinished papers I have lying about into some sort of order while I am there. Avila is an excellent place for writing, being an impossible one for reading as I carry no books with me.

Hoping all is well at Harvard, I am,

Sincerely yours,

To HENRY WARD ABBOT

OXFORD, MAY 29TH '87

Dear Harry,

. . . I have your note of May 12th and like your new view of absolute truth. But are you sure that this solves the question we were discussing? What you now say is that there are many absolutely (or perfectly) true judgments. Our problem was rather whether the reality is not equally well represented by various conceptions. I incline to the opinion that our intelligence has essentially a relative and partial function in the world and that its ac-

---

[1] John Stuart Mill.

quaintance with things is therefore partial and relative. No
thought we are even potentially capable of would exhaust the reality and take it all up within itself. Our conceptions are of course
part of the reality, but there is an infinite plus. My notion differs
from Spencer's [1] in this, that he makes an unknowable underlying
matter and mind, so that the unknowable lies as it were within the
known to explain it. This seems to me idle and vain. My unintelligible is simply the part of reality with which our intelligence is
not fit to deal, for I believe that our intelligence is not at the centre of things, but only at one point on their circumference. But if
by knowledge be meant any mode of actual palpitating presence,
however different from our own life, then I should maintain (inevitably enough) that all reality was knowable and known. . . . .

Sincerely

To WILLIAM JAMES

BERLIN, DECEMBER 18, 1887

Dear Prof. James—

I have been here since the first of November, going much the
same rounds as last year. I have discovered a Privat docent, Dr.
Simmel,[2] whose lectures interest me very much. I am also taking
Prof. Gizycki's Übungen on Kant's "Practical Reason". He gives
them at his own house on Monday evenings, and I find them interesting and Prof. Gizycki's vigorous Utilitarianism exhilirating. I
am taking some history with Prof. Bresslau,[3] and hearing a pleasant
ornamental course of Prof. Grimm's on the XVIII century.

Being under obligations to do something and not to waste my
time in occasional reading and theorising, I have tried to become

---

[1] Herbert Spencer. Many years later (1923) Santayana delivered the *Herbert
Spencer Lecture* at Oxford entitled "The Unknowable." See *Obiter Scripta,* pp. 162–
188.

[2] Georg Simmel, author of *Philosophie des Geldes.*

[3] Heinrich Bresslau, professor of history at University of Berlin.

methodical. I read with notebook in hand, and have one volume destined to contain the pearls of Ethical and another the nuts of Metaphysical wisdom. If I am expected to send something to Harvard as evidence of work not seen, I will try to bring a paper together out of some of these jottings. I do not do it for my own satisfaction, because as a matter of fact I am far from satisfied with these results of my reading. I want more time and more experience to sift them and show me where my real sympathies carry me. For on one point I am satisfied with my conclusions, and that is that it is our sympathies that must guide our opinions. I believe you interpreted something I wrote to you last year in the sense that I was disgusted with philosophy. There was certainly a change in that time in my attitude toward my studies but hardly a change in the studies themselves. In fact since I have been in Germany I have become optimistic about the prospects of philosophy. If philosophy were the attempt to solve a given problem, I should see reason to be discouraged about its success; but it strikes me that it is rather an attempt to express a half-undiscovered reality, just as art is, and that two different renderings, if they are expressive, far from cancelling each other add to each other's value. The great bane of philosophy is the theological animus which hurries a man toward final and intolerant truths as towards his salvation. Such truths may be necessary to men but philosophy can hardly furnish them. It can only interpret nature, in parts with accuracy, in parts only with a vague symbolism. I confess I do not see why we should be so vehemently curious about the absolute truth, which is not to be made or altered by our discovery of it. But philosophy seems to me to be its own reward, and its justification lies in the delight and dignity of the art itself.

Prof. Gizycki often speaks of you and of Mr. Salter.[1] He is interested to know whether we may soon hope to see your book on the human mind. I hear nothing this year about Harvard affairs. Loeser, who used to keep me well informed, has not written for a long time, and I do not even know where he is. Strong writes me that he is busy and contented, and is expounding Sir W. Hamilton to classes of two and three.[2] There are a great many Harvard men here this winter, Gates, Hildretto (85), Webster the mathemati-

---

[1] W. M. Salter, Mrs. James' brother-in-law.

[2] C. A. Strong was now teaching philosophy at Cornell University.

cian, Carpenter, Beal, Bullard, Watman, Von Klenze of my own class, and some '87 men.

I expect to leave Berlin about the middle of March and go to some smaller University for the summer semester. . . . I hope you will find time to drop me a line and tell me if I am expected to write something as holder of a fellowship. Wishing you and Mrs. James a very happy new year, I am sincerely,

To WILLIAM JAMES

BERLIN, JANUARY 28, 1888

Dear Prof. James—

I am much obliged for your letter,[1] as well as for your article of the perception of time which I received soon after. I understand perfectly what you say about my not profiting as much as I should from the Walker Fellowship. I keep myself tolerably busy, to be sure, but I hardly work with the energy and singlemindedness which one associates with the idea of a man living on a scholarship. And what I shall write will certainly not smack so much of a professorship of philosophy as if it were on the normal jerk of the knee-pan. But then it is very doubtful that I should ever get a professorship of philosophy anyway, and I hardly care to sacrifice my tastes to that bare possibility. I mean to ask for the fellowship for one more year, but of course I shouldn't expect to get it if there is a more thorough student who wants it. I am quite at ease about the duties that my supposed ability imposes on me, and by no means give myself up as a bad job. But you must understand perfectly how uncertain my

---

[1] James had written from Harvard (January 2, 1888) and told Santayana quite frankly what was expected of him if his Walker fellowship was to be renewed: ". . . . I know your ability, and also your way of talking small about yourself. But your ability imposes arduous duties. It seems to me that for a Walker fellow you are not profiting quite as much as you might by the resources of Berlin in the Philosophical line. . . . I can hardly defend your cause in the Committee, if on the whole you do not seem pretty definitely looking on the lines which lead to philosophical professorships. For that is the way in which the Walker fellowship is construed by those who administer it."

future is, and my preparations cannot be very definite until I know what I am to prepare for. Philosophy itself now-a-days is a tolerably broad field.

Simmel is a young man of sallow and ascetic look who lectures on pessimism and on contemporary philosophy in its relation with the natural sciences. He knows his subject like a German, and likes to go into the fine points. I go in to some lectures of Ebbinghaus's but am not taking anything with him regularly this term. Last year I took two courses with him, his psychology and his history of the same. I think him an excellent man, very clear and sound.

I had a short letter from Strong in answer to a very long one of mine, but have no recent news of him. I met his *fiancée* [1] in London last Spring as well as her family. She is very amiable and rather pretty, and it seems to be a very nice thing all round.

Hoping to hear from you again, I am

Very sincerely yours

To WILLIAM JAMES

AVILA, [SPAIN] JULY 3, 1888

Dear Prof. James—

I am glad to know that I have been reappointed to the Walker Fellowship, as that seems to show that I have not yet quite lost my reputation. I have left Germany, however, without any desire to go back there, nor do I think that I should learn or study much if I returned. I had thought of Paris as a possible resting place, but on the whole it seems to offer few advantages to me. I therefore intend to return to America. I have reached the stage where I must work by myself; but I have not enough motive force within me to accomplish anything without encouragement and stimulation from without. And it seems to me that I could employ the fellowship better at Harvard than anywhere else, since there I should have more people to talk with, and an atmosphere less favorable to

---

[1] Elizabeth, the daughter of John D. Rockefeller.

apathy. Then the advantage of a library managed on rational principles is not to be despised. I hope you will write to me soon and
tell me what you think of my plan. If you have any other to suggest
that seems to you better, I hope you will do so. But I dare say you
will agree with me that I could make as good use of my time at Harvard as anywhere. Three terms of Berlin have fully convinced me
that the German school, although it is well to have some acquaintance with it, is not one to which I can attach myself. After the first
impression of novelty and freedom, I have become oppressed by
the scholasticism of the thing and by the absurd pretension to be
scientific. In fact, my whole experience since I left college and
even before, has been a series of disenchantments. First I lost my
faith in the kind of philosophy that Prof. Palmer and Royce [1] are
interested in: and, then, when I came to Germany, I also lost my
faith in psycho-physics, and all the other attempts to discover something momentous. A German professor like Wundt [2] seems to me a
survival of the alchymist. What is the use of patience and inge-
nuity, when the fundamental aim is hopeless and perverse? I might
as well stick to Kant's Critique of the Practical Reason, or take at
once to dogmatic theology. Indeed, the whole thing has sometimes
seemed to me so wrong and futile, that I have suspected that I had
made a mistake in taking up philosophy at all, since all the professors of it seemed to be working along so merrily at problems that
to me appeared essentially vain. But I have remembered that this
very feeling of mine would make as good a ground for a philosophy as any other, if I only had the patience and the audacity to
work it out. This is what I hope to do in some measure next year.
I have already written a good deal, but in a loose and disjointed
manner. All needs rewriting.

I have come here to visit my father, and expect to remain here
until the middle of August, when I shall go to England, and thence
to America. I have been well, seeing a good deal of Berenson [3] and
Carpenter [4] at Berlin, as well as Emperors' funerals, and the rest of
it. Hoping to hear from you, I am

Sincerely yours

[1] George Herbert Palmer and Josiah Royce of the Department of Philosophy
at Harvard.

[2] Wilhelm Wundt.

[3] Bernard Berenson, who later became the famous art critic.

[4] Henry Barret Carpenter.

To WILLIAM JAMES

AVILA, AUGUST 7, 1888

Dear Prof. James—

Many thanks for your letter, and for your expressions of interest. I have not seen anywhere that residents can't hold the Walker Fellowship, but if such be the case or even if it be thought that non-residents have a better claim to it, of course I am quite ready to resign. The doubt you express about my "fulfilling the purposes, etc." was a reason in my mind for returning to Harvard. I fancy that if I were there I should run less danger of being considered an unprofitable servant. Being a foreigner and coming from a rather different intellectual and moral milieu, I have a lighter and less-conscience-stricken way of taking things, which produces the impression of idleness and frivolity in the absence of ocular proof that after all I do as much work as other people. You interpret my disillusions in the matter of philosophy rather too seriously. There is nothing tragic about them. I was drawn to philosophy in the beginning by curiosity and a natural taste for ingenious thinking, and my attachment to philosophy remains as firm as ever, as I said in my previous letters. These things never came to me as a personal problem, as a question of what was necessary for salvation. I was simply interested in seeing what pictures of the world and of human nature men had succeeded in sketching: on better acquaintance I see reason to think that they are conventional and hieroglyphic in the extreme. But the interest in these delineations is no more destroyed for me by not trusting their result or their method than the charm of a play is destroyed if it is not historical. Philosophy does not cease to be a field of human activity and as such to have its significance and worth, and I cannot see why one so inclined by temperament cannot make good use of his time in that study, as in the study of art or comparative religion. Renan has said that no one can be a good historian of religion who has not been a believer and who is not a sceptic: the same may be true of philosophy. I therefore do not think that my present attitude unfits me to study philosophy or to teach it, although I can easily imagine that others may not be of my opinion in this respect. I will therefore not throw up the fellowship on the ground that I have had a moral and mental collapse, a conversion to the devil, as it were, that unfits me, as insanity might, to hold any official position. I have had nothing of the sort. My notions about the possibilities of human thought and knowledge have gradually changed, and I have become convinced that most of our scheme of doctrine is built on false or arbitrary axioms. But this has been no personal crisis, no inner transformation. There have been moments when I have tired of certain authors, or certain problems, and in this mood I may have said something likely to be misunderstood. But the good authors, the sharp and radical thinkers, are still my delight and even my chief amusement, and I can imagine no more congenial task than to talk them over with other students. I have known all along that there was little chance of my being trusted anywhere with a professorship of philosophy; but I have taken this opportunity of study for its own sake and for mine, thinking that I could always live by teaching one thing or another, while I have not enough to live on without work.

This is frankly the way I feel about the matter. If it seems to you that under the circumstances it would be better to give up the fellowship, I am ready to do so. At any rate I intend to return to America, as it is a better country than this to get a living in, and for the present I can live with my mother. I shall probably arrive about Sept 15, when I hope to have the pleasure of seeing you.

Yours ever

To HENRY WARD ABBOT

[The seeds of some of the main themes developed in the *Life of Reason* are to be discovered in this letter.]

26 MILLMONT ST.
ROXBURY. [MASS.]
AUG. 6. 89.

Dear Harry,

. . . . . I must quarrel with your criticism of neo-paganism. In my case it may be true that it is forced (although I do not feel it so myself), I may not be able to free myself entirely from the oppression of a false idealism. But the question is a broad one: my lingering superstitions or yours are personal accidents. I protest against the notion that what is really joyous and lovely in life is for ever vitiated to all men because a fictitious and fanatical system has had great influence in the world. Your position is hardly tenable. You admit, do you not, that paganism is rational and satisfactory for men who have not been Christians? So that for our children, if we brought them up without Christianity, paganism would be natural and rational. That is, paganism is the human and spontaneous attitude of an intelligent and cultivated man in the presence of the universe. So that your consistent pessimism is but the unnatural reaction after an unnatural excitement and strain. The Hebrew religion and its twin offspring, and more than all, the Hebraising sects of Christianity, represent a false moral interpretation of life, a weight of responsibility and a consciousness of importance, which human nature repudiates. The Jews had the incredible conceit of believing they had made a covenant with nature, by which the mastery of the earth and all the good things thereof were secured to them in return for fidelity to a certain social and religious organization. Freed from its religious and irrational nature this covenant might stand for something real. Nature does award her prizes in return for fidelity to certain ethical laws: only these laws are natural: they are variable according to circumstances, and discoverable only by experience and study of history. But a religion, as it develops, loses hold of the natural significance and justification of its first principles. The fiction grows, the truth dwindles. So with the Hebrew idea. From recognition of the conditions of worldly success it waxed into the assertion of an inscrutable inward law with transcendent and imaginary sanctions. The crushing weight of delirious exhaltation is still felt, especially in Protestant communities. Catholicism is rational in its morals: its superstitions are in the field of fancy and emotional speculation: in conduct it has remained rational, granting the reality of the conditions of life believed in. In fact I have never been well able to understand the moral superstition of conscience and duty. Only when reading of or seeing cases of insanity has it become clear to me. X, for instance, has moral delirium, a fearful belief in right and wrong, without external sanctions, and of pathological origin. A touch of this insanity is what pervades society. And will you pretend to assert that life is not worth living if we are not mad? That only superstitious terrors give it value? that actual goods are worthless and fictitious and imaginary goods—in which is no enjoyment, no peace, and no loveliness,—are alone valuable? I confess, that seems to me pure madness. The world may have little in it that is good: granted. But that little is really and inalienably good. Its value cannot be destroyed because of the surrounding evil. But the greatest of all evils is surely that lunacy that convinces us that this little good is not good, and subverts natural standards in favor of unnatural and irrational standards. It is a form of insanity. And you know how the insane tinge sometimes all their experiences with a pathological horror or emptiness. That is just what you would have us do in the name of consistency. It seems to me that even supposing that our illusions are pleasant and consoling (which is not the case with moral illusions, atlhough it may be with purely imaginative and speculative fictions) the lesson of life is to give them up quietly and settle down, a sadder but a wiser man, on the new basis. And believe me, in respect to paganism, the new basis is the best basis. It admits more noble emotion, more justifiable ambition, more universal charity, than the old system. I cannot go on for ever: but I should like to show how we deceive ourselves in thinking that immortality, for instance, really added to our lives any value. An old man's enthusiasms, if he has any, are *naturally* for the world he leaves behind him, not for himself. Cf. Gladstone. F. Harrison may be a fool, but positivism, if truly pagan, seems to me good. But Goethe is the real spokesman of neo-paganism. I follow him.

Yours ever

To NORMAN HAPGOOD

[DECEMBER 16, 1893]

Dear Norman:

My answer must be also without any news of importance and with no other object than to get the pleasant illusion of a little confab with you. Today is my thirtieth birthday and I feel tolerably happy. The past has had its pleasures and the future will not be without its consolations.

As you know I made my peace with nature long ago, and I continue to feel that my vocation is found in the protest of quietness against an agitation which has not made out its rationality. Thought ought to lighten the burden of existence, to keep us from vanities, and square our accounts with the universe. The turgid thought that prevails in our day and generation is itself an unregulated passion, an imposition of the unnecessary, and an aggression against our natural contentment. It becomes clearer to me every day that both in teaching and living our need is simplification, measure and docility to the facts. How can such a spirit fail to lead us in the direction both of truth and of the greatest possible happiness?

To CHARLES W. ELIOT

7 STOUGHTON [1]
JUNE 23 1894

My dear Mr Eliot

I wish to express to you my regret that my whim in going to New London should have led to such unhappy results. I cannot apologise without hypocrisy for my way of carrying on the examinations, even if a more suspicious attitude could have prevented this abuse. But I lament that I should have undertaken an office which evidently demanded another kind of person. I should be sorry to think that this mistake had contributed to bring annoyance to you or disrepute to the college.[2]

Yours very truly

[1] Stoughton Hall, Harvard College.

[2] Apparently Santayana had been reprimanded by President Eliot for his somewhat lax manner of supervising the examinations of the Harvard crew-men, who were no doubt as interested in the impending boat race with Yale as in their scholastic laurels. Santayana went to New London in the capacity of a Proctor.

To GUY MURCHIE

7 STOUGHTON HALL
HARVARD COLLEGE
NOVEMBER 20, 1894

Dear Murchie:

Here is a bad consequence of our talk of the other night. However, being "the only begetter of this ensuing sonnet," you should be presented with the child—yours ever,

> You thought: "The vaporous world on which I gaze
> Why is it beautiful? Why in the dome
> Of silent heaven do the planets roam
> The patient reckoning of the hallowed days?
> Why do the resinous pine woods, the bays
> Grey 'twixt the islets, or the pregnant loam
> With keen sweet voices speak to me of home?
> 'Tis God within them hearkens to my praise."
> To yours he may: to me the frozen sod
> And barren stars are piteous, and no God
> Called to me ever from the sullen sea.
> Yet have I known him, in my soul apart
> Worshiped him long, and found him in your heart—
> What higher heaven should his dwelling be?

To GUY MURCHIE

7 STOUGHTON
DECEMBER 23, 1894

Dear Guy,

I was at the Bancroft's [1] last night and will give you an accurate description of all I saw. In the first place it was a smaller

---

[1] Mr. & Mrs. John Bancroft, He was the son of the celebrated historian.

and more intimate gathering than I had expected, some forty or fifty people, and no supper, so that you had a pleasant feeling that every one had come from a genuine interest in the event. Captain Flack [1] had arrived that morning, and complained of the discomfort of the night journey from New York (or New'york, as he called it.) His English is good but not very fluent. That fact as well as the trying situation may explain his seeming a little dull. I made a foolish attempt to amuse him. 'They say,' said I, 'That in America all men are born free and equal and all women superior to the men'—a joke from last year's Pudding play I think. He looked puzzled and said, 'Do they say *that?*' He is a well built light haired man, of the type that looks very youthful at a distance but rather oldish near to, like Dean Briggs. [2] He is of medium height, with a nice ugly face and altogether a naval appearance.—Here is an incident not without interest. An old lady I was talking to pointed out Miss Bancroft introducing Winslow Clarke [3] to the happy man. 'How pathetic,' she cried, 'the old lover meeting the successful one.' I knew nothing of such an affair but my dear gossip assured me it had been an old quasi-understanding among all the family friends. If it is true, it explains better why Clarke, whose friendship for me has been rather a memory of late, insisted on my going to supper with him and Jim Putnam, [3] as in the old days. We sat up until half past one over chicken sandwiches, devilled eggs, Camembert cheese, and beer, and talked of nothing but their college adventures, without a word about the present marriage— The bride-to-be seemed very happy and gay, and looked better than at the Gray's party. I told her that as I was something of a wanderer too, I hoped to meet her some day in an unexpected corner of the earth, and she was very gracious and friendly in talking about that possibility. Mrs. Bancroft was beaming. Mr. Bancroft was not, but sat in a chair and looked rather unhappy.

You must enjoy yourself and get thoroughly well during these holidays. It is very natural to be somewhat upset in one's senior year. One begins to see the end of college days and the perplexities of the future make one reflect. One discovers the difficulty of fancying any career that shall be wholly satisfying, even in prospect. We

[1] Of the Royal Swedish Navy, fiancé of Miss Pauline Bancroft, their daughter.

[2] Le Baron Russell Briggs, Dean of Harvard.

[3] Winslow Clarke and Jim Putnam were socially prominent Bostonians of that period.

have to begin to love the imperfect for the beautiful things it contains, and that takes discipline. The alternative is to mistake the imperfect for the perfect, which to my mind is a much sadder fate. But I am getting melancholy, which is out of season. I meant to send you a copy of the Apocryphal Gospels for Christmas, but the book had to be bound so that you will not get it until your return, when I hope to see you.

Yours ever

To GUY MURCHIE

NATIONAL LIBERAL CLUB
WHITEHALL PLACE
LONDON S.W.
SEPTEMBER 3, 1895

Dear Guy

I have taken my passage for the eleventh in the "Richmond Hill" which takes thirteen days to get from London to New York. The fare, however, is only ten guineas, and they say the ship is comfortable and empty. I join Russell tomorrow at Woodstock. My address until I sail is 87 Jermyn Street, and I hope if you feel like it you will write me a line to tell me your plans, and how soon you graduate from Coignet University.[1]

I have only a bad reason for writing tonight, which is the sonnet opposite. But you should forgive it, considering that it has (for us) a historical if not an aesthetic interest. Your Chapman [2] is not forgotten, but you must be patient; they are looking one up.

Yours aff'ly

[1] A humorous reference to the Villa of M. Coignet at La Terrace par le Touvet (near Grenoble), where Mr. Murchie was studying French.

[2] The translator of Homer, made famous by Keats' sonnet.

Brévent

O dweller in the valley, lift thine eyes
To where, above the drift of cloud, the stone
Endures in silence, and to God alone
Upturns its furrowed visage, and is wise.
There yet is being, far from all that dies,
And beauty, where no mortal maketh moan,
Where larger spirits swim the liquid zone,
And other spaces stretch to other skies.
Only a little way above the plain
Go snow eternal; round the mountains' knees
Hovers the fury of the wind and rain.
Look up, and teach they noble heart to cease
From endless labour. There is perfect peace
Only a little way above thy pain.

The end of this sounds as if it had been inspired by Mrs. Louise Moulton.[1] But it is written. Let it go.

To GUY MURCHIE

NAUSHON [2]
DECEMBER 1, 1895

Dear Guy

I am all alone here this morning and must write you a word simply because it is so beautiful a place that I want to tell you about it before the enthusiasm of the moment has time to cool. Cam Forbes, Harold Coolidge, Bert Dibblee, and I have come down for a couple of days, and the other three went off this morn-

---

[1] Louise Chandler Moulton, known as the "Duchess of Rutland Square" (South Boston), a genteel poetess, author of *In the Garden of Dreams,* etc.

[2] "On the sandy coasts of Cape Cod I repeatedly visited another young friend, Cameron Forbes, at Naushon, an island in Buzzard's Bay that belonged to his grandfather, Mr. John Forbes . . ." *The Middle Span.*

ing at four o'clock in the launch to shoot duck, leaving me to sleep the sleep of the lazy: the weather is crisp, clear and bracing, the water in all directions sparkling and blue, the woods ankle-deep in dead leaves, the crows caw away, the deer peep now and then from behind the bushes, and the sheep nibble what green grass they can still find among the moss and stubble. Just now a number of very philosophical kine are gazing at me through the windows. It is a lovely island: the harbour, beyond which one sees Woods Hole, is like those landscapes, all little hills and sheets of water, that the old masters like to put behind their Madonnas. I was here once before in winter and discovered how much more beautiful nature is then than in summer, at least to me. There is more variety of colour; all these browns, russets, yellows, and purples are blended in the subtlest and most interesting ways; there is an expression of sincerity, as it were, about the naked landscape that appeals to me immensely. There is more *truth* in this than in the season when everything is masquerading in green. The articulation of the branches is also plainer now, and they are seldom really bare. At the entrance of the avenue to this house there are two elms which may someday grow to be like those we admired, as you may remember, in front of the Lawrences' house at Groton. They are as yet not very big; but I wish I could paint them as they looked yesterday, with their perfectly . . . [rest of letter missing]

To GUY MURCHIE

CAMBRIDGE
MARCH 12, 1896

Dear Guy

The pen was literally in my hand to begin a letter to you when it was stopped by the arrival of your note and the new thoughts it suggested. It is pleasant to know that you are so well, and to know it directly from yourself. How I wish I could ride with you

over those snowy ridges, where I suppose I shouldn't be much hurt
if I was thrown a few times from the saddle. In time I should learn
to stay on, if I had a sufficient incentive. When you come back
(in a month or two *n'est-ce pas?*) we can go away for a day or two
into the country. You would make me very happy if you made up
your mind to come and stay with me here, but I understand that
it may not suit your plans. My visit to you on that Monday night
was *mal à propos,* and I felt it. You hadn't said Briggs [1] was to dine
with you and I had come in hopes of having a good talk. You had
done nothing to put me out, but it seemed necessary to get out
as quickly as possible, as that was the second time that day that I
had found myself stepping in inopportunely between you and
your friends. I am sorry if I betrayed my chagrin—that is what
you must mean by saying that I needn't have gone away without
even saying goodbye. Of course I said goodbye; not very elaborately, to be sure, since you used to dislike leavetakings, but you
may remember that I told you to come to see me again if you remained longer about Boston, and that in any case we should meet
in the other world. Wasn't that saying goodbye with a vengeance?

I continue to hear about your courtship from all sorts of
people. The general feeling is that you would be a lucky man, and
that you are carrying on a determined campaign. Your friends, on
the contrary, don't seem to like the idea, because they want you
to work out your own salvation, and not make a lifelong choice before you know what you will be and what you will want. My own
feelings are mixed. The match presents all the conditions which
you know I desire for you; it seems ideal— Yet I have a lurking
suspicion that your own reasons and deliberate choice are passive
in the matter; that you are being overpowered with encouragement, and that possibly your senses are driving you where your
judgment would not go. And besides I think marriage for you
extremely risky. You have not the gift of being easily happy or of
making others so. You are inconsequential, and the more one loves
you the more one must suffer from such vacillations of your sympathy. And if you married simply from boyish inclination, because
your senses drew you on and your heart was without defense, great
unhappiness might come to you both in the future. It is a revenge
the devil sometimes takes upon the virtuous, that he entraps them
by the force of the very passion they have suppressed and think

---

1 W. M. Briggs, classmate and room-mate of Mr. Murchie at Harvard.

themselves superior to. It is hard for a young man like you to distinguish the charm of a particular woman from that of woman in general, to distinguish affinity from proximity. Russell's misfortunes all sprang from his inexperience in this respect, so that the danger of it is very present to my mind. If you could weather this storm, the very experience would strengthen you and enlighten you for the future; and after a few years of life among men and women you could go to the woman you would be proudest to call your own, and say, "I love you with my whole soul and *my whole mind;* I have chosen you from all the world." That is a man's love, which is a better and safer thing than a boy's, and a kind you could offer, very likely, to this same girl when you came back to her with your character formed and your resolution made. It is the kind of love I should now feel for the woman of my choice, and the kind I feel for you too, dear Guy, who are a great deal more to me than any of my friends could be when I was a young fellow, and could not really know either myself or other men. There is resolution in this sort of love, it is the expression of character and not of chance. And I should wish you to come to it some day: it is worth waiting for. You will forgive this long sermon, and forget it if your mind is already made up. I have written all this because, if it happens to be in the line of your own reflections, it might help you a little towards clearness. If not, it will do no harm since you will pay no attention to it.

Of course you know that I sent a little book in payment of our bet, and that she wrote me a very ingenious note of thanks, in which she pretended to apologize for having deceived me. I hope she is not really sorry for having been so frank with me about you, because I valued that frankness very highly, as a tribute to my friendship for you. I hope you will keep it up, and tell me any important news there may be as soon as possible, so that I may know what to hope for.

I have made a new and amusing friend in the person of Mr. Robert Collier [1] of New York, a graduate of the Jesuit College at Georgetown and a great sport. His father is a sport also, keeps horses and hounds, hunts, is an intimate of Mrs. Ladenburg, and swims in money made by the publication of a series of dime novels and of I don't know what religious paper—My friend is living with his mother at the Empire, and deceives her into think-

---

[1] Son of Robert Collier, founder and owner of *Collier's Weekly.*

ing he is at Harvard College, while he only comes out to Cambridge to see a friend of his and lounge about, until it is time to go to dinner and to the Hollis Street Theatre where one of the troupe is his present flame. This pleasant youth has been at Oxford, knows something of the lighter contemporary literature, and is lavish with invitations. He came originally to ask me for advice about entering Harvard, which he means to do next year, and about the best way of getting into the best clubs. I asked him in turn if he knew the meaning of the word 'swipe'; he said no, and wanted to hear the derivation of it. I told him decency wouldn't allow me to explain that, but I described the thing at length, and when he went away he thanked me for having given him these hints about the social standards of the college.

Another episode: I went to see Mrs. Toy [1] the other day and was taken short, having caught cold from a sharp wind that had just sprung up. I was obliged to leave, saying I wasn't feeling well. But the law of compensation would have it that the next morning I should get a note from the lady, inviting me to come and nurse myself at her house, where she would make me very comfortable. See, even I have a Mr. James to take pity on my infirmities and put me up when I am ill. Of course I declined the offer, but I may actually go to spend a few days there in May, while I move my things from Cambridge to Longwood, where my mother lives. Mrs. Toy is a very good friend of mine: her attentions are of the kind that make one feel a little flattered, a little grateful, and a little annoyed. You know the kind I mean, don't you?—the kind your friends are apt to impose upon you.

I don't know whether this letter fulfills the requirements which Copeland [2] has been telling us a good letter ought to satisfy; it should contain a picture, and an incident, and be written in a style that unites correctness with ease. I am afraid I have forgotten those precepts, in my haste to tell you some of the many things I have had no chance to talk to you about, or at least to talk about enough. In the immediate future I expect to lead a monotonous life and you will not hear from me. But write if you feel inclined, especially if anything is settled about your plans for the future.

Yours ever

[1] Wife of Professor C. H. Toy of Harvard.

[2] Charles Townsend Copeland, Boylston Professor of English at Harvard.

To CONRAD SLADE

26 BANBURY ROAD,
OXFORD
AUGUST 11, '96

Dear Conrad,

It is a long time since I got your good letter and even longer since I read one of yours to Andersen.[1] From them I know that you are getting on well. Walter Cabot not long ago gave me news of you to the same effect. Now that I have come to a place where, having a geographical sense, I am conscious of being much nearer you, I must write and let you know it, as well as that in the course of the winter I expect to make you a long visit. My plans are as follows: Until October 1st I remain here—with the interruption of possible visits to friends—reading in the Bodleian and writing hard. The *"Marriage of Aphrodite"* [2] is nearly finished, and shall be submitted to you in due time. It seems to me less amusing than I had hoped, but not wholly bad, and capable of publication, with some expurgations for the sake of our Alma Mater. At the beginning of October I go, if I am admitted, which is not yet formally done, to King's College Cambridge, for a term, possibly for more. My idea is to go on with my writing, but at the same time to see something of people, and if possible read a little Plato, and see what the aesthetic religious and philosophical atmosphere in England is now-a-days. I should stay at Oxford, except that there is no way of getting into a college here which doesn't involve becoming an undergraduate again, which is impossible with my dignity and weight of years. But at King's they promise to take me in as a sort of honorary fellow—dining with the Dons etc.— and so I may go there. King's is a good college, I have a friend

[1] Andreas Andersen, the artist who sketched Santayana's favourite portrait of himself.

[2] The title of this play was changed to "The Marriage of Venus" and not published until after Santayana's death, in the book of posthumous poems and plays *The Poet's Testament*.

there, Wedd,[1] whom I met in '87, and the place has, you know, the loveliest and grandest chapel in the world, where before long —if it were not heretical and I didn't have a moustache—you might see your good friend in his stall dressed in his surplice! In January, or (if I stay for a second term) in March, I expect to go to Paris, and there I should like nothing better than to live with you, if you can find room for me in or near your quarters, and I could spend my time lolling in your studio and adjuring you to idealize your models. Then I should like to go to Italy and if possible to Greece, returning to Paris, probably, on my way to America. I needn't be back there before September '97, when my courses begin again. But I am never going to live at Harvard again; I am to stay with my mother in Longwood for a year, and if I remain at Harvard after that, I can either stay on in Longwood or take rooms in Boston. The idea of living in Cambridge without friends is intolerable to me, but in Boston I should have the ladies to console me and a more normal life for a man of my age than at the university.

This place is lovely, and I wish I could tell you how much delight I get from wandering about in it and around it. The solitude increases the charm; the place ought to be deserted. The sunlight here does wonders with the towers, especially St. Mary's and Magdalen, the latter one of the most engaging and satisfying towers in the world. I wish I could paint it as it looks at about seven in the afternoon when one walks along the High; the trees on either side frame in the picture, while the level sunlight gilds the eight pinnacles and the beautiful balustrade into the mellowest of golden grays. The stone gets gradually more mossy and rough as the eye follows the lines downward, and more clean white and silvery as it traces them up to the four gilt weather-vanes, that sparkle as they turn together majestically in the sun. That is the jewel of Oxford; but every where there are charming lanes and vistas, monastic seclusions for an amateur religion. I go often to evening prayers at Christ Church, and the more I hear them the more I am impressed with the diplomacy of the prayerbook; the non-committal dignity of it is worthy of a conference of the powers. —And then the country about is full of a quiet charm. If you follow the towpath up the river you come to Witham, if you follow it down to Iffley, both lovely villages, the latter for its

[1] Nathaniel Wedd.

church the former for everything. You never saw such nests of neatness and foliage; flint walls overgrown with ivy, thatched cottages with climbing rosebushes, little children half way between Kate Greenaway and Sir Joshua Reynolds, and inns with very refreshing cider and bitters. And beyond the fields in both directions are low hills, which tempt you to a two-hours healthy walk almost every afternoon.—My luncheon is on the table and my pen is getting used up; but I have written enough to give you an idea of what I am about. I feel very free and happy and while my letter of credit holds out I am going to forget all about being—or rather not being—a professor. Write to me soon and tell me what you are at work on, and everything else about yourself. My permanent address is care of Brown Shipley & Co London—

Yours ever

To GUY MURCHIE

OXFORD, ENGLAND
AUGUST 13, 1896

Dear Guy

I have been waiting a long time before writing to you in hopes of knowing what I was going to do, but everything is yet unsettled, and I write now so that you won't think I am forgetting my promise. Let me give you a little account of my adventures hitherto.

The *Parisian* in which I sailed from Quebec was horribly overcrowded, and there was on board a thing called the Canadian Rifle Team. However, we arrived in Liverpool in eight days, and had seen some interesting bits of the St. Laurence coast, and Belle Isle, which had still a good deal of snow on it. Icebergs were there in plenty, but not large or very impressive. The shore of Ireland was of course a welcome sight, and really pretty, with patches of the liveliest green. We entered the harbour of Londonderry, and then skirted the cliffs they call the Giants' Causeway. There is a strangely delightful and exciting sensation when one sails in a large ship very near the land, especially when it is rocky and pre-

cipitous, as this was, and overhangs your masts. From Liverpool I
went straight to London, where I staid a few days and then went
with Russell to a place in the Hampshire downs, within sight of
the sea, where he has bought a little cottage for his "cousin"—Her
mother was there to give respectability to the party. We staid four
days, which I spent very pleasantly wandering about alone a good
deal—Russell was suffering from a complaint that made walking
impossible, and besides, it was well to leave the cousins together,
as they only see each other once a week—. I walked about alone,
then, or rather among the most prodigious quantity of rabbits,
along charming dells and windy downs, and got my first whiff of
liberty and nature. From Telegraph House, so the little cottage is
called, having been once a signal station, by which messages went
from Portsmouth to London, I went to Windsor where I spent
a week with my friend Howard Sturgis. The house was filled with
people, a most entertaining and bewildering lot of them. There was
a Mrs. ———, daughter of ———, and at times also her husband,
a descendant of the playwright, but he was usually absent, attend-
ing to his stables and kitchen gardens at home. Although of such
literary ancestry these charming people are free from literature
themselves. The husband spends his leisure—when not occupied
as I said just now—in telling stories to make the married women
laugh, and the unmarried ones listen. The wife meantime tells
you with a sigh and a smile how sorry she is for the provincial
millionaire who is about to marry her daughter. These lovers
were also in the house, he a dapper nice little man of thirty nine
with forty thousand pounds a year, she a lazy big society belle
of some two and twenty, without the rudiments of anything but
a colossal selfishness. There turned up at various times for a day
or two, Story (Emma Eames' husband), a young Harcourt (son of
Sir William), various relations of our host, whom I was glad to
meet, and finally many people for single meals, including four
Eton boys, and Tom Motley, father and son, whom you may
have known at Harvard. The Eton boys were very nice, as were
two masters who came another day to luncheon and the School
itself, which I walked to repeatedly. One of these boys, the nicest
perhaps, was Waldorf Astor, who reminded me of my friend
Joe Hunt in his beardless days. I also thought of you, because it
seems to me that you were made to bring up such fine boys as these
in the way they should go. If you only had had a little Anglican

churchiness about you, you would have drifted into the sort of thing very easily. But the clerical element seems necessary—it gives a little touch of the highest propriety with the least possible constraint. The more I see of the Church of England the more I admire it, not, you conceive, philosophically or as a thing possible for myself, but as a masterpiece of social diplomacy, by which everything passes off with a vague dignity, a sense of spiritual elevation is attained, and no harm is done. A real religion, on the other hand, raises the imagination to a higher power, but makes it inapt, and an encumbrance to a man in the business of this world.

From Windsor I came up here, where I have been living very pleasantly and methodically. I read in the Bodleian, which is an ideal place for that, and write a good deal. My rooms are small but comfortable, my food plain but excellent, my landlady efficient but invisible. For the afternoon I have three favorite walks, each I fancy of about seven miles. One is to Sandford and Iffley, one to Marston, and one to Wytham. When it rains I feel less energetic. I wander about the town and drop in for evening prayers at Christ Church. Now the boy choir is broken up for the long vacation only the tenors and basses remain, and the anthem is usually in Latin—that gives the singing a monastic sound, and if I succeed in abstracting my attention from a few details in the foreground —such as the bicyclists and American tourists with their Baedekers for breviaries—I can fancy myself in Oxford as it was meant to be. To complete the impression the choir does not pronounce Latin in the English but in the to me natural continental way. I remember these words, for instance: Non nobis, Domine, non nobis, sed nomini tuo sit gloria; and another day: Beati mortui morientes in Domino. Hearing that, I couldn't help thinking of my friends Sanborn and Warwick Potter who cared for these things too, and who would have been glad, I think, to be here with me to listen.— I should remain in Oxford indefinitely were it not that, being in a University town, everyone says I ought to be in a college. I couldn't, however, join any college here except as an undergraduate, which is beneath my dignity and experience of life. At Cambridge, on the other hand, as you know, the situation is different, and it is not unlikely that I may go to King's for next term—I have been corresponding with Wedd about it, but nothing is yet definitely arranged.

I see few people here, the Dyers sometimes, and while the summer term was still going some Balliol people. Corbin,[1] whom you perhaps remember as a poet-athlete in '92, was there, and introduced me to some dons and undergraduates—no one particularly interesting. I like this seclusion: I seldom even read the papers, so that when I do I am startled at the references to things I know nothing of. What, for instance, has Cleveland[2] been proclaiming about Cuba? Something outrageous, probably. Don't forget, dear Guy, that I know nothing about you either.

Yours aff'ly

To CARLOTTA RUSSELL LOWELL

KING'S COLLEGE
CAMBRIDGE [ENGLAND]
NOV. 11, 1896

Dear Lotta

Many thanks for both your notes. When I got the first I never expected a second, as it is the part of prudence to thank an author for his book[3] before reading it, so as to avoid the necessity of lying about it afterwards. That you should have written both before and after is very gratifying, as it seems to mean that you liked the book better than you expected, and at any rate well enough to say something nice about it when this was no longer necessary. I am delighted that you found most of the book intelligible and interesting, and that you agreed with most of it. That is all I can now say for it myself, as there are already several things I should like to see put otherwise in it.

My life here is very pleasant and interesting, and perhaps a little luxurious. I try to chasten myself, however, with some tough Greek—the Parmenides and Philebus of Plato, which I am reading

---

[1] John Corbin, the writer and dramatic critic.

[2] Grover Cleveland, then President of the United States.

[3] *The Sense of Beauty.*

carefully—and with long walks among the clouds, which in this country come down to the surface of the land and especially of the water. The afternoons are very lovely, and the river with its many boats, blazers, bicycles, and coaches on horseback is a gay and pretty sight. My friends at King's have the flavour of their Port, sweet, mellow, and with lots of body, and it will be hard not to get so fond of them as to miss them when I go. My plan is now to go to Paris for Christmas, when we have five weeks' holiday, and return here for the Lent term, after which will come a little trip to Italy and in August, probably, America again.

Haven't the Russells [1] turned up? I should have been glad to have you meet, they are such nice people. He is mathematical and she humanitarian, but both are human at the same time.

You may tell Bob Barlow that my idea of writing about morals is not abandoned and that in fact some paragraphs are already set down, but it will take a long time yet to work out the scheme properly. It is a soberer subject than the "Sense of Beauty" and has to be constructed as solidly and compactly as possible, which means hard work. I also await the criticism of the learned on my first flourish, in case they should contain useful hints. Remember me to Aunt Sarah and your mother and believe me

Always sincerely yours

To SUSANA STURGIS DE SASTRE

[All of the letters in this collection addressed to "Susie" are to Santayana's half-sister, Susan Sturgis, who married Celedonio Sastre of Avila, Spain]

KING'S COLLEGE
[CAMBRIDGE, ENGLAND]
JAN. 14. 1897

Dear Susie,

Your good letter and the calendar find me this morning with nothing to do, and I am going to take the opportunity of writing

---

[1] Bertrand Russell and his first wife—the sister of Logan Pearsall Smith.

you a long letter and giving you an account of myself up to date. Let me say first, however, that I am very, very sorry about Celedonio's eyes, both for his sake and yours. Even if in the end the operation is successful, as no doubt it will be, there is the long anxiety, discomfort and expense to think of, and I see that the affair will involve a great deal of care and sorrow to the whole family. As to Eduardo's [1] smallpox, that would alarm me more if I didn't know from experience how lightly such a thing is thought of in Spain. I infer that no one else in the family has caught it, and that he himself is quite well again.

My life here is as quiet as possible without any excitements or notable variations. The people are much to my mind, being refined, simple and serious, but theirs is a slow fire and it takes a long time to get warm at it. Sometimes it seems as if the time for going away would come before I had really got into the ways of the place. I have made several valuable acquaintances, especially that of a man named Dickinson,[2] a tutor at King's, who is the type of everything I like and respect in the way of intelligence and feeling. I walk with him sometimes, and also with other young men, and we ask one another to lunch and breakfast, as is the custom in these parts. Dinner, as you know, is in Hall, and we go afterwards to a smoking room, where the papers are, to have coffee and perhaps a game of whist or chess; not that I play myself, as I prefer to do nothing when there is nothing to do. Perhaps what I shall carry away from this prolonged visit to England more than anything else will be a love for the fields and the country air; it was one of the dreadful lacks in our education that we had nothing of that, and I feel it now as a permanent incapacity and disadvantage; the last six weeks of Paris and London have made me feel the change, for already, I miss the country, and feel the oppression of pavements and walls, and the need of space and silence. Oxford last summer was a paradise in that respect, and I shall never forget my long solitary walks about that lovely region. The river here in the boating season is also beautiful, with its willows and broad fields, and the crowds of students in their bright blazers, and in every sort of athletic costume, moving about on the water and the banks. It is a very simple, youthful life every-

1 Son of Celedonio Sastre by a former marriage.

2 Lowes Dickinson.

one leads here, and Harvard in comparison seems constrained and corrupt. It is also more interesting, I must confess, and this Cambridge to say the truth is very dull. I should have stayed at Oxford if it had been possible to enter any college there except as an undergraduate (which I could not have become again with dignity at this late day.) Here they are beginning to admit graduates to advanced standing (I eat and live with the Dons, and am not subject to ordinary regulations) and therefore I had to come here or remain at Oxford unattached to the University, which would not have served my purpose. However, you must not think I am not satisfied with my experiment, I am: only more exciting and interesting surroundings could be imagined than these.

For the holidays I went to Paris and stayed most of the time (four weeks) with Guy Lowell and Joe Hunt. You may remember Guy Lowell as the man I went to Spain with some years ago; he is a son of the late Mr. Edward Lowell, whom I believe you knew. Joe Hunt is a son of the architect (now also dead). Both are studying architecture, and live in an apartment near the Panthéon. Above them are seven other American students, and all dine together in a very jolly way. They made me a temporary member of the concern (I paid for my share of the food, but was Guy Lowell's guest as to lodging.) It was very interesting to hear so much about the technique of architecture; you remember how you, being once interested in it for a feminine reason,[1] passed the taste on to me who have retained it ever since. I also learned a great deal about the ways of the Quartier Latin, went much to the theatre, and learned to know and love Paris as I had never done before. But after all what I valued most in that very pleasant month was seeing so many old friends—their names would mean little to you, but they were young men I had had about me at Harvard at various times, and grown more or less fond of—and especially Bob Potter and his wife. This is the eldest of the three brothers of whom you have heard me speak, of whom the second, Warwick,[2] died to the great sorrow of so many of us. It was delightful to me to see him again and find our old sympathies quite spontaneously revived. His wife, too, far from being a barrier between us, is the essence of sympathy, intelligence, and devotion.

[1] In her early days in Boston, Susan Sturgis was interested in a young architect named John Putnam. See Letter (May 18, 1936) to Mrs. Richards.

[2] The "W.P." to whom Santayana wrote two sonnets.

I am even on affectionate terms with the baby, the new Warwick; and altogether we have got on so well that it is arranged we shall go to Italy en famille in April. Mrs. Potter is to remain in Florence with the child and nurse, while Bob and I go on to Rome, stopping on the way at the more important places. We shall then return to Florence and Venice, and I expect to remain in Italy for some time after the Potters return to Paris, which will be about June 1st. I can't tell yet whether I can arrange to go to Avila. We can discuss that later. The idea of Greece is definitely abandoned: I have neither time, money, nor energy for it, especially as Loeser,[1] the person with whom I should have gone, has also given up the project. And to travel alone to a new country where I don't know the language or any of the inhabitants, even if that country is Greece, is now-a-days a prospect that does not tempt me. That is one reason why the idea of travelling with the Potters makes me so happy. I was going to Italy anyhow, but the possibility of being often alone in hotels or lodging-houses, without my books or a companionable fire, and with no one to discuss things with, seemed a little cheerless. I should have had to pick up travelling companions on the way, but that, you know, is a thing more easily done when one is not yet thirty three, and is less particular about other people and more amiable in oneself. I still expect to stay at Florence with Loeser, and at Fiesole (close by) with Berenson,[2] both art critics and old acquaintances of mine. Doubtless many other people will turn up, among them Boylston and Elsie Beal who will be on their way back from Egypt and Greece.—In Paris I saw Susie Minturn and her daughter Gertrude, at the house of her other daughter Edith Stokes, whose husband is studying architecture at the Beaux-Arts.

I came back to London to do a very singular thing—to give evidence in a *cause célèbre*. My unfortunate friend Russell [3] has been pursued by his wife with two great lawsuits already, which she has lost, of course, as well as her reputation. But exasperated by this, Lady Scott, the mother-in-law, got up a most abominable libel on her daughter's husband, had it printed in a disreputable hole, and circulated it anonymously in all the clubs and other places

---

[1] Charles Loeser.

[2] Bernard Berenson.

[3] The 2nd Earl Russell, elder brother of Bertrand Russell.

where Russell could have friends. He had no choice but to have her arrested, as well as her accomplices, and as the publication of the libel was proved against them beyond doubt, they took the impudent course of asserting that all it contained was true. Then it became necessary to disprove the various stories the libel contained, and as one of them was put at a time—June 1887—when I was with Russell at Winchester, my evidence as to what there occurred became useful. There were many complications in the case—as the death of one of the prisoners—and at last, after all had been done that was possible to ruin Russell's reputation—Lady Scott and her people threw up their case, and pleaded guilty. They were sentenced to eight months imprisonment, a year being the maximum the law allows in such a case. The matter thus ends, but it has been a most scandalous and disgusting affair, and even with the certainty of ultimate success, Russell and his friends have had to go through dreadful moments. It is not pleasant to hear one of one's best friends accused in public with the utmost art and deliberation, of all that is most shocking and dishonourable, and not to know how many people all over the world will hear only that accusation—never the disproof of it—and believe it. But the judge did his best to put things right in the end, and to vindicate Russell, who has shown a most admirable courage and patience through it all. But I shouldn't wonder if when Lady Scott comes out of prison she didn't do something even more desperate. His house was burned to the ground not long ago, and there was for a moment some fear it might have been done at her instigation. That however seems not to have been the case, but anything of the sort, even an attempt on Russell's life, would not be surprising from such wicked and vindictive women. I never heard of such characters in life or in fiction.

I will send you a French book or two at once: not that I am a particularly good person to get novels, as I don't read them myself, and seldom remember the names of those I promise to read on my friend's recommendation.

Love to all, and a happy new year from your affectionate brother

To GUY MURCHIE

KING'S COLLEGE [1]
CAMBRIDGE, ENGLAND
[1897]

Dear Guy

Your letter deserves an immediate answer, but can hardly have an adequate one, as I should have to cover a whole year of history and several of plans if I was to attempt to make up for such a long silence. You know already what I have been doing, although it is not true that I have been in Greece or Spain, but only in Italy for the months of May and April. The rest of the time I have spent here, with the avowed object of reading Plato, which I have done more in earnest, perhaps, than I myself expected. If you look at the elective pamphlet for next year you will see that I am offering a course [2] mainly in him. My teacher has been Dr. Henry Jackson of Trinity, a splendid old man, who knows the text of Plato better, perhaps, than he knows Plato's mind, but who is a very inspiring and jolly guide to one's own reading. I have heard him lecture twice a week, and he has been good enough to give me an hour besides to myself, and I have read with him several of the hardest and most crucial of the dialogues. Besides this I have seen some, not many, people, and written some, not good, verses. My pedestrian companion has been usually Morgan, who is at Trinity—Frederic Morgan, you know,—sometimes Wedd (whom you may remember) and the highly sympathetic and melancholy Dickinson of King's. The undergraduates here have little other charm than the great one of youth and innocence— There is a quietness and solidity about them that will make their Harvard cousins seem rather loud and rather cheap when I get back to them, but the great civic and manly virtue that prevails here gives people a sort of neutrality and dullness which will make me leave them without much regret. The place has not succeeded in making me love it—not that it has tried

---

[1] For further light on Santayana's life at King's College see Chapter II of *My Host the World.*

[2] In the Department of Philosophy at Harvard.

—as Oxford did long ago, with a passion that increases with every view of her sacred and profane charms. I was there for a week in March and for four weeks in June, often amused by the people I met and always very happy when alone. In spite of the deep differences between you and me, here is something we have in common —the greater facility of being happy alone. Is it because we don't care enough for our fellows or because we care for them too much? I know what most people would say, at least in respect to me, but I will give a much truer answer to the question, namely, that we are happier alone because our love of people is too great for their deserts and too little for our satisfaction. Nature deceives with more art, and never fetters the imagination so much as to bring about a disillusion afterwards. And then all her changes are due to our own inconstancy alone—which is the best sort of change— whereas people grow old and wicked as a matter of objective fact. These reflections, however, are parenthetical, and what I really meant to say was that at Oxford I saw George Griswold and F. Huidescoper and many of their friends, and in another direction the Delphic Dyer [1] and his robust family, now increased by the addition of one daughter, consequent upon a fat inheritance from a father-in-law. So immediately do well regulated households illustrate the laws of Malthus.

I am now at work on an exposition and defence of Plato's bad treatment of poets, whom, as you may know, he banished from his republic as trivial and demoralizing persons. There were solid reasons for that judgment even then—what would he have said of an age that believes in the moral dignity of a Wagner and a Browning? At the same time—and the vulgar logician might see an inconsistency here—I am giving the finishing touches to my own Lucifer— now a prodigious tragedy in five fat acts, with melodramatic situations and lyrical episodes all designed to effect the purgation of souls by pity of the author and dread of having to peruse his complete works. That, as Aristotle says, is the true function of tragedy.

I wish you all joy in your summer solitudes. When you return to Cambridge you may find me wandering homelessly about the streets and the Colonial Club, where I daresay you also now dine. In that case we shall have many a chance of exchanging our impressions of the past two years. I am not to have a room in Cambridge, but to live in Longwood with my mother. There are several reasons

---

[1] Louis Dyer.

for this: that three days in the week will thus be quite clear of interruptions and temptations; that it will be an economy; that it will mark more clearly the merely temporary status which I have, while they don't make up their minds about promoting me; and that it will make it easier for me than it was last year to give up Harvard altogether, if such is the final issue of things. I have had two Harvard lives already; this, if it lasts or not, must be a wholly different one. If they make me an assistant professor and I decide to stay indefinitely it will be time to look for a domicile, for I believe on the whole it would be better to live in Cambridge and do one's share in maintaining or establishing the academic traditions of the place. I sail on September 2nd in the "Sallia" for Boston, and hope soon after my arrival to have the pleasure of seeing you. But I should prefer that it might be here, where there is space and quiet, and the most exquisite verdure—if you could only turn up for a paddle in the river or a cup of tea in this room, which being Wedd's, overlooks the Backs, I should quite feel what I half feel already, that I am in a kind of dream.

Yours ever

To HUGO MÜNSTERBERG

75 MONMOUTH ST.
BROOKLINE [MASS.]
SEPT. 16 '97

Dear Professor Münsterberg

Your charming little volume had by some oversight not been sent on to me, and I found it here only the other day on my arrival. I didn't know you also yielded sometimes to poetical temptation, and I have read your poems through with great delight. It seems to me—although I fear my judgement of German verse isn't worth much—that they breathe the spirit of the lovable and inspired Germany of pre-Prussian days, and are truly ideal. What you have to say about America also hits me, especially that description of Yankee freedom—freedom to walk on the track! But you are too favourable to the ladies; they are so shrill. Thank you very much for sending me the book.

I am not living in Cambridge this year, but here at my mother's. Nevertheless I hope to have frequent opportunities of seeing you and Mrs. Münsterberg. It is a great satisfaction to everyone in these parts that you have decided to remain for good.

Yours very truly

To SUSANA STURGIS DE SASTRE

LONGWOOD [MASS.]
OCTOBER 18. 1897

Dear Susie,

It occurs to me that you will be interested in hearing something about Edgar Scott, Maisie's *fiancé*. He is a Philadelphian, very rich, and twenty seven or twenty eight years old. Although his health is in some respects not good he is a big and robust man, or at least was when I saw him some years ago. He was in the class of '93 at Harvard, but did not graduate, as the climate of Cambridge was not good for his weak lungs—this was the explanation I heard at the time from Warwick Potter, who was a good and ever-faithful friend of his. The gossips have given out others, but they may be regarded as false. He then went to Florida, and a year or two later bought a big steam yacht, the "Sagamore" in which he went around the world. It was on board this boat that Warwick died of cholera in October 1893.[1] Edgar Scott and Bob Potter came back to America with the body, and Maisie, I remember, came along from Philadelphia to New York to the funeral. As Warwick was no special friend of hers, it was clear that her interest in Edgar Scott and his experiences was what brought her there at that time.

[1] See *The Middle Span*, Chap. V, "Younger Harvard Friends."

I don't know what he has been doing since, but the present administration has appointed him second secretary of the American embassy in Paris, where he now is. He is coming back in December, if he can get leave of absence so soon, if not in February, when the wedding will take place, and they will go back to Paris immediately. The advantages of this match from a worldly point of view are great, and there seems to be an old affection also in the matter. The drawbacks are that Edgar Scott has not, it is thought, a good constitution, but has suffered some say from the lungs some from Bright's disease—just Uncle Robert's and Aunt Susie's maladies—and that there is drunkenness in his family, and a certain amount of wild oats in his own past. But the family seem to be pleased, and from what old Mrs. Potter and Austin her son tell me of Edgar Scott, I have no doubt that he is as worthy of a good girl's affection, and as capable of making her happy, as nine-tenths of our gilded youth.

I find things here quite as usual and everybody well. Living at home has great advantages, insuring quiet and freedom from interruptions for my reading and writing. At the same time, when I go to Cambridge, which is nearly every day, I have a chance to see a lot of different people and to propound philosophy *ex cathedra*. As to serious discussion of anything really interesting, that is impossible in this country, as there is here no cultivated public, only a few individuals with pronounced personalities, like Professors Norton and James, who don't lend themselves to easy conversation. I have to wait for my next visit to Europe, which I hope may be next summer, when I may come also to see you. People have been asking me about as usual, and I have been in Cotuit with the Codman's, at Beverley with Boylston and Elsie Beal, at Nahant with Robert and Ellen, whose children are nice, and go next Sunday to Manchester to the John Sturgises, where two of their English cousins, Marjorie Sturgis (Harry's eldest daughter) and Mildred Seymour are staying. Grafton and Howard Cushing will also be there, so we shall have a very distinguished house-party.

Cam Forbes, whom you may remember at Avila, has just lost his father—a loss more than usually painful in his case as there was the greatest sympathy and intimacy between father and son. He is coaching the football team this year and I see him often in Cambridge.—Julia Robbins is here, but very poor and very unhappy. Thinking of escaping again to Europe and, I suspect, of

marrying some foreigner and joining the Catholic Church at last.
How things come round in this world!—Give my love to Celedonio and the family

Your ever aff^{te} brother

To WILLIAM JAMES

60 BRATTLE STREET
[CAMBRIDGE, MASS.]
EASTER, 1900

Dear James

Palmer [1] has just sent me your delightful letter by which I see
with joy that you are full of life again in this season of resurrection.
May the revival be perennial for you and full of fruits! You must
have thought me very unfeeling not to write and make personal inquiries during all these months; it has not been for lack of concern
but merely from perplexity in finding the right moment and the
right words, as well as from the knowledge of how little my platonic sympathies would count in the midst of the affection of your
many friends. But I am as glad as any of them can be at the change
for the better, and full of confidence that you underestimate the
amount of energy that you will find again in yourself ere long.

I see that you have discovered me in the *Poetry & Religion* [2]
more than in my verses or the *Sense of Beauty,* although I fancy
there is no less of me in those other books. But there is more to
come, and although I daresay you won't like the *Life of Reason*
much better than you like my attitude hitherto, I think you will
find that, apart from temperament, I am nearer to you than you
now believe. What you say, for instance, about the value of the
good lying in its *existence,* and about the continuity of the world
of values with that of fact, is not different from what I should ad-

1 Professor George Herbert Palmer.

2 *Interpretations of Poetry and Religion.* (1900)

mit. Ideals would be irrelevant if they were not natural entelechies, if they were not called for by something that exists and if consequently their realization would not be a present and actual good. And the point in insisting that all the eggs at breakfast are rotten is nothing at all except the consequent possibility and endeavour to find good eggs for the morrow. The only thing I object to and absolutely abhor is the assertion that all the eggs indiscriminately are good because the hen has laid them.

You tax me several times with impertinence and superior airs. I wonder if you realize the years of suppressed irritation which I have past in the midst of an unintelligible sanctimonious and often disingenuous Protestantism, which is throughly alien and repulsive to me, and the need I have of joining hands with something far away from it and far above it. My Catholic sympathies didn't justify me in speaking out because I felt them to be merely sympathies and not to have a rational and human backing: but the study of Plato and Aristotle has given me confidence and, backed by such an authority as they and all who have accepted them represent, I have the right to be sincere, to be absolutely objective and unapologetic, because it is not I that speak but human reason that speaks in me. Truly the Babel in which we live has nothing in it so respectable as to put on the defensive the highest traditions of the human mind. No doubt, as you say, Latinity is moribund, as Greece itself was when it transmitted to the rest of the world the seeds of its own rationalism; and for that reason there is the more need of transplanting and propagating straight thinking among the peoples who hope to be masters of the world in the immediate future. Otherwise they will be its physical masters only, and the Muses will fly over them to alight among some future race that may understand the Gods better. . . .

Always sincerely yours

To SUSANA STURGIS DE SASTRE

OXFORD, AUG. 13. 1901

Dear Susie,

I have given up all idea of going even to Paris this year, and expect to remain here until I sail. It is a disappointment not to see you, but on the whole it seems best to put off that trip for another year, as I am in the midst of steady work and well and happy in this place. It has rained more or less lately so that the air is fresh and the country like an emerald. I drive about a good deal with some friends of mine, one of whom is a horse-dealer and the other (his brother) an actor.[1] The horse-dealer runs a coach and four to Blenheim twice a week and sometimes takes me when he is driving himself. You may think this very low company for a philosopher to keep, but you would be quite mistaken. He is a gentleman and in fact a great swell who has taken to keeping horses as the most congenial possible business. England is full of singular people of that sort. I have also been seeing something of Anglican monks who have a toy monastery here where they work in the garden with an expression of self-conscious beatitude on their faces. These contrasted types (I was introduced to the monks by the actor) keep me amused when I need a little change from my books and papers, so that I am having a good vacation and at the same time doing considerable work. England is not, as you naughtily say, the best possible world but it is the best actual country, and a great rest after America.

What you say about Rafael [2] makes me very sorry for the poor chap; he must be feeling rather sore. Farming is a good thing, but I am afraid there is not enough at Zorita for so many candidates as you have at home. You must tell us in your letters how the new projects for a *carrera* turn out.

Give my love to the family and tell them I hope to see them all next year.

Your affectionate brother

[1] See *My Host the World*, Chap. V, "Oxford Friends."

[2] A son of Celedonio Sastre by a previous marriage.

To LAWRENCE SMITH BUTLER

60 BRATTLE STREET
NOV. 28. 1901

Dear Lawrence

Many thanks for your nice letter. It was a great pleasure to hear from you, although, to be sure, I knew you were safe at home, far from the wicked orgies of the Quartier latin. We miss you very much in Boston. Aren't you ever coming to visit your old friends? You should come and gather the chorus of praise which we are raising about the big room at the Union.[1] It is the only noble room in the college and will give many people here their first notion of what good architecture means in practice. Façades and towers and details are one thing, but a beautiful place to live in, noble in colour and proportions, is something new in these parts and, it seems to me, invaluable. The Union seems to be a great success socially and gastronomically—although the ubiquity of ice water is a trifle chilling. The place is much used and the dining room (where I often go to eat) is crowded. Architecturally only the large room is of much consequence, but the rest seems serviceable and inoffensive. As to the gates, we have been suddenly blessed with too large a family of them; they look as if they had been all hatched in a hurry and had not yet got any feathers and hardly knew what they had come into the world for. But when the trees grow and hang about them again and the crude colour is toned down, I think they will seem all right and fall into a natural place in the landscape. The terrace in front of Palmer's house puzzles me a little, but I suppose some great pavilion is to back it up some day. I like to imagine it there, flanked with a few poplars standing high against the sky. However, this being Thanksgiving we ought to be grateful for what we have received up to date, without relying too much on favours to come.

I expect to be in New York at Christmas and will surely look you up. I am going out of town for a part of the time, to my friend

1 A Harvard social center.

Professor Strong's,[1] but I will write to you when I know my exact plans, so as not to miss seeing you.—I hope your father will soon be well again. This long illness must have been a great anxiety to you all.

Yours affectionately

To LAWRENCE SMITH BUTLER

60 BRATTLE STREET
DEC. 21 1901

Dear Lawrence

It was only last night that I heard you had lost your father, else I should have written before, because you know that my thoughts would turn to you at such a moment. I hope to see you soon—I go to New York on Xmas day and will look you up at once —but as one is not always inclined or able to say at odd times what is most in one's heart, I will write you a word now. This is an irreparable loss for you but not a bitter one, because it is in the order of nature that we should survive our parents and your father has lived to see you all grown up and to leave his memory and influence always with you. That ought to be a consolation for you. This world is so ordered that we must, in a material sense, lose everything we have and love, one thing after another, until we ourselves close our eyes upon the whole. It is hard for the natural man to bear this thought, but experience forces it upon him if he has the capacity of really learning anything. We should not set our hearts, then, on a material possession of anything, but our happiness should be made to lie in this, that whatever we possess for a time should reveal the ideal good to us and make us better in ourselves. Your family life has been so ideally happy and united (at least so it impresses your friends) that it must be doubly sad to suffer this cruel change; but you cannot lose that past happiness

[1] C. A. Strong.

altogether, because it was of the sort that brings happiness in memory and prepares one for meeting all the other events of life, sad and gay, in a right spirit, with a sense of what is truly good. The truly unfortunate are those persons—and how many of our friends are in this case!—who have never known anything worth living for, any noble and natural characters, any true happiness, or any beautiful thoughts and things. But those who have known such things and grown like them can never be truly unhappy because they carry the sweetness and truth within themselves which alone make a happiness that is worth having. Your nature and surroundings have opened this spiritual world to you more than to most people— that is why I have always cared for you so much—and that is a gift all the more to be grateful for in that it cannot be taken away.

Yours ever

To A. S. FULLER

NEAR LUXOR ON THE NILE
JANUARY 11TH 1904

Dear Fuller

There is a plan afoot which, if it is realised, will keep me in Europe for still another year.[1] In that case, you may keep my rooms[2] if you want them: if you don't, may I ask you to let me know, so that I may write to the landlord's agent giving them up.

I am at this moment going up the Nile with an impossible party of tourists, conscious of being no less grotesque than the rest of them. So many labour-saving-machines have left us no time for anything, else I should like to travel long in the East and yield for a time to its fascinations. People here seem to realise something of Faust's dream, to be young in body and old in spirit. What an amus-

---

[1] Santayana had been abroad on his Sabbatical year. See *My Host the World*, Chap. III, "Travels."

[2] The rooms in 60, Brattle Street, Cambridge, Mass.

ing place the world would be to such a creature. We sometimes speak of regretting lost illusions. What a silly idea! We may well regret lost powers, but the loss of illusions is an unmixed blessing. It leaves you free face to face with the facts and authorises you to profit by every real opportunity. The trouble is that, the Life of Reason being so largely in abeyance, people do not ordinarily lose their illusions till they have lost their passions, and then the real world, when they see it for the first time as it is, seems to them stale, not because it is real, but because they are played out.

I may perhaps go to Jerusalem and Damascus before returning to Europe. The donkey is losing its terrors for me and I now generally ride at the head of the party. Think what a party it must be!

Yours

To WILLIAM JAMES

[A reader with a taste for philosophy will find the following letter of peculiar interest in revealing Santayana's early efforts to escape the epistemology of the prevailing Idealism of the day.]

ROME, NOV. 29. 1904

Dear Mr James

Thank you very much for your two articles which have reached me here and filled an evening with very refreshing home-thoughts after the merciless biograph of mere phenomena which one gets in travelling. I am here with my old class-mate Loeser,[1] whom you will remember, and who wishes me to send you his love. He has an eighteenth century statuette of Locke with [sic] he wishes to present to you, but neither he nor I are quite clear about the possibility of sending it free through the custom house. I tell you of it so that you may mentally give him credit for his good intentions in case the object itself should never reach you.

Since I left America I have had glimpses of England, Belgium,

[1] Charles Loeser.

Holland, Germany and France, beside six weeks with my sister in Avila and almost a month in Florence with the advantage of being near Loeser and Berenson.[1] I am profoundly out of humour with "aesthetics", yet I have been feeling the new *douche* of it which these friends of mine have drenched me with as a rather invigorating change; one gets so dry in America with no food for the senses, especially if one is obliged to pump up theory every day. From here I mean to go on to Naples and Sicily, Egypt and Greece—all new ground for me; and I hope to return in the autumn a new man, with a fresh supply of "pure experience" and a budding crop of new ideas.

Your articles—apart from their intrinsic importance—have interested me particularly on account of a certain harmony which there is between what you make for and what I have fallen in with myself. Doubtless you have from of old let seeds fall into my mind which have sprouted there into what I feel to be quite native convictions; and it comes to me now as a rather surprising happiness that I can invoke your authority in support of a great deal that I feared might seem rash in my opinions. It is the general attitude which Bergson[2] also encourages, although of course it may be turned in various ways and expressed in various vocabularies. What I don't quite understand in your way of stating the matter is whether the conceptual world has *only* its immediate status. Of course every conception, taken existentially, is a part of the flux, which as you say is largely chaotic in its immediacy; but things and truths have also a systematic and more or less static dimension. For instance, if a candle which was nine inches long when left burning in an empty room is found to be six inches long on the observer's return, was it ever really eight inches in length? Of course the eight-inch candle will draw a potential sort of being from the philosopher's views, themselves immediate experiences of his; the *conception* that the candle passed through that phase will be an absolute item in the universal inventory. But the question seems to me to be whether the eight-inch candle has *only* that imputed being; or rather whether imputed being is not what we mean by reality and the immediate flux itself by appearance. The forthright intellect seems to be the life of the mind, and what it rests in seems to be alone important, true, or efficacious. The eight-inch candle is

---

1 Bernard Berenson.

2 Henri Bergson, the author of *Creative Evolution*.

something to be believed in, because in the material world which
the intellect has discovered it is a needful element that counts and
rewards our confidence in its reality. The materials which experience is composed of must therefore be credited with an existence
which makes them material elements and gives them a mechanical
order, since they exist *also* permanently, potentially, and beyond
our range.

If this is what is implied in your views—and I conceive that it
is—the result seems to be quite different from panpsychism and far
more rationalistic. According to panpsychism the eight-inch candle
exists only by virtue of its inconceivable psychic substance, that
mass of irrelevant experience of which a candle at best is but a remote symbol or effect. The real eight-inch candle is not eight inches
long and is no candle at all. It is perhaps a conclave of politic worms
electing an infallible pope to maintain that the universe is nothing
but a musical composition. According to your view—if I understand it—and to mine, on the contrary, the material qualities of the
candle themselves subsist, and it is a cylindrical white body that is
really eight inches long at an assignable instant. The world of science for us, then, would not be a mere fiction, but a real efficacious
order discovered in the chaos of immediate experience, a system
consisting bodily of the given elements, but of course involving
many more, and the longer subsistence of them. Am I right?

Please wish the various members of the department a happy
new year in my name and believe me

Very sincerely yours

To A. S. FULLER

ROME. DECEMBER 3, 1904

Dear Fuller

Your letter comes to remind me that a place I have often heard
of called Harvard College actually exists: it seems from here a
rather improbable myth; and quite an unnecessary complication
in the world, that has a complete history already. I am glad that

you take to your native country so well; I wonder why in a land where so much is potential the potential has not been allowed any place in philosophy, whereas an Aristotle, who lived in a finished world, made so much of the potential in his speculation. This is a sign, I suppose, that speculation is seldom a genuine expression of life, but rather a parasitic tradition expressing what is effete in the contemporary world.

Have you read Moore's [1] Principia Ethica? The book seems to contain a grain of accuracy in a bushel of inexperience.

James has sent me two of his new articles from the Columbia Journal. The one (or more) in Mind [2] I have not yet seen. Dickinson [3] writes to me from Cambridge: "I love W. James as a man. But what a singularly bad thinker he is!"

James' new statements do not seem to me to be bad insight, whatever may be thought of the logic of them. They point to materialism, which I believe may be destined before long to have a great rehabilitation. The material world is a fiction; but every other world is a nightmare.

Please wish Mrs. Burnett [4] a merry Christmas. I am delighted that you have kept my rooms, as your brother's youthful energies might have been too much for them. By the way, will you do me a favour, and in an idle moment cut off judiciously a bit of the red silk over my bed and send it to *Charles Loeser, 11 via Lambertesca, Florence?* Loeser has promised to get me some more stuff of the same shade, to make a coverlet of, so that my dreams may be as genteel and sumptuous as possible.

I am enjoying myself hugely and reading a good deal more than usual. Friends of mine turn up at regular intervals, and the sun shines, and humanity smiles about me almost without hypocrisy. I feel at home.

Your sincerely

[1] G. E. Moore, the distinguished English philosopher.

[2] The English philosophical quarterly.

[3] Lowes Dickinson, of Trinity College, Cambridge, England.

[4] The landlady of the house in 60 Brattle Street, Cambridge, Mass.

To SUSANA STURGIS DE SASTRE

JERUSALEM, FEBRUARY 17, 1905

Dear Susie,

The rains during the first week I spent here were so heavy that it was impossible to do the usual sight-seeing, and they have left the roads in such a state that it seemed imprudent to start on a long driving-tour such as I had planned. The other day when several of us went to Jericho and the Dead Sea two of our carriages got stuck in deep mud, and the horses had to be taken out while we waded to terra firma and help was brought to pull out the carriages. Such incidents, which do no harm in a short excursion when the town is hard by, might be serious in the wilds, when no halting place for the night might be within reach after a delay of several hours. I am therefore starting tomorrow morning for Damascus by way of Jaffa and Beyrout, a journey wholly by rail and steamboat. From Damascus I return to Beyrout and sail thence again for Athens via Smyrna. I expect to reach Greece about March 1st and you may address me there for a month or two directly, to the *Hôtel Grande Brétagne, Athènes:* if I don't like that place and go elsewhere I will let you know by the swift picture post-card.

The impression which the Holy Land makes on the traveller must depend more even than in other places on his point of view and his expectations. There are no ruins of architectural importance. Everything has been rebuilt at various periods, and now the town is a conglomerate of all sorts of buildings, chiefly shabby and modern. The shrines, at the Holy Sepulchre (which contains the supposed site of Calvary as well) and at Bethlehem, etc. are generally caves, and enclosed in a more or less imposing church. These churches are cut up into sections belonging to the various confessions, the Greeks usually having the lion's share. To make Jerusalem satisfactory as a place of pilgrimage one would have to possess unlimited faith in the traditions identifying the various spots, and even then I am not sure that much is gained for devotional purposes by knowing that the cross was planted here or there. The Catholic convents and hospices are numerous here and in good

order; the Dominicans have a pretty bran-new Church and college
and the Franciscans and Carmelites also have various establishments. There is a very large religious hostelry, where French
brothers receive pilgrims at eight francs a day; it is well built in
white stone with two elaborate chapels and other signs of prosperity. The older part of the town is inhabited by the Moslems
and Jews, the latter very numerous and divided into Spanish and
German Jews; the Spanish section still speaks a corrupt Castillian.
The Moslems are themselves of various nations: Arabic is the language of the country, but Turkish is that of the government, and
the Beduins, Turks, Syrians and negroes are strangely jumbled
together. A shepherd I met in a country walk spoke *in English*
and two other peasants in Italian. French, not very pure, is spoken
by all the educated natives and most shop-keepers. Costumes are
no less mixed. The country people still look Biblical, and from
their flowing white robes and bare feet you pass by insensible
degrees to complete European dress, modified only by the Fez or
tarbush which most natives still wear. Apart from this museum of
humanity what has interested and pleased me most has been the
landscape. It is arid and hilly, the slopes being often quite covered
with loose stones and ledges of rock peeping through the surface:
but there are also many olive-trees, and the deep gorges and the
dry beds of torrents make the scene most wild and varied. I had
no idea how easily one can dominate the whole country; from the
Mount of Olives, for instance, you not only can see the Dead Sea
but you can see quite across it, as if it were a pond at your feet,
while the mountains of Moab on its eastern shore rise high up
before you, like a wall of stone that you might touch with a long
stick. From hills only a little higher you can at the same time see
the Mediterranean; so that the ancient Jews could from a single
mountain-top view the whole land of promise. What an influence
this intimate familiarity with their country must have had on their
intense patriotism. With most nations their country is only an
idea, but for the Jews it was a sensible and tangible place, like
one's own house and garden.

The site of the Temple is still magnificent and a very pretty
round mosque occupies the place where the altar for burnt-offerings
stood in antiquity, just before the door of the Temple. The rest
of the enormous platform once occupied by the temples of Solomon
and Herod is now bare: only a few stone mosques and arches, and

a few trees rise above the immense pavement. Around stand several modern minarets and an old Christian basilica, somewhat "restored" and turned into another mosque. Those who are not Moslems are only permitted to visit these places on stated days and accompanied by a *cavass* or *gend'arme* from the consulate: Jews are never allowed to come in at all: this is because the Moslems also hold the Temple of Solomon sacred. They venerate some Christian shrines as well, for instance, the supposed site of the ascension, in which they believe: but they are indifferent to all that relates to the passion because the Koran says that Christ was never really crucified, but that a man resembling him was executed in his place, while he was translated like Elijah into heaven and will not die until the end of the world; after which he will rise again, and at the last judgment will stand on the Mount of Olives while Mohammed stands on the hill of the Temple; a rope will be stretched between and those souls that are able to pass over it will be saved, while those who fall in the transit will be lost. This last is not in the Koran, but is a popular conception.

I am perfectly well and feel well pleased with my journey so far, which is not so very expensive—about seven dollars a day since I came to the Orient, all included. I have been talking Spanish a great deal here with the South Americans that fill this hotel. They are for the most part from Buenos Aires and bubble over with self-satisfaction in their country.

Love to all from

To WILLIAM JAMES

ATHENS, HÔTEL MINERVA
MARCH 4, 1905

Dear Mr James

Thank you very much for your amusing letter.[1] Why didn't the Messiah come this year and leave me the more congenial task

1 James had written to Santayana from Harvard on February 8, 1905 urging him to accept the Hyde lectures in France for the following autumn and winter. "I cannot

of being a Paul to him and reducing his doctrine to dead dogmas and metaphysical Hellenisms? It is not too late, and if you are so well (which I am happy to hear) why shouldn't you stay in France for next year and leave it for me to follow, if need be, on the year after-next, or even later? My book, in spite of its five volumes, is not good to turn into lectures: it is *too concise!* My idea is rather to review my contemporaries, which I neglect in the book alto-gether, and to take for a subject "Contemporary Philosophy in England and America". Hyde [2] says you may wish to take that subject, or something like it, yourself, and if so, I could of course easily find a new title. I suspect, however, that you would be looking forward in your treatment, while I should be looking back—at least as far as Jonathan Edwards and the statuetted Locke.[3] So that even with the same theme we might make too [sic] sufficiently different symphonies to delight the Parisian ear with.

I have just arrived here from Palestine and Damascus, where I have received the usual impressions; I am staying here for two months, so that I look for the pleasure of doing a little peripatetic philosophy, under your distinguished guidance,[4] on its native heath —a heath being all that is left to philosophise over.

I hope you will like Spain and find it worth the inconveniences it will put you to.

Yours sincerely

---

believe," James wrote, "considering where you already are, and that your book [The Life of Reason] is ripe for being made into lectures, that you will refuse such an opportunity. I can't conceive a better man for our university to put forward among the first. The plan between Eliot and Hyde is to make me the lecturer the next year, 1906–07, and I am feeling so hearty again that I don't say nay. You the Baptist! I the Messiah! (That's the way it looks to my wife!) Pray write to me again and tell me how the whole thing is looking at your end."

[2] James Hazen Hyde.

[3] See letter (November 29, 1904).

[4] James later joined Santayana in Athens.

To CHARLES ELIOT NORTON

LONDON, JUNE 5TH 1905

Dear Mr. Norton

No letter [1] which I have received about my book has given me more satisfaction than yours. As you have never divided justice from kindness, it is hard not to believe that your approval is justified, even when expressed in such flattering and partial terms. I hoped that you would like the general intent and moral ideal that underlies all I say, although probably many arguments and tenets which I have ventured to propound may seem to you precarious and needlessly metaphysical. I am compelled, however, to use the tools of my trade and cannot altogether escape the controversial traditions in which I have been trained, much as I should have preferred if nature had consented to be a purer humanist. Nevertheless, some may be led in this way out of the fog and shown how the speculative instinct may be tamed and turned to moral uses in supporting and refining practical understanding.

With many thanks for your very kind letter, I am

Sincerely yours

[1] I am tempted to quote a portion of the generous and characteristic letter which Professor Norton of Harvard wrote to Santayana after first reading The *Life of Reason:*

"... If I were writing to a layman in philosophy like myself I should not hesitate to speak of the extraordinary range of your thought, the admirable ordering of it in a consistent system, its striking originality, and the display in it of the union of remarkable power of imagination with not less remarkable faculty of the understanding ... Now that you are away from Harvard I know not where to look for anyone who is truly meditating on the problem of life. Contemplation is an unfamiliar practice. Nobody seems to feel the need, or to say

'To many hours must I contemplate'.

The University is given over to facts, and regards thoughts with suspicion.—Come back soon, to redress the balance!"

To WILLIAM JAMES

BOX HILL, SURREY [ENGLAND]
JULY 27, 1905

Dear Mr James

I have just re-read, or read for the first time in some cases, the series of articles you have been good enough to send me. They have given me new light on many points—most important of all on the relation of "Humanism" to "Truth". It is perfectly clear that opinions are not all equally good on pragmatic principles, since some fulfil their pledges with advancing experience while others do not. I am inclined to think you would meet with less misapprehension and hostility on this score if you gave out, in dogmatic form, how you conceive "the final system of reality" (which you assume on page 3 of the article on "Experience of Activity") to be made up. I imagine you would say it is a historical system, its substance being feelings which may or may not be appropriated by persons. It would remain to work out a physics of these feelings, and to show how proposition might be essentially true or false descriptions of this historical flux.

I have got a clearer notion, I think, than I had when we talked in Athens, of what makes my way of seeing things puzzling to you —a mystery, you called it. You expect me to look at everything as I look on the things I don't believe in—religious myths, e.g.—which can have, of course, a symbolic or pragmatic truth. My nature, on the other hand, compels me to believe in something in quite a different sense, and this something is, in my view, double—material nature with its animation on the one hand, and logical or mathematical forms on the other. These are discovered by us, starting from sensation, and, in the first case, are tested by pragmatic sanctions. But we look to them in order to understand the origin of our experience (or its standard in signification) and I, for one, heartily accept them in that rôle. So I embrace materialism on pragmatic grounds—and on transcendental grounds also. The prohibition to believe which, in some expressions of it, pragmatism seems to impose, as if every opinion had to be symbolic and had to be superseded, is what I object to. It is too Hegelian. History, at least, must have a definite constitution, apart from the pragmatic value of knowing it.

With renewed thanks,

Yours sincerely,

To A. S. FULLER

AVILA, [SPAIN] OCTOBER 5, 1905

Dear Fuller

I write—breaking my habitual silence, to which I hope you have got used and indifferent—to ask you to do me several favours. One is to look at my copy of "Interpretations of Poetry and Religion", and see if there are *errata* marked on the flyleaf at the back, and if there are, to send the book to Charles Scribner's Sons, 153–157 Fifth Ave. N.Y. They have asked me for any corrections in view of a new edition.

Favour no. 2. Will you be an angel and send me to the Hôtel Foyot, rue Tournon, Paris, the following books, if you can conveniently pick them out of the heap—I don't know if they still sit on the shelves or have been compelled to yield to your own aids to wisdom.

> Spencer's First Principles.
> Green's Prolegomena.
> Ward's Naturalism & Agnosticism.

They are books for which I have a qualified admiration and I don't think it necessary to possess two copies of each. But I need them for reference in preparing my winter's lectures.[1] In payment for your trouble and the postage I will send you a Christmas present when I reach Paris. It shall be Bergson's books, if you haven't got them; if not, something else which you must select.

A letter which I got from you long ago gave me a very cheerful impression in respect to your state of mind and to things in gen-

---

[1] At the Sorbonne, Paris.

eral at Harvard. I trust that happiness is still unclouded, and that fat salaries and intelligent students are beginning to prevail—by students I mean candidates for the Ph.D., for the blameless tribe of moderate geniuses known as undergraduates no doubt ebbs and flows as sweetly as ever. Your letter also contained an interpretation of the Life of Reason which seemed original; what my own is may be a little clearer in the two volumes which I hope you have lately received; and it will be made quite unequivocal in the last volume,[1] to appear in the Spring. Some people say I am a pragmatist and some say I am not. On the whole, I agree with the latter, as pragmatism seems to involve a confusion between the test and the meaning of truth. I have been reading Mill,[2] and the psychologism of his theory repels me so much that I am sure I can't belong to any school which feels at home in it. Mill is a sort of ponderous and sober James. His temper and learning are admirable; his heart is in the right place; and his love of the good is honest. But his logic is a minus quantity, and the survival of dogma, psychological and theological, makes his conclusions pathetically personal and altogether unstable.

With best wishes

Yours ever

To WILLIAM JAMES

HÔTEL FOYOT, PARIS
DECEMBER 5, 1905

Dear Mr James

I am very grateful to you for your letter: I feel how *generous* it is, and how like you. I may say something about my book [3]—in

[1] *Reason in Science.*
[2] John Stuart Mill.
[3] *The Life of Reason.*

reply—if there is room at the end, but first let me answer your questions about the Sorbonne lectures.

As you may imagine my experience has been, so far, wholly unlike Wendell's.[1] He seems to have grasped with avidity every opportunity to see things and to know people, and seems to have lectured as if he was borne on a bubbling wave of international enthusiasm. I have come, thinking only of my subject, seeing only my personal friends, having only official relations with officials, and keeping away as much as possible from the American colony. Naturally I have enjoyed a great quiet, and am spending very little nervous energy on my work. The lectures themselves I find delightful to give—immensely *easy*. The Amphithéâtre Richelieu—which holds 800—is about half full. The acoustics are admirable and it is not too hot. The audience—fully half ladies, mostly Americans— is sympathetic. One feels that not everything is fully understood; those that have ears, let them hear, has to be one's motto. But every one is attentive, and I find improvisation easy in that *milieu*.

Of course, even if you wished to take things as I am taking them, it would be impossible. You are too famous; every one here speaks of no one in America but you; you would have enormous audiences and a host of invitations, all of which you would find it impracticable to refuse. Nevertheless, I don't see why you shouldn't refuse the American (the most persistent) set of them; and the French people, if I may trust my impression and experience so far, are perfectly willing to let one alone. Pierre Janet [2] has asked me to dinner—three weeks ahead—but none of the other Frenchmen I have met has even called on me, or suggested that I should call on him. Of course, I repeat, it would be otherwise with you; but my experience will show you that, in the abstract, people here have no Hyde-Wendell idea of the momentousness of this affair. In all frankness—since you ask me to tell you everything—no one—*no one*, American or French—mentions Wendell here without an ambiguous smile. He evidently made a damned— Wendell of himself. The Hyde foundation has been a success; audiences have been found; the idea of lectures in English is fashionable and politically opportune. But it is an incident lost amid a thousand others, a thing of importance to half a dozen persons. Paris

[1] Barrett Wendell, who gave the first course of Harvard Exchange lectures (1904–05) at the Sorbonne on the James Hazen Hyde Foundation.

[2] The distinguished French mental specialist of the period.

could live without it, and if a man likes the undertaking, as I do, from the purely personal, academic, scholarly point of view, he ought to attempt it. It is a delightful and a moderate task. The freedom of speaking in a foreign language among foreigners—I mean the intellectual room—is exhilarating. You can say what is *really true*. You needn't remember that you are in Cambridge, or are addressing the youth entrusted to your personal charge. I have never felt so grown up as I do at the Sorbonne; after our atmosphere, this is liberty. I am sure that—apart from the first lecture when the ice had been broken—I am lecturing better than I ever did before; and the audience is appreciative and lets itself be carried along.

All this may not help you very much to make up your mind about coming next year or not. It is hard for me to imagine exactly what points would be decisive to your mind. I can see no reason, however, why a winter here (except for the dark, chill climate and constant drizzle) shouldn't be as profitable and pleasant as one in Cambridge. Two lectures a week on a subject of which your mind was already full, wouldn't be a great strain; and if you hardened your heart a little against the impertinent homage of the public, I don't see why you shouldn't find this a good opportunity for writing down your thoughts.

I have spent, as you may have heard, some weeks with Strong [1] at Compiègne. We had many rather unsatisfactory discussions about idealism and mind-stuff. He tells me you are a convert to his theory: is this serious? I should think the same empirical reserve or abstension which makes you rebel against my materialistic Platonism would make you rebel against his reversible universe, perfectly concave and perfectly convex, matter lined throughout with mind. It is a scholastic artifice, *n'est-ce pas?* It is not science, nor nature, nor moral truth. Strong himself, let me add, seemed to me more heroic and admirable than ever and I enjoyed renewing our old friendship. I have left no room for more but if there is anything you wish I had touched on that I have left out, pray ask.

Yours sincerely,

[1] C. A. Strong.

To WILLIAM JAMES

HÔTEL FOYOT
PARIS, DEC. 6. 1905

Dear Mr James

I forgot yesterday to answer one of your questions, which I remember may be of importance to you. The lectures are at five o'clock in the afternoon on Tuesdays and Saturdays. I have no doubt they would change the hour for you if you wished. To everything they say "comme vous voudrez", and things here, as in England, seem to go by prerogative. You could also give as many or as few lectures as you chose—the great Hyde consenting.

Another omission. Blood's poem,[1] after about six readings, has become intelligible to me, and I like the thought very much, also the diction, but the *composition* is deplorable. Why can't people begin and end, and give one some indication of what they are talking about? As to the Tychism of it, it seems to me a good surface philosophy, a good expression of consciousness and the look of the flux. Of course what must be, if it must be, would never be known beforehand; and the machinery that may actually support our feelings doesn't deprive them of their dramatic novelty and interest, any more than the printed *dénouement* of a novel, extant in the last chapter, takes away from the dreamful excitement of perusing it and of wondering what will come next.

Now that I am launched I will say a word about some of the criticisms in your letter. You are very generous; I feel that you want to give me credit for everything good that can possibly be found in my book.[2] But you don't yet see my philosophy, nor my temper from the inside; your praise, like your blame, touches only the periphery, accidental aspects presented to this or that preconceived and disparate interest. The style is good, the tone is supercilious, here is a shrewd passage, etc., etc. And you say I am less hospitable than Emerson. Of course. Emerson might pipe his woodnotes and chirp at the universe most blandly; his genius might be

[1] *Reveries of One,* by B. P. Blood.
[2] *The Life of Reason.*

tender and profound and Hamlet-like, and that is all beyond my range and contrary to my purpose. I am a Latin, and nothing seems serious to me except politics, except the sort of men that your ideas will involve and the sort of happiness they will be capable of. The rest is exquisite moonshine. Religion in particular was *found out* more than 100 years ago, and it seems to me intolerable that we should still be condemned to ignore the fact and to give the parsons and the "idealists" a monopoly of indignation and of contemptuous dogmatism. It is they, not we, that are the pest; and while I wish to be just and to understand people's feelings, wherever they are at all significant, I am deliberately minded to be contemptuous toward what seems to me contemptible, and not to have any share in the conspiracy of mock respect by which intellectual ignominy and moral stagnation are kept up in our society. What did Emerson know or care about the passionate insanities and political disasters which religion, for instance, has so often been another name for? He could give that name to his last personal intuition, and ignore what it stands for and what it expresses in the world. It is the latter that absorbs me; and I care too much about mortal happiness to be interested in the charming vegetation of cancer-microbes in the system—except with the idea of suppressing it.

A more technical point. You say "activity" can be spiritual only. Is your activity, or sense of activity, not rather an ἐνέργεια [actuality] than a δύναμις [potentiality]? Of course I should be the first to agree that activity, in the sense of actuality and conscious stress, belongs only to consciousness or even to the rational and reflective energy of thought. But *efficiency,* in the sense of regular predictable contiguity with other specific events, belongs only to δύναμις, to the potential (= the potent.) In a dream there is the sense of activity, there is commotion and actualization, ἐνέργεια; but there is no δύναμις, no material efficacy, save through the underlying metabolism in the brain; the story in the dream stops short; its purposes evaporate. This may be contrary to common sense, meaning ordinary ways of expressing oneself; but it seems to me quite of a piece with common sense of a progressive sort, with science. It might be contrary to common sense to say that the sun is larger than the earth, but not to the common sense applied to the full situation. So this doctrine seems to me reasonable in its method and result, though as yet paradoxical in its language.

I have read practically no reviews of my book so that I don't know if any one has felt in it something which, I am sure, is there: I mean the *tears*. "Sunt lachrimae rerum, et mentem mortalia tangunt" ["E'en here the tear of pity springs/And hearts are touched by human things." Conington]. Not that I care to moan over the gods of Greece, turned into the law of gravity, or over the stained-glass of cathedrals broken to let in the sunlight and the air. It is not the past that seems to me affecting, entrancing, or pitiful to lose. It is the ideal. It is that vision of perfection that we just catch, or for a moment embody in some work of art, or in some idealised reality: it is the concomitant inspiration of life, always various, always beautiful, hardly ever expressible in its fulness. And it is my adoration of this real and familiar good, this love often embraced but always elusive, that makes me detest the Absolutes and the dragooned myths by which people try to cancel the passing ideal, or to denaturalise it. That is an inhumanity, an impiety, that I can't bear. And much of the irritation which I may betray and which, I assure you is much greater than I let it seem, comes of affection. It comes of exasperation at seeing the only things that are beautiful or worth having treated as if they were of no account.

I seldom write to any one so frankly as I have here. But I know *you* are human, and tolerant to anything, however alien, that smells of blood.

Always sincerely yours,

To GEORGE HERBERT PALMER

PARIS, DEC. 13, 1905

Dear Mr. Palmer

As the chief part of your recent letter (being about my book) didn't seem to require an answer, I have been forgetting that what you said about your own book [1] did; but I believe I had already written to you about it, saying I should be much obliged if you

1 *The English Works of George Herbert* (1593–1633), newly arranged and annotated and considered in relation to his life. By George Herbert Palmer.

would keep the volumes, as you suggest, until my return, as here
I have not only a sufficient load materially, but also too many occupations and distractions to leave me a quiet hour for poesy and
piety of George Herbert's somewhat remote sort. It must have
been a rare pleasure and consolation to you to do this labour of
love and to recover familiarly the habits and thoughts of so congenial and refined a spirit.

My lectures here are going on pleasantly and well before a
moderate audience composed in a large part of American ladies.

On another sheet (taking time by the fore-lock) I send you
my proposal for courses [1] next year, which I suppose will soon
have to be determined upon. Now that Perry [2] is a professor and
the author of a book *ad hoc,* it seems to me that he ought to go
on with Phil 1, b, which he will carry on much better than I should
or ever did. However, I am ready, of course, if it must be, to take
my share of that heavy and (as it seems to me) unnecessary burden.
Could I be relieved of it, there are several half courses or seminaries
that I might offer instead—besides the problematical Aristotle I
mention.

With best regards

Yours sincerely

To A. S. FULLER

HÔTEL FOYOT, PARIS
JANUARY 29, 1906

Your criticism, my dear Fuller, of my third volume [3] has this
defect, which I want to point out to you while the sense of it is
still hot within me. You make an *insincere* objection. Of course
there *might* be any number of finite gods making for righteousness,
as there certainly are some natural and human forces making for
it. But do you believe there are? In remote parts of nature we may

[1] At Harvard.

[2] Ralph Barton Perry.

[3] *Reason in Religion.*

well conjecture that some good is pursued and perhaps attained by beings inconceivable to us. But are these the gods of that living religion which you think I ignore? Of course the gods of actual religion are very confused and impossible monsters; but their essential functions, when discriminated and made articulate, seem to me to be reducible to the two I have insisted upon in my book. These are the *rational* values, the eternal sources and sanctions of what is sane in religious madness. The madness itself, in its psychological or dramatic texture, cannot be included in the Life of Reason, though of course it may be referred to in a description of that honourable fraction of our existence; nor do I think I have left this madness altogether uncharacterised.—As to my injustice to the Neo-Platonists—of whom Plotinus is of course the best and the most Hellenic—I am more inclined to plead guilty, because I know little at first hand about them, and you, in the full blush of your recent erudition, might easily refute me with quotations selected *ad hoc*. I know that Plotinus, as against even Gnostic Christians, stood for what he *called* natural and political goods; but nature and society were by that time transfused with a mystical solvent which rendered his official allegiance to them, I imagine, largely deceptive. And his followers made this illusion more transparent and quite let the ascetic cat out of the bag. . . .

Yours ever,

To SUSANA STURGIS DE SASTRE

GRAND HÔTEL & HOTEL TIVOLLIER
RUE DE METZ,
TOULOUSE
LE 29 AVRIL, 1906

Dear Susie,

I got your letter yesterday afternoon when I was leaving Carcassonne. It is raining this morning, so I take the opportunity to answer at once.

1st   I don't know what newspaper-cuttings about my book [1] they have been sending you. I have repeatedly begged them not to send me any, and they have finally stopped doing so: the reviews I have seen—one or two excepted—are quite incompetent and often written by people who have not even read a page of the book through. It is not worth paying any attention to what they say.— As to my teaching Strong "Catholic metaphysics", you must understand that my own philosophy *no es muy catolica;* it is independent of religion altogether, and looks at religion merely as at a historic and human fact—more or less appealing or beneficent, as the case may be. You have seen all you probably care to see of this attitude in my "Interpretations of Poetry and Religion". The attitude of my new book is exactly the same: but of course it deals with many other subjects as well as with religion.

2nd   Why should you be worried at Rafael's [2] going to "Mauriscot"? If he is to be long at Cartago isn't it much better that he should be normally settled there, with a domestic circle of his own, and smaller Rafaelitos to think about? He told me something about the affair: that you haven't seen the girl is nothing against her; you may see only too much of her some day. If you knew her and didn't like her, it might be something to complain of, although it would have to be put up with all the same.

3rd   Mr. Rockefeller is, . . . I understand, a little timid, and doubtless has detectives to protect him against "cranks" that might loiter about his house. But he is comparatively well, and has a new wig to make him beautiful: and he is coming to spend seven weeks at Compiègne this summer with the Strongs. [3] Mrs. Rockefeller comes with him; they are going to travel under an assumed name, to protect themselves from begging letters and indiscrete curiosity. Strong tells me that he has written an essay on the duties of rich men, which he is going to read some Sunday afternoon to his father-in-law. It points out that very large fortunes are truly "trusts": and that instead of being left to individuals of one's family they should be made into public funds, administered by some trustees of distinction, for the benefit of the community at large.—It is easy to give this generous advice when one is a philos-

---

[1] *The Life of Reason.*

[2] A son of Celedonio Sastre by a previous marriage.

[3] Mr. Rockefeller's daughter Elizabeth had married Professor C. A. Strong.

opher, and one's only daughter is sure, in any case, of being well
provided for. Strong himself is growing much more luxurious:
I think the old man has given him a million dollars, and it is
beginning to tell. . . .

Love to Celedonio and the family from

To CHARLES W. ELIOT

GRENOBLE, JUNE 23, 1906

Dear Mr Eliot [1]

The series of lectures which I have been giving in France,
ended here yesterday. The year has been a delightful one for me
personally,—except that my health has not been quite so good
as usual; together with the previous twelvemonth of travel, it has
given me a very refreshing change of scenes and of companion-
ships. Even in respect to my philosophic interests, I have found a
great deal that is new to me, and interesting, in the movement of
French speculation, which is very active at present and is carried
on in a most critical and open-minded spirit, as well as with a solid
foundation in scholarship.

My impressions about the value of the Hyde lectureship are
rather too complex to be expressed in a letter; I have accordingly
written the accompanying memorandum.[2] It represents my sincere
opinion upon this undertaking, when reflected on in cold blood.
It might give a wrong impression, however, of my personal satisfaction at the reception I have met with both from officials and
from the public. The post I have held is a delightful one; the
question is whether the general advantages of maintaining such
a lectureship are not largely factitious.

Mr Hyde has seen this memorandum and, I believe, has kept
a copy of it. With sincere regards

Yours very truly

1 President of Harvard College.
2 Deposited in the archives of Houghton Library at Harvard.

To CONRAD SLADE

75 MONMOUTH STREET
BROOKLINE MASS
MARCH 4 1908

Dear Conrad,

A great weight is lifted off my mind. My brother has decided to remain in America this summer, a decision which leaves me free to do what I like, and you know what that must be. My passage is taken for June 18 eastward and for September 10 westward, in the Hamburg-American Kaiserin and Deutschland respectively. First I go to England; but before July is far advanced I hope to be in Paris. If you are going to some idyllic place and would not think me an intruder, I might join you for a month or so. We might read—I am deep in history now, Gibbon,[1] Curtius,[2] etc.— and sketch. Perhaps you might give me a few lessons in drawing, or you might paint my portrait and immortalize us both. About September first it is not impossible that I may go to Heidelberg— it is the only place in Germany that tempts me back—to an international philosophic congress which is to meet there. I should see in the flesh a lot of ugly old men whose names I have seen in print all my life; and then I might go to Hamburg to make my friends there a few days' visit before sailing for my Peru—that is what Cambridge is getting to be to my mercenary mind.

When you get this send me a card with your surest address —I am never sure what it is—and I will forward you the first volume of the Arabian Nights, which I have read twice, once at sea and once on cold winter nights, and which has made both wildernesses turn for the moment into enchanted oases. And it is so funny! Only at times my Hellenic political conscience rebels against this irresponsible, unintellectual way of feeling life—all chances and surfaces and prodigies— Send me the second volume that I may have read it when I see you, and be ready to buy the next.

Yours affly,

[1] Edward Gibbon.   [2] Ernst Robert Curtius.

To SUSANA STURGIS DE SASTRE

COLONIAL CLUB
CAMBRIDGE [MASS.]
MARCH 18, 1909

Dear Susie,

It is several months since I last wrote to you, but as I know you get regular news of the family from Robert and Josephine,[1] I don't make a point of sending my bulletin as well. Nothing much has happened, except that Robert seems to be really going to Europe, and that, during the last week or ten days, Mother has been ailing a little, although she is now better, and about in the same condition as before her cold, or whatever it was—for I saw no particular evidence of anything definite. We had a "trained nurse" for three or four days. It was much better for Mother, as her little meals were prepared nicely, given to her with a certain authority, so that she took them, as well as her medicines, and she slept with her *window open,* which of course helped to prevent her feeling ill and faint in the morning, which is one of the chief troubles she had. But now that she is more or less herself again, and comes down to the dining room as usual, they have sent the nurse away, and we shall return to the old routine. For Josephine, the nurse was evidently a nuisance at first. Josephine was more nervous and anxious than ever, and hardly could sleep. But after two or three days, she seemed to me to be calming down, and if the nurse (or somebody like her) had stayed, I think Josephine would have learned to put off her responsibility for a while now and then, and to sleep and take an outing with more peace of mind. Robert and I have told her so: but she persists in being vague and conditional in all she says about taking a nurse or maid, and it will have to be postponed until mother has another ill turn. Poor Josephine is naturally looking thinner and yellower than ever, and is pretty nervous; although, luckily, she is not at all unhappy or sad. On the contrary, Mother's mental weakness seems to strike her as

[1] Robert and Josephine Sturgis, Santayana's half-brother and half-sister in Boston.

something humorous and appealing like the first notions of a young child: and she doesn't seem to be troubled about the future. What keeps her on the *qui vive* is whether Mother has sneezed, or worked longer than usual at her knitting, or breathed hard in her sleep, as if complaining. The great fundamental situation doesn't seem to weigh on Josephine at all. Is this merely that she is too much taken up with details to consider things in the gross, or is it that she is resigned to the ultimate issue, and pleased to give herself up to pious little cares in the meantime? Mother is now distinctly more feeble, both in mind and body, than she was when I arrived in the autumn. But she is without pain and almost without discomfort: and I see no reason why she shouldn't remain in this condition for an indefinite time, perhaps for years. It is for Josephine that the situation seems to me grave; how can she stand months and months of continual watchfulness, night and day, with no distractions, hardly any fresh air, no appetite, and very little sound sleep? I hope she will soon convince herself that a nurse is needed, just as one would be needed for a baby, and that she will learn to throw off a part of her cares. What may contribute to this is that Mother is really quite indifferent to who is with her, and if her little wants were being attended to, she would never notice whether Josephine had been away for five hours or for five minutes.

As to myself, I am much more settled and comfortable than I was when I last wrote. My rooms are satisfactory: pupils and other friends come to see me very often—I have tea ready for them every day from four to half-past five—and, best of all, I have been to New York twice and had a real change which amused and refreshed me remarkably. An old friend—Moncure Robinson—got me rooms, a whole apartment, at Sherry's, the very fashionable hotel at which he lives. I went out to lunch, dinner, and supper after the opera, every day, and on Sunday, even to breakfast. I saw a lot of very gay people. Their conversation is amusing and very *risqué,* but their manners are simple and excellent, and, for a change, I thought them delightful. One of the ladies I saw most was Mrs. Ralph Ellis, a sister of Ward Thoron's wife. The most interesting, however, was Mrs. John Jacob Astor, who is a very Parisian sort of beauty, about forty, with grey hair, but a girlish figure, and a superficial interest in things intellectual, covering a *fond* of sadness and of physical dissatisfaction. . . . This lady is one of the very few whom I look forward to seeing again when the occasion presents itself, and of keeping as a permanent link with the world. Of course she knows that she has made an impression on me, and she likes the idea. She has asked me to dinner since I came back, but I am not young and foolish enough to travel a day and a night for the pleasure of sitting for one hour next to any woman, no matter how charming.

My other friend Mrs. Bob Potter has been for a day in Boston. Her mother died suddenly and she came to America to arrange her affairs. I hear that she has inherited $300,000; it is probably much less, but it will help the Potters to live more as they like. They are now in Athens, and I expect, as Bob has given up his business in New York, that they will be in Europe most of the time in future. This is very nice for me, because it will help me to see them when I leave this country myself; and of course, in leaving it, I am far from wishing never to see my American friends again. It is only *their country* that I am longing to lose sight of. As a matter of fact, I have made my best American friends abroad, like Boylston Beal and the Potters, and I shall be able to see them as often, and to much greater advantage there than in Boston or New York. This is also true of my new flame, Mrs. Astor.

Is there any "Modernist" movement or party in Spain? I have been reading Loisy,[1] Tyrrell,[2] Paul Sabatier (who is a Protestant, but a great friend of the "Modernists") as well as the Pope's Encyclical "Pascendi" and other documents. As I expect to be here this summer, I have agreed to give two lectures on the religious situation in Catholic countries before the parsons that come to the summer school here, and I am anxious to get any general information that I can. What I read at Avila in the "Lectura Dominical", though little, is going to be a help. Of course, I know what the theoretic position of the Church and of her enemies is; but what these ignorant parsons want to hear is what are the tendencies of popular feeling. Are there any socialistic Catholics like Murri[3] in Spain? If you have any pamphlets or books that deal with this subject I should be much obliged if you would send them to me. Quite apart from my lectures, which will have to be very super-

---

[1] Alfred Loisy, author of *La naissance du Christianisme,* etc.

[2] George Tyrrell, author of *The Faith of the Millions,* etc.

[3] Romolo Murri, author of *La politica clericale & la democrazia,* etc.

ficial, the subject interests me in itself. I believe I have always been a "Modernist"; only it never crossed my mind that such an attitude was compatible with being a practical Catholic, much less a priest. How can they be so blind?—

Love to Celedonio and the family, with a great deal for yourself, from

To SUSANA STURGIS DE SASTRE

COLONIAL CLUB
CAMBRIDGE
APRIL 19, 1909

Dear Susie,

Thank you for your letter.—Mother, as you know, is getting on nicely, and we now have a nurse, —————, permanently established in the house. She is elderly, Irish, and Catholic, so that she eats in the kitchen and gets on with the other servants. She also prepares and serves Mother's food, does her room, sits there when Josephine is away, and makes herself as useful as she can, although Josephine doesn't give her a chance to take charge as much as she would like, and as would be advisable for Josephine's sake. They tell me that Mother is apt to be drowsy and somewhat restless in the morning, but in the afternoon, when I usually see her, she is placid and cheerful, busy with knitting or playing with cards, or folding papers and things. The only thing that is a little troublesome is that she thinks very often that she is not at home, and wants to go out to find her family—her father and mother, I think she means. But, with a little coaxing, she forgets this notion and settles down again, quite happy in her arm-chair.

You must have been sorry, and perhaps alarmed, to hear that Robert has given up his trip. It is a case of tender feeling on his part. There is no reason to think that Mother will not be as she is now at the end of the summer; but as she seems to like to see Robert, he feels that he had better stay. It is a natural sentiment, and I confess I thought it a little queer, considering Robert's character, that he should have planned to go away now. Of course, Mother forgets that he has come to see her as soon as he is gone, so that it makes no *steady difference* to her; but she seems to recognise him when he comes—that is, she is glad to see him, although she doesn't conceive that he is her son. Sometimes I think she imagines he is uncle Robert; but Josephine thinks I am wrong in this. . . .

My rheumatism is much better; only a little weakness in the right knee left. I take phosphate of sodium every morning, which is supposed to be like Carlsbad water, and it agrees with me very well, regulating the bowels as well as helping the rheumatism.

Since Robert is to stay, there is no reason why I shouldn't go; so that I have taken passages from N.Y. to Liverpool for July 14, and from Liverpool to N.Y. for September 18, in the big new Cunarder, where I find there are also single cabins to be had. I am sorry not to go to Avila, but the holiday is short, and I am thinking of spending it again chiefly at Oxford, where I have the Bodleian library to consult, and Bertrand Russell, the Earl's brother, to talk philosophy with. I am sailing so late on account of my lectures on "Modernism", which are to be on July 8 and 9. You ask me what "Modernism" is precisely. It is not anything precise; but as a general tendency, it consists in accepting all the rationalistic views current or possible in matters of history and science, and then saying that in a different sense, the dogmas of the Church may still be true. For instance, all miracles, including the Incarnation and Resurrection, are denied to be historical facts: but they remain, in some symbolic sense, theological truths. That is, they are normal ways in which religious imagination has expressed itself: and people ought to go on, in their devotions, using those expressions, just as they go on using a language or a style of dress that has naturally established itself. The Modernists say they are not Protestants, in that they wish to keep the whole doctrine and organisation of the Church and to develop it further, rather than to lop off parts of it. But they are free-thinkers, since they regard that whole doctrine and organisation as simply a human growth, symbolic only, and changeable. They also say (but this is a plain inconsistency) that there is a peculiar providence or Holy Spirit guiding the Catholic Church in its development, such as does *not* guide the Mahomedans or the Buddhists. This, however, is rejected by Paul Sabatier, a Protestant friend and defender of the Modernists.—Theologically considered, Modernism is untenable, like every theory of double truths: but I don't know how far it may express the filtering in of rationalism into the seminaries and among the clergy. Thank you for the *Lectura Dominical* of which one number has arrived so far. I didn't mean you to send it, as even if it mentions the subject, it will give a very onesided view of it. But I am always glad to read a little lively Spanish, and to get some hint of what is going on.

Love to all from

To SUSANA STURGIS DE SASTRE

COLONIAL CLUB,
CAMBRIDGE
MARCH 1, 1910

Dear Susie:

Yesterday Josephine showed me a letter of yours in which you say you want me to give you news of "high life" in New York. My visit there this year, though longer than last, wasn't so interesting, as I hardly saw any new people. Mrs. Astor (who has got a divorce from her husband) was not there, being in London presumably looking for a new spouse. I came across Jack Astor, however, at the Opera, and he did not assassinate me. My six lectures [1] took up a good deal of my time and energy, and the lunches and dinners I went to were rather conventional. At Mrs. Clarence Mackay's, however, the *food* was wonderful, and also the service. We were six people, four men and two ladies (no husband present) and we had a butler and four footmen, in red breeches and white silk stockings, pulled up very tight, to wait on us. Mrs. Mackay is a pronounced radical, weeps for the poor, and has a stamp with "Votes for Women" stuck on the back of her lavender and white note-paper.

[1] These lectures were delivered at Columbia University in February, 1910, and later composed the book *Three Philosophical Poets.*

Her hair is disarranged and poetical, and she affects a lace mantle or shawl. I suspect she writes poetry.—The Potters were in town, in a hired house, looking for a place in the country in which to settle down, with all their ancestral belongings. I saw them a good deal. Also Mrs. Ralph Ellis (sister-in-law of Ward Thoron) who is very gay and jolly, and rather handsome. Her husband also is a nice person.—Moncure Robinson was kind and friendly, getting me a great many invitations, and having me to breakfast, as all his lunches and dinners were taken up. He also talked of a motor-trip in France this summer, but that is very problematical.—In April I am going to repeat my six lectures (they are all written out and all I have to do is to read them) at the University of Wisconsin in Madison; and on the way I am going to read another lecture in Chicago. Madison will be a great contrast to New York, as it is a small place of 30,000 inhabitants (although the capital of Wisconsin) with a co-educational college. I shall be there about ten days, and it will be dull unless I can occasionally escape the attentions of the academic circle. In Chicago I may see amusing things, as the people who are to have me in tow seem to be semi-Bohemian, semi-rich, and semi-literary.

As to next summer, I don't exactly know what plans to make. Mother, as you know, is relatively well: but she is weaker every month, and it is impossible to say when the end may come. I have engaged my passages to Europe and back—for June 8th and September 17th—as if nothing were to be the matter. Robert (who had persuaded himself that mother could not live through the winter) will of course stay here, on the ground that she cannot live through the summer. It seems to me rather horrible to stay myself on that ground. Do you think I ought to? My presence might be of some use to Josephine, but also some trouble: and, if all went well, like last Summer, it would be all trouble and no use. Robert in any case would manage everything, and I confess the impulse to go away is very strong in me, even when I consider that the end might come in my absence. Mother does not know the difference, and Robert and Josephine could have things in their own way without criticism from me. I feel like a fifth wheel to the coach, that might as well roll off by itself. Mother gets up for a few hours every day, and has her food regularly. She does not speak coherently, and is too weak to walk. She sleeps and dozes most of the time, or amuses herself with picture-books, papers, and dolls. Sometimes, she seems amused and satisfied, usually rather listless. It is a strange sort of half-existence, but fortunately painless and without regrets.

Love to Celedonio and the family,

Yours affec^{ly}

To SUSANA STURGIS DE SASTRE

UNIVERSITY CLUB
MADISON, WIS.
APRIL 18, 1910

Dear Susie,

This place is, as you supposed, very much like a small Boston. The only peculiarity of it is that it is situated between three small lakes, and built on several hills, so that it is picturesque at a distance, although the houses are of the usual American wooden, nondescript kind. The university has some good buildings, and lawns, but is of course only half-finished, and full of architectural incongruities—one building brick and Gothic, the next stone and classical, the next a wooden shed, or a concrete store-house. The professors are very presentable, their wives more provincial than themselves, for they marry too young, and then, by their studies and contact with the world, outgrow the class they belonged to in their youth, and to which their wives belong. The students seem to be good fellows, not essentially different from those at Harvard, except that the extremes of fashion and poverty are wanting here. My lectures [1] are not such a success as they were in New York, because my ultra-modern, "superior-person" point of view is not familiar here, as it is in that very cosmopolitan and ventilated place —New York. However, some of the professors who come to hear me are very appreciative. Tomorrow, I am going to meet a class of advanced students who have been *studying one of my books!* It

[1] The lectures that later composed the book *Three Philosophical Poets*.

makes me feel strangely famous—although the sales of my books
rather indicate that nobody reads them.

I am glad that you think it is all right that I should go to Europe this summer as usual. I certainly hope to get to Avila in August, and I shall be glad to find you all as I left you two years ago.

With love to Celedonio and the family, and a great deal for
yourself

Yours aff^{ly}

To JOHN FRANCIS STANLEY, 2nd EARL RUSSELL

AVILA, JULY 29 1910

Dear Russell,

The cuttings you enclose interest me only as justifying an old
saying of Goethe's: *Die Engländer haben keine Intelligenz."* All
this sort of gossip is worthless, and this sort of controversy ridiculous. The Catholic Church is intolerant on principle, and the expression of this intolerance is limited only by the influence she is
able to exercise over the civil power. She would repress, and ex-
terminate, all heresy and schism, if she were able. To talk about
persecutions inspired by her as due to individual irritation or hot
temper is pure nonsense; and if English Catholics indulge in it, it
is because they must be ignoramuses, or cowards.

As to the sympathy you betray, however, with Ferrer,[1] and the
present instigators and perpetrators of murder (who are naturally
the defenders of Ferrer) I am separated from you *toto coelo.* The
attempted assassination of Maura [2] (the noblest figure we now have
in Spain) was the direct consequence of the instigation to such an
attempt uttered by Pablo Iglesias in the Chamber, and published
—without liability to prosecution for it—by all the papers. Just so

---

[1] A well-known Anarchist who was charged with having helped to instigate the
insurrection in Barcelona in 1909. He was later tried and executed.

[2] The Prime Minister of the Conservative Party.

the attempted murder of the King and Queen at their wedding had been instigated by Ferrer, and carried out by his young pupil Moraes. The insurrection in Barcelona was cruel itself; the repression of it was mild and much less than was legally warranted or (as I think) politically useful. It is the presence of cowards in the Government now, that encourages continued outrages and the disgraceful tone, in the revolutionary press in Spain and abroad, which makes it appear that the anarchists, who throw bombs, burn convents, and shoot at old gentlemen in railway stations, are the martyrs, and their victims the tyrants. It would be incredible, if madness and ignorance had not, since the world began, been the chief impulses that keep men talking in public. The tyrants in Spain are the anarchists and the revolutionary press; it is they that carry things with a high hand, and defend—and do—murder. But what is the use of talking about anything, however patent the fact may be, when what guides events, and people's opinions, is not justice or the facts in the case, but a certain party instinct, or sense for the direction in which they would wish things to move? Now, I am entirely able to feel that the whole society of Christendom (compared with that of Greece, or even with that of Islam) rests on a false and artificial basis; and I can share the hope of those anarchists, or other rebels, who dream of some future more naturalistic system of thought and life—say with free love, and without individual property.

But it is one thing to see the arbitrary and ultimately unstable character of a civilisation (every civilisation is essentially unstable) and another to set about destroying it by blind force. This latter system is hateful, because inspired only by hate: it has no ideal of a positive sort to inspire it, nor, if it had, could it attain that ideal merely by destroying what now exists. The want of intelligence is immense, that does not see that everything we have that makes (or might make) life worth living is an incident to the irrational, traditional civilisation in which we have been reared. All things are like language, which we must use, beautify, but not worship; and your anarchists are mere blundering dumb beasts, that sputter and howl, because they find the rules of grammar absurd and inconvenient. So they are, for people who are too stupid or too ill-bred to use them: but that does not make these people martyrs, or heralds of progress. It only makes them fit to be exhibited naked in cages, like other wild animals, and fed on raw meat through the bars.

I didn't mean to write a long letter, nor have I the least idea of modifying your opinion on these subjects. Only, I wanted to save you the trouble of sending me the chance thoughts of the provincial correspondents of the Daily News—Quakers or others.

Yours ever,

To ARTHUR DAVISON FICKE

3 PRESCOTT HALL
CAMBRIDGE, MASS.
OCT. 24, 1910

Dear Ficke

Your new book [1] has interested me very much and I must thank you, not only for sending it to me, but for the unusual pleasure I have found in reading it. The form you have chosen justifies itself in the result, for although I sometimes felt that the unrhymed passages might as well have been frankly in prose, the interest in the thought was almost always sufficient to carry me in pleasant unconsciousness over the details of the form. If you can attain *perfect* transparency and fitness of expression, and you are near attaining it, there will be nothing more to ask for in that direction.

I have noticed two or three impurities of idiom (or what seemed such to me) of the sort that a reader of American writing can hardly fail to slip into. What is it "to seek . . . fulfilment of the days that were my shame"? Or what is "infinite divertness"? And why should "day" be feminine? You will think this hypercritical; but, when I read poetry, I expect "integras accedere fontes", else I am not satisfied.

As to your prophecy itself (which is of more moment) all is convincing except the end. To my unilluminated mind it seems impossible that mankind should all be free, in any full sense of this word. They cannot be free if they don't exist; they can't exist, if they don't eat; and they can't eat, if they don't work. But to have to work, even if not to overwork, at definite tasks, hours, and places,

---

1 *The Breaking of Bonds,* (1910).

is not freedom. It is compulsion, and living willy-nilly in a once-determined groove.

You will forgive these frank observations, in view of the proof they are of the keen interest your book has aroused in me. It is splendid to find a real subject treated in the work of a young poet —or of any poet.

Yours sincerely

To SUSANA STURGIS DE SASTRE

COLONIAL CLUB
CAMBRIDGE
DECEMBER 23, 1910

Dear Susie,

A happy New Year to you and Celedonio, and the rest of the family.

Here there is no change. Mrs. Pollard, the nurse mother had until a week ago, is probably coming back; the one we have now is not unsatisfactory, but was not meant to be permanent.

I have read the article (largely from "La Croix") which you inclosed for me in a recent letter. My impression is that Catholicism in France—as elsewhere—may well gain in intensity what it loses in extension. Ceasing to be a matter of course for everybody, it becomes, for those who adopt it expressly, a personal conviction and affection; also a matter of party, a thing to be defended and propagated with zeal. This, however, is only the compensation for a very real and permanent loss—the loss of a dominant and pervasive influence over society. In a word, the Church is tending to acquire everywhere the sort of relation to the State and to society which it has in non-catholic countries; and you know very well that this position, while it has its advantages in the way of fostering strictures and zeal among the faithful minority, is not at all the position which the Church claims, and would like to preserve.

My object in writing today is to tell you that I have just accepted an invitation to lecture for six weeks next summer at the University of California. This invitation comes, probably, in the very latest year when I could have accepted it, and the chance to see the Far West, and what lies between (although I don't care for it particularly) ought, I suppose, not to be missed. The lectures will be mere shortened versions of those I give here, and will involve no preparation, while the fee ($500) will almost cover my expenses, and I shall save all I should have spent in going to Europe. I shall also be nearer Boston if there should be any need of my hastening back.

This cuts off the possibility of seeing you next summer: but I had hardly expected to get to Avila in any case, so that nothing is lost in that direction: and after one other winter, you may see only too much of me.

With love to all,

Your affectionate brother

To EDWARD J. O'BRIEN

3 PRESCOTT HALL
CAMBRIDGE
DEC. 26, 1910

Dear Mr. O'Brien

I am much touched by your thinking of sending me your paper on Jones's [1] poetry, together with those of your friends, and particularly with the inscription you have prefixed to it. But why do you canonise Lionel Johnson? I remember him very well in his last days.

Poetry in words, like fiction in life, is something which has ceased to be natural to me, and if I read Jones's verses I doubt whether they would impress me very much. No doubt the faculty of dreams may be as precious as waking, and less wearisome than

[1] Thomas S. Jones.

insomnia; but when one falls into prose, it is hard to rise again out of it. Another fiction which you amiably weave is the "quia multum amavit" which you apply to me. Any love while we have it seems great; but we must, in retrospect, reduce things to some proportion.

It is a pleasure for me to see that there is a school of the poetically minded round the corner, which we do not suspect the existence of here. The Stickney—Moody—Lodge School, well known to me, was turbid and turgid beyond endurance, in spite of flashes of gunpowder—for I will not call it lightning or genius. How interesting, if in Catholic circles, something simpler, tenderer, and more truly lived should arise in America!

Believe me, with best thanks and best wishes,

Yours sincerely

To MRS. FREDERICK WINSLOW

COLONIAL CLUB
CAMBRIDGE
MARCH 1, 1911

Dear Mrs Winslow

I shall be delighted to come next Tuesday, the 7th at half past seven. It is nice to know that you are well again, as your writing implies. As to your new son, I daresay he is a model of all a child should be, but for my part I am too prosaic and disillusioned to lavish any more unrequited affections upon objects unconscious of my regard. Besides, I am faithful to my Polly. It may be that in her young life she has sometimes forgotten me; but she has never re- fused to make eyes at me in my presence; while I am afraid I can expect nothing but stony indifference from her young brother, considering the disadvantage of his sex and age.

By the way, if you are having a regular dinner party on Tues- day, I should think it very, very nice of you to let me come some other day instead—I have absolutely no engagements—when I could really see you and make up for this long interval since our last talks.

Yours sincerely

To SUSANA STURGIS DE SASTRE

COLONIAL CLUB
CAMBRIDGE
MAY 16, 1911.

Dear Susie,

You have heard, of course, that there has been some change for the worse in Mother's condition: for a week she has had a slight fever, and has not rested so quietly as usual, and eaten less. When awake, however, she seems much as she did a month ago; she laughs occasionally and does not seem to have any pain or discomfort. I suppose this is simply one more stage in her slow decline: but it is remarkable how slow this decline is, and how steadily her system runs on, even with its lessening vitality.

I write today because I have had a very important interview with the President of the College,[1] in which we have agreed upon a new arrangement for my future work. I had finally been obliged to write to him saying that I meant to resign at the end of next year, twelve months from now: and he made a great ado about it, saying that it would never do, and that he would let me have all the free time I wanted if I would stay. After various suggestions it has been arranged that in future I shall be in Cambridge only four months the first half of each year, from October 1st to February 1st, and that besides I shall have leave of absence for the whole of the year 1912–13. I am to have half my present pay, that is $2000 a year, and half of that during the year I am away altogether. So that I shall be free for eighteen months after February 1st next,

[1] Abbott Lawrence Lowell was then President of Harvard College.

my holiday being thus advanced to half a year earlier than I expected. On the other hand, I am pledged to return for four months on October 1st 1913; but that is a long way off, and even if nothing intervenes to prevent it, there will be no need of repeating the experiment if I find it irksome. So that it seemed wiser and more accommodating to make this concession, rather than stick out for my original plan, especially as it makes my income larger and more assured.

I am leaving for California about June 15, and can be back as early as September 1st. Should circumstances demand, I could stay on here after February 1st, as I shall have my rooms for the whole season: but if it should not be necessary, I will sail then for Europe, and you may see me again before the winter is quite over.

I have not been to any dinners or other parties this winter, but I was in New York at Easter for a week, and have also visited Bowdoin, Bryn Mawr, and Williams Colleges, reading in each a paper on Shelley, the product of the Shelley Club I have had this year—a group of young men who came on Wednesday afternoons to have a cup of tea and read Shelley aloud. I am pretty tired of lecturing, but enjoy what reading I can do more than ever, and feel as if all the interesting things were still to be read and studied. I am writing a brand new system of philosophy to be called "Three Realms of Being" [1]—not the mineral vegetable and animal, but something far more metaphysical, namely Essence, Matter and Consciousness. It will not be a long book,[2] but very technical.

I continue to read *La lectura dominical* with pleasure, especially the *Cronica*. Spanish politics are extremely interesting, and I am pining for a season at Madrid, to understand them better.

Love to all from your aff^{te} brother

---

[1] It is interesting to note that Santayana's famous system of philosophy, *Realms of Being*, was first conceived by him so many years ago. It was not finally completed until 1940. In its final form it became *four* realms of being, a realm of *Truth* being added, and the earlier realm of *Consciousness* was later called the realm of *Spirit*.

[2] Not counting the Introductory volume (*Scepticism and Animal Faith*), or the various Prefaces, etc., the work ran to 854 printed pages!

To CONRAD SLADE

COLONIAL CLUB
CAMBRIDGE
JUNE 1ST 1911

Dear Conrad

I can't say I am very sorry, nor even very much surprised, that you are "still free". There was something a bit exotic about your proposed marriage, and your attachment was hardly violent enough to justify the step. Nevertheless, I am sorry there is to be no house to visit you in at Arles, and no little "nephews".

This summer, for a change, I am going to California! The University of California at Berkeley, has invited me to teach there for six weeks, and offered me $500, which will almost cover my expenses. It seemed a good chance to see the Pacific, like Cortes, before I die, and probably the last chance I should have, so I have accepted. So I shall not be in Oxford, or anywhere else within reach this summer, for which I am sorry. On the other hand, I have made an arrangement with the College here, by which in future I shall be here only for the first half of each year, from October 1st to the end of January. This arrangement begins at once, so that next February I shall turn up in Paris (or in Italy), and perhaps see you at once; or, in any case, before long, as I shall remain in Europe the whole of the following year, which is my "sabbatical", not needing to return to Harvard until September, 1913, and then only for four months. Whether I shall ever return after that is very doubtful; but I thought it wiser to make this arrangement than to insist at once on resigning altogether, especially during the life-time of my mother.

My friend Strong has taken an apartment in the Avenue de l'Observatoire, and has kindly invited me to stay there whenever I am in Paris. In fact, I am to have a room in his house with a place in which to keep my books and other belongings—almost a home! This will make it pleasant and economical for me to be often in Paris, and I count on seeing you constantly, for whatever your temporary impatience with the Parisian scene may be, you (like Strong) will never find another place in which you can really settle.

The news about your neo-classical head is excellent. Send me a photo of it, if you have one.

Your idea of coming to Oxford when I am there must be carried out some day—possibly next Spring. May and the early part of June are the best months there, unless you like, as I do, the place without the inhabitants. In mid-summer, however, you have the tourists instead, which is worse.

Yours ever

To PORTER GARNETT

UNIVERSITY CLUB
SAN FRANCISCO
AUGUST 15, 1911

Dear Mr. Garnett.

It has been a great pleasure, after seeing and hearing "The Green Knight," [1] to read the text at leisure, and the interesting introduction. As I told you, I am particularly pleased with the moral or "ritualistic" character of the whole, and now I appreciate better how many temptations you had to withstand in order to preserve it. In studying the text, which seemed to me very fine and well-sustained, I see that you have confined yourself to abstract or musical attitudes—the wood god simply *invited,* the Prince *suffers,* the Black Knight and Sathanas *bluster* and *threaten,* the Green Knight *cheers,* the King *relieves.* I mean that these attitudes are expressed without any indication of what circumstances may have produced them. They are abstract or absolute moods or sentiments. This may take away from the picturesqueness and fulness which your play might have had, if we had been told what cares Care

---

1 While in San Francisco Santayana attended the Bohemian Grove Play of that year—"The Green Knight"; and I am indebted to the Bancroft Library of the University of California for this interesting letter.

stands for, say in the case of the Prince and the various prisoners, or what form the liberation from care takes in each case. But I quite understand that this universality is desirable in a rite to which each participant may bring his own interpretation, his own care, and his own hope of redemption. Or perhaps later Grove Plays, that may be modelled on the principles you have laid down and illustrated so impressively, may take up now one and now another instance in which care is relieved by nature and beauty; and that would open up an infinite vista of variations upon your general theme.

Another point that seems to me very important is your *sincerity*. The pagan motive in Christian form is just what the spirit of the time can be expressed in. I am struck in California by the deep and almost religious affection which people have for nature, and by the sensitiveness they show to its influences; not merely poetically, but also athletically, because they like to live as nature lives. It is a relief from business and the genteel tradition. It is their spontaneous substitute for articulate art and articulate religion, and is perhaps the substance out of which these may some day be formed afresh. In conceiving a rite, carried on in the Bohemian Grove, that shall express this sense of "grace" coming from communion with nature, you seem to have hit on something wonderfully genuine and appealing and you ought to find a hearty response, and a general understanding of what you mean. Will you find it? It is not for me to say; but my impression is that it will be difficult, because rites and arts of this sort seem to require a nucleus of minstrels or hierophants that take them up as a sort of profession, and then diffuse them, by continual performances and settled forms of expression, to which the public gets accustomed. I am afraid our friends of the Bohemian Club are not quite ready to be the necessary chorus.

I was sorry to run away yesterday without saying goodbye, and thanking you for all your kindness, and for the absolutely unmatched opportunities you have given me of seeing what is best in Californian life. I shall never forget the Grove, and The Green Knight, and I hope I may have other chances of discussing it with you before I leave, which will not be for a fortnight yet. Thank you also for the beautiful book of the play.

Yours sincerely,

To SUSANA STURGIS DE SASTRE

COLONIAL CLUB
CAMBRIDGE
NOV. 7, 1911

Dear Susie,

In California, and again the other day in Montreal, I often wanted to write to you of the various things that I thought might interest you there or that suggested Spain and things un-American generally. But somehow the moment never came, as if some contrary impulse intervened. I felt as if you were not quite in sympathy with my present mood and plans, which mark a distinct and to me most welcome change in my life.

Mother remains about the same. She sleeps the greater part of the day as well as all night. When I see her—at about seven in the evening—she is almost always awake, or rather half-awake. Only on her "bright" days does she look up when I speak to her, or turn her eyes away from the doll or scrap of paper that she holds in her hand. Sometimes she smiles a little, but never says anything intelligible. The decline in her physical strength, if it exists, is almost imperceptible. Josephine,[1] I think, has become a little hardened to this situation, and is more willing than some months ago to leave Mother's room, and to interest herself in something else. The nurse is a bustling talkative creature, perfectly odious to me, and I avoid her as I should the plague. Josephine also suffers from her aggressive airs, but on the whole puts up with her for fear of a change for the worse, or of change itself, which in such a matter is always agitating. In her material business as a nurse, the woman is satisfactory and faithful. She is paid exorbitantly, so that she tries to please, as far as her bad breeding and tactlessness allow. Robert[2] seems to like her.

As the time for my departure approaches—I sail from N.Y. on January 27—I have considered what I could do to leave less to be done by others when the house is broken up, which I suppose

[1] Josephine Sturgis, his half-sister.

[2] Robert Sturgis, his half-brother.

will be before my return—if I return—in September 1913. My
own things are almost all disposed of, or will be before I go: but
the house is full of old truck that might as well be thrown away
now as later. I have proposed to Josephine that she should let me
do some clearing up: and with some hesitation she consented that
I should look over Mother's desk, full of old papers. In one day
I did it,—looking over everything separately. In one envelope I
found twenty four dollars in clean "bills", but not the larger sum
that was lost a few years ago. Many of the documents were interesting. I kept all letters from your uncles and aunts, and documents
relating to your father and our grandfather, among the latter his
U.S. (or rather Virginian) naturalisation papers, his appointment
as Consul, signed by Andrew Jackson, and a testimonial of affection from the townspeople of Winchester.[1] These letters and
papers—not bulky at all—I have left in Mother's desk, for Robert
to examine if he likes. My father's letters, I have taken possession
of myself and I have been reading them with almost unmingled
pleasure. When I have finished—they are very numerous—I may
write you something about the impressions and doubts they raise
in my mind about the inner history of our family. In any case, I
mean to take them to Avila, where the other half of the correspondence is, I suppose, in the large packages in my desk, which
I have never opened. Your letters to Mother I have, in agreement
with Josephine, burnt unread. We thought that would be what
you would prefer to have us do, unless you wished to see them
yourself: but I don't think you would care to. I read my own
letters to Mother before burning them. They were very impersonal and I learned nothing from them that I didn't personally
remember. The other chief contents of Mother's desk were thou-
sands of paid bills and notices or coupons or yearly accounts.—I
found no letters at all from Dª Victorina or Mercedes [2] or any
(except very old ones) from other friends.

By the way, as I am going first to England and Paris, I shall
stop in Avila—though only for a few days—before I go to Madrid.
This will be in February. You can then tell me if you think Mercedes really wants me to go to her. I can well imagine that, at
close quarters, that project might please her less; and I might be

---

[1] See *Persons and Places*, Vol. I, Chap. 1, "Time, Place and Ancestry."

[2] Two old Spanish friends of the family.

freer in a hotel. But I want to spend some time in Madrid in any case.

Love to Celedonio and all the family from your affectionate brother

To SUSANA STURGIS DE SASTRE

COLONIAL CLUB
CAMBRIDGE
DEC. 7, 1911

Dear Susie:

I am very sorry if you have been *debanandote los sesos* about what I could have meant by saying that I thought you were not in sympathy with my present mood. What I meant was (chiefly) that I am very sick of America and of professors and professoresses, and that I am pining for a sunny, quiet, remote, friendly, intellectual, obscure existence, with large horizons and no empty noise in the foreground. What I have seen in California and Canada—apart from the geography of those regions—has left no impression on my mind whatever. They are intellectually emptier than the Sahara, where I understand the Arabs have some idea of God or of Fate. Where did you get the impression that anything in California could have affected my opinions or sentiments? When there, in my Italian restaurant, or in Montreal among the ultra-British Scotch-Canadians I saw, I felt almost out of America, so much so that I once said inadvertently to someone in San Francisco that I soon had to go back *to America*. That is why, from those places, I felt like expressing myself: because when I am here in the midst of the dull round, a sort of instinct of courtesy makes me take it for granted, and I become almost unconscious of how much I hate it all: otherwise I couldn't have stood it for *forty years!*

As to your supposition that I am removing myself "farther from God", apparently in some deliberate manner, I certainly have no consciousness of such a plan. My opinions in philosophy have not changed essentially for twenty years, although they may have settled and grown less plastic with time. In respect to the Church, I think I am in greater sympathy with it politically than I was previously, because the radical people I know are proving to be such Hottentots and so wholly ignorant of the art of living and of the art of thinking. The Church is an integral part of European civilisation, as it has been for the last thousand years and more. The "satanic" onslaught on it which you lament is a symptom of a general transformation, which will take hundreds of years to become definable in its results or ideals, and which is tending to destroy not the Church only but all institutions, including private property and national governments. The French Revolution was a first and violent shock of this earthquake; others will follow from time to time, I suppose, until, long after we are dead, everything we know and care about has disappeared. Now, I sympathise with the self-preserving instinct of formed things more than with the destructive forces of nature, such as democratic envy, fury, and ignorance are. Therefore I sympathise with the Church more than with its enemies: but I think the latter must prevail more and more in the world in our time. I also think that after the deluge, life and order are bound to reassert themselves in some form—doubtless a wholly new one. I should not be hostile to that new order for not being Christian, as I am not hostile to ancient Greece. But we don't know what that new order may some day be, and meantime the revolution is destroying everything noble and beautiful which actually exists, or which can exist in our day. It is producing nothing but vulgarity, shallowness, and a suicidal waywardness in the "emancipated souls"—like those of the Infanta Eulalia. These people are positively *loathsome*. They do not understand the creative and moral principle of anything, least of all of what they are themselves.—They are *silly traitors*. Yet, without in the least knowing what they are about, they are ploughing up the ground in which the seeds of new things are to take root. For, as Hamlet says, "so runs the world away".

I will write to Mercedes [1] before long. Would it simplify matters if I was a "lodger" and not a "boarder" at her house, do you think? I should rather like being free to explore the cafés and restaurants, and not be tied down to hours, especially at a

[1] Mercedes de la Escalera, an old friend of the family.

place so far from the centre of the town. I could have my chocolate
in bed, and go out for lunch and dinner, as I did very pleasantly
in Paris.

Love to all

To JOHN FRANCIS STANLEY, 2nd EARL RUSSELL

COLONIAL CLUB,
CAMBRIDGE.
JANUARY 2, 1912

Dear Russell,

Your letter of some months ago has somehow remained unanswered. Although I had several things to say in reply, and have
been thinking about you especially, because in looking over my
old papers I have come upon a lot of your letters and reread them
all, being carried back to 1887 and the following years, when all
that happened to you was so much a part of my life. I can see now
how great an influence you had on me. It was an influence for
good. It seems almost as if I had gathered the fruits of your courage
and independance, while you have suffered the punishment which
the world imposes always on those who refuse to conform to its
ways. You may say you are content, but with your position and
character you ought to have had a greater career. Isn't it, at bottom, because you have tried to combine liberty with democracy,
in your personal as well as political alliances, and *liberty and
democracy are really incompatible?* I will explain what I mean
by word of mouth (it would take up too much paper) if you are
in England. I expect to reach London on February 1st. Send me
a line c/o Brown, Shipley & Co. 123, Pall Mall.

Yours ever,

To SUSANA STURGIS DE SASTRE

ON BOARD R.M.S. "OLYMPIC"
JAN. 29, 1912

Dear Susie,

We expect to reach Plymouth tomorrow at about noon, after a voyage of just six days. The weather has been wintry, with winds, rain, snow, hail and rather rough seas, and the ship has rolled merrily, like the old-fashioned craft: nevertheless, size helps, for the motion is slow and majestic, and most of the passengers (I among them) have kept well and not missed a meal in the dining-room.

In New York, the one day I was there, I went out to lunch, tea, dinner, a play, a musicale in a private house, and the ball given by the Whitelaw Reids to the Duke of Connaught and his family. I was in bed, however, by half past twelve, as we stayed only a short time at each place. I saw some agreeable people, and some striking costumes and jewels.

It is probable that I shall have to go to Cambridge on an official mission from Harvard, to see if I can get someone there to go to America for next winter in the capacity of a temporary professor. I have not been in the English Cambridge for years, and shall not be sorry of this occasion for revisiting the place, where I still have some friends.

I will write again (or send a card) when my movements are decided upon.

Leaving my rooms and disposing of all my possessions was very fatiguing; but I am now quite myself again, though I shall be glad to sleep in a motionless bed, with fresh air, and walk on *terra firma*.

Yours aff^ly

Memorias a toda la familia.

To SUSANA STURGIS DE SASTRE

QUEEN'S ACRE
WINDSOR [ENGLAND]
FEBRUARY 6, 1912

Dear Susie,

I have just got a telegram, like one you must have received also, saying that Mother died yesterday. Josephine had written on Jan. 24, saying the doctor had been to see her twice, and found her better; but I can't gather whether this means that she had been ill before that date, or whether the change for the worse came later. I am anxiously awaiting particulars, although, so far as Mother herself is concerned, I imagine there was little except a decline into more complete unconsciousness. But the external circumstances must have affected Josephine and Robert, and I very much wish to know how Josephine has borne up—or rather is bearing up—under the shock and the immense change in her own life. If she has gone to Robert's house, I am not at all confident that she will find it easier to fall into a new way of occupying her time. I have answered Robert by cable, asking whether Josephine will join me. The last day I saw Robert he said it would not be possible for him to leave Boston immediately after Mother's death, but would require a good many weeks in which to arrange all the matters of business involved, and he seemed to think too that it was not advisable to cross the Atlantic in March—why, I don't know exactly, since the chances of bad weather are not so very much greater than in April or May. So that if poor Josephine is stranded and ill at ease, I think she might find a friend, or even mere acquaintance, to cross with, and I might meet her where ever she landed, and go with her to your house. If she decides to wait till Robert is ready, I should of course go to see her on the way, but I don't think it would be well for Robert and me to go to Spain together. I will either go to see you before they come, or put it off till Robert has left you. I have written to him today that I will not leave England until I hear more fully from him and Josephine.

I hope you will not harrow up your own feelings and make yourself ill over all the past and present horrors which this event brings to a head. We were certainly not unprepared for it; it was inevitable, and has been delayed longer than we could have hoped. Nothing remains but to heal the wound, especially in Josephine's case, as best we may.—I confess I do not see any solution that is altogether promising, as to how and where she is to live.

I suppose you will write to me, or have already written, and then we can put our heads together and see what can be done.

What a tremendous change this is! Mother was the absolutely dominating force in all our lives. Even her mere existence, in these last years, was a sort of centre around which we revolved, in thought if not in our actual movements. We shall be living henceforth in an essentially different world. I hope you and I may be nearer rather than farther from one another in consequence.

I know Celedonio and all the family will be full of kind and sympathetic sentiments towards us all on this occasion: by your letter of Jan. 10, which Josephine has sent me, I know they are well, and send them my greetings.

Your affectionate brother

To MRS. FREDERICK WINSLOW

MADRID, APRIL 2, 1912

Dear Mrs. Winslow:

Does Mrs. Warren describe as "glimpses" the brief hours of rapt contemplation during which we gazed at each other across the tea-table, surrounded by Lady Lawrence, Miss Honor (not Beauty), Mrs. Osgood and several semi-attached young women and emaciated young men. *Es war ein Traum!*

I have followed—somewhat slowly—the general plan I had for the rest of the winter and spring. In England I visited my usual hosts, and went besides to Cambridge where I slept in a medieval dungeon, in the Clock Tower of Trinity College, being the guest of Bertie Russell: I sentimentally evoked memories of the past by walking on the tow-paths and watching the college eights practice; I dined in Hall, saw Dickinson [1] and other old acquaintances, and altogether drenched myself in diluted emotions. It was terribly cold, particularly in bed.—In Paris I was only a few days, and did nothing worth mentioning, except to visit the apartment where I am to live next month, and after, with my friend Strong. It is very suitable, but I could imagine something more luxurious and Byzantine, if I put my mind to it. Possibly, if I find Strong docile, I may add a few touches of frivolity to the solemn scene.—In Avila, while continuing to suffer from the cold, I found my sister [2] and her family as usual, and stayed nearly a fortnight; whence I came here, to begin life with my new mate, Mercedes.[3] We get on beautifully, I eat a lot (having had only one colic so far), walk a lot, and have even managed to do some real work, having had one or two spells of industry and absorption over my books and papers. I hope to get out a book of essays,[4] including the Shelley, in the autumn. This is only by the way, not being one of the three post-professorial works which I have *in petto*. My native town is, for the most part, rather mean and ugly, and the people of a low type; but the newer parts are pretty, almost distinguished; the *nice* people have a great deal of charm and naturalness, as well as feeling: the amusements really amuse, the Churches are churches, and the sun and sky are like the Platonic ideas of these things. The weather, though variable, is often delightful, and the Park and promenades are fine. So that I am quite happy here, and should be glad to return next winter, if my sister Josephine were here and wanted me to keep her company. As you perhaps have heard, she and my brother Robert are sailing at the end of the month. I shall see them in Paris, when they pass through, in May, on their way to Spain.

The photograph of the little angel does not do him justice, but merely serves to remind me of how sleepy and metaphysical he looked when I saw him in his crib. As to Polly, she is not sufficiently in evidence, but here too my memory can supply the diffi-

---

[1] Lowes Dickinson.

[2] Susana Sturgis de Sastre.

[3] Mercedes de la Escalera, an old friend of the family.

[4] *Winds of Doctrine.*

culties of merely *suggestive* art. The figs, prunes, and ginger came
in very well, and I observed no ill effects of indulging in them—
with some moderation to be sure. The voyage was not smooth nor
very agreeable in other ways, but I wasn't positively sea-sick, and
went to all my meals like a veteran.

It is one o'clock, and at any moment Mercedes, who is gadding
all day, will knock at my door and cry—*Jorge!* so that I may not
have many more minutes to finish this sheet in. We dine at one
and sup at eight—call it lunch and dinner, and it would be quite
English. The food, however, is very Spanish, and excellent; only I
eat too much. There is a restaurant, called "The Ideal Room" (in
English) which almost deserves its name, and where I usually have
tea; the waiters have silk stockings and shoes with silver buckles,
and at about six there is a great gathering of ladies with daughters,
young swells, and foreigners. The bull-fighting element, with its
many camp-followers, is excluded by the prices (tea is 15 cents!)
but is to be found next door, at another café, and opposite in great
numbers. It is very picturesque in appearance and even more so
in language; the love of talk, and of a sort of constant play-acting
in real life, is extraordinary here. It is as among the ancients, and
explains the origin of Greek drama and eloquence—perhaps of
all literature.—Mercedes must have found some particularly griev-
ous wrong to right this morning; but my stomach wants to be
given something to do, while my brain says *basta!*

Thank you and Fred very much for your kind messages.

To SUSANA STURGIS DE SASTRE

MADRID
APRIL 8, 1912

Dear Susie,

During Holy Week I tried to see the things you recommended,
not always succeeding; but I got glimpses that were interesting of
several functions. Mercedes [1] got me a ticket, through the Duquesa
de la Conquista, for the *Lavatorio* in the royal palace; but evidently

---
[1] Mercedes de la Escalera.

they had been very lavish with them, for it proved impossible to get into the hall, and inside there were shrieks and fainting-fits. I saw the procession, however, in the gallery, very well: and I have of course seen the King and Queen, and other royalties, on many occasions. Yesterday I went (as you suggested) to San Francisco el Grande, and heard the music. It was a mass by Perosi, very nice by itself, but sung as I thought too furiously, and without taste. The organist was the most obstreperous, and the singers seemed to catch the infection. But they had fine voices.—The singing in the body of the Church seems to have been given up.

The other day, when I was peacefully having tea outside the "Ideal Room" in the Calle de Alcala, I found before me, when I got up to leave, the spectre of a woman! It was Manuela,[1] with a parcel wrapped in a newspaper under her arm, who suggested that we should go for a walk: and dragged me up and down the most solitary alleys of the Rebiro, by the light of the full moon, before she thought it time to go home. Our conversation, however, was not sentimental. I have been a second time to see them and delivered your boa, which Mercedes did up scientifically in a very compact form. Juan [2] comes sometimes in the evening and we go out to a café or small show. I think he wanted me to take him to the big bull fight yesterday, but I preferred to go alone; today I am going to the Primera de Abono, to sit next to Mercedes' cousins, the Manfredi boys, whom I have not yet seen. Don't tell Celedonio that I have been to bull-fights, if you think it would shock him.

Yours aff[ly]

P.S. I am thinking of staying here until the 22nd, when I might go to you for a week.—Thank Celedonio for his card.

[1] Manuela Santayana, a cousin. See *Persons and Places,* Chap. XIV, p. 221, "First Return to Spain", for an amusing account of matrimonial schemes.

[2] Juan Santayana, brother of Manuela.

To *ABBOTT LAWRENCE LOWELL*

PARIS, JUNE 6, 1912

Dear Mr. Lowell:

Your letter about the proposed lectures at some French Universities reaches me when I was about to write to you in a wholly different sense. The death of my mother, which occurred shortly after I left America, has made a great change in my personal situation, leaving me without a home in Boston and with most of my close friends and relations living in Europe. It seems clearly to mark the moment when I should carry out the plan I have always had of giving up teaching, returning to live in Europe, and devoting myself to literary work. Each of these things is an object in itself sufficient to determine me, and the three conspire together. The plan which you kindly proposed and we agreed upon last winter, that I should continue to spend four months of each year at Harvard, certainly had many advantages; but it was a compromise. I hardly think we could have been faithful to it long. I should not have attained my object of a change of life, and I should not have left the field open for you to choose my successor. In any case, under the changed circumstances, I could not bring myself to return to Cambridge. I therefore enclose a formal resignation of my professorship, and I hope you will not ask me to reconsider it. This is a step I have meditated on all my life, and always meant to take when it became possible; but I am sorry the time coincides so nearly with the beginning of your Presidency, when things at Harvard are taking a direction with which I am so heartily in sympathy, and when personally I had begun to receive marks of greater appreciation both from above and from below. But although fond of books and of young men, I was never altogether fit to be a professor, and in the department of philosophy you will now have a better chance to make a fresh start and see if Harvard can secure the leadership of the next generation, as it had that of the last.

As to the lectureship in France, it is not proper that I should now be a candidate for it; but having some experience of the matter

I should say that, unless the study of English here has made great strides since 1906, audiences really able to understand English lectures cannot be found except in Lyons, Bordeaux, and possibly Caen. There is the danger that, for the listeners, the courses should degenerate into exercises in pronunciation or exercises of patience. The fee of 500 francs seems small. It would cover expenses for the fortnight, but it would offer no compensation for the work of preparation nor for the other energies which such an undertaking uses up. I found the provincial capitals usually delightful and the officials kind; but a second visit might be less stimulating, and I think a new and younger person might profit by it more and might arouse more interest in the place he visited.

If there is anything connected with this or any other matter in which I can be of service, I hope you will call upon me. Believe me sincerely and gratefully

Yours

To MRS. FREDERICK WINSLOW

I TATTI
SETTIGNANO (FLORENCE)
DECEMBER 6, 1912

Dear Mrs Winslow

Your kind letter reached me in Rome, where I have been for six weeks, after a trip to Sicily, and other wanderings, and I have kept it ever since to reread and answer, and to look at the two photographs (of which I like one, Polly's), but somehow the spirit has not been propitious until this morning. I am at the Berenson's,[1] very handsomely entertained, and enjoying the contrast from the solitude of the tourist in a crowd, to the conversations of the ultra-learned and all-judging aesthetes in a villa, and I shall enjoy the change back to solitude even more, perhaps, when it comes. Last night we even went to a dinner—at Lady Sybil Cutting's, widow

---

[1] Mr. and Mrs. Bernard Berenson.

of my friend Bayard Cutting—and it was very pleasant getting home and going to bed after it. Berenson is full of *esprit,* and there is a stream of distilled culture flowing over us continually in the form of soulful tourists and weary *dilettanti* who frequent this place; but I really enjoy best talking with my friend Strong [1] about things-in-themselves when we go for a walk together or to a *café* in the town of Florence. He is here at Fiesole, overseeing the building of a villa, which is to be his "home" (he thinks); and I am expecting the arrival of Loeser [2] also, who is married, and about to become a father. These friends will probably induce me to stay in Florence for some time, if it doesn't prove too cold and bleak for me. . . .

As to work, I have done a lot, though as yet I have nothing to show for it, as even "Winds of Doctrine," though in print, is not yet out. You shall have a copy as soon as it is published, which I hope will be in January or February. The Shelley paper is in it. It was a terrible piece of work getting it off, and took me all summer; the essay on Bergson [3] is only a selection of reams that I had written about him, and the essay on modernism is also patch-work, and I am afraid it shows it; revising and rearranging old stuff is harder than composing afresh from the beginning: but on the other hand there is a loss if one doesn't use what was written under the direct inspiration of one's reading. In Rome, where I was absolutely free and happy, I did a good deal on both the "Three Realms of Being" [4] and the "Dialogues",[5] and even burst into poetry, something that hadn't happened to me for years: but both these undertakings are formidable and I cannot expect to finish either for two or three years. The system of philosophy, probably, will be ready first. Next year I hope to be able to go to Cambridge to talk it over with Russell and Moore,[6] with whom I agree and disagree just enough to make discussion profitable.

My sister Josephine seems to be getting on well in Spain, but

[1] C. A. Strong.

[2] Charles Loeser.

[3] Henri Bergson.

[4] At the time, Santayana had not distinguished a *fourth* Realm—*The Realm of Truth*—in his system of philosophy.

[5] *Dialogues in Limbo.*

[6] Bertrand Russell and G. E. Moore.

her plans for the future are still unformed. I suppose she will re-main there. My love to Fred and the young ones and best wishes for you all for Christmas and the New Year.

Yours sincerely,

To MRS. FREDERICK WINSLOW

FLORENCE, DECEMBER 31, 1912

Dear Mrs Winslow

Thank you very much for the pretty calendar with its kind message. It has found me still here—though rather restive—re-tained by my friends, Strong and his daughter, Loeser and his wife, the Berensons, etc, but driven on by the bad weather—London couldn't be more wet and foggy—and by a certain dislike I have taken to the place and to the life of the aesthetical colony in it. Rome is far more to my liking—larger, nobler, more genuinely alive, and more appealing to wide reflection. In Florence it is rather the quaint, incidental, and hopelessly archaic that people feed their imagination upon. The landlord of my hotel complains that the stream of tourists has dwindled, and that people who came to spend the winter in Florence now go to Cairo instead. I can perfectly sympathise with this change of fashion, and though I am too lazy and fond of solitude to go to Egypt with the smart rabble, I am going for awhile to the Riviera, to catch a glimpse of the sun and sea, on my way to Andalusia and thence to Madrid.

My sister-in-law Ellen [1] has written me a Christmas letter in which she speaks of you and says your children are splendidly healthy, which is all that can be required of them at their tender age; and I hope they will continue to look angelic and to behave accordingly. Nowadays, I daresay the angels play tennis and foot-ball, just as formerly they used to brandish flaming swords and to spear dragons. I have also heard from Mrs. Toy,[2] your favourite

[1] The wife of Robert Sturgis.

[2] The wife of Prof. C. H. Toy.

Fuller,[1] and the Schofields [2] (this last on business, but with friendly and social frills) all of whom put together give me a vivid picture of Boston, with its old heart and its new subway vibrating merrily together. It doesn't seem to me much more remote than when I was there; and I am surprised to see how much life everywhere is now like life in America. Except Boylston Beal, I hardly know anybody who seems to stop to consider what it all comes to—and he is a trifle captious in his judgments. It is a sort of tobboggan-slide; but I assure you it is far more comfortable and far more interesting to roll off as soon as possible into the soft snow by the way, shake oneself together, and look on. My friend Strong does the same thing and we sympathise entirely on every subject except mind-stuff (which I insist on calling by another name) but he doesn't get as much fun out of it as I do. He is far more charitable and hasn't an enormous sense of humour. And I am a little afraid, when his Villa at Fiesole is built (a part of it was washed down by the rain the other day) he will find the moral atmosphere of the place less satisfactory than the Tuscan air. He will be roped into the Anglo-American aesthetic ring, and the sparring ladies will make him dizzy. On Christmas he actually had to go to Lady Sybil Cutting's fancy-dress party, dressed like a decadent Roman, with a ridiculous false beard, a hired tunic with tinsel embroideries glued on, pink stockings, and a scroll in his hand (the plans for his villa, I suppose). Margaret [3] went as an ancient Egyptian. He was ill next day in consequence.

Isn't there a chance that you should come to Paris some summer? Fred didn't seem to be overwhelmed with patients in Nahant; you might let your house, and take an outing without any additional expense. If you ever can manage this, it would be such a pleasure for me to show you my Parisian haunts . . . When I get back from Spain . . . I expect to settle down in the avenue de l'Observatoire [4] for a long stay—perhaps for ever! I feel now as if I had sufficiently explored the ground, and that my future wanderings will be merely trips.

Yours sincerely

[1] Prof. B. A. G. Fuller.

[2] Professor and Mrs. William Henry Schofield.

[3] The daughter of C. A. Strong.

[4] With Strong in his apartment at no. 9.

To B. A. G. FULLER

MADRID, MARCH 18, 1913.

Dear Fuller

Yesterday, when I arrived here, after many wanderings, I found your good letter of Feb. 21. Many congratulations on your final appointment, consecration, and holy marriage with old mother Harvard. I suppose, after a year or two of your permanent instructorship and preceptorship (whatever this may be) you will rise automatically, like the souls in the Paradiso, to higher and higher spheres till you are lost in the exceeding light of the absolute focus —by which I don't mean the Presidency of the College, for I am speaking of spiritual things. It is a very nice prospect for you; responsibility will keep you seriously at work, and you will have enough leisure—with the occasional leaves of absence which you can ask for—to write judiciously (don't write too much, like me) —and to travel, while at 'Tween Waters [1] and at Cambridge, even in termtime, you will not lack pleasant occupations of varied sorts to refresh your mind and keep you human. Let me congratulate you very sincerely, and your mother also, to whom this must be a great satisfaction. It is a satisfaction to me as well, because I feel as if you and I were members of the same party, stood for more or less the same things, so that you will be taking my place, now that I have decamped—and you will be doing under far more favourable conditions what I should like to have done. The times have improved, for one thing, and people, if not more enlightened positively than they were twenty years ago, are at least less hide-bound and parochial, and I sometimes think American good will may shortly be extended even to people with ideas! It will be a great pleasure if, in a few years, I come to visit you and find everything so much improved and humanised as I believe it will be. The material improvements will be interesting to see too—the subway, the Freshman college, the new Library, the new bridge, etc. etc. I will bring a set of ultra-sublime lectures to read to the ladies in the New Lecture Hall, at 4.30, and then you will waft me in your

[1] Professor Fuller's country home outside Boston.

motor—for you will have a motor then—to 'Tween Waters, to imbibe a cocktail (with a dividend) and discuss the Epicurean gods —with imitations! and, so to speak, demonstrations in the life.

I have been so lazy about writing that I don't know how far back to go in my account of my doings—if doings they can be called. After my trip in Sicily I was in Rome, quite preternaturally happy, for six weeks! but as the happiness was earthly after all it could not be complete, and I had a bad attack of my bronchitis. The depression which this caused, and the urgent missives of Strong and the Berensons, who wanted me to go to Florence, finally got the better of an instinct which told me that Rome was the place in which to stay for the winter. I went to Florence, staid ten days at the Berenson's, moved to the town, and saw a lot of people, from Strong and his daughter, to rather grand people at Lady Sybil Cutting's, who holds a sort of little court at the Villa Medici in Fiesole, close to Strong's new house. It was not satisfactory on the whole; the climate of Florence at that season—December—is beastly, and the expatriated anaemic aesthetes and the Jews surprised to find that success is not happiness made a moral atmosphere not wholesome to breathe; so I fled to the comparative innocence and moral simplicity of Monte Carlo. I took a small room flooded with sunshine and overlooking the toy port of Monaco, and I established a routine of life, going always for the same walks and to the same restaurants, which enabled me to rest thoroughly, and to do some little work. The gilded hall of the Casino did not swallow me up; I went there only once, on the first day of my sojourn in the place, and never returned, as I found it crowded and dingy, full of uninteresting middle-aged people, not even fascinatingly ugly or obviously gnawed by all the vices. They were for the most part fat greedy Germans, millionaire sausage-makers in appearance and in smell. I went sometimes to the theatre, and I saw several amusing ultra-Parisian things, to make up for the Teutonic real life about me. Above all, I delighted in the climate and in the old town of Monaco, to which I walked up every day, and where I sometimes read or wrote in the gardens. The only friend I came upon in all that time was X, who was living just beyond Nice, with a lady variously described as his wife, his *bonne,* his mistress, his model, his cook, and his mother. She might be any of these, as far as appearances went, and several at once, most probably; at any rate, she was very amiable, and the pair seemed quite happy.

—The advancing season, and the fact that my unmarried sister [1] was to be alone here in Madrid for the rest of this month (the friend with whom we stay having been called away to Vigo) made me finally quit the Riviera and return to Madrid; and this is the end of my story for the present. I expect to be back in Paris, with Strong, by the middle of May. He tells me he has finally got everything in his system clear and straight, and I have made some progress also in mine—I mean, in my next book the "Three Realms of Being" [2]—so that our discussions promise to have a new aliment, which they much needed. Excuse this blot, and this briefness; but I am hardly settled here yet, and have many letters to answer.

Yours ever

To ARTHUR DAVISON FICKE

9 AV. DE L'OBSERVATOIRE
PARIS, JULY 18, 1913

Dear Ficke

Your "Twelve Japanese Painters" and your article on "Winds of Doctrine" reached me long ago and both, in very different ways, gave me a great deal of pleasure. Perhaps you did yourself a little violence to praise or at least to condone *everything* in my book. It would have been right to blame anything that really seemed to you unreasonable; I am not sure that I shouldn't have been even better pleased if you had blamed something, for then I should have felt that in most matters you had made observations and judgements similar to mine, and been confirmed in them myself by that. The warmth of your tone is very exhilarating—like liquor— but the ardours of bout-drinking friendship, even in philosophy, are short-lived. I am grateful to you for your evident wish that *other people* should appreciate me and see something good in what

1 Josephine Sturgis.

2 See Letter (May 16, 1911).

William James once called my "diabolisms"; but what does it matter what *other people* think? If we care too much about persuading them we may disturb their peaceful conventions to no good purpose, since they will never get anything straight, while we blunt the edge of truth in our own words.

Your Japanese book has done something for me that I have long been praying for—given me a hint of how Japanese painting should be understood. I have asked several other people—Denman Ross, Berenson—to guide me in a matter very foreign and mysterious to me, and they have never said anything human and philosophical enough for me to understand it. They have merely said: this line is good, this design is beautiful, and left it at that. In your poems I find at last the first ray of light. It is the glimpse of life at some instant, of some ungrounded bird-note of life caught as it vibrates, we ask not why or in what a world; it is some shimmer of passion expressed economically, keenly, with wonderful dexterity, and without any comment; and it is (perhaps this is your personal addition to what the Oriental felt) a responding sentimental passion or moral comment inspired in ourselves. Tints, lines, attitudes, stuffs all have a certain hypnotic power, a sensuous magic that enthralls us if we gaze at them intently. This I have always known, and it is the fault of our Renaissance (from the sixteenth century to the middle of the nineteenth, and even today among the academic and conventional artists) not to have felt this sensuous quality enough, to have had no natural idolatry, but to have been interested in a pompous completeness and discursive literary reports—Zolas on canvas. What you teach me is that the Japanese are not merely sensuous but lyric, that it is the charm, mood, unrecoverable secret of some "witching hour" that they sing to us; and that as they feel this function to be sufficient for the painter, they are led naturally to that wonderful simplification and wonderful proficiency which they exhibit. Is this at all right, or like what you feel?

As English poems I also like your pieces; here and there, perhaps, you want to say things too elaborately (unlike your Japs) and slip into prose; but often your touch is exquisite like theirs. I keep your little book at hand and swear by it.

Yours sincerely

To SUSANA STURGIS DE SASTRE

OXFORD
OCTOBER 1, 1913.

Dear Susie,

. . . Here I have been working very steadily; my book, however, hasn't got all the benefit of it, as I have been writing other stuff—some half-poetical dialogues [1] that I have long had in mind and one of which was actually written and published long ago in a review. When this spurt of inspiration is over, however, I shall go back to the solid work, and I count on being stimulated especially by talking with Bertie Russell in Cambridge. I saw him at his brother's, but we didn't have more than one or two opportunities for quiet discussion. He is a logician and mathematician, strong where I am weakest, so that it is not always easy for us to understand each other on these abstruse points. However, we feel sympathy even in our diversity, and that is why I am anxious to put my view on some subjects (not on all) before him and to learn his more accurately. However, in the end every philosopher has to walk alone.

Oxford is beginning to take on its normal aspect, and I almost regret the idea of leaving as I like the place much better than its sister and rival, Cambridge: but I suppose the lodgings I have will soon be let, and I shall have to quit . . .

Love to all

Your affectionate brother

[1] The first drafts of the well-known *Dialogues in Limbo.*

To B. A. G. FULLER

45 CHESTERTON ROAD
CAMBRIDGE, NOV. 10, '13
[ENGLAND]

Dear Fuller

This morning I have received the package of notebooks, etc, which you were good enough to send me. As a thank-offering for your trouble I am despatching a book I have just read and found rather interesting "The Eighteen Nineties" by Holbrook Jackson. Perhaps, as you are so much younger, you will not be reminded of your own times, as I have been, by these reports, but it will do you no harm to be reminded of the preceding generation. I found the chapter on Francis Thompson particularly interesting.

Since I settled down here I have not done so much work as I had been doing at Oxford, because I have had more distractions, seeing people and reading odds and ends, as well as making one or two escapades to London and beyond. Bertrand Russell, on the whole, is not a very trustworthy thinker; he has the fault common to the political radicals of being disproportionately annoyed at things only slightly wrong or weak in others, and of flaming up into quite temporary enthusiasms for one panacea after another. His theory of the natural world is Mill-ish and almost Humian; [1] it is, in comparison with the reality of nature and even of experience, what the report of a battle might be in the mind of a telegraph wire through which a full description of it had been sent. There would be a perfectly adequate representation of everything in dots, dashes, and pauses, but no blood, no passions, no drama, no heroes, and no poor devils. On the other hand, Russell's lectures on logic (one or two of which he has shown me) are very clear and enlightening. You will see what a delightful and witty creature he is personally; I hope Harvard and Boston will not weary and depress him. That is the danger.

This place seems to me this year to have a new beauty. For one thing we have had a wonderful spell of golden autumn weather,

---

[1] John Stuart Mill and David Hume.

with the most beautiful afternoons, like landscapes by Poussin, and the lower River, with the trial eights and the fours has been gay and amusing in the way you know very well. I walk sometimes with Dickinson [1] (fuller than ever of Chinese sweet-reasonableness) or with Lapsley,[2] in whose rooms I sometimes meet the flowering undergraduate of the period—very smiling, as they didn't use to be, half stifled with little emphatic bursts of enthusiasm, and vaguely earnest about socialism, Ulster, land-reform, his next essay, or his next match. It is all a little flighty and girlish, and one has to let it blow past like a gust in a garden. I somehow feel more foreign in England than I did fifteen years ago or even ten years before that, when I was first here. It seems rather an unseizable life, without ideas or achievements clear and notable enough to appeal to the outsider. It is a chaos of half-measures and immediate aims; and even the philosophers are casual, personal, intense only in spots, and essentially heretical. All roads still lead to Rome and unless you place yourself there you will never be in the heart of the world or see it in the right perspective. To be a Protestant is to be cross-eyed. In America that doesn't matter, because there is nothing to look at there, but here, where everything has depth and is historical, it makes priggish limping scholars, and funny squeaking one-eyed philosophers. To make amends, I see there is really a little poetry being written in England; it is amiable, sincere, tender, manly. Read the collection "Georgian Poetry, 1911–1912" published by the "Poetry Bookshop".

My best regards to the survivors of the Department.

Yours ever,

1 Lowes Dickinson.

2 G. T. Lapsley.

To LOWES DICKINSON

45 CHESTERTON ROAD
NOVEMBER 26, 1913

Dear Dickinson

It has been a great pleasure to read your reflections on America.[1] I think you say very true and profound things about that land, and about the contemporary world. There is nothing, I think, that can justly give offence. No doubt Americans would take what you tell them more seriously if your tone were more jocular. What you say about advertisements—both the aspect and the psychology of it—could easily be made amusing; and it would then be a welcome criticism instead of a disagreeable and panic-stricken one. The reader in any case will smile, and it would improve your case if you could smile with him. It also occurs to me that a little redistribution of the parts might help to leave a stronger impression at the end. Of course there is and can be no art in America at present; and to speak of this at the end looks a little as if one's attention had been drawn away from the living facts and forces in the case into private musings.

There are also two small points on which I think you would seem to Americans not to have quite understood them. No one there is interested in the miracles in the Gospel. Of course, I know what you mean—the religion of James, Mrs. Eddy, etc.—but if you said that they *ought to be* interested in the miracles, wouldn't you make your point even clearer, without asserting anything apparently contrary to fact? The element in the Gospel which Americans really care for is the teaching of "good-will" and "service", with the necessary cheery self-abnegation and steadiness. It is what Matthew Arnold called the "method", without the "secret". The only thing to which they feel they ought to help others is material well-being; nevertheless there is a certain solemnity and tenderness in their sense that they ought to help, which is truly religious.

[1] *Appearances; Notes of Travel, East and West.* (1914) Santayana no doubt read some earlier articles, in the *Manchester Guardian* or *English Review,* that were later reprinted in the book.

The other point is about Mollycoddles. The term, so far as I know, is purely Rooseveltian; you put into it a rather different and more positive element—genius, independence, spirituality. These elements are absent from the American meaning of the word, which on the other hand implies that a man is a coward and a "quitter" (perhaps a more usual slang synonym), so that your assertion that Voltaire is a Mollycoddle is not plausible. Shelley is one on his feminine side, but not because he was revolutionary; and Socrates is one only if you regard him as a fretful sophist. Professors (according to Roosevelt) are Mollycoddles, not because they are rebels, but because they are not. Think of the American professor—mediocre, seedy, hungry, and hen-pecked—and you have the Mollycoddle in all his purity.

I also think (though this would doubtless not occur to your American readers) that there is a parasitic "red-blood", namely, the muscular Evangelical Christian of the school-master type. I shouldn't wonder if some German "idealists" and Jewish historians of art were also parasitic red-bloods, because they defend or promote ideal interests by the methods and in the spirit of "hustlers". Were not the Crusaders, when they took Constantinople, and some of the Popes, parasitic red-bloods too?

Now that I am started upon my own hobbies, I can't help adding that you ought not to be so dubious about the possibility of art and poetry in a peaceful world. The stress of war and suffering is not a needed element to stir the imagination or to give pungency to the representation of life. When life is turbulent, art has to make harmonies out of strife, but if life were placid, it would more easily make harmonies out of placidity. Think of all the distant poignant vistas, and all the profound renunciations, and all the exquisite charming fugitive moments that would fall to a soul living the life of reason in the midst of this world clearly understood. And think of all the amiable arts, both of the Greek and of the Dutch sort, that would be fostered by a well-ordered polity. No: the idea that horrors are required to give zest to life and interest to art is the idea of savages, men of no experience worth mentioning, and of merely servile, hunted sensibilities. Don't tolerate it.

Yours sincerely

To OLIVER WENDELL HOLMES

SEVILLE, JANUARY 21, 1914

Dear Mr. Holmes

I need hardly say that it is a great satisfaction to me to have your letter and to see that my book [1] pleased you enough to make you write it. I think there is a sort of background of agreement among all men, especially those of the same generation, although publicists often obscure rather than represent it, being taken up with party controversies or special causes. I am not a great philosopher, but in my separation from the world of action, and now even from the academic world (for I have retired from teaching) I feel that I can distinguish the normal and inevitable lines of human opinion from the modish flourishes that overlay it. This is my solid standing-ground outside and around special systems, of which you speak with an insight which goes to my heart. In "Winds of Doctrine" this fund of human orthodoxy is assumed rather than formulated: but I am trying to give it a more explicit expression in a book [2] on which I am now at work. I daresay you, and most judicious people, would have much to quarrel with and correct in this systematisation of common sense which I am attempting; but after all my training has been that of a technical philosopher, and I feel I owe it to my *Fachgenossen* to put my conclusions into their language, and not retain the unfair advantage of seeming reasonable by not admitting clearly the implications of my suave opinions.

I am now a wanderer, almost without impediments of any sort, and fortune may take me any day to Washington or Boston, where it would be a great pleasure to see you again. My centre is supposed to be in Paris, at n° 9, avenue de l'Observatoire, where the few books are that I have not wished to part with. I am there regularly in the Spring and early summer—in case by any chance you should find yourself there.

It was really very kind of you to write and to give me the encouragement of so much sympathy from so welcome a quarter.

Yours sincerely

1 *Winds of Doctrine.*

2 *Realms of Being.*

To SUSANA STURGIS DE SASTRE

LA PENINSULAR—SEVILLA
JAN. 28, 1914.

Dear Susie,

By this time I feel quite settled and happy here. My cough has disappeared with the cold and rainy weather, and I have come to find the hotel quite tolerable. The food is good enough if one makes a judicious selection of dishes, and I rather like monotony in food, e.g. I have an omelette and fried fish and a bit of *guisado* or rice and two or three oranges for lunch every day, and no wine. It seems to agree with me; and if I went to a better hotel I fear I should find many worse things—tourists, for instance. This is a small place, with some old German women and business men living permanently and a very moderate tide of Spanish people coming and going. Not a single English or American person yet! Then my room is quite delightful, with so much sun that I already have to close the blinds not to be dazzled. I am in the *principal,* looking out on the main Square, and almost in it, as I hear and see everything that is going on. I get up and have my chocolate at 9, and dress at 12. After lunch I go to a café—always the same one, and the same table, if possible, where the waiters are now my friends and bring me the illustrated papers—and then, with a notebook in my pocket, in case of inspiration, I start on my walk, through the Delicias into the country. On the way I watch the steamers loading and unloading, and if it is warm I sit in the gardens for a while. Tea I take on my return to the city, this at quite a different and more fashionable coffee-house, where there are ladies and foreigners. Then I usually come to my room again, and read or write until dinner, which I have about 7.30. There is a good electric light over my table, by which I am writing now. In the evening, I return to my first café, in the Sierpes, overhear and sometimes join in conversation with some of the *habitués,* and then go to the theatre. I have seen a lot of things, good, bad and indifferent, with and without local colour; but half the amusement is in seeing the people. I affect the *dias de moda*—tonight it will be at the *cine* in the teatro de San Fernando, the largest and best in Seville. In this way I see the beauty and fashion of the place, better than in their carriages and autos in the Delicias. Seville is a true and homogeneous capital city, like ancient towns, with its aristocracy just as native as its lower classes. I find it very *simpatico*. Tomorrow we shall have the novelty of the arrival of the court. I suppose they will drive by my window in the morning—there is hardly another possible route—and I shall have other opportunities of seeing them during their sojourn, which I understand is to be for less than a fortnight.

As you see, I dawdle and amuse myself a good deal, but at the same time I manage to work every day for two or three hours: and this is enough to keep my mind engaged and give me the resource of a settled occupation in the background, to which I can always return. I am in no hurry about my book,[1] but if all goes on as it is going now, I might actually finish the first draft here. In Paris, later, I should still have much revising and curtailing to do: writing in so desultory a fashion, I repeat myself a great deal, and this has to be remedied afterwards.

If I continue as well pleased as I am now, and the heat, flies, and mosquitoes don't become intolerable—I have already killed three mosquitoes in my room, but there are arrangements for a mosquitoe netting over the bed—I may stay until after the *Feria* and bull-fights in April. I don't expect to stop at all in Madrid, but to make straight for Avila and Paris.

Love to Celedonio and the rest of the family from your affectionate brother

---

[1] *Realms of Being*. The work on this book was interrupted later in the year by the outbreak of War, and Santayana put it to one side, and did not finally complete it until 1940. What was originally intended to be a rather concise single book, eventually became a mighty work of four volumes.

To B. A. G. FULLER

SEVILLE
FEBRUARY 7, 1914

Dear Fuller

Your good letter, written the day after Christmas, has been stranded for three weeks at the first hotel I went to here, when I was with my sister. Yesterday I went to see if they had nothing for me, and I found five letters, yours among them, naturally to my great joy.

They will persecute you, like all the Apostles of sweetness and light, and especially of liberty, that thing unknown to America; it was foretold of the Lord. I trust, however, that you will be victorious in the end and become one of the patriarchs of the orthodox church—I mean of the life of reason. I note with pleasure that you are to be in Paris in the summer. You will find me there, and you will tell me, I hope, all about these physical and moral transformations which Harvard is undergoing. What I hear from time to time confirms me in the feeling that I quitted most opportunely. The wonder is that I endured and was endured so long. The only Harvard that in any measure held my affections and with which I could have almost identified myself was that of the "nineties"—or rather, of 1890–1895; but the awful cloud of Eliot [1] then overhung it, and made life impossible. Before and after that, Harvard was only an accident and a temporary necessity in my life; and especially since I became a professor I did nothing but save money so as to get out of it *quam celerrime*. It took a great many years, partly for other reasons, and I wrote a great many bad books in the interval: otherwise it seems a stretch of desert. However, I have still senses and life enough left to see, and perhaps to do, something: and I am perfectly happy. "Of course he is", said an Italian scholar of peasant origin at the Berensons, [2] when this confessed beatitude of mine was reported to him, "Of course, *he has such a strong digestion!*" . . .

[1] C. W. Eliot, the President of Harvard College.

[2] Mr. and Mrs. Bernard Berenson.

Russell [1] knows America and goes there with his eyes open: I imagine he would be grateful to be left alone as much as possible. His philosophy seems to have taken a new turn—to construct the universe out of sense-data. If this be realism, it is marvellously like empirical idealism. It has the same minimising and "nothing but" quality: it is a substitution of means for ends and of an analysis of knowledge for the object of it. Since I discovered this I have largely lost my interest in Russell as a thinker: but he is a very amusing person. There is a strange mixture in him, as in his brother, of great ability and great disability; prodigious capacity and brilliance here—astonishing unconsciousness and want of perception there. They are like creatures of a species somewhat different from man.

I spent a delightful autumn at Cambridge, staying on until the end of term. Besides Russell, I saw Lapsley [2] often, and he was very friendly and sympathetic, lending me books, and asking me to feasts, both in Hall and in his rooms, where I saw some of the undergraduates of the period. The weather was extraordinary— a continual delight. I came to Spain for Christmas, when the cold set in; and very cold and uncomfortable it was (in the house) in Avila, and Madrid, and even here in Seville, when we first arrived. My sister and her friend left me after about a week, and I have established myself in a more modest hotel, where no tourists go, and where I can work very nicely in the morning, and sometimes for awhile in the late afternoon. My book is getting on well: I have hopes of finishing the first draft here, and in that case I might have it ready for the press in the autumn. The rest of the day I spend in the most delightful saunterings and musings. I take a small note-book in my pocket, in case some pearl of thought needs to be strung as I walk the streets, or sit in the *Delicias*—truly delicious gardens, or even in the masculine atmosphere of the *cafés*. Spring has set in full, here, and everything is as human, simple, engaging, and warm as if one were living in antiquity. O blessed Meditarrean, [sic] where man is man!

Yours ever

[1] Bertrand Russell.
[2] G. T. Lapsley.

To SUSANA STURGIS DE SASTRE

QUEEN'S ACRE,
WINDSOR. [ENGLAND]
AUGUST 5, 1914.

Dear Susie,

I don't know whether you are getting the letters I am writing you: this is the third during the last few days. There is nothing new to say, but the stress of excitement somehow impels me to write; and if by chance one letter goes astray, you may get another. None from you or Robert or Josephine has reached me for some time, but I am hoping to have one soon.

Howard [1] and his household are as usual. He is less overcome by the war—of which he of course "disapproves" sadly—than I had expected: in fact everyone everywhere seems to take this prodigious outbreak very seriously and calmly, with a reasonable sense of how human and how inevitable unreason is. It reminds me of the mock phrase in Don Quixote: la razón de la sinrazon etc: only this is sober earnest. My sympathies are naturally with France and England, and with the blameless unfortunate Belgians; yet I feel no anger against the Germans. They are carrying out a brave and heroic determination to be the masters of Europe and to rule by force of arms, industry and character. It is not very different from the principle that has animated strong aggressive nations in all ages: only it is more deliberate and conscious—a little rude and conceited as well. Perhaps the sense of power and of "duty" has turned their heads a little, and they may be rushing to their destruction—or rather to their discomfiture, because no great nationality can be destroyed until it dissolves inwardly. It is hard to say whether what is guiding them is infatuation or consciousness of their destiny. If they win, with all Europe against them, it will be because they deserved to win, being morally the stronger.—I am going on Friday to Oxford, and shall probably remain there indefinitely, until we see how things are going.

Love to all from your affectionate brother

---

[1] Howard Sturgis, a distant cousin.

To MRS. FREDERICK WINSLOW

OXFORD, AUGUST 16, 1914

Dear Mrs Winslow

The shock of war seems to have been necessary to knock me out of my comatose state of mind and unconsciousness of the lapse of weeks and months since I received your last kind letter. I am now very restless, hardly knowing which way to turn, what to hope for or what to expect. My plans are upset and my sympathies lacerated. Happy the man with a country, and faith that it is of course always in the right, and will of course be victorious! To me, it seems a dreadful indignity to have a soul controlled by geography. If you are born east of this frontier—one religion, one language, one history, one dominating passion; if you are born west of it— another religion, another language, another history, and a deep desire to knock the other man, and not yourself, on the head! You may say it is the difference in people's racial soul that originally made that frontier, so that after all you are born on the side to which you belong. But that only turns the comedy into a tragedy; for why should my soul be racial at all, and why should mewing be a delight to it, and barking an abomination? I try—in vain, I am afraid—to transcend this kind of fatality and to consider fairly what is at stake and what would be the moral value of the victory for the dogs or for the cats. I say to myself (not from the heart, perhaps) that France, though amiable, is played out and rotten (a sort of Anatole France, in fact); that the British Empire is a pious sham, and must soon go in any event; that Austria and Germany represent clericalism and discipline, and that if Christendom is capable of a new lease of life at all, it could only be by their victory and sobering influence; and that perhaps it is better that man should recognise sour duties than no duties at all. When I try to take that line I immediately feel the conviction rise that Christendom and clerical duty and discipline are pious shams and hopelessly played out too; and that those who work for them politically are inwardly more rotten than the avowed anarchists. In fine, I don't at all know how we can discover whether it would be better for the world that we should be all overawed by Germany and turned into pompous prigs, or that we should be allowed to go to the dogs in our own natural way.

I have come to Oxford in the fond hope of finding peace—but this war is too atmospheric, it pervades every retreat. By the merest chance the cataclysm found me in England: I had come from Paris to do some shopping, and see a few friends, intending to return in a fortnight: but now I don't know at all when I shall get back, or whether I shall go to Italy for the winter, as I had intended. No place seems to beckon, and all to repel. During the last year I have had two happy perfect seasons—three months at Cambridge in the autumn and four months at Seville in the winter and spring. Both places, in their different ways, afforded solitude and stimulation, and I could read and write and walk and feel alive and fit for great illuminations. I seemed there to be growing mellow, very mellow—"extra ripe", as the man said to recommend his bananas; but since I left Seville, and began to feel the friction of more or less unsympathetic friends, I seem again the poor, uncultivated, shallow caged-squirrel-soul that the world makes us. My book has advanced—especially in my own mind, it has got more firmly knit together—but it is not finished, and the last smelting and recasting is yet to be done. Perhaps in Rome—if I get there this winter—the hills and the Gods will favour the work.

You must be at Nahant now, Fred playing tennis like a champion and you and Polly teaching the baby to know such things as he ought to know at his age—leaving him to find out the others for himself. I suppose the old rocks and the old fossils of Nahant surround you as usual, and everyone is concerned deeply to do as many uninteresting things as possible in the most competent way. Dear old Boston, what an unlovely place it is! Don't you ever miss Buffalo, and wish to transplant Fred and the children there?

Your friend Apthorp Fuller [1] was in Paris not long ago and gave me the most dismal account of Harvard College and its philosophy. (By the way, I hear Münsterberg [2] upbraids England for betraying the cause of Teutonic *Kultur*. But might not this be acquired by Englishmen, Frenchmen, and even Russians, seeing that its purest present champions may combine it with descent

---

[1] Prof. B. A. G. Fuller.

[2] Hugo Münsterberg.

from other heroes than Siegfried? Isn't Boston flooded with German music and German philosophy, without needing to be policed by German officials?) My poor brother [1] is in Spain, uncertain how to get back to State Street and Duty and to Bay State Road and Happiness. All because a Servian student shot the Archduke Franz Ferdinand! And people still say that Reason governs the world!

Yours sincerely

To SUSANA STURGIS DE SASTRE

LONDON
AUG. 24, 1914

Dear Susie,

This afternoon I receive at the same moment two numbers of the ABC,[2] which you send me, and word from the bankers that Robert is sailing on Wednesday from Cadiz in the "Infanta Isabel". I am glad he has taken this determination, for I think it is the simplest and safest way for him to get home. He will also get there sooner than if he had come north in order to embark.

The Spanish papers, although of course they are belated, contain a more impartial view than the papers I see here, which even when they quote German reports, emphasise only what is obviously exaggerated or false in them, so as to make them seem absurd. The interview with a German officer of the general staff, for instance, in the ABC of the 15th instant, is very illuminating. It shows how *competent* the Germans are, even when their vision is dense and their sentiment narrow. He gives out the exact plan which is being carried out, and I almost think he foresees what must be the result, at least of the campaign in Belgium. This sort of thing gives me more perspective, and helps me to prepare for the disappointments which are in store for us here—I say "us", because it is impossible

---

1 Robert Sturgis.

2 A Spanish magazine.

not to share the sentiment of people about one, when it is strong and steady and one has no contrary passion of one's own. My natural sympathies are anti-German, but I can't help admiring the sureness and the immense patient effort which characterises their action. If they overpower "us", I am not sure that the world will be ultimately the worse for it. I say this, I confess, partly to console myself for the news of the German victory—I don't know yet how complete—which has been given out this afternoon. We are told that "Namur has fallen"—but we are not told if that is all, and I fear there is a lot more to tell. Perhaps the Avenue de l'Observatoire may be bombarded, and Strong[1] be relieved of the trouble of deciding what to do with his furniture, and I with my books! It would be rather amusing, and as far as that is concerned, I shouldn't weep over it. But how much anguish everywhere, and all for what?

Yours aff^{ly}

To SUSANA STURGIS DE SASTRE

LONDON
SUNDAY, OCT. 11, '14.

Dear Susie,

Your letter of the 3rd reached me yesterday, taking a week. Thank you for the notice about the direct line from Falmouth to Bilbao. For the moment I think I will stay here: I go to Cambridge tomorrow, and if I don't find suitable quarters there I can always return to Oxford or retire to Bournemouth or Torquay, to what they call the English *Riviera*, which they say is balmy and comparatively cloudless. As a matter of fact, since I have been in England, we have had hardly any rain. It would be very nice to get back to Spain— as you say, Italy had better be left out of the reckoning for the pres-

---

[1] C. A. Strong, who shared an apartment with Santayana on the Avenue de l'Observatoire in Paris.

ent—but if possible I should like to go *via* Paris, and I can easily wait until Christmas and see what the facilities for travel are at that time.

When I said in my last long letter that England would be "strong at the finish" I didn't quite mean that I feel sure her side will be victorious: Germany is materially and morally prodigiously strong. So far, while she has not taken Paris nor maintained her invasion of Russia from East Prussia, she has had the upper hand, both on land and sea, and now with the possession of Antwerp she may attempt the long premediated attack on the English fleet and coasts by sea and air. If the Russian advance in Southern Poland should collapse, and the British fleet should be crippled (not impossible contingencies) Germany might become unconquerable, and the war might have to end in some arrangement not unfavourable to her, because she would be free to prepare even more thoroughly for the next war against weakened opponents.

I shall be glad to see the *Corzeo Español* [1] when it arrives. It is quite intelligible that the Catholic party should back the decline of Masonic France, heretical England and schismatic Russia. A new Holy German Empire, even if the Emperor was nominally a Protestant and had to be tolerant to his 200,000,000 Moslem *protégés,* would give the Church a great backing. Politically and morally she would be countenanced and respected everywhere as she has not been since the Reformation. In other ways, too, a universal German ascendancy would not be without its splendours, and I am by no means sure that this development of things is not as desirable as any other. Things cannot remain as they are, and the Americanisation of the Universe would be even a worse fate. But my heart, I confess, is with the French, English, and also with the Russians, because they all three, in various ways, make for individual freedom, and for the security and delightfulness of life. They are the peoples who wish to be left alone, because they know how to make themselves comfortable and happy. The German system is one of strain and of artificial aims: it is a sort of orderly night-mare. For this reason I can't help thinking that the Mediterranean countries would obey their true instinct in sympathising with the allies, as the liberal and paganised parties in them actually do. And that need not involve any disloyalty to Christianity. The German spirit

[1] A Spanish journal.

is very anti-Christian at bottom, although in its demands for order and discipline it may find an alliance with Christianity useful for the moment. The German spirit, however, is that of "Absolute Will", as their philosophers call it. It is unregenerate. It trusts, like the heathen Northmen, in strength, will and inward instinct or illumination. It has no consciousness of sin, or of the vanity of the world or the passions. The Cross never had, and never can have, any meaning for it. In its heart it never believed in another world, but always looked forward to a sort of heroic suicide or "twilight of the gods"; for the very people who are now planning a great German era for the whole world are perfectly conscious that that era, too, must pass away in time. It will be merely a *beau geste,* lasting a thousand years ending in the tragic and romantic extinction of the race and its glorious "Kultur". This is a heathen ideal, not a Christian nor even a pagan one, as the Greeks and Latins conceived paganism, which meant a modest and permanent alliance with the gods of nature, and a life as pleasant and intellectual as possible.

I have sent you several books and will send you one or two more, concerning the crisis: if you don't care to read them, please lay them aside anywhere, and I will relieve you of them when I come and can rearrange my belongings.

Love to Celedonio, Josephine and all the family.

Your affectionate brother

To MRS. FREDERICK WINSLOW

CAMBRIDGE, [ENGLAND] DECEMBER 11, 1914

Dear Mrs Winslow

It shocks me to see that Christmas is upon us and no answer yet sent to your last good letter. The War has destroyed my *moral.* At first it really quite upset me—more than I thought anything could —besides interfering somewhat with my material movements. I was caught in England, and here I remain, partly because all travelling is difficult and partly because this is the place where under the circumstances my feelings are least accerberated by daily con-

tacts with hideous unreason. Of course the newspapers and the political speeches are full of cant, even here; but the living people,
especially the young officers, are pure of all malice and intentional
passion—really wonderful in their disillusioned courage and humble gallantry. No manufactured hatred here, no politics and philosophy *per order*. Germany was never more studied or better understood; and if the natural antagonism crops up here and there, it is
less unjust than was the former sublime unconsciousness that there
was a Germany at all. And Germany deserves to be opposed, because she pushes: she would deserve to be hated if anything could
deserve that, because she cultivates hate. But whatever the military
result will be, there is nothing to fear from German *Kultur*. Even
if you and I and Polly and little Fred and big Fred were conquered
and annexed by the Fatherland, it would make no difference, because we should conquer *it*. Every German in three weeks would
be as much like us as he could make himself: and as to the Germans
remaining (poor things!) in the Fatherland itself, as soon as they
heard of my philosophy they would be so ashamed of ever having
been Germans that I think they would all pretend—like so many
of them that I have found about—to be Swedes and Swiss, and not
Germans at all. Germans elsewhere are as harmless as a snow storm
in the tropics; they may do good but they will never remain snow
flakes in doing it. Perhaps in America you are not quite so obsessed
as we are here by this War: but I shouldn't be able to shake off the
consciousness merely because others were less preoccupied: on the
contrary, it would become a worse thing—like a private sorrow.
Here one can work it off, because everyone is thinking of nothing
else. I have read and am reading all the German books I can find
that throw light on their attitude, and I have begun to write about
it—not particularly because I want to, but because it is impossible
to think seriously or consecutively on any other subject. And the
whole world puts on a new face in view of this extraordinary present reality. The wars in Herodotus (I have been reading that) and
all he says about those forgotten nations and tribes take on a strange
naturalness and vivacity: of course, that was what they *had* to be
doing. It is only the silly superficial chatter of busy people, perfectly unconscious that they live over an active volcano, that becomes remote and inconceivable.

My landlady here makes me quite comfortable, but I am nevertheless somewhat restless. I am going to Brighton for the holidays,
for a little change of sea and air, but expect to return here, where

Bertrand Russell and other friends keep me from feeling too solitary. I ought now, according to a long laid plan, to be in Rome or at Fiesole, where my friend Strong is already inhabiting his villa, and was expecting me for a long visit. My instinct, however, since the war, is rather to go to Spain. But I fear the cold and pro-Germans, and I don't want to be disgusted with my own country. So here I shall stay for the present, until the sky clears a little and we see what is going to happen. My love to Polly and little Fred (if they are not pro-German) and best wishes to you all for many new years.

Yours sincerely

To SUSANA STURGIS DE SASTRE

OLD SHIP HOTEL,
BRIGHTON.
DEC. 14, 1914.

Dear Susie,

. . . I came here today in just three hours from Cambridge, stopping in London to get some money at the banker's. It was a rapid journey—

Cambridge	12 noon
London, King's Cross Station	1.15
London, Victoria "	1.55
Brighton	3 o'clock.

I kept my taxi waiting ten minutes at Brown Shipley & Co. while I did my financial errand; but the close connection left me without any lunch. However, I had beef sandwiches with my tea at four, and feel particularly well—I have just dined!—so that going lunch-less is perhaps good for the health. One is apt to overeat in England, on account of the damp climate.

My impression of this place—my room, the hotel, and the general aspect of Brighton, which I had never seen in winter—is rather agreeable and I may remain here a month or so. It is a great change from the scholastic and dowdy atmosphere of Cambridge. It is a haunt of pleasure seekers, and there is a sprinkling of convalescent officers with the devoted females of their family dancing attendance. The "Parade" or street along the beach is four miles long— splendid for an uninterrupted walk; and the theatrical and other gay people make it amusing. In spite of the drizzle this afternoon, it reminded me of Nice! The war seems to affect the place only at night, when all bright lighting is forbidden, and the darkness (similar to that in which London is plunged) is rather impressive, and makes the surge of the breakers on the beach very much more impressive. On a clear night it must be very poetical. This compulsory darkness is supposed to be a precaution against Zeppelins or against a sudden landing of a German army: but I can't think there is much danger of either here, as Brighton is no port, but a long shallow beach, where landing would be impossible and where Zeppelins would hardly waste their bombs: nor is it on the way to London from Germany or Belgium. Anyhow, everyone here is perfectly cheerful and happy to take their chances. At the station I saw some wounded Indians, just arrived from France, going to a camp for convalescents not far from here. They were rather fine-looking, with the true Oriental impassibility. [sic] The entrance of Turkey into the war has added very much to its geographical picturesqueness. I think it may also facilitate the issue, as Turkey may be made to pay the price, and satisfy the allies, in case Germany and Austria are not defeated decisively enough to be interfered with themselves.

I enclose the stamps (some of which Pepe [1] may not have) which came from Paris with the manuscript of my book, which is now in my possession, as well as the letter of credit I left in Paris. Strong writes from Fiesole that now he is reconsidering the question of the apartment in the Avenue de l'Observatoire, and may not give it up after all, as next Spring it will be impossible for him and Margaret [2] to go to Germany as he had planned. So that my books and clothes (which remain in Paris) can probably remain undisturbed indefinitely! Strong wants me to go to Fiesole now, but I think I shall stay in England for the present.

Love to Celedonio and all the family from your affectionate brother

[1] A son of Celedonio Sastre by a former marriage.

[2] The daughter of C. A. Strong.

To B. A. G. FULLER

22 BEAUMONT STREET
OXFORD, AUG. 4. 1915

Dear Fuller

Are you sure that I haven't written to you for so long? I think I remember penning an epistle from Cambridge, but it may have been longer ago than I think, or it may have been stopped by the Censor. However I will tell you today the little I have to tell.

First, as to your letter. Without knowing the new people in the philosophical department at Harvard it is hard for me to judge whether you would be happy with them or they with you. I have preached to you by example; but example is really no maxim, since cases are different, and trying as I can well see that you might find professing for life, it would have the advantage of justifying your existence before Mrs Minerva Grundy, and of keeping you in contact with old habits and old amenities—for there *are* amenities at Harvard, at least while you are there. But I can't take the teaching of philosophy seriously in itself, either as a means of being a philosopher or of teaching the young anything solid: they merely flirt with that for a year or two instead of flirting with something else. Philosophy is not a science; it might be a life or a means of artistic expression, but it is not likely to be either at an American college. So that, substantially, I shouldn't feel that you were missing anything if you abandoned the whole thing. You could still read and think and write, if you had anything to say; and you could still live with your friends and be an ornament to Sherborn. When the war is over I may go on a visit to America, and then I will knock at your gate, and we can talk all this over at leisure.

Is your "primer" to be a work of art—the first chapter on "What is philosophy" rather suggests that—or is it to be a handbook for cramming on the day before an examination? In the latter case, I shouldn't introduce any views of my own, for they will be learned by heart and deposited on the examination paper like a chemical precipitate of your best thoughts. I should begin with

Thales [1] and water which is refreshing, wholesome, and unforgettable.

I too am writing a book [2]—the Realms of Being are in abeyance until the noise of explosives subsides—and bits of it are appearing in The New Republic; also other articles, for somehow the war, in making me very unhappy, has made me very prolific in a miscellaneous way. I have even attempted to write verses again, but in this I have failed. However, I spend my whole time over books and papers, hardly seeing anyone or opening my lips for weeks and weeks. I don't suffer from solitude, but I have suffered a good deal —less lately—from the war. You may say, "Why less lately, when things have been going from bad to worse?" Because I am weary of it all, my feelings blunted, and my mind resigned. The cries of this camp or that are folly: what does it mean to fight for "our very existence", or what to "crush militarism?" That is all rot. Germany will annex more or less land; England will be safe enough at home with conscription and a lesson in the futility of liberalism and the shocking incompetence of politicians. Everybody will be poorer— not a bad thing altogether—and we shall be able to travel about untorpedoed until the next scrimmage. *Voilà.*

I send you, with comments, part of a letter I received today.

Yours ever

To SUSANA STURGIS DE SASTRE

22 BEAUMONT STREET,
OXFORD
SEPT. 26, 1915.

Dear Susie,

Strong [3] and his daughter Margaret arrived in England ten days ago. I went to London to see them and afterwards they came

---

[1] The earliest recorded Greek philosopher, who taught that water, in all its forms, was the principle of everything.

[2] *Egotism in German Philosophy.*

[3] C. A. Strong.

on here and established themselves in my old lodgings in the High, where Strong still is, while Margaret is visiting various friends in or near London. She is to go to Newnham, one of the girl's colleges at Cambridge, although her father for a while seemed to be afraid that bombs and even licentious soldiery might burst upon her there, and endanger her life or at least her honour. His mind now seems to be reassured—although the danger from bombs is real, though of course the chances of being actually hit are infinitesmal. I now come to the point, and my reason for writing all this, which in itself can hardly interest you. Strong, while his daughter is in England, wants to remain here too, so as not to be separated from her by some possible interruption of travel between England and the continent. Hence as he will not return to Paris or Fiesole for the present, there is no incentive for me to go to either place. This, added to the difficulties of travel on account of passports and other formalities, points to the advisability of my remaining where I am —possibly until the end of the war. I am very well, and (but for the war) perfectly happy: I see interesting people, work enough, and live economically. The only reason for moving would be the desire to see you and all the others at Avila again: but on the other hand I don't think if I went to Spain under the present circumstances my stay there would be long or altogether pleasant. Peace and neutrality there do not extend to the mind, while here, on account of the very excitements and griefs of the war, there is a sort of common understanding and even zest in the air which is not unpleasing; at least one knows what to expect in people and can live without friction. My idea is to stay in Oxford till December and then to go to some watering place like Brighton, Bath, or Bournemouth, to spend the darker and colder months, returning here again in the Spring, when Oxford is at its best, materially and socially.

I am going tomorrow once more to Moncure Robinson's for three days. Lord Russell [1] has returned from Rhodesia (where he went to inspect a gold mine of which he is chairman) and I shall probably go on a visit to him before long. They say he is about to marry (being just divorced for the second time) the Countess von Arnim,[2] a novelist, English but formerly married to a German, and

[1] The 2nd Earl Russell, elder brother of Bertrand Russell.

[2] The author of *Elizabeth and Her German Garden*.

a lady with grown up daughters (a thing of evil omen, for any day Russell may elope with one of them). At least this third spouse is a person of more character and education than her predecessors, but I have no expectation that the marriage will be happy or lasting.

Another person I have lately seen (for the first time) is Henry James. He is seventy three, and not very well in health: but he was entertaining, and greeted me in particular very effusively and even affectionately, giving me the delicious sensation of being a young man whom one's respectable and distinguished elders wish to pat on the head. If he had done so materially as well as metaphorically he would have found as little hair there as on his own.

You see I have been very gay of late: and I could tell of other curious people I have been seeing. Now that I am frankly and unmistakably an old gentleman, I find my place in the social world more congenial than formerly, especially in England where people exact nothing and do not pester one with forced conversation, as in the U.S. Both kindliness and malice seem to fall more gracefully and ripely from an old tree than from a stripling; besides as people are no longer interested in one's person they take one for what one *says:* and that is a boon.

Love to all from

To MRS. FREDERICK WINSLOW

OXFORD, NOVEMBER 4, 1915

Dear Mrs Winslow

The children, and what you allow me incidentally to spy of you and your engaging husband, appear to less advantage in their photographs than in my memory. I especially resent seeing little Fred in goggles instead of a nimbus. However, disillusions rain upon us these days from every side, and you know my philosophy has always been that disillusion is the only safe foundation for happiness. I am therefore waiting sadly for the end of the war; I wish I could go to sleep and wake up at the peace—whatever it may be, so that I might begin at once to readjust myself to fate. Now we don't know what our fate is—although I have a shrewd suspicion—and the horror of life and the horror of death oppress together. Extreme situations they say bring out one's true character; and I am sorry to observe that these overwhelming events make me more selfish than ever. I find myself arguing with myself against my few remaining affections—not that for you and yours, which brings no remorse with it, but my affection for England, for instance, or for the life of reason. I say to myself: "Why do you care for that hopelessly dissolving and unrealisable thing? Why don't you love the dear good Germans—such well-equipped animals—instead? Why don't you reconcile yourself fundamentally to everything in the world being unjust, irrational, and ugly? You might then sleep peacefully, and not tremble every morning when you unfold your newspaper". But it won't do: I have suppressed the newspaper, as I gather quite enough from posters and conversation and the extras which I can't always resist buying in the evening: but I can't suppress the unrest. And what every fresh person tells you who returns from the front is so horrifying—I meet them everywhere—that one is not allowed to forget the troubles of others in one's own comfortable and stupid routine of life. Sometimes, when I have written and sent off some article or had a drink (which is not more frequently) I have a moment of peace. Otherwise all is war, war in the world, in the mind, in the heart, in the family—because my sister,[1] who is the nearest person to me now, is a rabid and relentless pro-German. Of course I don't write to her about the matter, and she probably doesn't suppose that her way of feeling makes me unhappy, but if I said what I think it would be this: "You imagine that my sympathetic way of tolerating absurdity and fiction in religion will extend to perversity and fiction in politics; but not at all. If one were not governed in religion by emotion and imagination one could have no religion at all—for imagination and emotion are the substance of it. It is to be tolerated and respected nevertheless, because men have no adequate knowledge and no trained courage in respect to their destiny: they therefore have to make believe something or other, and that is their necessary religion. But politics is a matter of fact, of history, of morals; perversity in that is intolerable. See how people have to die for it". But if I said this to my sister she would think it wicked nonsense and be as much

---

[1] Susana, who was living in Spain with her husband Celedonio Sastre.

distressed about it as I am at the wicked nonsense which she luxuriates in about Germany and England.

About my movements there is little to say. I have found nice lodgings here, I take long walks, often lunching on bread and cheese and a glass of "bitter" at some country inn. Strong is here, also other old and new friends. I don't do much work, although I am supposed to be writing three separate books. Perhaps you have seen my articles in the "New Republic". They are my chief sign of life at present.—Thank you so much for writing.

Yours sincerely

To LAWRENCE SMITH BUTLER

OXFORD. NOV. 13. 1915

Dear Lawrence

Mʳˢ Potter writes me that you have lost your mother, and I know what a great sorrow that must be for you. For almost anybody the death of a mother cuts deeper than any other bereavement, it strikes more at the roots of one's life and seems to require a new beginning and almost a new character in oneself. One becomes a senior, a person of the older generation, whose past is buried out of sight of the world, and has become strange and mysterious to other people, and almost to oneself. But in your case there must be something more, because you all lived in such complete sympathy, like contemporaries, and all kept young together. Your mother was one of the most perfect and ideal mothers I have ever seen, absorbed in her children and living their lives without sentimentality and without interfering with their liberty. She deserved what she obtained, which is so rare, that you all remained about her after you were grown up, not from necessity, but by instinct and through affection. I am sure you must have made her as happy as she made you.

More than once since I left America I have been on the point of writing, but put it off, perhaps expecting that you would turn up some day in Paris, where I have had my headquarter's, at my friend

Strong's (once a professor at Columbia) at 9 Avenue de l'Observatoire. I have asked about you when I have come across any of our common friends, like Moncure Robinson—but never heard of any change in your way of living. Now perhaps you will get married at last, as we have all expected you to do these many years. No doubt for the present you are not thinking of that. If you feel lost and troubled by the foolish noise and flurry that you probably see about you, in that extraordinarily loud New York, it occurs to me that you might find something to do that would at once be worthy of your sorrow and help you to forget it if you came to France and did some work for the wounded. Mr Harjes (of Morgan Harjes) has an American ambulance in which some of my young friends have been employed; and if you had your own motor perhaps you might join some purely French ambulance corps, if you preferred that. I believe my friend Pierre Abreu has done so. Those who have helped in France all seem to be very much deepened and steadied by it, as are the French themselves by this war. I am not one of those who say that anything so fearful is *good* for people, better than what they might have seen and felt in times of peace: but it certainly contains compensations for all the hardening and suffering which it brings—that people live in the presence of the terrible realities of this world, instead of nursing their comfortable illusions.

The war has made me very unhappy, and incidentally has upset all my plans. I have found nice lodgings in Oxford (where I have always liked to live) and am waiting for the storm to blow over. I may go to America for two months next year, if the war lasts; but I am longing, when peace returns, to go back to Paris, Spain, and Italy. Now the journey is troublesome, and I don't want to be nearer the horrors of war (since I am useless) than I can help. Here we feel much bitterness and disappointment at the course things are taking, but the young people are splendid, and material life goes on much as usual.—How nice it would be if you should come here for a few days! You probably have no idea of how much affection—at least for me!—I have always felt for you, and what an unmixed pleasure it is to remember you, as I do very often.

Yours affectionately

P.S. Excuse this scrawl in pencil. I am writing at a country inn, one of those to which I now walk out to lunch whenever the weather is

fair—to lunch on bread and cheese and a glass of beer, which is all
these places afford— But the skies and fields are very beautiful, and
I like the solitude—

To SUSANA STURGIS DE SASTRE

22 BEAUMONT STREET,
OXFORD
JUNE 22, 1916.

Dear Susie,

You shall certainly have my book [1] as soon as it is out, which I
hope will be soon, as the proofs are all corrected. It is a very small
book, and I hope very clear. Meantime I am sending you another,
on somewhat the same subject, written by the Countess von Arnim,[2] now married to my much married friend Lord Russell.[3] She
has lived for eighteen years in Germany with her first husband, and
her view of German egotism is more amusing than mine. Of course,
it is a caricature: but my colleague at Harvard, Professor Münsterberg,[4] could furnish episodes not less extravagant drawn from real
life. For instance, once when I happened to be crossing the Atlantic
in his company (much against my choice) he said to me with a great
air of importance: "People don't know it, but it is surprising how
many people are sailing in this ship simply because I am here. For
instance, there is a young lady I have been successfully hypnotising,
to cure her of the obsession that she is—quite miraculously—to
have a child" etc. etc. I shouldn't wonder if to other people he said
that I had taken the ship on his account too, though I suppose not
quite for the same reason.

I was at the Russell's lately for three days, and made the new
bride's acquaintance. She must have been pretty, and is still slight,
and of course much cleverer than any of her predecessors—except

1 *Egotism in German Philosophy.*

2 The author of *Elizabeth and Her German Garden.*

3 The 2nd Earl Russell, elder brother of Bertrand Russell.

4 Hugo Münsterberg.

in venturing on this marriage which I hardly think will last more than a year or two longer—like the war.

I expect to go to London again for a few days in a week or two.

Strong has left England. "Overjoyed to be again in France" he wrote me on a postcard from Havre. By this time I dare say he is in Switzerland taking his cure.

I am delighted to see that Celedonio is himself again. Thank him for his message.

With love to you all from

To ROBERT BRIDGES

22, BEAUMONT STREET
DEC. 23 [1916]

Dear Bridges,

Your address [1] is full of "wisdom" and I have read it with great pleasure keeping in mind what you said about not agreeing with me about "reason." I see that you use it here as a synonym of "intelligence": perhaps I tend to think of something else when I use the word: but I don't discover any material divergence between us as to the good, which is the root of all important differences between peoples. As to the *machinery* of reasoning, instinct, etc. we are all in the dark, and our philosophies move in the region of rhetorical symbols. When we speak of reason governing an animal or governing the world, do we mean simply that the good is being realised somehow, or that abstract terms and discourse are running meantime through somebody's head, or do we mean something further? It seems to me all a chaos of conventional phrases and verbal psychology, by which we describe variously the same undisputed facts.

I hope you are all having a pleasant Christmas at Chilswell.

Yours sincerely,

[1] "The reference is to 'An Address to the Swindon Branch of the Workers Educational Association', given on 28th October, 1916, by Robert Bridges, and in particular to the passage in it about 'Reason'." [Sir Edward Bridges, son of the poet-laureate.]

To ROBERT BRIDGES

3 PARK STREET,
TORQUAY
MARCH 19, 1917

Dear Bridges,

There is a Spanish proverb (I daresay not Spanish originally) that says: *Bien vienes mal, si vienes solo,* and I am afraid your second misfortune is worse than the first.[1] However, if your son is doing well, even if his wound leaves sad traces, it will be some comfort to you and Mrs. Bridges to know that the worst is over and to be relieved of the strain of anxiety, which must have been hard to bear during all these months.

I think I shall stay here until after Easter, and then on my return to Oxford I will make enquiries at Merton Lane or at Corpus, in the hope of finding you still there. I shall also make a pilgrimage to Chilswell to view the ruins, which I am glad to know are not total.

Events are so thick and so overwhelming of late that I live in a sort of continual suspense, waiting for the next morning's paper. Ought we, who are mere spectators, to be glad or sorry that we live at such a time? I think on the whole I am glad, although I could wish to be younger so as to have borne some part in the struggle, and to have lived to see its fruits which I rather think will be good. The 1880's and 1890's, which were the years in which I began to look upon the world intelligently, left an impression on my mind which I should like to feel had been wholly erased by experience of a better age.

Yours sincerely,

1 The first misfortune was the fact that Robert Bridges' house had been partially destroyed by fire; the second, that his son had been wounded in France.

To LOGAN PEARSALL SMITH

22 BEAUMONT ST. OXFORD
MAY 9, 1917

Dear Smith

A collection of extracts: how wonderful! Loeser once had a statuette of Locke, which he meant to give to W*m* James.[1] When James heard of it, he exclaimed: "A statuette, that is fame indeed! Anybody can have a statue, but a statuette is true immortality." So I say: any one can fill a shelf with his complete works; but a book of elegant extracts is for the few only, the few who, like Browning and me, have written wisely but too much.

To be quite frank, I had vaguely thought of paying myself this compliment some day, when the ontology[2] was finished, and I might find an egotistical pleasure in my old age in turning over the good things I had once been capable of saying. But by all odds, it is better that you should do it, if you are inexplicably so inclined. It is an overwhelming compliment to me, and a great service at the same time, because I think not only my style but my ideas will gain by being loosened from the academic and professorial mortar in which they have been set, because of the trade of system-building. I shall probably be much enlightened myself by beholding my naked little collection of ideas. . . . .

Egotism in German Philosophy is being translated into French —not by a man of very great wit, but by a worthy wounded officer[3] interested in philosophy and solemnly convinced of the diabolical character of the German mind. I am revising his work, and so far we have not quarrelled.

Yours sincerely

[1] See Letter to William James, Nov. 29, 1904.

[2] The contemplated system of philosophy, *Realms of Being*.

[3] The French edition was called *L'Erreur de la Philosophie Allemande* (Nouvelle Librairie Nationale, 1917). It was actually translated by two men—MM. Guillaume Lerolle and Henri Quentin. The former is, I believe, the "wounded officer" that Santayana refers to.

To LOGAN PEARSALL SMITH

Dear Smith

All my books—and most of my clothes—have lain neglected in Paris since the beginning of the war: I have only one or two copies —quite fresh—of my last book, and one of Poetry and Religion, just sent me by Scribner. Even in Paris I have, I think, only one copy of most of my volumes. And such things as proof sheets are eschewed by me the moment the corrected text appears. So that I can't provide the *corpus vile* you require for your anatomical labours.[1] Are pencil marks—which could be easily erased—incompatible with Chinese veneration for the printed page? If not, wouldn't it be quite simple to have the sentences you choose and mark, type-written on small loose sheets or cards, which could be afterwards conveniently shuffled as much as we desired? And perhaps, being all of the same size and shape, they could go to the printer, when definitely arranged, without requiring to be recopied. . . .

As to arrangement, I am glad that you don't intend it should be chronological. I don't evolve: we all have to grow up and to grow old, but what bears evident marks of immaturity or decay in our faculties ought charitably to be disregarded: the rest will have no other essential variety than that which is due to varying subjects and moods. The order should be the order of the subject-matter, or at the least (if the subject-matter is vague) of types of expression; it shouldn't on any account follow the dates at which the fragments happen to have been penned or rather published—because many things written now may have been first conceived thirty years ago, as old scraps of paper sometimes prove to me in the most startling fashion. I sometimes think we all die at twenty-five and after that are nothing but walking corpses, with gramophones inside.—It is a comforting thought when one reads the "roll of honour".

[1] Pearsall Smith was engaged in preparing his anthology, to be called *Little Essays Drawn from the Writings of George Santayana*.

I rather expect to go to London for a week or so in July. Will you still be there? If not, and there is any point to talk over, I will gladly go up at any time for the day. I like Oxford better for an occasional change of scene and *breath of the city*.

Yours sincerely

To LOGAN PEARSALL SMITH

22 BEAUMONT ST. OXFORD
JUNE 30, 1917

Dear Smith

Your titles and arrangement seem most complete and systematic, and I wish, after this, I might be an Inquisitor and burn all my other volumes. Four hundred pages are certainly as much as anyone in this world has a right to have written. I am curious to see the selection you have made and no doubt can suggest some omissions if they are required. For instance, do you think that people will care to hear what I have to say about love? That is not, as we said at Harvard, my "department".

I have been busy revising my French translator's version of "Egotism", which is now finished. Boutroux [1] is decorating it with a kindly and complimentary preface. I never had (until you undertook to distill my essence) such an honour done me in my life.

For the moment I am putting off going to town, as I wish to finish a paper [2] I have promised for an American book, written by a lot of professors in collaboration, which is to give the *coup de grace* to all philosophical errors. When this is done (it may take three or four weeks) I hope to find you still in London . . .

1 The distinguished French philosopher, Émile Boutroux.

2 "Three Proofs of Realism". In *Essays in Critical Realism; A Cooperative Study of the Problem of Knowledge.* Macmillan, 1920.

To *LOGAN PEARSALL SMITH*

22 BEAUMONT ST. OXFORD
OCT. 9, 1917

Dear Smith

I have been looking over the product of your friendly labours, and have read some of the sections entire. My feelings are mixed. Now I am overcome by the ecstasy of a doting parent, now by a sense of how ridiculously dead, old-fashioned, and thin all this argumentation and "viewiness" of my early days was or has become. I suppose both judgments are exaggerated, and that what I like is not much better than what I hate, and the wayward psychology not much worse than the epigrams. Perhaps on calmer consideration, I shall reconcile myself to these inequalities. As to your selections, my impression is that they are too long, and that a great deal of dead wood could be plucked out of them. If you are not in a hurry, perhaps you will let me indicate in some way (say with a blue pencil) the parts that seem to me unnecessary. On the other hand, I had expected more single sentences and detached paragraphs: my impression is that what I have to say is better conveyed in these occasional epigrams than in any of my attempts at argument or system. I am glad you have not made a collection merely of *pensées,* because that is cloying and distracting: but perhaps short passages interspersed among the longer ones, when on the same subject, might relieve and give point to the whole. If you didn't mind waiting six months or a year (so that without self-indigestion I could myself read over all my works) I might send you a small collection of these loose stones, to put into your edifice if you thought they would improve it.

If these suggestions, especially the second, don't appeal to you, there is nothing said: I am only telling you frankly what my impressions are. The only thing I should like to insist on is the omission here and there of arguments or opinions of which I no longer approve—and there is a whole family of them. I was hardly aware before how much my philosophy has changed since "The

Life of Reason". That book now seems to me hopelessly lost in the subjective, not that the subjective is not worth expressing, but that it should never be confused with the natural or historical facts.

Yours sincerely

To LOGAN PEARSALL SMITH

22 BEAUMONT ST. OXFORD
DECEMBER 4, 1917

Dear Smith

The ten volumes have arrived and I have set to work with such ardour that I have already finished the first volume of the L. of R.[1] and half of the S. of B.[2] The latter is written in a very genteel style—only a few lapses into the jargon of American philosophy. But the L. of R. is really scandalous in its confusion, both in language and in thought. I feel strongly that, *Deo volente*, I must rewrite this whole book: it could easily be purified, shortened, strengthened, and filled out logically.[3] I find two good things in it, which make it worth while to attempt a revision, one is the general idea—the doctrine as well as the subject—and the other a certain warmth and boldness in the description and interpretation of particular points and episodes. This last, of course, is what we are after for the present, and you have already selected the best passages: but there are some others that I think might be put in— I have made a great collection, subject to further selection—while in those you have taken there is a great deal of alloy—mere argumentation or psychological twaddle—that I want to cut out.

As the worst passages in the L. of R. will be just those left when our excisions are all made, I should like to keep the mutilated

[1] *The Life of Reason.*

[2] This second abbreviation stands for an early book—*The Sense of Beauty.*

[3] It was not until the last year of his life that Santayana finally accomplished this task in the new revised one-volume edition of *The Life of Reason.* (Scribner's, 1953)

volumes as a perpetual thorn in my conscience, and a stimulus to this necessary revision, if the book is to be rescued from the flames. As these books seem to have been the copies you possessed, may I have the pleasure of sending you a complete set—with the *American binding* to the S. of B., not this dreadful vegetative-aesthetical cover! I mention this before having the books sent to you, in case you have other copies, or for some other reason don't wish to be burdened with a fresh set.

Yours sincerely

P.S. I reopen this note to thank you for the lists and the extra pages of the books which have come by this morning's post.

If my harvest, when piled up, makes too vast a haystack, I will send it back to you with a hope that you may take it in hand again, and choose out of what I have chosen the sections that seem to you most interesting. You might, for instance, take out the aesthetic and religious sections, and leave out all the technical philosophy.

To MRS. FREDERICK WINSLOW

22 BEAUMONT STREET, OXFORD
APRIL 6, 1918

Dear Mrs. Winslow

So poor dear Julia Robbins is no more! Although I was never (whatever she may have hinted) positively in love with her, I used to write her long literary letters in my callow days, when she was still a heathen—of the old Boston type. Of late she still preserved a place for me in her gallery of "geniuses I have known", in the line, but *magno intervallo,* with Cardinal Merry del Val and the young consumptive at Davos that she on the whole decided it was her duty to give up, on account of the disparity in their ages and his tragic state of health: although I always thought these two reasons balanced and cancelled one another, and that perhaps there were other obstacles. In fine, Julia and I were very good friends, and she never despaired of my salvation, and no doubt prayed for my re-conversion—when it was partly my unconscious influence that converted her, or prepared her to be converted. She and her sister were desperately brave: everything of theirs had to be felt and believed to be most superior and beautiful; and when the bluff had to be dropped in one direction, it was put up all the more desperately in another. The Church was her last refuge, and I can't help thinking a very suitable one, although the strain would have been less if she had had a more reasonable family and set of acquaintances.—I am really made sad and pensive by this news, which I had not heard—not that I am "sorry", because at this date it is not an event to be particularly set down as unfortunate—but because her whole life and being were so pathetic, so hopelessly hopefully desirous of everything that was not.

As to myself, there is no change to speak of: I have been rather busy writing—in my lazy way—although as yet there is nothing in print to vouch for it. I gave a lecture in London this winter,[1] facing an English audience for the first time; it was, at bottom, quite like the same kind of audience in America. I am going to give another at the Cambridge summer session in August. Meantime besides my big book I am preparing another little one on the war, or rather on the psychological question, how governments and religions manage to dominate mankind, in spite or (as I shall say) because of their irrationality. I am thinking of calling it "Dominations and Powers".[2] In view of it I have been reading all sorts of things to fill the *lacunae* in my knowledge of which I am made aware as I write. For one thing, I am reading the Bible from cover to cover—something I had never done before—and Josephus [3] as a commentary. I am well, and, in spite of everything, very happy in my thoughts and in my country rambles. I am now in love with a new walk and tea-garden—in the direction of Nuneham and the Harcourt's park, which I often traverse, taking a local train back filled with munition-workers.

As to the war, I have grown a protective cuticle, and suffer less from it than during the first two years. I then expected a German victory; during the third year I began to have hopes that the Allies might get together, and even that the Russian revolution

---

[1] The Third Annual Henriette Hertz lecture. Reprinted, with some alterations, as Ch. V of *Character and Opinion in the United States.*

[2] This famous work was, actually, concluded some thirty-three years later!

[3] An ancient Jewish historian.

might help. Now that the opposite has happened—at least for the time being—and things look pretty black, I have fallen back on a sort of grey leaden sea of philosophy, where I find all human purposes and ambitions, all likes and dislikes, benevolently neutralised by the hidden forces that at once create and defeat them. My feeling is that, however things shape themselves in the immediate future, the world is going to take a new direction in which the "aims"—oh, vanity!—of both parties will be submerged. Something in me tells me that the Russian Bolsheviks are right—not in their conduct, which has been scandalous and silly—but in their sense for values, in their equal hostility to every government founded on property and privilege. At any rate, though I take up the paper every morning with a beating heart, I lay it down with a sort of inward smile, as if someone said to me (the Lord, as they have it in the Bible) *"never mind"*.

I can't believe that you in America are really in this fray; it seems a drama in a different language. But I believe in American energy and power of cooperation. What is lamentably wanting all round is *Intelligence!* What little men, what helpless minds! Thank you for breaking this long silence and giving me news of your domestic hearth.

Yours sincerely

To LOGAN PEARSALL SMITH

22 BEAUMONT ST. OXFORD
MAY 24, 1918

Dear Smith

Trivia [1] is hardly a book to be read consecutively and only once: nevertheless I have done so, and I need hardly say with the greatest pleasure. It is not only the style and tone, so familiar and at the same time so exquisite that delights me, for you know I can't

[1] Perhaps Pearsall Smith's best book.

very well separate style from thought: it seems to me that the form in which a thought is cast is a part of its quality, and that the quality of the idea itself is only a deeper sort of form or style of expression: it too, like verbal form, expresses a reaction of the mind and its habits upon objects, rather than the objects themselves; for ideas are not objects at all, but only views of objects. In your manner, therefore, I find and relish your way of thinking. Where did you get your humility? I thought that was an extinct virtue. And I very much like your love of pleasure, and your humour and *malice:* it is so delightful to live in a world that is full of pictures, and incidental *divertissements,* and amiable absurdities. Why shouldn't things be largely absurd, futile, and transitory? They are so, and we are so, and they and we go very well together. But I am afraid you don't quite think so, are not quite reconciled to yourself and the world as you find them, and feel that it is *ignominious* to grow old, and slant your umbrella against the wind. Now, if what is our inevitable fate is *ignominious,* I understand what Bridges [1] says of Trivia, that it is the most immoral book ever written, although every word of it can be read aloud. But I don't think so; it is not immoral at all unless you take it to be complete and ultimate, which of course is the last thing you would think of pretending. Your point is to be incomplete, fugitive, incidental. Yet the devil of it is that if you don't suggest or keep in reserve a firm background, a religion or philosophy that enables you to face and to judge all these small delights, and say to them ἔχω οὐκ ἔχομαι, [I enjoy; I am not possessed] then the thing becomes ultimate and complete for you against your will. That is the danger and the trouble with Trivia: you *must* have a philosophy, even in fooling, or the fooling will be spoiled and made bitter by having to take the place of the philosophy that is wanting: and the sweet treble will crack. What I wish you would do is to write another Trivia, or two more (since Trivia had three faces) and make your bow to Luna and Hecate also, after having shown us Diana tripping across the flickering glades. Humility is not weak, it is just. Heraclitus said that justice presided over the flux, because such things didn't *deserve* to last for ever.

You see I take Trivia very seriously, and I hope you will think it a compliment, and not mere ponderosity on my part.

Yours

1 Robert Bridges, the poet-laureate.

To LOGAN PEARSALL SMITH

22 BEAUMONT ST., OXFORD

MAY 29, 1918

Dear Smith

Please tell Mrs Berenson [1] that I had been looking forward with pleasure to seeing her, but I can't very well go to London this week, so that I hope you will let me know when she is again in town, as usually I am quite free, and always glad to come to see and hear what is going on in your hospitable circle, which to me represents the centre of the intellectual world. Oxford, very decidedly, does not. It is a sort of celestial epicycle—an eccentric and back-handed convolution suspected by some to have no real existence, except in the mind of the ancients. Physically, however, Oxford is really heavenly in these days: I have had today a most delightful day, walking in the morning through Nuneham Park (where an ostrich made faces at me, and threatened hostilities) to lunch (very well) at the Harcourt Arms, and walk back to Littlemore through fields covered with flowers and made companionable by cuckoos, peewits, and larks. I wonder if the iteration of the cuckoo's note ever really made husbands uncomfortable. I think it well might, because repetition can persuade us of anything.

You are quite right in your defence of Trivia and her right to be as light and charming and irresponsible as she will. It was only here and there that I felt as if a touch of something else was needed for complete felicity; where the cadence, as it were, seemed incomplete. When we have a talk, I also want to protest against a technical heresy which my inquisitorial *flair* has detected in one place; it touches the separate existence of mind and body, which Aristotle and I do not admit in this world any more than in the other. However, that has nothing to do with what you wanted your pretty Trivia to be: only these darlings do turn out to have unsuspected depths in their natures sometimes, and do tragic things much to the surprise of their fond parents.

Thank you very much for writing.

Yours sincerely

[1] Mrs. Bernard Berenson, the sister of Pearsall Smith.

To ROBERT BRIDGES

22 BEAUMONT STREET
JULY 11, 1918

Dear Bridges,

Many thanks for your kindness in enquiring after me this morning. I have not been positively ill, but struggling with the symptoms of my old bronchitis, and feeling generally slack.

Obeying your prohibition I haven't written to thank you for "The Necessity of Poetry" [1] or to tell you how much I liked the goings on in the Market Place of the Subconscious. That is more to my taste than "Concepts", and I think you pay our friend Campion [2] too great a compliment in calling him to witness in the matter. These "concepts" are mythological symbols. We don't at all know what it is that develops a thought or a passion in us. It is not literally a concept, because that means only a static essence, one of the forms which our thought (if it were conscious) might fall into at one moment. The *motif* is more like a dramatic personage, or consecutive dream. That is why I like your Market Place and its hubbub: that is *frankly* mythological and far more adequate.

If the weather and the state of my inner man permit, I will come to Chilswell on Sunday afternoon in the hope of seeing you.

Yours sincerely,

[1] "An Address given to the Tredeger & District Co-operative Society in November, 1917." [Sir Edward Bridges]

[2] George Goring Campion.

To ROBERT BRIDGES

22, BEAUMONT STREET
JULY 18, 1918

Dear Bridges,

Your objection to the word "consciousness" and even "conscious" which latter at least I use *mente conscia recti,* makes it hard to explain that I don't assert that a thought cannot be thought about. The *essence* thought of once may of course be thought of again, and the *fact* that it has been thought of before may be thought of later. But *attention* itself doesn't offer an objective to contemplation. If people chose to deny that attention existed or was diverted from one object to another, the only experimental evidence we could offer would be indirect. We might point out the way in which the eyes are turned or the brow knit; or we might point out that objects sometimes come into view at intervals and with such a variable intensity as can hardly be attributed to their own nature. But these arguments could be eluded by saying that neither of these facts is what we mean by attention. Attention is interpolated by us into our view of those facts in what we conceive to be their natural relations and their way of hanging together: but attention is not to be found among the observable facts themselves. This is all I meant to assert.

I agree that "instinct" is more "intelligible" than thought, if we mean more pervasive, fundamental, and "natural": because nature is, or should be, the standard of naturalness. But philosophers (Bergson included) do not understand anything inwardly, they do not plunge downwards towards the depths. Their art is merely to reform or extend discourse on its own level: and those who are not judicious add that this level is the deepest or the only one that exists.

I hope we may soon have a chance of talking about all this.

Yours,

To B. A. G. FULLER

22 BEAUMONT ST. OXFORD
SEPT. 10. 1918

Dear Fuller

It is a real pleasure to hear from you. I knew that you were in France officiating in some useful capacity, but had no definite address. Some six months ago I sent a pamphlet to you at Sherborn but I daresay it never reached you. The Harvard world seems far away and not very enticing; Heraclitus was right, I think, in believing that *Dike* presides over the lapse of things, and that when they pass away, it is high time they should do so. If you go round the world after the war, I hope it will not be at a hurried or an even pace, and that you will spend three quarters of the time of your journey in the places which after all are most interesting and where there is most (for us, at least) to discover—in western Europe. Then I shall hope to come across your path and perhaps even to make some excursion in your good company; this long confinement in England, though pleasant in itself, is beginning to grow oppressive, and I often think with envy of those in Paris or beyond. At the same time, I hate to face suspicious officials, and any unusual difficulties and complications in the machinery of travel; so I have remained in my Oxford headquarters now for three years, and expect not to abandon them until the war ends.

For the moment I am spending a few days with Moncure Robinson and his sister Mrs Chetwynd and her nice family; and expect to go to London to see the new Russian ballets. Do you remember our first night at the Châtelet and the sensation caused by *L'Après-midi d'un Faune?* I haven't seen that sort of thing since those distant days. The routine of my life has been broken only by some invitations to give lectures about things connected with philosophy or the U. S. I accept, and the obligation compels me to put pen to paper and give shape to floating memories and ideas.

My good friend Strong [1] has had a bad time—laid up with a

---

[1] C. A. Strong.

paralysis of the legs—and is still hardly able to walk. The attack fortunately came on when he was at Val Mont [1] above the lake of Geneva, a place he likes and where the doctors inspire him with confidence. He hopes soon to return to Fiesole; meantime I have been separated from him and have missed him, for in his quiet dull way he is the best of friends and the soundest of philosophers— good ballast for my cockleshell. We are both contributing to a volume [2] that Durant Drake is getting together in defence of the Old Realism; it is to be a sort of competitor with the New Realism and the pragmatists' Creative Intelligence. I am also deep in a book to be called Dominations and Powers [3]—a sort of psychology of politics and attempt to explain how it happens that governments and religions, with so little to recommend them, secure such a measure of popular allegiance. Of course, behind all this, is the shadow of the Realms of Being, still (I am sorry to say) rather nebulous, although the cloud of manuscript is already ponderous and charged with some electricity in the potential state. I don't know if any lightning or thunder will ever reach mortals from it.

I hope the translation of your Plotinus [4] into French will materialize. There seems to be a wave of interest in him—and that is better than toying with Bergsonism.[5] I suppose the motive is the same—a desire to escape from reality; but Plotinus is willing to migrate into the supernatural, whereas the enemies of the intellect only desire to feel their own pulse. They are valetudinarians scared at the sight of the doctor and taking comfort in keeping their eyes shut tight. Neo-Catholics and Neo-Platonists at least have a world of fancy on which to exercise their faculties and train their hearts. . . .

Keep the inner fires burning; it will be such happiness for me to feel their genial warmth when we next meet.

Yours ever,

[1] A clinic near Glion-sur-Montreux.

[2] *Essays in Critical Realism.*

[3] This work was laid aside and not finally completed until 1950.

[4] *The Problem of Evil in Plotinus.*

[5] The philosophy of Henri Bergson.

To ROBERT BRIDGES

22, BEAUMONT STREET,
SUNDAY
[1918]

Dear Bridges,

Your good impressions of the French translation of my book [1] comfort and relieve me a good deal, because the sense that, do what I might, I couldn't get the translators to understand certain passages has weighed upon me, and kept me from enjoying with a free mind the greater part of their work, which is indeed excellent. I shouldn't at all wonder if the translation had a better fortune in the world than the original. At any rate it will not fall so much into the hands of the surviving academic idealists, whose philosophic home is in Germany.

Of course, you mustn't be bothered with Pearsall Smith's selections: [2] you have already made a contribution (which I will see is included) about the symptoms and the disease: if anything else occurs to you and you will let us know it shall be incorporated also: but only if it happens to come to mind. I tremble myself at the prospect of having to read over my *opera omnia quae exstant* (for the verses and the innumerable philosophic articles may be regarded as lost for good) in order to rescue my favourite *bons mots*. I think Pearsall Smith has made his selections too long: he consents that I should shorten them and add a sprinkling of loose sentences and maxims of my own choosing; and he kindly says he has had his fun, and will let me have my way and take my time with the matter. I am busy at the moment with something else, but will begin the process of cutting down what has been chosen already, leaving the additions until later. If such a book is to appear at all, it ought not to contain *dead wood*.

I am sorry not to have been of the party on Thursday: I am going to Mrs. Morrell's today, when Mrs. Warren will be there.

[1] *Egotism in German Philosophy.*

[2] For the anthology *Little Essays Drawn from the Writings of George Santayana.*

I have copied what you say of the French translation and sent it to the author of it: he will be better pleased than by any compliment from me, which might be merely perfunctory.

Yours sincerely,

To LOGAN PEARSALL SMITH

22 BEAUMONT STREET
OXFORD, MARCH 9, '19

Dear Smith

Your letter makes me rather ashamed of myself not only in the matter of the Selections [1]—of which more anon—but for not having written or seen you for so long. The fact is I have spent the winter in a mentally comatose condition, doing very little but read the papers and a few odd books, and pottering away now and then at some one of my many half-written things. Inertia has also invaded me in respect to travel, and I have put off all attempts to get to Italy this Spring. I mean to go to Spain first—in the summer or autumn—and then to Fiesole, when Strong returns from America, where he is going for the summer. What has contributed to my uselessness has been an illusion about my lectures on America: I thought they were practically ready to be sown together into a volume; [2] but in filling out the paper on James [3] and Royce [4] I got into a terrible mess; and that one lecture has now expanded into four chapters. I believe I am out of the wood in this matter now: and as soon as it is done and sent to the publishers I am going to return to the Selections; you shall have them back, I assure you, before I leave England. It is of course not for lack of

[1] For Pearsall Smith's anthology—*Little Essays Drawn from the Writings of George Santayana.*

[2] *Character and Opinion in the United States.*

[3] William James.

[4] Josiah Royce.

time or any material difficulty that I have neglected this matter. The reason is that I get sick of my old paragraphs, and of thinking of style apart from substance, and simply *can't* keep my mind applied to the task. But when I am fresh I have great hopes that we may make a good book out of it, one fit to take the place of all I have written until lately. . .

My own unhappiness about the war disappeared on July 18, 1918, and indeed in a certain sense had disappeared earlier, because although I thought the Germans might win a nominal victory, the Russian revolution seemed to me to have sealed the fate of the German system and its essential ambitions; I felt we had passed into another theme in the symphony, and that Hegel and Bismarck were in the same category as Torquemada and Philip II. But in July, 1918, we saw that the German machine was *already* cracking, even in a military sense; and since then it has been all a matter of more or less delay, suffering, confusion, and muddle, but not a question of a new illustration of Dominations and Powers in the person of *Deutschtum über Alles.* That is what I had feared during the first two years of the war, and what made me very miserable: not that I couldn't reconcile myself to a German Age—I could stand a Chinese, an American, or a Bolshevik Age perfectly —but that I was sorry for France and England, and very sorry at the thought that the Latin tradition might be cut off, or disfigured into a Teutonic classicism. Of course, as you say, we have no peace in prospect: but peace is in the grave. Existence is fundamentally in flux—that is a conviction and expectation to start with; and we are merely returning the movement, perfectly sensible before the war, which is bringing about the dissolution of the age of luxury and respectability in which you and I were born. Let it dissolve! Of course much horror and injustice will be involved in the process—but much would have been involved also in maintaining the old order. I am not afraid of the people. It is their leaders that are odious, but they will either succumb and be discredited, or they will become fashionable tyrants and patrons of the arts like all the bosses that preceded them. At least, that is my prophecy.

I hope your pleasant convalescence will continue and that I may before long come to you, laden with the revised Selections.

Yours sincerely

To *LOGAN PEARSALL SMITH*

22 BEAUMONT ST. OXFORD
MARCH 16, '19

Dear Smith

What you say about the selections exactly expresses my own feeling. I have already rearranged the passages with a view to an architectural effect which a few titles, like mouldings, can help to bring out. I have looked up the pages you suggest for the first "essay"—if you think we can call the book "Little Essays"—and I think it will do, only the references to Spinoza must be cut out, and perhaps a sentence or two supplied from other sources. I mean to use the single sentences and epigrams which I have collected *only* in case they can be used in this way to give point to or to sum up longer passages. As you see, I take a great interest in this affair, in spite of my apparent apathy, and have hopes of making it a success. The arrangement is already far advanced; also the finding of titles.

There are two other reasons why a synthetic view of my books in this form is desirable: that I have written too much and repeated myself in a way which only the bad habit of daily lecturing can explain, if not excuse; and that there is a real vacillation or incoherence in my expressions, because I take alternately and without warning now the transcendental and now the naturalistic point of view; i.e. I sometimes describe the *perspectives* of the senses and imagination, and sometimes the natural sequence or relations of *facts*. Of course both things are worth describing, and there is no inconsistency in the differences which exist between the two views; but it is a grave defect not to have made it clear how this difference arises, and why it is inevitable and indeed makes the chief interest in the drama of thought. . . .

Yours ever

To LOGAN PEARSALL SMITH

RICHMOND HILL HOTEL
[RICHMOND, SURREY]
JUNE 20, '19

Dear Smith

You see, I am still where you last saw me—or rather, very nearly in the same place, because after going away to town in the hope of getting my passport properly endorsed, I have returned to a still better room on the top floor of Wick House, with a really magnificent view on two sides and the feeling of being in a castle tower overlooking some smiling champaign— It is quite delightful as a retreat for working: only marred by the necessity of descending to the dining room two or three times a day.

The reason for my return here, as you may conjecture is the obduracy of the French authorities who will not give a *visa* for one's *beaux yeux,* but require all sorts of proofs of business activities, services during the war, living to earn, wife to rescue from starvation or dishonour, or some other work of moral or national importance. It is still possible that I may get away next week, if Cerberus is satisfied with a sop (which he has asked for and promised to be appeased by—but what are promises to Cerberus?) in the form of an affidavit that I really lived in Paris before the war. I wonder how Berenson [1] manages to travel so like a lord or an Irish emissary: is it his business or his fame that propitiates people, or his American nationality?

I should be sorry not to see Strong, who has been philosophically rather lonely as well as laid up physically for the last year: otherwise I should be really glad to give up all thought of travel and return to peace and happiness at Oxford.

You are very generous in wishing me to have all the profit of the Little Essays, if profit there is to be: let us not have a quarrel of disinterestedness about it. But it would really be simpler for me if you took half the royalties, let us say, to invest in the beautiful book which should serve as a memento of your labours. I am

[1] Bernard Berenson.

not a connoiseur in books; but it occurs to me that the right thing
would be a copy of the *great* Essays of Bacon or Montaigne, with
an inscription witnessing that seeing thou hast been faithful over
little essays, thou shalt be made master over great essays. If I return
to Oxford, I will ask Blackwell if he has an attractive edition of
either of these, and send it to you so inscribed.

Thank you very much for wanting me to come to Big Chilling.
Of course I should like to, but can make no plans at present. Thank
you, too, for Mrs Berenson's card, from which I am happy to infer
that she is quite well again.

Yours

To ROBERT BRIDGES

9, AV. DE L'OBSERVATOIRE,
PARIS
SEPT. 18, 1919

Dear Bridges,

Your letters make me a little homesick for Oxford, although
I am having a very nice time (in my own way) here among all my
books and papers, and under the stimulus of such delightful scenes
as meet one wherever one goes in this place—more normal, more
Roman and human, than what is man-made at Oxford,—because
the fields and trees and skies, and that mesh of little streams, are
another matter. I am confirmed in the intention to return to Oxford for good—but it will not be for the present, because I don't
want to go until I am ready to shift my head-quarters, which is not
yet the case.

I won't attempt to answer your letter *seriatim,* although each
of the things you tell me prompts me to say something, but I can't
let Plotinus lie under the imputation you throw on him of not
being a "good philosopher." If you mean that his system of the
universe is not a map of it, is not scientifically correct or in scale,

of course I agree. But it seems to me a very great system, very "good philosophy", and I am glad that the mystics in Oxford are taking him up, rather than pretending to find comfort in Hegel or in the meretricious psychology of Bergson. The doctrines of Plotinus are flights in the same direction as the doctrines of Christianity: they are not hypotheses intended to explain facts, but expressions invented for sentiment and aspiration. The world, he feels, is full of the *suggestion* of beauty and goodness, but of the suggestion only. In fact, it betrays and obliterates everything it tries to express, like an inscription in invisible ink that should become luminous only for a moment. And his question is: What does the world *say*, what does life *mean*, what is there beyond, 'εκεî [yonder], that might lend significance and a worthy origin and end to this wonderful apparition and to our passionate love and passionate dissatisfaction in its presence? His system is an elaborate answer to this question. It is not a hypothesis but an intention, and such rightness as it has is merely fidelity and fineness in rendering moral experience. Of course all those things he describes do not exist; of course he is not describing *this* world, he is describing *the other* world, that is, deciphering the good, just beyond it or above it, which each actual thing suggests. Even this rendering of moral aspiration is arbitrary, because nature really does not aspire to anything, and each living thing aspires to something different, in divergent ways. But this arbitrary aspiration, which Plotinus reads into the world, sincerely expresses his own aspiration and that of his age. That is why I say he is decidedly a "good philosopher." It is the Byzantine architecture of the mind, just as good or better than the Gothic. It seems to me better than Christian theology in this respect, that it isn't mixed up with history, it isn't half Jewish, half worldly. It is the Greek side of Christian theology isolated and made pure; and that is the side of it which seems to me truly spiritual, truly sacrificial and penitentially joyful. That it is terribly superstitious and turns all physics into magic is an integral part of its poetic and expressive virtue. Every passion, every force, must be a devil or an angel, because it is agreed to begin with we are looking for the *spirit* in things.

I didn't mean to go on in this way, especially as really I know Plotinus very little: but I feel a great power in him, a sublime illusion, as if some plant or some pensive animal had laboriously spun the moral dialectic of its own experience round itself, and called it the universe. I have actually seen, and read, that first volume of the translation [1] to be published by the "Medici Press"; of course, except in the extracts at the end, it doesn't come to the core of the matter, which is in the Vth and VIth Enneads. The translator has eccentric notions of what the vocabulary of philosophy should be: he doesn't stick to the traditional renderings and leave it to the reader to put new life into them, which after all is the safest course. He tries various paraphrases of his own, which of course bias and distort the meaning, even if they have a certain value of their own as interpretations.

Do you ever see the Athenaeum? I have kept on writing for it, although to be quite frank I don't like the review as a whole, and don't read it; but there is no other that I know of that would publish my effusions, and it is a great relief to have them in print. What is once out is done for, and one doesn't have to think of it any more.

Are you going to America? If your society for the purification of the language is going to cleanse those Augean stables, I don't envy it its labours. Why shouldn't the English language of a hundred years hence be as different from ours as ours is from Shakespeare's? I know you say he pronounced as we do: but we don't write like him. The Americans have a great love of language for its own sake, and will develop new effects, if not new beauties. As one of them used to say whenever anything was censured: Let them have their fun!

Yours ever,

To B. A. G. FULLER

LE BALZE; FIESOLE, JAN. 10. 1920

Dear Fuller

It is never too late for good wishes or for letters from you, and it has been a real pleasure to get this missive of yours, which has

[1] The translation by Stephen MacKenna.

arrived together with renewed sunshine—I am writing in an open loggia, quite warm, and squinting at the paper on which Apollo is pouring all his rays and dazzling me even in reflexion—and at the moment when I am planning to start for Rome, and spend three months there in solitude and enchantment. I staid at the Avenue de l'Observatoire until the end of November, when Strong came back alone from America—his daughter Margaret remained in New York, to get a taste of winter gaieties with her rich relations. She is returning here in a day or two; and Strong will no longer miss me if I run away. He is not able, poor man, to do more than crawl about unsteadily with the help of a stick, and as he doesn't like driving, he becomes at times rather depressed with sitting in the stuffy library, reading the literary supplement to the Times. When the sun is out, he feels more cheerful, and in fact is perfectly well as to his inner man, eats, sleeps, and looks like a young man and is deeply interested in his improvements in this villa, which is getting to be rather grand on a small scale, since it is condemned to cling to a ledge, like those of the Purgatorio, on the steep side of the hills of Fiesole. When Rome becomes too hot, I expect to return to Paris, and to leave Spain for next winter. I miss England, but don't mean to go back there until I go for good, taking my goods and chattels from Paris, and settling down, probably in Oxford, for the rest of my days.

You hint—and we all feel it—that the disturbance of the war and the deterioration of man which it has brought to light have lost little of their horror by the advent of a nominal peace: never-theless personally I am reconciled to the end of the world—the Christian genteel world—and not afraid of futurity, even if it should take the form of Bolshevism. Heaven and hell are relative and *essentially prospective;* by the time we get to either we begin to see that each of them has its other side. I think to be born under Bolshevism would not be worse than to be born in Boston: it would have its virtues, although not always those which we may personally be most inclined to practise. Your picture of Harvard and its back-stairs philosophy is indeed horrible: but it was not very satisfying even in the consulate of James & Royce when we were younger. In England philosophy seems to be tolerably unprej-udiced and varied at present. There is no commanding intellect, but for that very reason, perhaps, there is a sense of movement and of opening vistas which I think rather encouraging. I am so much absorbed, however, in thinking out my own ideas that, being too old to take up with new things, I am not at all troubled by the shifts of persons and notions in the academic world: and as for Harvard philosophy, it seems not to exist. Does it? Here I have been reading various books that Strong has in his library, for *he* buys books; one is by Broad [1] of Trinity, Cambridge, groping but light-minded; and of course I read what Bertie Russell writes, although, as you know, I think he has relapsed into the British original sin of empiricism, and all his intelligence and keenness will not help him out of the consequent impotence and artificiality.

I am *glad* you are leaving Harvard; you are old and ballasted enough by this time not to be upset by the silliness of Mrs. Grundy; devote yourself to your garden and books and horses, come to see us often in Europe, and write what the spirit moves you to write, not in self-defence or in protest against anybody, but for the love of picturing what there is to picture. You will "do" infinitely more "good" by assuming such an attitude and performing such a function than by joining any tug-of-war team that may want you to pull hard on one side—no matter on which—because it is theirs—or yours.

Here, good living and the presence of other persons have rather kept me from doing anything but reading; but I have had the proof of my "Little Essays" (selections from my books made by Logan Pearsall Smith) and written one or two "Soliloquies". These may make another incidental book before long. My book on James & Royce,—to be called "Character and Opinion in the United States", for it spreads out a great deal over things American in general—is in the press. You will see these three books, I expect, within a year. Strong has persuaded me to work at once, with all the energy I have, on the "Realms of Being", and I am resolved to do so, for fear that I may die (although I am in perfect health at present) before it is finished. There may therefore be a pause in my apparent fertility after these little triplets are born.

Yours ever

[1] C. D. Broad.

To ROBERT BRIDGES

PARIS, AUG. 29, 1920

Dear Bridges,

Logan Pearsall Smith has just sent me a copy of your paper in the *London Mercury* about the *Little Essays*. I don't subscribe to the press-cutting agencies, so that I remain for the most part in blessed ignorance of what people say or don't say about my books, and in rare cases, like the present one, where I should have been truly sorry to miss the evidence of understanding and friendship which a review contains, it usually reaches me sooner or later in some round-about way. I hope the delay in the expression of my appreciation of your so warm, so sympathetic, and in itself so pleasant paper has not made you think for a moment that I could be indifferent to it. The mere fact of your taking the trouble to write it at all is a great honour to me, and of course the publisher has already seized on your flattering phrases to put into his advertisements: but what in my own mind is most precious and interesting in your criticism is precisely the indication of your own views where they diverge from mine: I hadn't understood so clearly before exactly why you seemed to regard some of my opinions about poetry and about Christianity with a certain kindly wonder, as if they were strange and excentric or at least amusing paradoxes. But now I think I see better, both what your view is and what you suppose mine to be, and consequently why you find a certain perversity in me at those points.

I won't say that the differences between us are wholly verbal, because I suspect there is some (perfectly legitimate) diversity of temperament and allegiance behind them: but I think they are, so to speak, semi-verbal. I mean that such words as materialism or Christianity or religion or poetry, besides being used for many different definable objects, carry an opprobrious or eulogistic connotation which often drowns and hides all their other meanings. For instance, if Christianity is used eulogistically, to mean whatever is best or truest in the belief and sentiment of people calling themselves Christians, I should agree with you that London in the nineteenth century, or that the social ethics of the future, may be more Christian than Rome in the fifteenth or any other century: because

I should be inclined to admit that what is best and truest in Christianity is that tender humanity which it borrowed from late Judaeism and which, touched with poetry and disenchantment, shines so beautifully in the maxims of our Lord: but I submit that if that had been the sole or the chief inspiration of the Gospel, there never would have been anything called Christianity in the world. In other words, the feeling you or I may have as to what is best and truest in this religion, does not determine its actual essence, or what distinguishes it from other religions or from the absence of religion altogether. To get at this essence or anything approaching it, we must add to that Jewish philanthropy and tenderness a particular historical and supernaturalistic philosophy, intended to buttress that sentiment, and actually qualifying it and transforming it into specifically Christian charity such as in itself it is not: there must be not only love of men but love of sinners for the love of God. This would be no better than a cant phrase unless it was inspired by such eschatology and such supernaturalistic hygiene for saving the soul as the Christian Churches have developed: and it is these doctrines and forms of discipline that I am thinking of when I talk of Christianity. Otherwise one might have to admit that Socrates was a better Christian than Saint Paul, and Buddha than Saint Dominic: and perhaps one would have to deny that Luther and Calvin were Christians at all, which (on account of their theology) I should hesitate to do.

Much the same misunderstandings arise in the matter of poetry and its relation with philosophy. By philosophy I don't mean true philosophy—far from it. And it would not occur to me that if totality of view and a sense for the ultimate raised Dante to the highest level of poetry, he would descend from it because we afterwards decided that his conception of the world and of man's place in it was not correct: correctness has nothing to do with it. Homer and Virgil are just as comprehensive—if not perhaps so earnest or consecrated—as Dante: and as the geography of Homer and the agriculture of Virgil lose nothing by being scientifically obsolete, so the astronomy and theology of Dante lose nothing by being so. My contention is only that their dignity as poets would fall immeasurably if they had had *no* geography, astronomy, theology, or agriculture: in other words, if they had not attuned their minds to the world as they conceived it, but had conceived no world and—to be frank—had had no mind.

I like what you say about matter and the capacities of the

atom: and I have laughed aloud, like an idiot, at your final story and the capacity of the Sphinx to "be there" when it no longer appears in the bill. I should admit the fair impeachment if you boldly called me a platonist, and a materialist as well. This contradiction disappears if we take seriously the profoundly platonic doctrine that natural philosophy and theology (in the Platonic system) are *necessarily mythical.* This does not preclude a scientific analysis of phenomenal nature, although Socrates and his pupils did not attempt it. Their despair about science was premature, as is that of Bergson: but a student of physics (which is the true metaphysics) may perfectly lend himself to platonism in the poetic and discursive expression of his own mind, and in his moral philosophy. Only he must beware of supposing, as the dogmatic platonists do, that in his platonising he is going *deeper,* as well as higher, than in his natural science. He is not going deeper: he is mythologising.

In a few weeks I am off to Spain, where I expect to spend the coming winter. Often a longing comes over me to walk round Christ Church Meadows,[1] and I ask myself why I put off returning to England. On the other hand, all those scenes are so vividly before me that they could hardly be more so if I revisited them, and I am still writing "Soliloquies in England" abroad!

It would be a great pleasure to hear from you and know how Chilswell and all its inhabitants are faring—

Yours sincerely,

To LOGAN PEARSALL SMITH

PARIS, AUG. 30 1920

Dear Smith

Thank you very much for your kind letter, received a few days ago, and for the cuttings about *Little Essays,* which arrived this morning. I am very glad to see Bridges' charming paper; quite

---

[1] In Oxford.

apart from what it says about us that is flattering and useful (to Constable)[1] I like the good humour and kind feeling running through it all. I am writing to him about it, explaining that I hadn't seen it until this day.

I agree with you that the book makes a nice appearance and in dipping into it now and then, it has seemed to me that it struck its notes clearly and pleasantly, and that people might like it, if they only could be brought to read it. This is perhaps true of most books of poetry, or of prose that has been digested and distilled like poetry. I feel that I owe you a debt of gratitude for having persisted in the plan of disengaging these passages from their original—too professorial—context. My early books were written too much under the pressure of American public sentiment—I don't mean that this influenced my opinions, or even my style, very much, but that it made me write to justify my existence and make sure to myself that I did have an intellect: but I should have had more, perhaps, if I hadn't been in such haste to exhibit it. My comfort is that you have saved these fragments from the wilderness of the top shelf, and that I am not yet too old to recast the more theoretic parts of my reflexion into a system that may be better articulated and more closely knit than my old divagations.

I am afraid my shameful carelessness about writing letters has caused me not to thank you as yet for your *Stories from the Bible*, which I see you have greatly expurgated and reduced in bulk from your original manuscript, parts of which you read to us some time ago. As I told you then, I think the satirical strain is so much better in it than the farcical strain, that it is almost a pity to have the latter in it at all: I mean that your parody of the commentators and your suggestions (as in the case of Jezebel's kindly feelings towards the religion of the peasants) of what the facts may have really been, are far too witty to require the introduction of modern slang or other anachronisms. But this was probably your original joke in the matter, and the higher flights suggested themselves afterwards.

I am sorry that my inertia has proved too great to suffer me to go to England this summer. Strong leaves me the day after tomorrow for Aix-les-Bains, and I shall probably stay here until Margaret returns, so as to see her and act as official guardian while she is in Paris: then I am going to Spain for the winter. In the summer

1 His publishers in England.

I count on going to England at least for a few weeks, when I may have the pleasure of seeing you.

Yours sincerely

P.S. The translator of my "Egotism in German Philosophy" into French, Lerolle, writes asking if you and I have any objection to his undertaking a translation of "Little Essays". It is only fair to add that he is a person of various employments and uncertain ways; but (under careful watching) a competent translator. His French, at least, can't be very bad, since the Academy gave him a prize for his version. I suppose you have no objection to letting him make the attempt if he likes, although we must not count on his perseverence. What say you?

To WILLIAM LYON PHELPS

PARIS, SEPTEMBER 8, 1920

Dear Phelps

I am much pleased to have your letter and your review of the *Little Essays*. All the first part of it makes me feel as if I were reading an obituary notice by anticipation, and I can almost imagine some Phi Beta Kappa orator, in the not very distant future, spreading this sort of roseate sunset glow over my uneventful history and limping personality. I don't object to the headlines; Harvard in the 1890's being me, and America Today being you; and I think the view of the Yard has much the same quality of cautious idealization. Yours is not a cubist portrait of your humble servant, nor yet a Dutch inventory of his features and circumstances. I think it is very good and fair, if one allows for the friendly partiality you do not disguise, and also for a certain glamour or pathos of distance that already bathes our memories of youth. The only fact that is wrong is your saying that my mother was an American; she was Spanish—we never spoke English together—but had been first married (in Manila) to one of the Boston Sturgises, so that my half-sisters and half-brother belonged to that once prosperous and always agreeable tribe: and it was in consequence of this connection, and money matters concerned in it, that we went to live in America. A point of interpretation where I feel that you are also somewhat misled, or at least reticent, is in regard to my reasons for leaving Harvard. Weariness had something to do with it, but weariness with lectures and with the "problems" of technical philosophy rather than with college committees, on which I seldom appeared. They knew I was no good at business! But my chief motive was a life-long desire to live in Europe and—which is only possible here —to be left alone. In respect to higher things, most of what you say pleases and satisfies me greatly, especially your mention of Schopenhauer: that is to hit the nail on the head. There are only two points in which perhaps you don't understand me: it seems to me unfair to suggest that, unlike the wizened Morley, I am not frank about immortality; a scholar like you ought to know that the platonising or Spinozistic things I say about it, taken in an ideal sense, are the *original motif* of this doctrine in the European tradition: the notion of ghosts or of resurrection has been merely confused with it, and it is no compromise or hedging on my part to separate the two views once more. The other point is about liking life, and the poets who relish it. My disgust at Browning is not because he loves life or has it abundantly, but because he doesn't love it (as Dickens does, for instance) for what is *good* in it, but for what is base, tawdry, and pretentious. I protest against being called a snob; what I love is what is simple, humble, easy, what ought to be common, and it is only the bombast of false ambitions and false superiority, that I abhor.

Before the war I was on the point of going to give some lectures at the University of Wisconsin, and at Columbia, but I doubt now whether I shall ever cross the Atlantic again. I have my headquarters here, and go away at intervals. Last winter I was in Italy, now I go to Spain, and I was in England throughout the war. All places, where there is an arm-chair within and something human to see without, are much the same, and I lead the same life everywhere. You will find me somewhere on the beaten track whenever you next come to these parts.

Yours sincerely

To GEORGE STURGIS

PARIS, AUGUST 14, 1921

Dear George

Your good letter of July 25th, coming after your telegram, told me just what I most wished to know about your father's [1] last days; and I very much appreciate the clear way in which you put everything. In respect to money-matters, I am a *true* philosopher (not a mere professor of Phil. 10, 12, etc) and my one wish is not to hear about them, but to cash cheques and be happy. Your father was inestimable to me and to your aunts [2] in this way, because besides being so affectionate and loyal, and taking so much pains, he was very clever at it, and made us far more prosperous than we ever expected to be. I can't speak for your aunts, although I think your aunt Josephine at least will be of my way of thinking, but my own chief desire is that things should go on as much as possible as they did before, and I will gladly sign a power of attorney in your favour if you will send me one. If you know your father's books, you must have noticed that your aunt Josephine and I are not extravagant persons—I hope not miserly, but accustomed to an inexpensive way of living. I am also, at last, beginning to get something out of my books: so that a large income is a secondary consideration for us. What we desire is security, and the absence of care. So that if you will take charge, and incline to the side of prudence, we will bless you from the bottom of our hearts. It is also, I suppose, no secret to you that virtue on your part, in this case, is likely to be its own reward, as you and Josephine [3] are our principle heirs—at least, as things now stand: but I warn you that if when accounts begin to come in, I see ruin and starvation before me, I will put the *débris* of my fortune into an annuity, and when my end comes there will be nothing to dry your tears.

I expect to be in Paris, at 9 Av. de l'Observatoire, until the middle of October: but you had better get into the habit of think-

[1] Robert Sturgis, Santayana's half-brother.

[2] Susana Sturgis de Sastre and Josephine Sturgis, Santayana's half-sisters.

[3] Sister of George Sturgis.

ing that my address is % Brown Shipley & Co. because I move about a good deal, and shall probably be much in England in the future; and in any case the delay is not more than a day, if letters from America come by way of London.

When you have time and feel like it, I should be glad if you would write about yourself and Rosamond [1] and give me some idea of your life and surroundings.

                    Yours affectionately

To Mrs FREDERICK WINSLOW

To *Mrs FREDERICK WINSLOW*

PARIS, AUGUST 23, 1921

Dear Mrs Winslow

What a kind letter this is which I receive from you this morning! I always felt that you and Fred were the best friends I had during those later years in Boston, and there was no house where I was happier or felt more at home, so that all the kind things you say do not surprise me, although they bring a fresh pleasure, and I believe you mean them. It would be a treat to find myself once more in Clarendon Street, and to see the children in the present stage of their existence—because you and Fred I know would be just the same; but it is impossible to combine everything as one would wish, and with the years it becomes harder and harder for me to interrupt the routine into which I have fallen.

Robert, like others of the Sturgis tribe, was a very loyal, affectionate, candid soul; he loved whole-heartedly what he felt was good and what appealed to his feelings. Once won over, he spared no pains or trouble, and lived without stint in the life of others. But his misfortune throughout his life was that his perceptions were not equal to his feelings; he irritated people, and that was the reason why he had comparatively few friends, especially among men. I very well remember him as a boy—how pertinacious he was.

[1] Wife of George Sturgis.

We had pillow-fights—very unequal contests, as he was twelve and I was three: and as he had been forbidden by our mother—who had a very severe sense of justice—to take away any part of my supper without my consent, he used to put out his tongue and say that, *if I liked,* I might give him a bite of my omelette; and he did this so persistently, that I sometimes gave him a little—a very little—to get rid of him. He meant this as a lesson in generosity, to teach me to be unselfish; but I am afraid that I was a poor pupil, and that it was only he that learned to distribute his omelette in generous portions to everybody about him. During the last few years he and I have been on better terms than we had ever been on before. He said, after seeing me in Paris in 1913, that my moral character was much improved; and I too came to appreciate better the value of his strong points, and to rely on his judgement in a way which, I dare say, conciliated him. He was a treasure in the way of taking all earthly cares off my back and that of our sisters, and we have to thank him not only for being relatively well off, but for the sense of being devotedly and untiringly looked after, where we were incompetent. I don't know what will become of us now; but I rely on the momentum he has given to things, to carry them on smoothly until our own end comes. George seems to be a nice clear-headed young man, and has written his aunts and me very nice frank letters about his father's illness and death, his own marriage, and our future arrangements.

I have been working very hard all summer on the Soliloquies [1]—which will be my next book—and which are now finished. This leaves the field comparatively clear for the *magnum opus;* [2] but as I can never reduce myself to one project, I have taken up again an old one, which is to write a novel. It is to be entitled The Last Puritan, and to contain all I know about America, about women, and about young men. As this last is rather my strong point, I have *two* heroes, the Puritan and another not too much the other way. To make up, I have no heroine, but a worldly grandmother, a mother—the quintessence of all New England virtues—and various fashionable, High Church, emancipated, European, and sentimental young ladies. I have also a German governess—in love with the hero—of whom I am very proud. I did a good deal on this novel

[1] *Soliloquies in England.*

[2] *Realms of Being.*

last winter in Toledo,[1] where I was absolutely alone for two months: but I reserve it for slack seasons, and am not at all sure it will ever be finished, much less published . . . One of my friends —a widow—tells me she is sure I shall fail in the love scenes. I shan't, because there won't be any . . .

Yours sincerely

To SUSANA STURGIS DE SASTRE

HOTEL MARINI,
ROMA
NOV. 16, 1921.

Dear Susie,

Rome yesterday reverted to its usual aspect, with cabs, trams, and I believe most of the scheduled trains; at any rate I was able to move from my first hotel, which was in the modern and foreign part of Rome, to this old one in the centre, which I think I shall like better, although it is not of the first class. The patriotic *fascisti* who were marching with flags about the town have also disappeared, and if the sun would only shine and it would stop threatening to rain (it has actually been raining a great deal for the last fortnight) I should be quite happy.

I write to you at once, now that I am settled and that things have returned to the normal, as I don't know what you may have heard about the disturbances here. All I saw of them was absolutely innocent, and the streets without carriages and without newspapers were rather improved, and looked more as they must have looked in the good old times. Yesterday, when the first newspapers appeared, it was amusing to see everyone lost in the absolute intensity of his reading, though there was little in them after all: but masculine man has become a paper-reading animal, and hungers for that thin nutriment when he is deprived of it by any chance.

[1] Spain.

I haven't been able to make out what the strikes were about, or how they have been settled; I shall have to wait for the foreign papers to throw some light on the essential facts. The Italian sheets are filled with the exploits of the *fascisti*, which as far as I know had nothing to do with strikes, but were a demonstration à propos of the patriotic ceremony of burying the "Unknown Soldier".

I was glad to get away from Fiesole which, as I believe I said in my former letter, is not to my taste, as Strong has been caught in the life of the Anglo-American colony, and no longer lives with his old simplicity. He will probably join me here later when he himself gets tired of living like a rich man.

I want to send a Xmas present to Pepe's boys: should I send Pepe money, or send it to you, and in what form, and must I send something for Rafael's little girls also? [1]

Love to all from

To LOGAN PEARSALL SMITH

ROME, DEC. 2. 1921

Dear Smith

In Florence they told me that you were in America having an operation, and I am glad to hear, in spite of the delicate or indelicate character of it, you are on the way to a complete recovery. I hardly expect to be in Florence again this winter, having settled down in the sort of . . . town hotel which I like—The Marini— to solitude in a crowd, and steady work.

This taste of mine for living in the midst of a noisy, vulgar rush of people, most of them ugly, with whom I have nothing to do, will perhaps hint to you why I am not altogether in sympathy with your judgement on America. Not that I disagree with your characterization of it; they say it has changed even in these last ten years, but not essentially. I could perfectly recognize, though the genteel tradition may then have been stronger, that America had

---

1 Pepe and Rafael were Susana's step-children.

"no interest for the life of the mind" was "without a head", and "alien". But why do you call this condition "lying fallow" and "deterioration"? Isn't the judgement of the American people rather the opposite, namely that its condition is constantly improving, and its labours splendidly fruitful? Not for the "mind", which in our lips means, I suppose, the liberal or aristocratic life, the mind turned to pure reflection and pure expression and pure pleasure. But why need all the tribes of men sacrifice at our altar? I agree that it is barbarous and tragic to strain after merely conventional ends, by attaining which nobody is the happier, but everyone is sacrificed to some fetish. But isn't America happy? The old genteel America was not happy; it was eager to know the truth, and to be "cultured" and to love "art", and to miss nothing that made other nations interesting or distinguished; and it was terribly and constitutionally unhappy, because with its handicap and its meagreness of soul and its thinness of temper and its paucity of talent, it *could* not attain, nor even approach, any of those ideals. But is the new America unhappy? Does it feel that it is living in a desert, and thirsting for the gardens and the treasure-houses of the Arabian Nights? I think not: it wants simply the sort of life it has, only more of it. It wants comfort and speed and good cheer; it wants health and spirits, and a round of weddings, foot-ball games, campaigns, outings, and cheerful funerals; and it is getting them. In the midst of this, as a sort of joke (and you may make a business of joking) there is a patter of sophomoric art and lady-like religion—never mind what, if only it is new and funny. Why not? When I was at Harvard, from my Freshman days on, I "belonged" to the Lampoon: and that seems to me a sort of symbol or oracle: I belonged to the Lampoon just as much in the philosophical faculty, as I did in the Lampoon "sanctum". It was all a pleasant hard-working exuberance *by the way;* there was not, and could not be anything serious or substantial in it. But notice: *all* learning and all "mind" in America is not of this ineffectual Sopohomoric sort. There is your doctor at Baltimore who is a great expert, and *really knows how to do things:* and you will find that, in the service of material life, all the arts and sciences are prosperous in America. But it must be in the service of material life; because it is material life (of course with the hygiene, morality, and international good order that can minister to material life) that America has and wants to have and may perhaps bring to perfection. Think of that! If material life could be made perfect, as (in a very small way) it was perhaps for a moment among the Greeks, would not that of itself be a most admirable achievement, like the creation of a new and superior mammal, who would instinctively suck only the bottle? Imagine a race perfectly adapted to elevated railroads and aeroplanes and submarines, with a regular percentage of a neutral sex to serve as "school-marms", and not the least dissatisfaction with the extremes of the weather, the pains of childbirth or toothache (all pains being eliminated) or English as she is spoke by three hundred million Americans! I submit that such a race would be as well worth having and as precious in its own eyes (and any other criterion is irrelevant) as ever were the Chinese or the Egyptians or the Jews. And possibly on that basis of perfected material life, a new art and philosophy would grow unawares, not similar to what we call by those names, but having the same relation to the life beneath which art and philosophy amongst us ought to have had, but never have had actually. You see I am content to let the past bury its dead. It does not seem to me that we can impose on America the task of imitating Europe. The more different it can come to be, the better; and we must let it take its own course, going a long way round, perhaps, before it can shake off the last trammels of alien tradition, and learn to express itself simply, not apologetically, after its own heart. Of course, I don't mean that I feel confident that America will ever produce a true civilisation of a new sort; it may all come to nothing, as almost all experiments in nature do; but while the experiment is going on it seems only fair to give it a chance, and to watch it sympathetically.

I have sent to London for *Vera*,[1] but with the strike of railwaymen which is threatened, I don't know when I may get it. The proofs of the Soliloquies [2] have not yet begun to arrive—everything is slowly adapting itself to the *minimum of labour per man,* which is the ideal of the labour parties. Being lazy myself, I rather sympathise with our new masters, the proletariat, but I am sometimes afraid that they will be beguiled, will not really accept the simpler life which their ideal would impose on them, as well as on the rest of us, and will simply succumb to their old masters, or to new ones no less ungentle, after having made all this row for nothing— The

[1] A novel by the author of *Elizabeth and Her German Garden.*

[2] *Soliloquies in England.*

longest of my Soliloquies, one on Dickens, by the way, has some phrases in it very like those of your letter. You will find it in the November number of the Dial, if you ever see that production. It is frankly sophomoric, and that is why I have enjoyed contributing to it, as I did to the Harvard Lampoon.

Yours sincerely

To GEORGE LAWTON

ROME, MARCH 29, 1922.

Dear Mr. Lawton,

It is always pleasant to be urged to do something on the ground that one can do it well; and I have some sympathy with your cry: No more metaphysics.[1] I am nevertheless at work on a book of philosophy (which I do not like to call metaphysics); it will take a year or two; after that I promise you to renounce the subject—except as an ingredient in pleasanter things. The "Three Proofs of Realism" is only a short paper, and has already appeared. But now I come to the part of your advice which I don't mean to follow at all. Criticism is something purely incidental—talk about talk—and to my mind has no serious value except perhaps as an expression of *philosophy* in the critic. When I have been led to write criticism it has never been for any other reason; and you don't know me at all if you suppose me capable of *reading up* Meredith or Thomas Hardy or any one else who hasn't come in my way, in order to describe them to other people. If you like that sort of vicarious literary nourishment, read Croce, or any other competent person who sets out to express the impression which literature has made upon him. But I should advise you to read the originals instead, and be satisfied with the impression they make

[1] When a student of philosophy at Columbia, Dr. Lawton had written to Santayana and urged him to give up metaphysics and devote all his time to literary criticism. We are all indebted to Dr. Lawton for his youthful enthusiasm, as it was the occasion of this remarkable letter.

upon you. You know Plato's contempt for the image of an image; but as a man's view of things is an image in the first place, and his work is an image of that, and the critic's feelings are an image of that work, and his writings an image of his feelings, and your idea of what the critic means only an image of his writings,—please consider that you are steeping your poor original tea-leaves in their fifth wash of hot water, and are drinking slops. May not the remarkable sloppiness and feebleness of the cultivated American mind be due to this habit of drinking life in its fifth dilution only? What you need is not more criticism of current authors, but more *philosophy:* more courage and sincerity in facing nature directly, and in criticising books or institutions only with a view to choosing among them whatever is most harmonious with the life you want to lead. For as Dryden (or is it Pope?) says, "If you think the world worth winning, think, oh think it worth enjoying." I accordingly intend to devote such years as may remain to me exclusively to philosophy; although I hope the form in which it will be expressed will not lead you to call it metaphysics.

Yours very truly,

To GEORGE STURGIS

9 AVENUE DE L'OBSERVATOIRE
PARIS, APRIL 25, 1922

Dear George

I have just returned to Paris from Italy, and am looking over my arrears of letters in order to start the season with a clear conscience. I am afraid I haven't yet answered your interesting letter of February 20th in which you gave me an account of the various investments of which I am the happy but semi-conscious possessor. It all sounds very safe, prosperous, and up-to-date, and if I ventured to make any comments, they would be hopelessly trivial and unbusiness-like, and hardly worthy of an old editor of the Harvard

Lampoon, since I can think of nothing but double meanings for American vitrified products preferred, and the furnishing of light heat and power to such important parts of the world as Saint Louis, Mo. not to speak of medicine for England Scotland and Wales. I am only sorry that I am not supplying a little medicine to Ireland also. I vaguely remember trying to furnish a little light to little groups of obscure minds in some dark corner of Sever Hall: [1] but it never entered my thoughts to supply all Boston with heat and power as well. This only shows how we do our best actions without knowing it, and how we may be laying up pleasant surprises for ourselves against the Day of Judgement.

I am glad to hear that you are to build yourselves a house and home. You may not know that I only just missed being an architect and have always taken a great interest in houses—in the planning no less than in the architectural effect—and I should be glad if you would send me some sketch—if you have one not too large—of what you are to build, or some photo of it when done . . .

I expect to remain in Paris all summer—at least.

Yours affectionately

To MRS. FREDERICK WINSLOW

NICE, NOVEMBER 16, 1922

Dear Mrs Winslow

Two letters, two sets of Sargent decorations,[2] and I don't know how many months are being put down by the Recording Angel to my debit: but I console myself with the thought that you have had a thick volume of Soliloquies to overhear whenever you chose, and that I have been writing so much else—"Scepticism and Animal Faith: Introduction to a System of Philosophy" is in the press—that I may fairly be excused for neglecting to put pen to paper out

[1] In the Harvard Yard.

[2] Reproductions of the murals in the Boston Public Library.

of school hours. However, reform is better than repentance, and I will give you some account of myself—although as you know nothing ever happens in my little world.

I spent the summer very pleasantly in Paris, working on the above-mentioned volume. I wasn't at Strong's, because his daughter Margaret was about, and his apartment is too small for three, a maid, a dog, and ten thousand hat-boxes. I found a quiet cool hotel near the Palais Royal, and lived there in a top room like a true philosopher, dining every evening with the Strongs. They are my most constant link with human affairs. Strong himself, in spite of his lameness, has developed a new geniality (in every sense of this word), composes fables, reads the Latin classics, travels by motor, builds baroque staircases in his garden at Fiesole, and altogether plays the part of the opulent man of letters of the eighteenth century. It is a great satisfaction to me to see him so happy, in spite of his physical infirmity, and to find him blooming intellectually in his old age after having been all his life rather cramped in expression and rigidly professorial in his interests. I think the Anglo-American colony in Florence has had a great effect on him, and *thawed* him thoroughly. Perhaps he has also caught from me the idea that a serious philosopher may be playful on occasion. He has just been to Rome in his motor with his architect, who is an invaluable friend and factotum, and I expect he will turn up here later in the winter. I have not wanted to go to Italy nor to Spain this year, because I want to finish the big book—and turn to the novel! When that comes on the *tapis,* if I am as well as I am now, I shall go the rounds again to Avila, Seville, Rome, Fiesole, Venice, etc. because those scenes will not distract me from the *fun* which I shall be having. Composing a system of philosophy is not such an easy matter, and when once the thread of interest and the momentum of the argument are lost it is sometimes weeks before the engine can be made to run again properly. Therefore I need absolute solitude, such as I have here—that is, solitude in casinos, cafés, restaurants, theatres, and rambles in the midst of swarms of idlers, villas, motors, and palm-trees. But to return to the Strongs: there is the question of Margaret. Everybody (including herself) wants her to get married, and she has plenty of suitors and of money; but somehow she doesn't make up her mind. This prolonged coyness on her part has a curious effect on the lives of two elderly philosophers, her father and myself, because it keeps us both waiting with one foot in the air, until (she having established herself) we may know

where to set it down. I for my part would like to settle down somewhere for the rest of my days; but I don't like to go to England, for
instance, and leave Strong altogether; and yet I can't live with him
while she is about, because then I feel I am staying in a rich man's
house, and not sharing rooms with a fellow-student—which is the
sort of existence that Strong and I affect when we are alone.

This summer I had several visits from strange quarters. The
Rev. Dr. Zampa came to spend a few days with me on his way from
Michigan, where he has been lecturing on Biblical exegesis (in
Latin, if you please) at a Polish Catholic seminary, back to his native Umbria, to the castle of La Petroia in Gubbio, which is his
ancestral seat, and which I am invited to visit some day. He is furious with prohibition and doesn't find the American Catholic clergy
very spiritual: he says they are like the Apostles—before the coming of the Holy Ghost. I also had a visit from young Warwick Potter and his bride, who was Harriet Amory; I enjoyed their company very much, and thought them both delightfully simple and
unaffected. But it seemed to me they were a little more *plebeian*
than the older generation. Is this usually the case?

Now as to the Sargent compositions, of course it is not fair to
judge of them without their colour and in imperfect reproductions; but they seem to me very vulgar. What I wanted to discover
was how he had finally treated the long walls of the staircase hall
in the Public Library; because he told me himself,[1] many years
ago, that one long wall was to exhibit the Sermon on the Mount
and the other the Reformation. I was really more interested in the
idea of the composition, than in the composition itself; the two
semi-circles being very imaginative and learned in a historical way.
As a painter Sargent belongs to the spiritual world of Zola; he has
the nineteenth century curiosity for things historical, decorative,
and exotic: but he has no leaven of his own to make the dough rise.

My nephew George Sturgis—with whom I correspond affectionately on business and other matters—tells me that Polly Winslow is "great", and that young Fred [2] is a nice boy "but quiet", because he wears glasses. You see George knows I take an interest in
them; but his descriptions are imperfect and do not set the reality
before me in a satisfying way. But he seems to be a wide-awake
young man and an optimist like his father. I had an amusing dream

[1] See *My Host the World.*

[2] The children of Mrs. Frederick Winslow.

about him; he had written a letter, and it began by announcing
that one of my investments might not yield the usual interest next
year: then it went on, step by step, to make matters worse (and I
was astonished afterwards that in my dreams I showed so much
more business knowledge than I have when awake) by the most
ingenious gradual transformations; until at the end he said he had
75 cents left in all; but that it would be all right, because he had
put them into the Louisiana lottery, and was sure of the first prize.
Then I awoke. I haven't told him of this dream, because it might
suggest doubts of his stewardship which I don't feel in reality, at
least not consciously. Love, best thanks, and best wishes from

To GEORGE STURGIS

NEW YORK HOTEL, NICE
JAN. 18, '23

Dear George

. . . Yesterday your letter arrived with my yearly account, for
which I am much obliged. It is much more than satisfactory; it is
invraisemblable, and hard to believe quite real. I can only repeat
what I understand made you laugh in one of my previous letters
about the miraculous fountain of dollars. By the way, I am afraid
that my way of expressing myself is too poetical for business. My
father used to say that every old man had his own rhetoric: and
that is probably my case; and you must study Santayanese as a special language, particularly if you want to read the Soliloquies.[1]
For instance, when I said you were the presiding genius over that
miraculous fountain of dollars I didn't mean by genius any extraordinary intelligence—although I have no reason to deny that you
may not be a genius even in that sense. What I meant was that you
were the presiding sprite, fay, goblin, or demon over the said fountain: in other words, I was talking mythology, which happens to
me rather often. So on another occasion when I said you were an
optimist, I didn't mean that you took too rosy a view of matters of

---

[1] *Soliloquies in England.*

fact, but that you were full of the zest of life and confident about the value and the success of what you undertook—a sentiment which is healthy and natural in any energetic person, and characteristic (for obvious good reasons) of America. And certainly so far, in your capacity of attorney, you seem to justify any amount of optimism. Your aunt Josephine will be snowed under by her millions, and I expect will ask you anxiously not to send her any more.

Thank you too for the new photo of Bobby.[1] In amount of hair and in the form of his equatorial regions he rather resembles *me:* extremes meet, but there is a difference between the baldness and rotundity of youth and those of age. To quote my father again, there is a Spanish proverb which says: "Man has two childhoods, one means life and the other death, but in both he has a jolly time". At this moment, however, I am hardly having a "jolly" time, because I am leading an extraordinarily quiet life, coming home in the afternoon, after a little walk in the sun, and having supper served on a tray in my own room, so as to avoid the evening air which becomes suddenly very cold and penetrating and dangerous to my chronic bronchitis. But I am well entertained nevertheless, at present reading the proof and preparing the index to my new book, "Scepticism".[2] I have also written, at odd moments, several chapters of the novel, which I think now will really come off, although not yet for some years . . .

Yours affectionately

To MRS. FREDERICK WINSLOW

NICE, MARCH 19, 1923

Dear Mrs Winslow

You have been very good in satisfying my curiosity about Sargent's paintings,[3] and also in throwing the incredible Island and campanile of Venice in the River Charles. As to Sargent, I feel that

---

[1] The baby son of George Sturgis.

[2] *Scepticism and Animal Faith.*

[3] See *Letter* (Nov. 16, 1922).

he belongs to the past generation, and (being the youngest of men myself) I think him an anachronism. This material fulness and realism, and these descriptive literary intentions, are foreign to "modern art". We are now spiritual, simple, eccentric, combining Il Greco with the Russian ballet. I was especially glad to see the design of Sargent's "Our Lady of Sorrows",[1] because this was what we had talked about in that voyage in which we happened to be in the same ship. But the twenty-five years or more that have intervened, in which he has painted little but fashionable ladies, and perhaps has not gone back to look at the old Spanish images, have had a strange effect on his conception. The face is (at least in this photograph) quite empty and doll-like, and the hand seems to be pressing a bouquet flirtatiously, and not a broken heart. The faces of the good old Spanish images are very beautiful, and tragic, a combination of the grand lady and the saint. And how characteristic of him to put in the tall candles into the picture! A mere extraneous feature, but one that strikes the tourist in the Holy Week processions at Seville. . . .

I have been reading a new book of Freud's and other things by his disciples. They are settling down to a steadier pace, and reducing their paradoxes to very much what everybody has always known. Einstein I do not attempt to read: I am willing to have a maximum of "relativity", but I wonder if they have ever considered that if "relative" systems have no connexion, and no common object, each is *absolute:* and if they have a common object, or form a connected group of perspectives, then they are only relative views, like optical illusions, and the universe is not ambiguous in its true form.

When I was ill with the grippe, the doctor, I think, gave me some "dope" or other: anyhow my imagination was very active and I scribbled in pencil four chapters of my novel, including the end; but I have not dared to reread them, for fear they may be pure nonsense. There *is* a love scene, but the hero is only 17 and the heroine 10. However, I thought it a lovely love-scene in spite of what my friend the widow prognosticated—that my novel would be interesting but the love-scenes failures. People never believe in volcanoes until the lava actually overtakes them.

Yours sincerely

[1] In the Boston Public Library.

To JOHN FRANCIS STANLEY, 2nd EARL RUSSELL

PARIS, SEPT. 5. 1923

Dear Russell,

After four years' absence I am returning to England in a fortnight, to remain at least until October 24, when I am to give the Spencerian lecture [1] at Oxford. I hope there may be a chance of seeing you in the interval.

Yours ever

To JOHN FRANCIS STANLEY, 2nd EARL RUSSELL

BROWN SHIPLEY & CO.,
123, PALL MALL, S.W.1.
[LONDON]

Dear Russell,

If you leave it to me, I will certainly come. I don't believe that anything has really happened to alter our relations to one another which were always tacit and expressed in conduct rather than words. You now say more than you ever *said* to me, even in our young days, about being "attached to me"; you *must* have been, in some way which in spite of my cold-blooded psychology I don't pretend to understand. In that case, why drop me now, when certainly there has been no change on my side except that involved in passing from twenty to sixty? Let me come, anyhow once, and we can judge better whether everything is as usual or whether the barrier you speak of—which certainly is not "Elizabeth" [2] or her affairs—really exists.

Shall it be next Tuesday, and if so, what train shall I take?

Yours ever,

[1] "The Unknowable"; the Herbert Spencer lecture.
[2] The Countess Russell.

To ROBERT BRIDGES

DOVER,
OCT. 31, 1923

Dear Bridges,

Your delightful "experiment" [1] reached me this morning, just when I was lamenting leaving England without having been to see you. I left Oxford immediately after my lecture, hoping to return for a longer stay; but meantime the bronchitis that is always knocking at the door forced its way in, and I am fleeing to Italy, in hopes of not having such a winter as the last was, when my health hardly allowed me to do anything worth mentioning—

"Polly" is so interesting in himself, that your metrical devices are lost, so to speak, in the general pleasure and interest which one feels in reading. I suppose this is the greatest triumph of composition: but it leaves one in doubt whether it is the art of versification or the simple vision of Polly that produces the effect. Many of your lines, however, convince me that the Alexandrine without rhymes, might be a good substitute or variant for the blank verse of English tradition.

My glimpse of England after four years has left me with mixed feelings. I fear my English days are over. Nothing I could now see or feel would be likely to equal the memories I have of other days, which, if not the beaux jours of England, were at least my beaux jours and which it is almost a pity to overlay with sadder impressions. Oxford is very much itself in spite of obvious crowding, and the flocks of women on bicycles which come round the corners of New College Lane. *Sunt lacrymae rerum* but so mixed with pleasure that all regrets become impertinent.

Yours sincerely,

[1] "The 'experiment' is a poem of R. B., called 'Polly' of which a few copies were printed privately in 1923 and distributed by R. B. to his friends. It was later reprinted in *New Verse*." [Sir Edward Bridges, son of the poet-laureate].

To ROBERT HILLYER

[I am grateful to Mr. Hillyer for the following note:

"I have always had the deepest admiration for Santayana's sonnet sequence . . . but I remember that in the first edition of the Sonnets one of them began

A wall, a wall around my garden rear
And hedge me in from the disconsolate hills. . . .

In the Scribner edition of 1923, he changed the opening of this sonnet to something quite inferior. I wrote him a respectful remonstrance and received the letter that I here copy for you."]

⌈FIESOLE, FLORENCE ⌉
⌊ NOVEMBER 9, 1923⌋

My dear Mr Hillyer

That anyone should resent a change in one of my sonnets is in itself such exquisite flattery that I can't resist telling you why that change was made. "Garden rear" [1] has a ridiculous familiar sense—and only one—to an English mind, and as my new collection was made for the English edition (Scribner's is only a reprint) it was imperative to avoid such a snag. Certainly the original, if the *double entendre* is not suggested, was better. Nor is this the only case where I have been forced to make unwelcome changes in order to avoid comic effects.

Yours very truly

[1] Santayana changed the opening line to
A wall, a wall to hedge the azure sphere. . . .
thus avoiding an expression that might provoke the contraction of an eyebrow in England.

To HENRY WARD ABBOT

ROME, DEC. 12. 1923

Dear Harry

Someone has sent me a clipping from the Boston Transcript —what an odour of old maid comes from those words!—in which you resuscitate some old memories of ours and incidentally supply your address. There has long been a suppressed impulse in my nervous system—not strong enough to produce any Freudian phenomena—to write to you, and ask what has become of you in these thirty years, and also what has become of our friends Herbert Lyman, Ward Thoron, etc.; for although Boylston Beal has sometimes mentioned them, I see him rarely, and usually when political matters are so absorbing that we have no time for private gossip.

As to me, you know all that can be told and probably can guess the rest. My health is good, and I manage to avoid most of the troubles that most people bring upon one another, by keeping to the life of a wandering student, which has been my ideal from my earliest days. I do nothing that seriously disturbs my digestion or my agreeable isolation; and I read and write when the impulse comes, and not under pressure. Sometimes my literary projects become something of an incubus, and I ask myself whether I shall live to carry them out: but what does it matter? I have already had my say: although I confess that I am still young and enthusiastic enough to feel that what I have *in petto* is far better than anything I have yet done, and that it *must* see the light. You may be surprised to hear that the most lively of these embryos is a novel.[1] I began it long, long ago—in the early '90's—as a story of college life: that part has now receded into a mere incident; not that my heroes have become much older, since on the contrary I have gone back to their childhood and parentage, but that the scene has widened, and the fable—it is all a fable—has become more organic, knit more closely around the central *motif*, which is Puritanism repenting, but unable to reform.

---

[1] *The Last Puritan.*

Haven't you written any novels? It is the only living art, and now it seems possible to print what in earlier days we hardly ventured to whisper.

Your old friend

To HENRY WARD ABBOT

ROME, JAN. 16, 1924

Dear Harry

As another thirty years will put us beyond the possibility of writing letters (in spite of monkey-glands) I am going to answer you at once, while the iron is hot. It is very flattering to be so faithfully read by an old friend—how did you discover the Spencer lecture? [1] I find that old friends and old pupils usually think they know me well enough as it is, and leave my writings alone. But you were always a literary gourmand (or gourmé) [sic] and I see you haven't changed at all in this respect nor in your erotic preoccupations. My hero (in the novel) whose name is Oliver (after Cromwell) Alden (after John Alden of the Mayflower and Longfellow's Poem, his supposed ancestor) is a *natural* Puritan, and it is not his sexual suppressions that make the thread of the story, at least not on the surface, but his general discovery that it is *wrong* not to live naturally, not to tell the truth about important things, as well as about trifles, and not to make hay while the sun shines. But he is very much too fine in texture and feeling to be happy in his world, or to succeed in the things (including love-making) which it expects him to attempt: and so he peters out—which is so terrible a quiet tragedy that I have actually cried over the writing of it! But I mustn't describe my chicken while it is still in the realm of essence only, and I don't know when the book will be

[1] *The Unknowable;* The Herbert Spencer Lecture delivered at Oxford, October 24, 1923.

done. For the moment I am absorbed in the System [1] and, at odd times, in the Dialogues in Limbo, which will begin to appear in the Dial at once, and will probably compose my next book. They are a general criticism of things modern from an ancient (or normal) point of view: and they are *purple*—more so than the Soliloquies, I think, which I regard as my sincerest book so far: because colour with me, as with Latins generally, is more spontaneous than form, although it may not be thought so by northern critics. Besides, in my old age, I have become far more sentimental and even benevolent. I couldn't write now those sublimated love sonnets, nor Lucifer (of which they talk of making a new edition): they were a perfectly sincere *conviction*, but they were not an actual experience; they were an evasion of experience, on the presumption (quite just when you are young and on a high horse) that experience would be a ghastly failure. The lady of the sonnets, far from being the one you absurdly mention, is a myth, a symbol: certainly she stands for Somebody, not always for the same Somebody, and generally for a hint or suggestion drawn from reality rather than for any specific passion; but the enthusiasm is speculative, not erotic: I had been convinced by Plato and the Italian Platonists: I had not been obliged to make the Pilgrim's progress in person. Love has never made me long unhappy, nor sexual impulse uncomfortable: on the contrary in the comparatively manageable form in which they have visited me, they have been *great fun*, because they have given me an interest in people and (by a natural extension of emotion) in things, places, and stories, such as religion, which otherwise would have failed me altogether; because in itself, apart from the golden light of diffused erotic feeling falling upon it, the world I have been condemned to live in most of my life would have been simply deadly. I have never been anything but utterly bored and disgusted with the public world, the world of business, politics, family, and society. It was only the glimmer of sport, humour, friendship, or love falling over it that made it tolerable. In the last ten years, in spite of the war, I have been able to keep out of that insufferable medium, and have consequently been much happier. Here in Rome, for instance, the world is pleasing: it seems always to have cared for things worth having; it is congenitally beautiful, born to enjoy itself humanly,

[1] The *Realms of Being*.

and straightforward in its villainies and its sorrows. I walk about, knowing no one and speaking to nobody, and I feel that everybody understands me; and what is more and greater, that everybody is at work for the sake of the very things I am inwardly at work about, human liberty and pleasantness breaking through the mesh of circumstances and laughing at it. The political atmosphere here is good also: I am in great hopes in respect to the Latin world: the German and Anglosaxon shams have been discredited—representative government, for instance—and people are daring to be themselves. The church too is a good thing—much better than "science", —and a part of the game.

You don't tell me anything about your way of life, or about our old friends. What you say—or hint—about the power of Gompers [1] surprises me. I thought the U.S. was in the hands of the big business men. Or is Gompers on their side? I understand little of what I hear about America nowadays; but the people I see are so full of health, good-will, pleasantness, and money that I can't believe things can be seriously wrong there—I mean, granting the American postulates—work, progress, democracy, and whoop-her-up. Those who rebel against America are doomed to fail even in what America is busy about, and of course in everything else. Everything good in the ultimate sense will long come from Europe only, and from Latin Europe, because the Graeco-Roman tradition is the only life of reason afoot. Remember what Norton [2] used to say so sadly: Primum Graius homo! [3] And last, too in the spirit.

Your old friend

[1] Samuel Gompers, the Labor Leader.

[2] Professor Charles Eliot Norton of Harvard.

[3] *Primum Graius homo mortaleis tollere contra*
Est oculos ausus primusque obsistere contra.
Lucretius. 1.67
A Greek was he who first raised mortal eyes
And lodged his daring challenge to the skies.
King.

To GEORGE STURGIS

HOTEL BRISTOL, ROME
JAN. 16. 1924

Dear George

. . . My late friend Moncure Robinson (who hob-nobbed only with Vanderbilts, Morgans and dukes) used to say I was the richest person he knew, because I didn't spend half my income; but it would be truer to say that I am "beyond riches and poverty", because I eat, drink, spend, and keep no accounts, and yet nothing happens. Or rather, the unexpected happens in receiving in one year (apart from Constable's [1] cheques) $760 from Scribner for my literary productions! By the way, in view of this sum (which will be reduced very much next year, I expect) I have written to Scribner to send me my royalties direct in future: because my account at Brown Shipley's [2] is getting near to the point (£1000) at which they begin to give interest, and it seems foolish to leave all that money there without getting any return. I might draw most of it out, but I prefer to add to it, and have that little nest egg hatched, even if the brood is rather measly, because at any moment I may want to set up a little establishment of my own, and a lump sum at hand would be convenient. My way of living half with Strong and half alone in hotels, has great advantages in that freedom from care and from possessions which I value so highly: but there is instability in it, especially so long as Margaret Strong continues to hover over us, an unmarried angel; and as I have now passed my sixtieth birthday, I shouldn't mind a fixed abode. But the trouble is all in the inclination of the earth's axis, which makes it impossible to live anywhere all the year round. It might be possible in England, if a catarrhal old man could live in England at all; but almost anywhere else, either in summer or winter, one is practically obliged to decamp: and then what is the use of settling at all? However, I foresee that if a furnace is put into the apartment

1 The English publishing-house.
2 The London banking-house.

at 9, Avenue de l'Observatoire, as there is talk of doing, I might stay there at any and every season, when I chose.

I have received an invitation (declined with thanks) from Prof. Palmer [1] to read a poem at the Phi Beta Kappa at the next Harvard Commencement, the said poem to be about Beauty, and to occupy not less than ten and not more than fifteen minutes in the reading: for which I should receive $50, travelling expenses, and the honour of appearing on the same platform with the President of Yale, the Orator of the occasion. This is what comes of being really a great man. . .

Yours aff^{ly}

To BENJAMIN A. MORTON

ROME, MARCH 14, 1924

Dear Mr. Morton:

It was very kind of you to send me *The Veiled Empress* and I have read not only the last three pages, but the whole book, and gazed long at the illustrations, especially the Cross Street and L'Impératrice. My father and mother—though before my birth— lived for many years in the Tropics, and the quality of that life has a fascination for me, almost as if I had tasted it in person. The rest of your narrative is not too romantic to be credible, and as to your theory of history—which is what you wish me to speak of—I think it is certainly right on its negative side, but its positive side is hardly made explicit enough to be accepted or rejected absolutely. By the negative side I mean your disbelief in grand impersonal principles governing events: that is a pure superstition proper to a certain moralistic philosophy of history, essentially Jewish and adopted by the Hegelians. It is not to be found in the great ancient historians who, like Homer and Shakespeare, see in public affairs only the play of private passions. Saint-Simon is another observer who testifies to the same fact—indeed, it is the

[1] George Herbert Palmer.

natural and orthodox view; so that I hardly think you should call it "new", although no doubt you may have rediscovered it. At the same time I should suggest this doubt or rather this complication; the circumstances under which individuals act, as well as all their religious or national prejudices, belong to their backgrounds; so that both in its sources and in its effects their private passion may not be merely theirs, but that of their age or class; and in this way something typical or generic may be found in the parts played by leading men. Herodotus sees history as a duel between Europe and Asia, and we may see the same continued in our day, as between personal and national individuality on the one hand and the great average on the other. But I think these are only optical effects or total perspectives, not causes. Now the ambiguity which I still find in your view relates to the causes of personal decisions, on which we agree that public events are dependent. Are these decisions merely personal and metaphysically "free", or could we, with sufficient information, trace them back to inevitable instincts, *plus* circumstances? Your Aimee, for instance, is represented by you as caring for Martinique, Josephine, France, and Christianity; so that her personal initiative has ultra-personal sources, and she is a sort of meeting place of influences rather than an absolute arbitrary creator of her own will. That the human brain and heart are the central office, so to speak, where all messages are received and re-sent, and that without such delicate personal, often inexplicable redirection of forces there would be no human life, morality, or history, I think is certain; but I am afraid we should get into hopeless difficulties if we tried to stop at the *conscious* origins of our actions and feelings. Consciousness is a very superficial thing.

I have wondered a little how seriously you take the suggestion that Napoleon's divorce sounded the knell of his fortunes. It also seemed to me probable that Mahmoud, in making peace with the Russians so unaccountably, was following the British policy of a balance of power; because it would have been useless to get his provinces back if he had had a French High Commissioner—or Napoleon himself—in his own capital. I can hardly imagine a Sultan seriously shocked, like a good American husband, at the wickedness of divorcing a childless wife.

Yours very truly,

To C. J. DUCASSE

Dear Mr. Ducasse:

It is no ordinary note of thanks that I owe you for your book on "Causation",[1] because at an age when one has abandoned the hope of learning anything new, you have really taught me something which I hope to keep by me and to incorporate into my philosophy—namely, that causation is not a law but an observable derivation of fact from fact in particular instances. In one sense, like Columbus' egg, this is not new to me; and you say Mercier and Joseph have pointed it out; but though I have seen both gentlemen (and they are very different) I have not studied their writings, and it is not probable that I ever shall. In fact, something of the sort is said or hinted, by the way, in my "Scepticism and Animal Faith"; but I can't give you a reference, as I have no books here. If I remember, I say there that when not an arbitrary assignment of magic influence, cause is "the principle of generation in nature"; but this phrase (if it *is* this phrase) is loose and ambiguous. I meant, however, that the birth of thing from thing is causation— which is what you, in your clearer and more explicit language, now confirm me in believing.

Heartily as I agree with your main thesis, I had a feeling that perhaps you were not in dramatic sympathy with Hume and Mill in their analysis, and avoided the issue that was uppermost in their minds. Even at the end, when you enumerate the senses in which one may ask "why" effect follows on cause, you do not mention what I suspect was their problem, namely, what *internal relevance* there was between cause and effect, to be the *reason* for their sequence. People expect to have an insight into this connection, such as they have in action, or in an answer to prayer, or obedience to an order given, or the execution of a plan. In such cases an image of the consequent is a part of the antecedent, and seems to announce and usher it in; in deduction also the consequence follows because it is contained in the premises. On this ground too identity

1 *Causation and the Types of Necessity.*

of substance binds the material and the product in nature more closely together than if they were unsubstantial disjointed perceptions. The change of forms remains unexplained, which you rightly say is all that requires a cause; yet the continuity of substance, which needs *no* explanations, partly reconciles the observer to that change (which it also keeps within limits) and so gives him a feeling that causation is intelligible, or ought to be so, beneath its actual working. People, in a word, desiderate a dialectical or moral unity in natural sequences, and it was the absence of this desideration that Hume and Mill pointed out.

There is a point at the end, in respect to the nature of philosophy, which I am not sure I understand. Is it a mere valuation on the part of the idealist that makes it "true" that the model of nature is within his mind, not his mind an item in the world of nature? Can the opposite valuation on the part of the materialist render the opposite equally "true"? And is the "liberalistic" view that both are true, or that neither is? And if the latter, what is the "true" liberalistic relation of mind to matter? I am puzzled by the (very prevalent) habit of calling truth a value. There may be a value in discovering the truth, or some part of it; but what I understand by the truth (and I think I am following your maxim in this and sticking to current usage) is something waiting to be recognised and perhaps valued, but not ambiguous or variable with human interest in it.

Yours sincerely,

To C. J. DUCASSE

CORTINA, JUNE 28, 1924

Dear Mr. Ducasse:

I have not yet thanked you for your article in defense of "Ontological Liberalism", with which I entirely agree (save perhaps at one point about which a word presently) and which interests me particularly now that I am at work on "Realms of Being." Your analysis of the problem, exhibition of the verbal character of it, and of the eulogistic meaning of "reality", seem to me all admirably true and clear. But now as to the point of possible divergence.

If "real" is a eulogistic term relative to private interests, it should be left (shouldn't it?) to the tender mercies of poets and newspapers, and when *we* use it in our speculations it should be in our concomitant capacity of human babblers, without giving it any importance, except rhetorically.

As you probably know, or will when you read my first chapter of "Realms of Being" in the "Journal," [1] I am in the habit of using the word "existence" instead of "reality" (because the "non-existent" is not indifferent to me) for a *presumptive* sphere, defined by me as that in which beings have external and variable relations, or in other words, as contingent and in flux. Being defined in this way, the existent is or includes all that is dynamic, and therefore all that interests practical people in their transitive thoughts; and it includes all action, movement, and conduct. It might be called Americanly real. But (as you show) it need not be real for the oyster, the poet, or the mystic. Now, is it or is it not incompatible with "Ontological Liberalism" to confine the word "existence" to this dynamic realm, to nature? Is this contrary to good English usage? And if so, is not some name of the kind to be given to a sphere which, in one sense, forces the recognition of its emphatic reality and arbitrary limits upon everybody, since it conditions the *existence* even of his most rapt contemplation or most passive pleasures?

Yours sincerely,

1 "Some Meanings of the Word 'Is'." (*Journal of Philosophy*, July 3, 1924). This article was later altered considerably before it became the first chapter of *The Realm of Essence*.

To GEORGE STURGIS

CORTINA D'AMPEZZO
JULY 29, 1924

Dear George

Following a suggestion of yours I have begun to write an Autobiography, and almost at the beginning I feel the need of a document which you may possibly have seen among your father's papers. It is a testimonial of friendship and admiration presented to your great grandfather José Borrás by the citizens of Winchester, Virginia, in 1832 or thereabouts.[1] If I remember it was rather yellow and torn, and you had better not send it to me; but its phraseology is quaint and old-fashioned, and if you have it at hand and could have it copied, I should be much obliged. This residence of José Borrás in Virginia was the source of my whole connection with America, the English language, and the Sturgis family: because the reason my mother married your grandfather George Sturgis [2] of Manila was that she spoke English and had sympathetic feelings towards America, where she lived in her early childhood: and the rest all follows from that marriage.

I am staying on here, surrounded by rugged Alps, because I find I am comfortable and can work easily. The first part [3] (there are to be four in all) of my "big book" is finished, and I believe the rest will be easier to put in shape. It rains a great deal and though the sun is hot at midday (when it shines) cool if not cold weather soon comes on, and the nights are always fresh. It is a most beautiful valley, and in my walks I sometimes feel a wonderful elation, as if I were a real poet and lover of nature, which I have always believed I was not.

Yours aff^{tly}

---

[1] See *Persons and Places,* Vol. I, Chap. I, "Time, Place and Ancestry."

[2] After whose death she married Santayana's father—Agustín Ruiz de Santayana.

[3] *The Realm of Essence,* being Book I of *Realms of Being.*

To ROBERT BRIDGES

CORTINA D'AMPEZZO
AUGUST 15, 1924

My dear Bridges,

Your boldness in going to America at all rather astonished me, but once having taken the plunge I can well imagine that you found it tolerable, and even appealing to that vague tenderness for mankind which I suppose is in all our hearts. Often, in these hotels in which I live, I am annoyed at the American parties that loudly take possession of the next table, and deluge me with commonplaces and bad slow jokes, and then, if something obliges me to "make their acquaintance" and, as it were, to become one of their party, I immediately lose all consciousness of their trying tones and sentiments, and am entirely absorbed by a sort of contagious kindness and hearty simplicity which reigns among them. I am glad to know that you and Mrs. Bridges have not only survived the ordeal, but profited by it in health and energy. How nice and quiet Chilswell must seem!

You speak of my "desertion of England." I don't feel that I have deserted: I have got my discharge. There is no place I should rather spend the rest of my life in, if my free inclination were omnipotent: but I should have to make myself younger, less sensitive to chill and damp, less disinclined to travel (because I shouldn't like to give up my other haunts, Avila, Rome, Paris) and able to find a place simple but comfortable enough, in which I could work without interruption. When I was in England last year I was not well and not comfortable. Possibly it was for this reason that I felt that everything was somewhat changed, materially and morally: less peace, less deference, less facility in obtaining services or small comforts. It was very like America. If I lived in England now I fear I should feel that sort of *pressure* which drove me away from America—that same difficulty in escaping and being at peace. The resource of living quite in the country is not open to me, unless I took a house and servants, which of itself would be perdition. Of course, I hope soon to return to Oxford, but in the summer, and when I have no definite work in hand. At present I am deep in "Realms of Being": but even under the most favourable circumstances, it is hard to remain faithful to such a task, and last winter in Rome, for instance, I turned to quite another project, and wrote some "Dialogues in Limbo", which will probably see the light before the other book is finished.

I think I have heard of Mencken, but who is Owen Young? My Americana are very ancient.

You don't know how pleasant it is to hear a good word said of my chapter on Royce.[1] I *did* enjoy writing it, not only "maliciously" but also imaginatively, in trying to call up the complete figure and tragedy of such a man, a patient voluminous straggling mind, with a sort of childish insistence and stubbornness in fundamental matters—puzzled and muddled, and yet good and wise. It is not a complete picture—I hadn't the facts before me and could not have made public use of them in any case: but I think there is enough to sketch the personage in outline, and strike the characteristic note. Of course, his friends and disciples were angry: it was so unlike an obituary notice. One (a pragmatist, I suppose) said that my account would be true in twenty-five years, but was utterly false today.

Here there are so many English people that when I go to tea in "The English Tearooms" I might almost be at the "————". I peeped in there when I was last at Oxford, but found it so disgustingly changed that I immediately went out again. Cortina is a good place for the pedestrian. I don't mean only for the Alpine adventurer, but for the peripatetic philosopher: clouds and frequent rain keep the summer cool—almost too cool; and the noisy Italians in the hotel do not seriously disturb me in my own corner. Besides, I like Italians.

Yours sincerely,

---

[1] *Character and Opinion in the United States*, Chap. **IV**.

To ROBERT BRIDGES

HOTEL BRISTOL
ROME
JAN. 8, 1925

Dear Bridges,

Of course I had nothing to do with the choice of a collective present [1] for your birthday, nor with the idea of such a present, but I was very glad to join the others when I heard of it, for the very reason that it seemed a way of concentrating the "fuss" and sparing you separate and endless congratulations; but I am afraid you had to endure them as well. However, it is all over now and I hope that this somewhat impertinent celebration has not left you too much fatigued or feeling at all older.

Your poem [2] in the *London Mercury* has a magnificent breadth and a *saturation* (especially in the unrhymed parts) which is always a marvel to me in English poetry of the genuine sort. I have tried, in my literal rationalistic way, to unravel the exact meaning of your dream. Is it that the church is the only refuge for spiritual minds? In a very different way—through the more and more frankly confessed mythical character of exact science—I too have been recognising of late that the church is a normal habitation for the mind, as impertinent free thought never is. But there remains the old misunderstanding, the forcing of literature into dogma, and the intolerable intolerance of other symbols, where symbols are all. Here in Rome, in the Pincio and the Villa Borghese, I often watch with amazement the troops of theological students of all nations, so vigorous and modern in their persons, and I ask myself whether these young men can truly understand and accept the antique religion which they profess—especially the Americans (very numerous) with their defiant vulgar airs and horrible aggressive twang. Could the monks of Iona and the Venerable Bede have been like this? Was it perhaps after some ages of

---

[1] "The collective present for R. B's 80th birthday was a clavichord." [Sir Edward Bridges]

[2] "Come si quando" (November 1924).

chastening that the barbarians could really become christian and could produce a Saint Francis?

It is probable that I shall be in England during the coming summer, and I shall not fail to spend at least a few days in Oxford, when I hope to see you. In July and August it may be possible to erase the unpleasant impression which October and November left on me when I was last in England.

Here I lead a very pleasant regular life, seeing only an occasional pilgrim who comes to peep into my cell. I have finished a volume of *Dialogues in Limbo* which are still simmering in my mind, so that I can't judge whether the dish will be at all appetizing when served up cold to the public. Meantime, I have plenty of other projects to occupy me, and Rome, for comfort and for stimulus, is everything that I could desire.

I will send you my new book, but publishers are very slow, and I may appear in person before my missive.

Yours sincerely,

To PIERRE LA ROSE

HOTEL BRISTOL, ROME
MARCH 19, 1925

Dear la Rose,

I have been waiting for a moment of inspiration in order to describe to you my feelings about the new Lucifer,[1] but weeks and weeks are passing, and I must not put off thanking you, even if perfunctorily, for all your devoted labour and art in executing this generous project. It makes a beautiful book, and seems to lift the poem itself into a new category. Nothing remains except that someone should make an opera of it—it would be, duly abridged, a splendid libretto—and that some other wizard should design the stage-settings in the style of Bakst. I have often in secret thought

---

[1] The de luxe and revised edition of Santayana's "theological tragedy."

of it actually on the stage! There is an absence of female parts, but
Turel could be a Soprano, and in the fifth act there are the god-
desses, while of course the angel choir could be feminine too. And
this leads me to speak of details. When you wrote that you had
printed the chorus in blue, I had some misgivings; but on seeing
the pages, with the red caption in the corner, and the long rather
narrow page (to which I am quite reconciled) I was really delighted: Those are the best pages in the book; and I instantly composed a motto:

'Tis *Taste* that prints the
mystic verse in blue,
And robes the Angels in
their azure hue.

As to the misprints you mentioned, "He Drinks", is harmless—
might even be taken for a subtle Catholic protest against Prohibition. . . .

The black binding with its gold ornament pleased me very
much, and also the gorgeous Pompeian lining: it would do very
well for the lining of the black cloak which Lucifer should wear
in the Opera. If this was a concession to the fashion of the hour,
I without being aware of the fashion entirely approve of it. Also
of the title-page; and the monogram repeated here seems to me
the best and boldest of your designs for letters. The others are in
no less perfect taste, as are also the head-pieces, but I think you
err if anything on the side of safety and delicacy: I seem to miss
emphasis, concentration, and variety in the patterns of the blacks
and whites. The red tail-piece at the very end is an exception; here
you have given Mephistopheles the last word in a fashion which
I can only call naughty. Or perhaps you let yourself go because
there you are in the atmosphere of editions, copyrights, and publishers' announcements, and the sacred theme of the book has become irrelevant. As you know, my idea of Lucifer is that (like my
"Poem") it is a book of devotion—thank you, therefore, for the
black and gold—and should properly be a small volume, in fine
clear print, with decorations (if any) themselves favourable to meditation and concentration of spirit. But granting the folio, and the
necessary absence of pictorial decoration—nobody alive could illustrate Lucifer, even in head-pieces or small friezes such as I might
fancy, like those in the small Virgil that Joe Stickney once gave

me—I am wholly satisfied with your *sympathetic* presentation; and in itself, as printing and typographical design, it will no doubt receive on all hands the commendation it deserves. I am not myself a connoisseur in the matter, but all my instincts are flattered, and the book is an unmistakably precious and beautiful object.

"Dialogues in Limbo" are in the press, but I have no notion when they will appear.

Yours sincerely,

P.S. A fourth copy of Lucifer has reached me safely. Many thanks.

To ROBERT BRIDGES

9 AVENUE DE L'OBSERVATOIRE,
PARIS
AUG. 8, 1925

My dear Bridges,

You are such a good friend that you understand one's silence as well as one's words, and I needn't apologize for not writing and thanking you for your previous (engraved) letter and the photograph attached. I am glad my Dialogues do not seem to irritate you or offend your feelings, as I fear they may those of many a reader—if many people read them. They are not, of course, being mine, a work of erudition or even of retrospective fancy, and I am not at all sure that the extant sayings of Democritus and the rest will justify everything that I put in their mouths. I use them only as Platonic types for points of view which are natural to my own mind, braver and more truly ultimate than my accidental personal opinions, such as I assign to The Stranger. And there are two things which I should be much pleased if people found in this book, although I am afraid they won't: one is a *connected* doctrine and theme, the other an assimilation in spirit, though not in language, between Greek and Indian philosophy. I have long thought that the earlier Greeks had virtually the same wisdom as the Indians, and that it was only an accident of race and rhetoric that they seemed physiologers rather than religious mystics. My

Democritus is intended to establish between his "atoms and void" on the one hand and his "normal madness" on the other precisely the same opposition and connection that the Indians established between Brahma and Illusion. I think myself that this is the only right physics or metaphysics: but it is only half of human philosophy. Socrates (who is nothing in physics, or a mere child) is brought into supply the other half, the self-justification of Illusion, because it is the moral essence and fruit of life: and the "Secret of Aristotle" (which I am much pleased that you take to kindly) is the means of harmonising the two points of view, and proving them to be not only consistent but indispensable to one another if the nature of things is to be understood at all. Socrates defends human morality against religion no less than against naturalism (which are not fundamentally enemies) and he is right politically: but both science and religion, in their profound unison, make this political humanism and ant-morality seem rather small and accidental. Both science and religion, not being on the human scale, do violence to the human point of view, which at the same time they show to be excusable and inevitable in a spirit expressing an animal life and generated by it. Is this a hard saying? If not, why are people so slow to understand it?

I have been in Spain and expect to return to Rome for the winter, but my local habitation makes little difference to my way of life. I still hope to return to England, which means Oxford and Chilswell, before very long.

Yours ever,

To MAURICE FIRUSKI

ROME, DEC. 23, 1926

Dear Mr. Firuski

I am glad to hear that Charles Pierce left copious materials yet unpublished, but I am not at all the person to undertake editing any portion of them. Find some young philosopher or mathematician, in whose career such deserving work might be of use and profit. I saw Pierce only once, at a lecture after a dinner at Wm. James's. He had a red nose, a straggling grey beard, and an evening coat that seemed lopsided and thirty years old. As to his life, save that it was retired and, they say, bibulous, I know nothing: but if you can enlighten me, I shall not be incurious. As a philosopher Pierce has come late to be recognized, but his quality is unmistakably good, far better logically than Wm. James's, and anything speculative from his pen would be welcomed, I think, by the learned public.

Where did you get the impression, I wonder, that I am planning a translation of Don Quixote? Many years ago Updike proposed such a thing to me: I tried the first page and found it impossible: moreover the extant translations are excellent.

My novel has been lying fallow, but I hope to devote myself consecutively to it as soon as I have dispatched volume one of my "Big Book"—"The Realms of Being"; and this I hope will be before I leave Rome this winter. Meantime I have composed a little book, now being printed, which may interest you in your spiritual exaltation, since it is precisely about "Platonism and the Spiritual Life". It is very short, but very sublimated: written all at one go last summer at Cortina.

Please give my best wishes to la Rose, and tell him that it would give me real pleasure if he would write to me about anything, or send me anything that he may have published.

Is it true that "Lucifer" is sold out? If so, congratulations.

Yours sincerely,

To *VAN WYCK BROOKS*

ROME, MAY 22 1927

Dear Mr. Brooks

Although I am not sure whether I owe the pleasure of reading your book on "Emerson & Others" to your initiative or that of your publishers,[1] I would rather thank you personally for it, be-

---

[1] Mr. Brooks' publishers, E. P. Dutton & Company, had sent Santayana an advance editorial copy of *Emerson and Others*.

cause I have one or two things which I should like to say, as it were, in private. Your pictures of Emerson are perfect in the way of impressions: not that I knew him (he was dead, I think, when I first reached America, aged 8); but that, whether true to the fact or not, they are convincing in their vividness. But just how much is quoted, and how much is your own? Am I to believe—I who haven't read the Journal and know little of the facts—that Emerson was such a colossal egotist and so pedantic and affected as he seems on your pages 39 and 40? Or have you maliciously put things together so as to let the cat out of the bag? Sham sympathy, sham classicism, sham universality, all got from books and pictures! Loving the people for their robust sinews and Michaelangelesque poses! And for the thrill of hearing them swear! How different a true lover of the people, like Dickens!

You apologize because some of your descriptions applied to the remote America of 1919: I who think of America as I knew it in the 1890's (although I vegetated there for another decade) can only accept what I hear about all these recent developments. On the other hand, when you speak of the older worthies, you seem to me to exaggerate, not so much their importance, as their distinction: wasn't this Melville (I have never read him) the most terrible ranter? What you quote of him doesn't tempt me to repair the holes in my education. The paper I have most enjoyed—enjoyed immensely—is the one on the old Yeats. *His* English is good: *his* mind is quick.

One more little protestation. Why do the American poets and other geniuses die young or peter out, unless they go and hibernate in Europe? What you say about Bourne [1] (whom again I haven't read) and in your last chapter suggests to me that it all comes of *applied culture*. Instead of being interested in what they are and what they do and see, they are interested in what they think they would like to be and see and do: it is a misguided ambition, and moreover, if realised, fatal, because it wears out all their energies in trying to bear fruits which are not of their species. A certain degree of sympathy and assimilation with ultra-modern ways in Europe or even Asia may be possible, because young America is simply modernism undiluted: but what Lewis Mumford calls "the pillage of the past" (of which he thinks I am guilty too) is worse than useless. I therefore think that art, etc. has a better soil in

[1] Randolph [Silliman] Bourne.

the ferocious 100% America than in the Intelligentsia of New
York. It is veneer, rouge, aestheticism, art museums, new theatres,
etc. that make America impotent. The good things are football,
kindness, and jazz bands.

Yours sincerely,

To J. MIDDLETON MURRY

ROME, NOV. 1, 1927

Dear Mr. Murry

. . . A heretic, I should say, had to be a believer: he had to
maintain a principle while denying some of its consequences. I
am a free-thinker or sceptic: and my sympathies in religion are
with the orthodoxies—not with one, but with each in contrast
to its heresies. I am therefore not a heretic: but you are right that
my share in the spiritual life is more vicarious than personal, if
a complete ascetic renunciation is understood to be involved in
it. Such insight as I may have comes from poetic indolence, or
speculative ecstasy. I *can* feel the sweetness of saying no, and the
greater joy of leaving the daisies growing in the field rather than
plucking them to wilt in my buttonhole.—I thought my little
book [1] made my position quite clear: but I have a more formal
treatise, about to appear, called *The Realm of Essence,* in which
I speak more than once of my personal attitude towards the ambition of those who aspire to be pure spirits. I do *not* share it.

Yours sincerely

[1] *Platonism and the Spiritual Life.*

To GEORGE STURGIS

HOTEL BRISTOL ROME
NOV. 27, 1927

Dear George

Apparently, to judge by what you say in your letter of Nov. 15, it is a long time since I have written: I am sorry, and I can't say it has been because I was too busy or because I had nothing to say, which are the grown-up and the childish excuses for such delinquences. In Paris I spent rather an exciting summer, being a party to a sort of run-away match. Don't be alarmed; it isn't I that was married, but Margaret Strong; only in the absence of her father I had to officiate as sponsor, or witness, or giver-away, or whatever you call it. There were two weddings,—a week apart—which was an absurdity in itself: after the first one, at the *mairie,* I gave the party a breakfast: we were only six persons, and it went off very well. At the second wedding, which was in the American Episcopal Church, I had to lead the (married) bride up the aisle, in the conventional fashion. People said: *Voilà le papa!* but I felt like a fool and rather like a fraud. The Chilean *chargé d'affaires* gave a reception for us afterwards, and the bride was much admired with her "golden" eyes and her nun-like tulle veil. I ought to have said that the bridegroom is an . . . but rather fashionable Chilean named Jorge Cuevas . . . Strong in Switzerland was left out in the cold, except for my letters. He finally telegraphed his consent and blessing at the very last moment; and now having seen his son-in-law, he is quite reconciled or rather positively pleased . . . They are at Luxor in Egypt for the winter, so that all here is peace for the present.

I am sorry we can't have another bottle of *Asti Spumante:* I never indulge in it myself when I am alone—I will draw the rest of my letter of credit ($1000) before New Years, and shall be in no hurry for the new one; but send one for $4000, when it is convenient.

Yours aff^tly

To J. MIDDLETON MURRY

HOTEL BRISTOL, ROME
DECEMBER 8, 1927.

Dear Mr. Murry

Thank you for the copy of my article on "Revolutions in Science".[1] There are one or two phrases in it that I should like to correct: I suppose you will send me the proof when the time comes. It might be better to address it to me directly to Rome, Hotel Bristol, where I shall be all winter.

You are easily victorious in your article "Concerning Intelligence" in *The New Criterion:* at least a person who said long ago that religion *is* poetry can't help thinking so. But it seems to me that you aren't just to St. Thomas. Words had a precise meaning in his mind; "faith" excludes "reason" because it is a name for the *supplement,* beyond proof, in which our sensations are bathed:

Praestet fides supplementum
sensuum defectui.[2]

Moreover, the whole world to him was like a children's theatre, that could be delightfully pulled to pieces and put together again, not with a loss of illusion, but with a masterful knowledge of why and how the illusion came about, and was intended. The earthly and the heavenly, the rational and the miraculous made one tapestry: the distinctions were not arid, because they were internal to the work of God, and friendly.

Yours sincerely

[1] Reprinted in *Some Turns of Thought in Modern Philosophy,* Chap. II.
[2] [Let faith provide a supplement for the deficiency of the senses.]

To LOGAN PEARSALL SMITH

HOTEL BRISTOL, ROME
DECEMBER 21, 1927

Dear Smith

My memory is not good for references, and I am without books here; but all your quotations have a familiar sound, and I have no doubt they come from something of mine—from what book or article I can't tell you. I am sorry to be so useless, especially when you are overwhelming me with your constancy to my muse, and paying me the compliment of associating my words with those of such great wits. I shall be curious to see your anthology and it may induce me to read Hazlitt, Halifax, and Selden, who are all unknown to me. But it is hopeless, so late in life, to fill up the lacunae in one's education. I tried the other day to read Moby Dick, but in spite of much skipping, I have got stuck in the middle. Is it such a masterpiece as they say? On the other hand, I am not too old to enjoy some novel authors: and what do you suppose was my joy at finding the theory of essence beautifully expounded in the last volume of Proust, (the second of *Le Temps Retrouvé*) and made, in a manner, the pivot of his immense work! Do read it, page 14 to 20, if you haven't yet done so. My excursions into the other world are not so remote from experience as you seem to think: we live in that world; we only move in this one.—What you say of your neighbour who likes my philosophy makes me think of another disciple of mine who is now in London. He is a young American named Daniel Cory, who is a sort of unattached student, and has understood my books—at least the later ones—better than anyone else that I know of. As he has nothing urgent to do, I have got him to help me in straightening out the MS of the *Realm of Matter,* which is to be my next, and I hope culminating, book. I am going to take the liberty of giving him a card to you, and perhaps you can also introduce him to your neighbour: anything he learns from you or from him in the way of judicious criticism of my works or ideas, will be useful to him and indirectly to me; because he isn't shy, though devoted, and tells me where I go wrong.

Cory is also a disciple of Berty's [1] and is studying under him in London.

Rome is very like London in these dark, cold days: but a sort of Socratic sign, saying No! intercepts all my projects of crossing the channel.

Yours sincerely

To WESLEY FULLER

ROME, DECEMBER 23, 1927

Dear Mr. Fuller

It is hardly possible for me to write anything for the Latin School Register: [2] too much time and space separates me from that world. Yet I don't like to disregard your request, and I am sending you a few lines of translation from Catullus, which I happen to have at hand, as a token of remembrance and good wishes.

Yours truly

A FRAGMENT FROM CATULLUS

O misero frater adempte mihi, etc.

You, brother, snatched, and I bereft,
My whole life crushed, no drop of sweetness left,
My whole soul buried in your grave,
My soul that lived but by the love you gave!
All my life's pleasures, with you dead,

[1] Bertrand Russell.

[2] I am grateful to Mr. Fuller for the following information:
"I was a Second Classman at the Boston Latin School and a member of the staff of the Latin School Register, our school publication. I . . . set about seeking contributions from our most distinguished alumni. Naturally I wrote Mr. Santayana . . . It was in response to this request that I received the reply I am sending on to you . . . Needless to say, it was the highlight of the issue, indeed of the year and, I suspect, of many, many alumni issues. I do not believe it has ever been published elsewhere."

My studies all, my joy in all is fled.
Why speak, why call? I am not heard.
Your sweet voice, brother, answers not a word.
Never till death, never that face again,
Never that smile: yet love shall still remain.

To *JOHN LIVINGSTON LOWES*

ROME, JANUARY 3, 1928

My dear Mr. Lowes

Your letter offering me the Norton Chair of Poetry for next year fills me with pride, and I wish I were free to accept so honourable an appointment. But I am deeply engaged in my *opus magnum* (as I call it), and the second volume [1]—being on a subject, the universe at large, of which Professor Norton would not have approved—is so exacting, that I am afraid it would not be prudent, even if it were possible, for me at this moment to turn my attention in an entirely different direction. Indeed, I hardly know what substance for lectures on poetry I should now find in my own mind: it would require a new birth. Moreover, my retirement has long been so complete, that I should tremble at the physical and social commitments involved in being again a public lecturer, even among old friends and under such exceptionally tempting conditions. I must therefore beg you to present my heartfelt regrets and thanks to the committee and to President Lowell for the great honour which they have done me, and to believe me

Very gratefully yours

[1] *The Realm of Matter; Book Second of Realms of Being,* Scribner's, 1930.

To J. MIDDLETON MURRY

HOTEL BRISTOL, ROME, FEB. 9. 1928

Dear Mr. Murry

I am glad you are writing this article for the *Times* about the coincidence between Proust & me. Of course, being independent, the approaches are not identical. I don't find it necessary to have *two* phenomena, separate in time, in order to "purify" the phenomenon by considering it out of its accidental relations: but the result is the same. I also should observe that an essence has no interest in itself: it is merely innocent, being non-existent: but Proust seems to find it interesting, however trivial the occasion may be which calls it up. Here I feel that he is too inhuman, idiotically aesthetic, and tediously non-moral . . .

Yours sincerely

To GEORGE STURGIS

HOTEL BRISTOL, ROME
MAY 7, 1928

Dear George

I send you the deed of trust and the schedule of securities, which I received this morning. You see I can be expeditious when I see the way clear, and in a jiffy I discovered the American consulate and, I hope, did the thing up brown.

The vagueness of the bequest to Harvard was intentional. It may be hard to find just the right man for the Fellowship even in the wide field of poetry, philosophy, theology, and the Harvard Lampoon: and when you remember that I hope to die a novelist, almost anyone not a chimney-sweep can hope for my legacy.

You are right about the reason for a Spanish child not having the same *last* name, although he has the same *surname*, as his father: the last is his mother's family name. As to the *middle* name, as in the case of Manuela (Ruiz de) Santayana (y) Zabalgoitia, it is not necessary. Ruiz was originally our family name, Santayana being a place; but my father and his brothers got into the habit of using Santayana exclusively, for the sake of brevity. But the addition of the mother's surname, now usually without the "y" prefixed, is legal, and necessary in a document. So you will find that your aunt's will is signed "Susana Sturgis Borrás". The Parkman is optional, and the husband's name is not, in Spain, a wife's name at all. She may be described as the *wife,* or politely, the *lady,* of so-and-so: but her name remains what is was originally. Calling your aunt, as she liked to be called, Susana Sturgis de Sastre, is not strictly correct; she was Doña Susana Sturgis y Borrás, señora de Sastre. The last words are a title or description, not a part of her name, as if you called me G.S., wedded to Metaphysics.

I am pleased with the arrangement by which you provide for the Spanish bequests out of the Trust fund, and I agree that it will be better to keep all my money in America, *où il fait boule de neige,* or grows like a rolling snow-ball; let us hope it will not melt in the same manner. When I go to Avila I will make a Spanish will to cover the remaining trifles and provide for my literary executor. And if I save by not spending all my income, will the savings become part of the trust, or will that be a separate fund?

Yours aff^{tly}

To ROBERT BRIDGES

HOTEL BRISTOL,
ROME
MAY 10, 1928

My dear Bridges,

How can you doubt that I shouldn't read with the greatest eagerness the advanced sheets of your Poem, if you will send them? This, even if you didn't heighten my curiosity and pleasant expectations by saying that I shall find in it a philosophy akin to my own. I see by what you say, and gather from various quarters, "The Realm of Essence" has been more kindly received than I should have expected. The professors persist in thinking me an amateur, and the literary people are not really interested, because the subject eludes them; yet some impression seems to be produced—more than by my "Dialogues in Limbo", which seems to me so much better written a book, with more colour, than "The Realm of Essence." But there is a tide in these matters of criticism which sometimes is found rising and sometimes ebbing or at the low-water of indifference and fatigue. We mustn't quarrel with the moods of our critics.

I am afraid there is little prospect of journeys to England on my part for the present. I expect to be in Paris in June, but if I go further it will be to Spain, where family affairs may call me. When the next volume of "Realms" is finished, which I hope will be next winter, I shall feel freer, and may travel again a bit for pleasure: my present movements are simply to avoid oppressive or dangerous climates, according to the season.

Do send me the three cantos; I shall be in Rome, at the Hotel Bristol, at least until June 1st.

Yours sincerely,

To C. J. DUCASSE

ROME, MAY 16, 1928

Dear Mr. Ducasse:

Since my post-card of yesterday I have read your article.[1] I agree with your general thesis and with the conclusions at the bottom of p. 185, but your arguments and your categories are not always those which I should use. In what might be called classical philosophy art meant command over instrumentalities and meth-

[1] "What Has Beauty to do with Art?" (*Journal of Philosophy*, March 29, 1928)

ods: it might be abused, but it was the moralist's duty to watch over it and see that it was directed towards the ultimate and harmonious service of the soul. Beauty, on the other hand, was one side of the ultimate good. Art was called fine or beautiful, in so far as it was directed towards this good: but a material work of art, or a method, had to be judged not only on this ground, but in view of all its effects. A beautiful work of art might be evil in that it flattered falsehood or vice; but to a truly refined taste only that could be wholly beautiful which was wholly attuned to the health of human nature. Now-a-days all this has been confused and lost sight of. In radical quarters beauty is not regarded as a good, but art is respected as expression—but expression of what? You say, of feeling. Swearing then would be art, but acting, if done for money, and (as they say it should be) without actual feeling, would not be art. Croce—with whom I don't agree in anything else— says that the beautiful is a hybrid concept, meaning partly the expressive and partly the attractive (simpatico); and certainly erotic standards and similar sensuous preferences have much to do with it. But "art", in the modern world, is a pure affectation and self-indulgence on the part of a Soviet of ill-educated persons, who have no discernment of the good in any form, but only a certain irritability and impatience to put their finger in the pie.

There was a point in your letter which I meant to have spoken of, viz., about "animal faith" extending to propositions. This shows that you don't feel at all the force of this word which I use, and perhaps abuse—*animal*. The animal organism is wound up, and has certain potentialities which it discharges upon occasion: the sentiment which accompanies this discharge, when it is conscious, is a *vague, wordless* confidence or premonition. It is not a proposition to be verified, because it has no terms. That is why I call it faith, not belief. It is not in the least necessary to conceive the future, or to assert that it exists, in order to jump out of the way of a vehicle. The mechanism of the body reacts, and the mind is merely carried along in a forward and open sympathy. So in perception: animal faith does not prophesy future sensations; it recognises present opportunities.—After all this, I needn't say that your letter and article have greatly interested me.

Yours sincerely,

To WILLIAM LYON PHELPS

ROME, NOVEMBER 2, 1928

Dear Billy

You always bring with you, even if you come only by the post, a sort of Gulf Stream of warmth and kindness. I have said that old sonnet (written in 1884) [1] over to myself—I find that I still remember it—and although the words are too much spaced, thinly scattered over an empty waste, like the scrub oaks over a ploughed field, which in Spain are called a wood, yet the whole is perfectly limpid, and I can imagine that emitted in a rotund voice in a hushed religious atmosphere (do people still cough in the Yale Chapel?) it might have a good effect. In any case, I appreciate your appreciation, and I hope our combined exhortation will encourage your young people to have Faith—in themselves!

I have been in Spain—no harm resulting—and afterwards at Strong's in Fiesole: now I am trying to bend all my remaining energies to finishing vol. II of Realms of Being.

Affectionate greetings to you both from your old friend

To SIR DESMOND MAC CARTHY

HOTEL BRISTOL, ROME
NOV. 16. 1928

Dear Mr. MacCarthy,[2]

Here are "a few remarks" which I found lately in an old notebook and which I have revised. It occurs to me that you might be willing to publish them in *Life and Letters* because though rather

---

[1] The famous sonnet "O World, thou choosest not the better part".

[2] Who later became Sir Desmond.

oracular they are so short. Or you might choose one or two and leave the others. If so, please send the MS. back, as I have no other clean copy.

Please tell Berty Russell, if you see him, that I was immensely amused at his diagnosis of "Catholic and Protestant Sceptics", and in particular of myself. But I don't like his saying that I dislike the Founder of Christianity: has he read my "Lucifer" or the dialogue about "The Philanthropist"? It may be a biassed interpretation, but I take even the eschatology, and the coming of the Kingdom, in Christ's mouth, to be gently ironical and meant secretly in a spiritual sense. So understood, I accept his doctrine and spirit *in toto*.

Yours sincerely,

To C. J. DUCASSE

ROME, NOV. 24, 1928

Dear Mr. Ducasse:

There are many points in your letter and article—many thanks for both—with which I feel agreement, especially that separation of *beauty* from "art" and the psychology of artists which you excuse yourself for making. Nothing could be more different, and nowadays more disconnected. But I am afraid, on the whole, I should make a mess of any introduction to your book.[1] Not only am I beyond my depth in other work, but this entire matter of psychology and aesthetics has become remote to me. I still notice and enjoy the beautiful, but seldom in works of art; rather in *light,* and the effects of light, casual and momentary, on objects, whether the dome of St. Peter's or the Italian flag hanging in the streets. I also feel as much interest as ever in what literary men and artists are up to; not aesthetically so much, as morally and politically; they express, not a wish or an emotion, but a fatal state of society. When I say "fatal" I don't mean deadly—it is often quite

---

[1] *Philosophy of Art* (1929).

lively—but inevitable, and historically curious. This human or symptomatic character of the arts makes it difficult for me to take seriously questions of approval or disapproval, pleasure or pain, supposed to be felt by casual observers; and much less can I take seriously academic theories about these problematic aesthetic reactions. The artists themselves, in their judgements, are partisans and children; but their works may be good.

I say all this—which hardly expresses my seasoned judgement, but only a mood—in order that you may forgive me for not complying with your request to write an introduction to your book. It is more than I could undertake.

Yours sincerely,

To THOMAS MUNRO

ROME, DEC. 13, 1928

Dear Munro:

It is very good of you to send me your little book,[1] which not only reminds me of you (which is always pleasant) but carries me into an interesting living world from which I am too far removed. I can't say that your book is good, beautiful, and true, because that would be to substitute thrills for clear thinking: let me say instead that it seems pleasantly reasonable and open-minded, and, of course, highly characteristic of the *milieu* in which it has taken shape. In so far as this is academic, philosophical, and American it is not so very different from what it was 35 years ago, when I wrote *The Sense of Beauty:* and I feel for you, caught in the same snags and compelled to thresh the same old straw. But there is another quality in discussion now—not in your book only—which has fallen upon the world since the days of my youth. You must remember that we were not very much later than Ruskin, Pater, Swinburne, and Matthew Arnold: our atmosphere was that of

[1] *Scientific Method in Aesthetics.*

poets and persons touched with religious enthusiasm or religious sadness. Beauty (which mustn't be mentioned now) was then a living presence, or an aching absence, day and night: history was always singing in our ears: and not even psychology or the analysis of works of art could take away from art its human implications. It was the great memorial to us, the great revelation, of what the soul had lived on, and had lived with, in her better days. But now analysis and psychology seem to stand alone: there is no spiritual interest, no spiritual need. The mind, in this direction, has been *desiccated:* art has become an abstract object in itself, to be studied scientifically as a *caput mortuum:* and the living side of the subject —the tabulation of people's feelings and comments—is no less dead. You are yourself enormously intelligent and appreciative, and so is Dr. Barnes, but like a conservator of the fine arts, as if everything had been made to be placed and studied in a museum. And in your theory of taste—do you mention taste?—you (like Dewey) seem to me to confuse the liberty and variability of human nature, which the naturalist must allow, with absence of integration in each man or age or society: for if you felt the need of integration, you would understand that fidelity to the good or the beautiful is like health, not a regimen to be imposed, by the same masters, upon men of different constitutions, but a perfection to be jealously guarded at home, and in one's own arts: and you will never have any arts that are not pitiful until you have an integrated and exclusive life. However, I am far from denying you the possibility of happiness, and wish it for you and Mrs. Munro, with all my heart—even if it be happiness in a museum.

Yours sincerely,

To STERLING P. LAMPRECHT

ROME, JAN. 28, 1929

Dear Mr. Lamprecht

Your beautiful article on Me Now and Then [1] has just come under my eye: it is so friendly in its criticism and so penetrating in its analysis that I ought merely to thank you for the satisfaction, and very gentle correction, which it brings me. The end in particular is perfect: if you look at my "Dialogues in Limbo", in which the "Stranger" is simply myself, you will find confirmation of your judgement out of my own mouth.

Nevertheless, it may be a more loyal way of acknowledging your interest in my way of thinking, if I attempt to explain one or two points where, without positively misunderstanding what I meant, you seem to be at a greater distance, more foreign, as it were, to my thought, than you are in your so sympathetic interpretation as a whole. 1st a technical point, on p. 546. "Essence" is more concrete, as I understand it, more *interior* than you suggest, when you say that the essence of beauty is not lovely. That is to substitute names for things: the essence of beauty is loveliness itself. All that can be said is that without animal life and capacity for intuition the essence of beauty could not be realized: and *if* you had no preference for life, no heart, you would not come within range of the good in any form: not even of the spiritual life *as a form of salvation*. Perhaps, then, you forget that in analyzing the spiritual life, I do not forget (I hope) that it is *life:* if it becomes pure Being it ceases to exist. And this leads to 2nd the relation of the spiritual to the rational life. Suppose that instead of mysticism I was considering taste: the poet or musician may, in moments of ecstasy, lose himself entirely in the intuition of his ideal theme. It is a limit to one movement in the Life of Reason. To revert to humanity and morality he has to consider the healthfulness of such

[1] Professor Lamprecht writes me that he had published an article entitled "Santayana Then and Now", and that the above letter is the reply sent him by Santayana after perusing his paper. "The opening phrase about 'Me Now and Then' is a triumph of graceful condemnation of the venturesome critic!"

rapture: he has to re-introduce it into the political life. Yet the moral world (being animal and spontaneous in its elements) does have those windows. I have been looking out of one lately: but, as you seem to suspect, with no intention of jumping out of it.

Yours sincerely

To GEORGE STURGIS

GLION, SEPT. 1. 1929

Dear George

You will have seen by my drafts that I have not moved from here all summer. It is not a place I like for itself, and it is not easy to take elderly walks without first making a journey to the water-level; but as you know, at first I came on Strong's account, and then have stayed on in order to finish my book, and also because Cory, who had come to help me with it, liked the place, danced with the neurotic ladies, played tennis with the consumptive clergymen, and seemed to be enjoying himself. *The book is now done,* and Cory is leaving tomorrow with the MS. of the last chapters, which he will have typewritten in Paris, so that we may make a final revision of the whole before it goes to the press. The book is called "The Realm of Matter", and was frightfully difficult to write, as I fear it may be to read.

In October Cory is returning to Florence, where he is going to be secretary to Strong, who also has a philosophical work in the slips. I shall probably go to Strong's myself shortly, and stay until October 15, which is my usual time for settling down at the Hotel Bristol. I am a little afraid of having fresh attacks of my bronchial cold: if so I may go further south, even possibly to Greece or Egypt, as now that the book is done I shall feel more free and irresponsible in my movements . . .

I am glad to know that family and business matters are all going well. My best love to Rosamond and the boys, as well as to yourself from

To *JOHN FRANCIS STANLEY, 2nd EARL RUSSELL*

FIESOLE

OCT. 20 1929

Dear Russell,

Since I received your letter of Sept. 14, I have reread Lionel Johnson's Winchester letters, including the introduction, which I am interested to know is written by you. Apart from the precocity of this correspondence, it throws a good deal of light on what we all were in the 1880's. For a practical man like you, although you have not forgotten Lionel himself, all that must lie now very much in the limbo of almost incredible things. For me it is different, because external things and the fashions of the times make very little difference to my thoughts, and what we were then is almost as present to me, and more interesting, than what we are now. In respect to you in particular, it was you as I first knew you, in 1886, and for five or ten years after that, that have played a leading part in my life, although of course, even then, I was very much in the margin of yours; since then, it has been only the momentum of that youthful attachment, which was very deep on my part, that has kept up what you call in your "Life" our *"long acquaintance"*. You minimise even your friendship with Lionel, in this very book: and I quite understand how you come to do it. You obliterate very soon your own feelings, when the occasion is past, and you never understand the feelings of others—it is part of your strength. But it causes you to make little mistakes which, in some cases, might have unpleasant consequences. I remember that of late years at Telegraph House, you several times called me Sargeant: that slip of the tongue—natural enough then—showed how completely the past had dropped for you behind the horizon. Perhaps you think now that I am *inventing* this "past." Read Lionel's verses "To a Spanish Friend" and you may recover a little of the atmosphere of those days.

Do you wish to keep the identity of B and C in Lionel's letters a secret? If not, I should be very glad to know who they were.

Yours ever,

P.S. I find it increasingly hard to visit England—read "My, not my, England" in the last number of "Life and Letters"—and I haven't been in America for 17 years.

To ROBERT BRIDGES

ROME,

NOV. 4, 1929

My dear Bridges,

The Testament of Beauty has splendidly filled for me the last two days, although the feeling that you were expecting comments on its philosophy somewhat troubled my pleasure, and I shall have to re-read many parts of it to enjoy their full savour. You charge me to tell you, not what I approve, but what I fall foul of: it is hard to do, because what I approve of, or rather relish and delight in, is clear: it is the episodes, the pictures, the judgements, the wise reflections: whereas what I fall foul of is obscure: it is the system of philosophy which you say is so much like my own. But before I come to that let me confess that besides the qualities which I expected—saturation, abundance, picturesqueness, colour—I lighted on one which I didn't expect at all, and found myself laughing aloud at your wit and naughtiness—for instance at page 48. Your prosody, of which I am not a very competent judge, seemed to me to justify itself, and carried me along buoyantly: I sometimes seemed to hear echoes of Milton and Wordsworth, and once or twice—you won't mind, I hope—of Walt Whitman, for instance, "Now like sailing-ships on a calm ocean drifting", or "Rangeth up here in place for the parley of this book."

But to come to business: I am not sure whether you mean to discuss only the life of reason, neglecting the universe in which it occurs, or to identify the two, or to represent the universe as somehow antecedently subservient to the life of reason and exclusively designed to make that life possible. Evidently the universe subserves the life of reason in so far as the latter exists and prospers; and if your "Ring", and your general ultimate monism, meant only that there was correspondence and harmony *there,* where and in so far as correspondence and harmony exist, it would be very true, but perhaps hardly worth saying. But if you mean this "Ring" and this pre-established harmony to describe the whole universe, I should decidedly reject that view: because I am convinced that the relation between things natural and things moral is forthright and unreturning. It seems meaningless to me to say that Mind or the Good is at the origin as well as at the summit of things (when they have a summit), because there can't be intelligence or value before there is a natural world with specific animate beings in it to describe and enjoy it in their specific ways. Then, and not till then, a certain segment or strain in the material world (materially and dynamically imbedded in much else that remains morally irrelevant or hostile) becomes Parent and Food for the spirit, and a Harmony sustaining the beautiful. But that, in the outer always persistent chaos, is an accident, an islet in a sea of infinite indifference.

The case is similar in regard to your transposition of essences into influences. To see them in that light is to see them humanly, in so far as they become important or guiding ideas for us: they are then names for influences of which we do not understand the true mechanism. Indeed, I should go further and say that, in *that* relation, they are not even influences, but only impulses or virtues in ourselves: because no idea or goal would be influential unless we were initially directed upon it. Between those particular chosen essences and the effort of life, issuing in beauty, there is evidently the circularity and reciprocity which you describe: but that is not because they are essences, but because they are chosen, so that the marvel is a tautology.

I should therefore agree with you completely if it were understood that you were traversing the life of spirit only, and leaving out all physics and logic: but even then so exclusive an interest in the moral side of things, ignoring their natural basis and ontological surroundings, leads into ambiguities and illusions: the relative becomes absolute and the absolute relative. If you admitted openly, as I do, that the impulses which determine the direction in which the good and the beautiful may be realized are specific, local, and temporal impulses, I think your judgement, for instance, of the Catholic church would be more sympathetic than it is. For why does the church accept a myth (as I agree with you that it is) and pass it off for true history and eschatology, and for a scientific truth wider than any natural science, and extending natural science on the same level of natural fact? Because without this supernatural environing world, invented to suit the human conscience, spiritual and moral life would be precarious, and its forms while it subsisted would be innocently and endlessly divergent. There would be no "Ring", no far-off divine event, except imperfectly in each case, and relatively to that little creature. Now I accept, and have almost come to prefer and to love, this miscellany of many contrary transitory beauties and virtues: sometimes you seem to me to love it too, and to be content with it: but then again your "Ring" and your "One Eternal" seem to assert a dominant moral unity and Hebraic plan in all creation. If you really demand this, you ought to become a Catholic: because *The unnaturalness of nature as we find it,* its need of a supernatural complement before we can bear to live in it, is implied in any ascription of dominance to the good. The good in nature is not supreme, and it is impossible that it ever should be: in any living thing the beautiful must be involved, and the good partly realized: but it is an omnimodal beauty and a dispersed multitude of contrary goods. If we rest there, we must resign ourselves to our own bird-song, and to an eternal war of contrary virtues imperfectly realised. The vigorous fighting conscience, the dogmatic religious impulse, will not put up with that. Therefore it seems to me that the church, in its preposterous myth, shows a great experience of the world and a deep understanding of what human religion is: and when you speak of *"lumen ademptum"* [1] your own light seems to have failed you. I am as well aware as you are of the enormity of subjecting nature to the catechism and making the universe stand on its virtuous head; yet I profoundly pity and reverence the desperate faith which when forced to admit the death of its Beloved invents his resurrection.

My "Realm of Matter" is now in the publisher's hands and I hope before many months to send you a copy, as an inadequate thank-offering.

Yours sincerely,

1 Robbed of vision. See Virgil. Aen. Book III l. 658.

To J. MIDDLETON MURRY

HOTEL BRISTOL, ROME.
DEC. 11, 1929

Dear Mr. Murry

I have read "God" [1] with much interest, and am happy to think that perhaps my books have been of use to you in your heroic struggles with so many misfortunes and perplexities. My own course has been relatively smooth: I have had no "mystical experience" and have not been obliged to extricate myself from the tangle of Protestantism and Moralism. For that reason, probably, I am not able to share your enthusiasm for D. H. Lawrence, Dostojewski, Nietzsche, or even Goethe. They may be invaluable in bringing one to the conclusion that things moral are natural, and simply the fruition of things physical—in which latter the psyche, or principle of life, must be included. But I gathered all that in my youth from Aristotle and from my own reflection (as I have described at length in "Dialogues in Limbo") and those romantic solvents were unnecessary to my own liberty. I see their strength, but I don't need their influence. Goethe of course is full of wise reflexions, like Bacon: but when his romanticism droops, he becomes, like Bacon, a ponderous worldling: not a ray of spirituality in either of them. I am puzzled about what you find in Keats: is it there? As to your reconstruction of Christ, you know that I have no faith in such things. Like everybody else, I like to assimilate the sense of the Gospel to my own insights: and I have no objection to *poetic* interpretations of Jesus, if they continue his legend and are faithful to his sacred character as tradition preserves it—according to the maxim of Horace about fidelity to characters once established by the poets. But these reconstructions have no historical truth: documents are lacking, and the imagination of the modern poet is hopelessly transformed. On single abstracted points we may, of course, have reasons for forming particular judgements: and there are *ideas* which we may study and understand in them-

[1] *God: being an introduction to the science of Metabiology.* J. Middleton Murry (1929).

selves, apart from the biography of their author, who probably did nothing but adopt them. What you call Christ's "amazing" idea of God seems to me to be one of these. In substance it is the commonplace of all Eastern religion: you say yourself that it is found also in India and China; yes, and in the Stoics and the Mohammedans: in fact in everybody except the unmitigated Jews. It is the universal *"sursum corda"—"habemus ad Dominum"*. If we ventured on hypotheses about the personal context in which this idea existed in Christ, we might say that is was merged with that of Jehovah and (as you explain) with that of a Messiah: and there was also a good deal of assimilation of the divine Being to the governing principles of this world. For instance, besides your favourite text about the sun and rain, there are texts about the wheat and tares, the harvest, and the burning. Elevation above human interests did not exclude perception of what those interests required: they required conventional morality, and even an established church. I was glad to see you so bravely identifying genuine Christianity with Rome; but there is one point which, if I had the pleasure of talking with you, I would try to convince you of: and that is that the "supernatural" is the most harmless thing in the world, and not arbitrary. It is merely the ultra-mundane: it is governed by its own principles, of which there is a definite science, and it is the truly and fundamentally natural, of which our conventional or scientific nature is only a local, temporary, and superficial mode. Of course, the *revelation* of what this ultra-mundane sphere contains is "fishy" and itself inspired from below: it is like our modern Spiritualism; but that doesn't prevent the general notion of an existing sphere beyond our sphere, but touching it and sometimes penetrating into it, from being legitimate, if only the evidence for it were not drawn from the wrong quarter.

You are a modern, an "intellectual", and I am an old fogey: that is probably the reason why I balk at your emphasis on "newness". Aren't you confusing newness with freshness or spontaneity? True religion, true philosophy, like true love, must be spontaneous, it must be fresh: but why should it be new? There is no harm in a new species of rose, if nature drops into it, or horticulture succeeds in bringing it forth under electric reflectors, and by judicious grafting: but surely the beauty even of the new roses, if genuine, and not simply a vile worldly fashion, is independent of the accident that such a form was previously unknown. Evolution is a fact, and we must be grateful to it for the good things it brings forth: but the good in each of these things lies in their own perfection and harmony with themselves; and the date of them makes no difference in their happiness. Am I wrong?

I have just received Whitehead's new book on "Process & Reality", in which I expect to find much instruction. His point of view is in some respects like yours, and you must value so expert an ally. But why such "newness" in vocabulary? Both you and he bewilder us with your pseudo-technical terms, most of which, I am sure, could be avoided by a little precision in the use of old words.

Yours sincerely

To GEORGE STURGIS

HOTEL BRISTOL, ROME

DEC. 20, 1929

Dear George

I am reading the proofs of my new book,[1] and expecting Cory —you know he is my young disciple, who has been helping me with my work, but is now in Florence, assisting Strong—to spend Christmas with me here. Early in January we are to have a royal wedding, and apparently much festivity.

We are having the first spell of cold weather—not very cold —but so far the winter has been pleasant, and I have kept well. It is true that I am carrying out various methods of treatment recommended by doctors and dentists in the hope of dying in the remote future in perfect health.

Will you please send the enclosed note to Mr. Sadakichi Hartmann, P.O. Box, 372, Beaumont, California, with a cheque for $100. He is—you have sent him money for me before—an impecunious poet, old, and in ill-health; and although I am a

[1] *The Realm of Matter.*

little tired of his begging letters, this time he has forced my hand by sending me three very nice Japanese prints. I have no idea of their value, but they are not common, and the least I can do is to supply him in exchange with some bread and butter.

I am coming to have a lot of unknown correspondents: not all of them ask for cash; but most of them do, which in view of the spiritual gifts which, as they say, they have already received, is in order, I suppose, to prove that I am not one-sided.

Best wishes for the New Year, for all of you, from

To J. MIDDLETON MURRY

HOTEL BRISTOL, ROME
DEC. 21, 1929

Dear Mr. Murry

Thank you for your letter which relieves me of a certain feeling that perhaps my own epistle had been impertinent. You are very good to take it in good part. I see that I was vague and obscure about the "supernatural".[1] What I meant was that, *for those who believe in it in some definite form,* there is a science of it, as there was of oracles and omens, or of Karma and the methods of lightening it, or of sacraments, grace, indulgences, etc. These sciences show that the supernatural is never conceived as anything but the rest of the natural, the background of fact and law behind our human experience and conventions. It seems to me almost certain that such a supernatural sphere must exist, and that our world is an incident in some larger flux of existence: but evidently the difficulty is to learn anything about that ulterior region. We can get on very well without such knowledge: but if we feel unhappy in that ultimate ignorance, we can hardly be satisfied except by some alleged revelation breaking in into our world by miracle. This, I take it, is the way in which belief in the supernatural, and in a definite science of

[1] See Letter [Dec. 11, 1929].

it *up to a certain point,* can be grafted upon the life of reason. It is so grafted, for instance, in Dante.

I have not yet made much progress in Whitehead's book, but if I am tempted to write about it, you shall have the review.

Yours sincerely

To HENRY SEIDEL CANBY

ROME, JAN. 16, 1930

Dear Canby

That opiferous cheque for $100 which you said you had directed your secretary to send me has never arrived. Isn't it yet ripe, or has it gone astray?

I was a little surprised at the tone of Lippmann's reply to my article.[1] I thought he would be pleased, and certainly I had liked his book very much; but apparently he requires us all to share his vague hopes of "high religious" worldly organization, and is angry if we are attached to some different political ideal. I am sorry. And I was also a little vexed at the preliminary anecdote, not for the tone of it this time, but because it was historically inaccurate and missed the point of the story. I remember the incident very well: it must have been in 1907–8, when I had the beard which you have immortalized in your Review, but which was shaved off some 20 years ago. I enclose my official portrait, in case you wish to exhibit me again when I die, or before. But to return: I said in my lecture that if some angel without a carnal body appeared to me and assured me that he was perfectly happy on prayer and music, I should congratulate him, but shouldn't care to imitate him. Some of the class laughed: and at the end of the hour, Lee Simonson (what has

---

[1] The article was entitled "Enduring the Truth", and appeared in *The Saturday Review of Literature,* Dec. 7, 1929. It was intended to be a review of Walter Lippmann's book *A Preface to Morals.* The same issue contains a brief "reply" on the part of Mr. Lippmann.

become of him?) showed me a caricature of myself, looking very dissipated and very French, repeating those words to a vast female angel of a very insipid sentimentality in the heavens. These particular youths seem to have found it comic that I should always carry a stick and gloves, and no coat: but I was a good pedestrian in those days and that was natural to me. The point of my lecture was not, as Lippmann says, absorbtion in pure Being, but the relativity of ethical ideals: which I wish he had taken more to heart. But Simonson's sketch was amusing, and has made me remember the incident.

Yours sincerely

To J. MIDDLETON MURRY

SAINT GERMAIN, JUNE 22, 1930

Dear Mr. Murry

I have just finished your article in *The Criterion,* on *The Detachment of Naturalism.* I am delighted with it, not merely because I agree with every word of it, but because you put these things in a personal and moving way which heightens their clearness, and probably will make them intelligible to many who, at another angle, might miss them altogether.

The only thing which I should be tempted to add to your exposition is that the detachment of spirit, or of understanding, is itself an inevitable aspect or moment of natural intelligence. To see things as they are, or in their truth, by variously exchanging, balancing, and thereby transcending any one private station or interest, is the condition of seeing them usefully in the larger economy of life. There is nothing antinatural in reflection, imagination, or impersonal hypothesis. We must discount our personal equation —sensuous organs, passions, etc.—in order to calculate correctly the movement of things, in which our animal existence and passions are interpolated. But in thus serving our natural life our intelligence has detached itself, in idea, from the bias of that life: it has become impartial and disinterested. It can therefore, to that extent and in that relation, constitute a spiritual life detached from the person and lost in the truth: although materially it remains a function of animal intelligence, with its material organs, and its roots in the free play and requisite transpositions of animal fancy.

Your article is a fresh and eloquent exposition of Spinoza's "intellectual love of God".

Yours sincerely

To J. MIDDLETON MURRY

HOTEL VOUILLEMONT
15, RUE BOISSY D'ANGLAS, PARIS
AUGUST 17, 1930

Dear Mr. Murry

I have just finished reading—with great care and delight—your *Studies in Keats*.[1] They give me much information which I never had, and a new insight into Keats' mind. In the days when I read English poetry he was always my personal favourite. I found him warmer than Shelley, and liked a certain frank sensuality or youthfulness in him, a certain plebeian innocence of great human interests: I called him the Cockney Genius, and thought him luscious rather than intellectual. I see now how wrong that was, and that he was really intuitive and contemplative. Intuition, as you say, is nearer to sensation than to reasoning thought. It has a spiritual quality, by virtue of its disinterestedness, quite apart from the character of the object contemplated: but the nature of this object—whether it is physical, historical, botanical or dramatic—nevertheless has a great influence on the human value of the poetry expressing our intuitions. I still feel that there was a certain weakness in Keats—not (I now see) in his spirit, or in the elevation of his thought, but in his psyche, in the principle of health and

[1] Oxford University Press, 1930.

integration in the natural man. And I don't say this in a niggardly mood, as if I wished to find some fault at all costs in so wonderful a creature: I say it because your discussion seems to reveal to me a theoretical confusion consequent in him upon that weakness. Spiritual insight no doubt *transcends* moral preference, as it transcends scientific dogma: but it does not *obliterate* either the one or the other. The pure intellect—which is also an animal exercise and carries a joy of its own in merely exerting itself—dominates good and evil, truth and fancy with an equal pleasure: but that contemplation is superadded. It doesn't in any way correct or remove the judgements proper to the psyche, and imposed on her by her actual relation to the facts. We are not ultimately constrained "to love all Facts" or to say that "all Fact is beautiful". That would be callous and wicked: just as it would be idiotic to affirm all ideas and to say that all propositions are true. It is only the essences exemplified in evil or false objects that, to a sublimated spirit, may be as interesting and contemplatively as welcome as the essences of objects which, in this world and for the creatures living here, are evil or false. And in the same way, I should wish to make a distinction about the maxim "Beauty is Truth, Truth Beauty".[1] If we define Truth as "Fact that is loved", truth would become identical with Goodness or excellence in existing things: but Beauty extends to much that is not Fact, and is an excellence felt in contemplation, not like Goodness, proper to things in their dynamic capacity or uses. Of course, we may define words as we like, but it seems to me an abuse of language to define Truth as an accident of Love. Beauty is that: but Truth is the eternal form of the Facts, in all their relations, whether anyone loves them or not. That the intellect, in its disinterested contemplation, may understand all facts with pleasure, does not justify us in saying that this pleasure makes the truth of those facts.

Would the following be a fair transcription of the passage [2]

[1] The celebrated conclusion to the *Ode to a Grecian Urn.*

[2] The passage in question is from a famous letter of Keats to Benjamin Bailey, dated November 22, 1817. (I have preferred to follow the punctuation and capital lettering of the original MS., rather than the more readable transcript in Mr. Murry's book).

"I am certain of nothing but of the holiness of the Heart's affections and the truth of Imagination—What the Imagination seizes as Beauty must be truth—whether it existed before or not—for I have the same Idea of all our Passions as of Love they are all in their sublime creative of essential Beauty."

Santayana's interesting rendering of this passage must be taken as an effort to on pp. 35–36? "I am certain of the Heart's right to assert the excellence of that which it loves. All the passions create true excellence, whether their objects ever exist or not". This kind of excellence is evidently the sort that the poet discovers and celebrates: it is Beauty whether it be Truth or not. Beauty is fiction even before it is truth.

My article on "The Genteel Tradition at Bay" is getting involved in all sorts of side-issues; but I am in hopes of finishing it soon, and if it is too long for one issue you might either abridge it or publish it in two numbers.

Yours sincerely

To HERBERT J. SELIGMANN

PARIS, SEPT. 22, 1930

Dear Mr. Seligmann

It is very pleasant to be reminded, after so many years, of the sympathy which existed between us when we were teacher and pupil; and I am glad to see that the Firebird [1] that was then already stirring within you has not been smothered by the pressure of circumstances. I remember that your mother secretly wrote to me —I suppose after twenty years or more that secret need not be kept —to express her anxiety about your temperament and inclinations: she feared perhaps that you might be unhappy in the world. I judge by certain indications in this little book that the world has not been too unkind: yet you seem, at bottom, not to be very much interested in it, only in images and in a certain spiritual freedom which transcends all accidental facts. Images, sensual and atmospheric, can't be well described in words, and you are troubled like all contemporary poets, by a medium which is inappropriate, and of which

---

make explicit what Keats might have said if he had been trained to think philosophically, and clarify his key concepts—like Beauty, Truth, Imagination, etc. And only a Santayana would be qualified to suggest such an audacious alternative version.

[1] *Firebird and Other Poems* (1930).

you haven't an adequate command: because language is a splendid
medium in itself, if you are an artist in it, and if your interests are
dramatic or intellectual: but pure images rather require to be
preserved in painting or created by music. Your verses, in this
direction, are simply so many proofs that images do arrest you, and
that things and events do not: there is a philosophy for you, and a
characteristically modern one. It is well expressed in your "Brook-
lyn Bridge": but it seems to me that, for a poet, this is rather a
confession of impotence; because the world if mastered and exploited humanly, ought to be far more interesting to the mind and
heart than sensuous images which remain meaningless. When I
came to the Firebird proper, at first I supposed that of course it
was Love; but after reading, it seemed rather to be Truth: in any
case, here is the spirit passing beyond the images and the facts into
some abyss where it feels more at home. Every one has his own way
of feeling and expressing these ultimate things, but there is much
unanimity among mystics of all ages and religions, and we shouldn't
quarrel about vehicles and accidents when it is precisely accidents
and vehicles that we wish to transcend. Thank you for remembering
me: you see I haven't forgotten you.

Yours sincerely

To HENRY WARD ABBOT

VILLA LE BALZE
FIESOLE OCT. 4, 1930

Dear Harry

If I send you my books, it is because various little articles of
yours in the papers have proved to me that you haven't forgotten
our old confabulations on ultimate things; and I wish you wouldn't
let your attention become entangled in matters of style; style is
only a cumbrous vehicle, though an inevitable one, for what I have
to say; and without pretending that my views are of much im-

portance measured by the standard of absolute truth, which after
all is in nobody's hand, I think you might be interested in them
as confessions and moral insights of an old friend. You say I am
hard to read: I have heard that before, yet it surprises me because
I take the greatest pains to be clear, not only in language but in
thought, and am a very simple commonplace person in my opinions.
Everybody ought to say: "Of course: that's what I've always
thought, only I didn't expect a philosopher to see it". I said this to
Strong (with whom I am staying at present among these Tuscan
hills) and he explained that the difficulty in reading my books
came from the ornaments, which interfered with the attention and
made the reader lose the outline of the thought. Is that it? If so I
can only say that the ornaments, for me, are a spontaneous concomitant of the sense, like gestures in animated discourse: they are
necessary, if you want to reach the true ground and flavour of the
ideas. All language is rhetorical, and even the senses are poets. But
people compare books with other books, not with experience.

Yours sincerely

To THOMAS MUNRO

HOTEL BRISTOL, ROME
JANUARY 7, 1931

Henceforward, in the galleries of Europe, it will be easy to distinguish the children of light from the Philistines: they will carry
a green book [1] instead of a red one.—Thank you very much for
your Christmas present, and let me congratulate you on the just-
ness, as well as the enthusiasm and the knowledge, to be found in
your handbook. I have looked up certain key works (like Raphael's
La Disputa del Sacramento, and the Gauguin at the end) and I
think you are admirably fair in distinguishing the qualities—
whether fashionable at this moment or not—which characterize

---

[1] *Great Pictures of Europe* (1930).

the most different schools. This is all the more admirable when your heart is (or was) so generously set on the love of the ugly ducklings of art; but you have a scientific conscience as well as a fresh enthusiasm, and you have not been willing to blind yourself to the beauties of those works which to you personally may be less appealing.

To B. A. G. FULLER

ROME, MAY 25, 1931

Dear Fuller

After I had finished the proofs of your Aristotle, the two volumes [1] arrived, and I have now read the Socrates and Plato. I am partly reconciled to your international American and jocular medium; for I see that really you are not writing a history of Greek Philosophy at all, but a review of what the professors—chiefly English or Scottish—now say about it. You might have carried the joke out, and composed a perfect satire on all these controversies, on the theme which you indicate in several places, that the two and seventy sects come out by the same door wherein they went. And this is always the back door. All these professors are outsiders and interlopers, and the first thing to do if you had wished to study the ancients themselves should have been to become a believer in them, and to have let all these modern egotistical critics lie buried in their own dust. Plato and Aristotle speak for themselves, *if you trust them,* and if you want guidance, you have it, within the school and its living traditions, in the Neo Platonists the Arabians, and the Scholastics. Two points, for instance, would at once drop out of the discussion, 1st the supposed transformations and contradictions in the systems, with the whole trivial question of dates; 2nd the importance of the problem of evil. As to the first, I found it more annoying in Aristotle than in Plato, in whom (especially if you accept the letters) some chronological variations

[1] *History of Greek Philosophy.*

may really be traced; but in either case, it is impossible for any author to say (or to develop) everything at once; he must study one subject first and then another, and the order of these subjects, and his age, may naturally colour the discussion, and give it a different emphasis or point of approach: but to speak of an evolution or self-contradiction in mature masters like Plato and Aristotle is a piece of modern insolence and pedantry. As to the other point—the origin of evil—I came the other day in Maritain on the observation that this is *not an important subject in philosophy:* and naturally not for a Platonist or Aristotelian, because in that system the creativity of the One is accidental to Him. He may be the absolute good in himself and our ultimate good also: but the fact that there is evil too, and separation from the good, is our business and misfortune, not a blemish or a fault in Him. So the attribution of evil to matter or to accidental wilfulness or to malice is a question of history: and your argument about God "letting go" loses all its urgency if we remember that "matter" is by definition indeterminate. When any essence "lets go", matter (or the contingent, whatever you may call it which is crucial for *existence*) is ready to become anything: i.e. matter, left alone, will deviate or go wrong of itself—wrong, I mean, from the point of view of the essence which we happen to look to. You may then say that matter is attracted by the devil, or the seat of free-will, or simply chaotic: these are all ways of describing the same earthly fact. God lets go when we lose Him.

I shouldn't have bothered you with these old carpings, which you will think wrong-headed were it not that in reading your Plato I have more than once been arrested by the extraordinary sympathy and understanding which you display in revealing the true inwardness of the system, for instance, at the end of the chapter on love. Page 201 is sublime. Why then not have interpreted Plato in this fashion throughout, paraphrasing and re-thinking his own thoughts? You could do it, if you cared. But the confounded Protestant professors have got you to paraphrase them instead.

I hope you will have a good press and a good sale. You are modest in your professions, and really do much more than you propose and promise to do. But merely as a review of reviews or set of lectures about all other sets of lectures, your books may be useful: and certainly they will keep the reader awake.

Yours sincerely

To HENRY WARD ABBOT

ROME, JUNE 10, 1931

Dear Harry

Many thanks for introducing me to Miss Millay. I had seen her name, and possibly (if she ever wrote for *the Dial*) I may have read some piece of hers before: but all was lost in that terrible bog of false poetry into which I hate to step. Poetry, in the sense of versified passionate eloquence, seems to be a thing of the past. But I see that Miss Millay takes the bull by the horns and *dresses up* her poetry in the magnificent ruff and pearls of Queen Elizabeth. It is a wonderful performance: very rarely did I feel that the sawdust of modern diction was trickling out of the beautiful fancy-dress doll. The movement, and in particular the way of repeating and heightening a word, like a theme in music, are unexampled, as far as I know, in any contemporary performance. When it comes to the thought or the morality, just because it is somewhat genuine and modern, there is less nobility: a woman who was really in love and gave herself too freely to a lover who, liking her well enough at first, got tired of her in the end. The case demands repentance and sublimation, both of which Miss Millay avoids, in her evidently pragmatic philosophy. But without sublimation or repentance the feeling could not rise to the level of the versification. It is like very good Latin versification, such as is still occasionally produced by the well-educated.

I am at work on *The Last Puritan* and often wish I could show you a passage and ask you if it seems to you true to the life—to the inner life especially—of our old-fashioned friends.

I agree that the last years of life are the best, if one is a philosopher.

Yours sincerely

To GEORGE STURGIS

NAPLES, OCT. 4. 1931

Dear George

Since your last letter, which reached me here the other day, things have got more mixed up than ever in the financial world. I am not frightened, as I have no real desire or intention to have a motor, and I suppose there will always be enough left, of our fabulous wealth, for me to pay for spaghetti. Long ago I wrote you some philosophical reflections on the absurdity of living well on invisible property: but you said I must have been talking with Bertrand Russell—I don't think I had, at least on that subject; I am not a *modern* or *liberal* socialist; but I feel in my bones that our form of industrial society is very precarious, and that it will disappear, perhaps rather soon, as completely as the mediaeval or the Graeco-Roman civilizations have disappeared. I went the other day to Pompei, where there is a well-preserved Roman house now to be seen. It made me wish I had lived 2000 years ago: it was so very beautiful and so very intimate: all the sources, and all the ultimate objects, of life were then close at hand, visible, and obvious. Shouldn't it always be so? We live lost in a spider's web of machinery, material and social, and don't know what we are living for or how we manage to live at all.

Your prophetic uncle

MRS. C. H. TOY

To MRS. C. H. TOY

HOTEL BRISTOL, ROME,
NOV. 12, 1931.

Dear Mrs. Toy

On rereading your last letter, I am shocked to see that it is of July 10, and presumably unanswered! Four months gone by insensibly, every day very like every other. I didn't stay in Venice long, my room at the Danieli being uncomfortably hot and the difficulty in taking walks—which I had overcome on other occasions —proving insuperable. I moved almost at once to Cortina d'Ampezzo, and found it pleasant and, after the month of June, cool enough for walking and writing. I have rewritten and (I say to myself) *finished* the Prologue and the first two parts of the Novel,[1] "Ancestry" and "Childhood", bringing Oliver down to the end of his seventeenth year. This is perhaps a third—possibly more—of the whole in length, but not in importance; for I am discovering that the Novel, like *Lucifer,* really turns out to be dramatic, although I had conceived it as merely philosophical. Even the second part, on Boyhood, seems to move with some acceleration, and to have a perceptible, even if yet not violent, *wind* running through it. At least, this is the impression it makes on my own mind, as the condemned portions are chipped off gradually, and the statue appears. It may be only the fond fancy of a parent, or of an amateur sculptor.

Being tolerably satisfied with this result, I am thinking of suspending work on the novel until next summer, when very likely I shall go to Cortina again, and of devoting this winter to the *Realm of Truth,* which is so far advanced already, and so short, that I hope to be able to finish and publish it in 1932. The novel in any case will take much longer, if it is ever finished at all. Of course, incidental things always arise to distract one from one's plans. Now I have got an irrepressible desire to write an article [2] on The Good *versus* The Infinite, or the Difference between Western and Eastern

1 *The Last Puritan.*

2 "The Prestige of the Infinite."

Mysticism. The cause of this rash plan is double: a book by Julien Benda [1] (do you know of him? A French Jew who dislikes Bergson) on the relations of the World to (the infinite) God, and a Spanish book by a Carmelite friar on Saint John of the Cross. The article is begun: it is an interruption; but how can I help it?

The Bushes [2] (of Columbia) have been here; also "Elizabeth" of the German Garden. The latter told me some interesting things about her late husband, my old friend Lord Russell.[3] In the first place we both agreed that it was most satisfactory—much more so than anyone could have hoped—that he should have been rehabilitated and rewarded at the end with a place in the government: you know, I suppose, that he was successively Under secretary for Transport and for India in the late Labour government. But he and "Elizabeth" had had the most bitter quarrels and had long been separated. She says marriage is a horrid thing, and that nobody ought to be *bound* to anybody else. Have you read her last book, *Father?* It is another picture of the evils of domestic tyranny, although in this case neither of the two domestic tyrants pilloried is a husband. She has built herself a house, with a garden in which things at last are able to grow, on the hills behind Cannes: and one of her husband's relations was coming to stay with her, and was being greeted with waving scarves and eager smiles at the garden gate, when the visitor's long face and solemn air made the hostess ask what was the matter.

"Frank!" cried the newcomer, with tragic brevity . .

"What about him now?"

"Dead and cremated!"

And this was the way in which "Elizabeth" received the glad tidings that she was once more a widow. She says she was never happier in her life. She also told me that Bertie had presented himself at the House of Lords to take his seat, but had been rudely shown to the door: a brother must wait eleven months for the sucession, in case his bereaved sister-in-law should have a posthumous male child. This law, with modern manners and morals, opens vistas of curious possible plots: I shouldn't wonder if "Elizabeth" took advantage of one of them.

---

[1] *Essai d'un Discours Cohérent sur les Rapports de Dieu et du Monde.*

[2] Professor & Mrs. Wendell T. Bush.

[3] The elder brother of Bertrand Russell.

All this merriment may seem heartless at the death of a husband and an old friend: but "Elizabeth" and I are known to be heartless: at least, for my own part, I feel so much the *continual* death of everything and everybody, and have so learned to reconcile myself to it, that the final and official end loses most of its impressiveness. I have now lost almost everybody that has counted for much in my life. You are almost the sole exception: because Strong, a lifelong if not at all a romantic friend, has developed an attitude towards me which is as unpleasant as it is unexpected. I have become, philosophically and intellectually, his *bête noire*. Personally we are still good friends: we keep up appearances, and this summer and autumn he has actually followed me to Cortina and to Naples (where I have been for a month) and spent a few days near me at each place. But there is always a tension beneath. He has reverted to strict Puritanism in his moral sentiments, and regards his father (who had a very red nose and married again at 85) as a model of human character. And he has recovered also all his American pride, and feels that it is unseemly and unworthy that I shouldn't endeavour to think and write like other American professors. My theory of "essence" is anathema to him, although for some years he innocently adopted it: he doesn't like my last little book on *The Genteel Tradition:* and as to the novel, of which at his request I showed him the first three chapters, he told Cory that it ought to be burned. Cory has no doubt been the accidental cause of a part of this transformation. Cory at first was *my* friend only, and helped me with *The Realm of Matter.* When this was finished I was going to let him go home and look after himself: but Strong said he envied me such a secretary, and asked him to stay and work with *him.* And quite naturally, I suppose, Strong began to resent the fact that, in our technical divergencies (which have always existed, and not caused any serious trouble) Cory should follow me rather than himself: and he began to work to convert Cory, partly by persistently and overbearingly imposing his own view, and partly by doing all he could to disparage and condemn me. Isn't it sad? Let me give you a sample of the process. In one page of an essay on Whitehead which Cory has written,[1] —he is partly Irish and has warm feelings—he had said that he was a "disciple" of mine, had called *The Realm of Matter* a "great

[1] *Dr. Whitehead on Perception,* Journal of Philosophy. Vol. XXX No. 2.

book", and had used the term "essence" once. Strong, in reviewing the essay with him, didn't rest until "disciple" was changed to "person influenced by", "great book" to "recent work", and "essence" to "datum". If you asked Strong how he could be so mean and ungenerous to his oldest and almost his only friend, I think he would say that he felt it his duty to protect Cory from making unfortunate slips which would discredit him as a critic among the professional philosophers: and that nobody would take him seriously if he began by saying that he was simply following me. There may be some truth in this, and I don't regret at all that Cory should correct his essay as required. But what do you make of such want of feeling, and such a bitter undercurrent of tyranny? Poor Margaret! [1] I understand now better than ever what she must have suffered. Cory himself is very unhappy about it all: but what is he to do? Strong is supporting him, and has put him in his will.

I hope I am not indiscreet in telling you all this, but it is very much on my mind and as I said, you are the only true friend left to

To MRS. C. H. TOY

ROME, DECEMBER 13, 1931

Dear Mrs. Toy

With some hesitation I am sending you a book [2] which you may have read already, which you may think horrible, and for which they may make you pay duty, because although the book spiritually speaking is intensely American, this is an English edition. The author is a young graduate of Princeton, and I (being very stupid at catching author's intentions) can't quite make out what he is after. Is it a realistic study, or is it a bitter denunciation with a latent summons to repentance? In spite of the awful dialect

[1] The Marquise de Cuevas, the daughter of Professor Strong.

[2] *This Our Exile,* by David Burnham.

his characters speak— (always "home", for instance, for "at home")
—and their pitiful moral impotence, I have read the thing through
with great interest. Tell me, are people nowadays really like that?
And is America really so helpless and distracted? I don't know
whether I have told you that last summer I read "Babbit" [1]—not
the Harvard Babbit,[2] but the true classic; there the prophetic intention is evident, although no suggestion of the direction appears
in which salvation may come.

You asked me in a previous letter whether I liked the idea
of building a chapel at Harvard for a war-memorial. Yes, I like it.
A chapel isn't a meeting-house: it is, or may be, just a shrine or a
monument. Here in Rome there are often two or three churches
in the same square; they are not needed for popular worship; they
are acts of homage in themselves, as public statues would be. And
at Harvard, where the existing Chapel is so hideous, the new one
might serve its commemorative purpose and at the same time (in
one transept, perhaps, or in one corner) supply a place in which
morning prayers could be recited for those who wish to hear them.
The main part could be left open, without pews, and could be a
sort of Harvard Westminster Abbey for monuments to her distinguished sons. They might set up even a bust of ME there someday, in the philosophers' corner. By all means, a Memorial Chapel!
—but not in the style of Memorial Hall.

To return to *This Our Exile,* I notice what must be a deliberate practice of mentioning insignificant details—how people
sit, whether it takes two matches or one to light a cigarette, etc—
and this, apparently, quite passively, in a sort of realistic effort to
record experience just as it flows through one man's consciousness.
Proust—as you must have heard, even if you haven't read him—
also made a point of introducing infinite details: but his had two
qualities not found here, nor in Joyce: the medley of impressions
and memories has, with him, a *poetic* quality, you feel the sentiment, the guiding thread in the labyrinth; and in the second place
the details themselves are beautiful or interesting, they are selected
by an *active intellect.* What appals me in this picture of young
American life is the passivity of it, the incapacity of everybody to

[1] By Sinclair Lewis.

[2] Professor Irving Babbitt.

swim against the stream of mechanical automatisms carrying the world along. It is life in a luxurious inferno; everybody rich, ignorant, common, and unhappy. Or am I quite at sea, and have I missed the point?

Yours sincerely

To JAMES HAUGHTON WOODS

ROME, DECEMBER 26, 1931

Dear Woods [1]

Your invitation (apart from the honour of it, and in such company!) is tempting in many ways, and if anything could bring me to plunge again into academic life, it would be your letter. But there are insuperable obstacles, the most easily stated of which is this: that, as you know, I am trying to write a system of philosophy of which two parts are still unpublished, and I am 68 years old. If the eight or ten lectures required for the William James foundation could have been carved out of these two books, now in preparation, I think that would have decided me to accept—in spite of the social and other commitments to which such an acceptance would lead. But the *Realm of Truth* and the *Realm of Spirit* are not possible lecture-quarries: and it would be rash, if not impossible, for me to turn away from them now, and compose a book— and it would need to be a careful and a lovingly-written book for such an audience—in an entirely different key. That is only one difficulty; there are others with which I won't bother you. It is most regretfully that I sum them all up, and ask you to look to some younger and fresher quarter. Please thank the Department in my name for the honour they have done me, and believe me

Sincerely yours

[1] Chairman of the Department of Philosophy at Harvard.

To GEORGE STURGIS

HOTEL BRISTOL, ROME
JAN. 18. 1932

Dear George

Your letter, accompanying your yearly account, sounds rather serious, and I am afraid you have been having an anxious year and are still feeling the strain and uncertainty of the crisis. I hope you will soon be able to feel secure, even if not so well off as you were formerly. As for me, the fall (of about one half, as I calculate it) in what would have been the value of my property at the top prices, leaves me perfectly happy. I seem to have saved $15,000 during this calamitous year, after spending all I wished to spend: and unless the decline should continue and income be reduced to less than a quarter of what it now is, I should suffer no inconvenience. Even if I lost everything, and became a pauper, I should be all right, if my health continued to be good. I could easily earn my living by writing and lecturing. Harvard College has just invited me to be the Wm James professor for 3 months, receiving $5,000, and I have declined, because I prefer to go on with my writing, as planned: but in "case of push" I might have accepted. And I have recently declined several other profitable engagements to lecture in America.

I see you take my political speculations seriously: I hope they deserve it, but am not quite sure. The collapse of "capitalism", or what I call invisible wealth would not involve communism: people might still own houses and land, ships and merchandise, as people did in antiquity, and down to recent times. Private property is a natural thing, because men like to possess, and are unequally capable of creating or holding their possessions: so that there are *naturally* rich and poor people. Communism has a great theoretical attractiveness: but it can be established and maintained only by a deliberate effort and a very strong government, as now in Russia, or in the Catholic religious orders. I think it would be a good thing, if it could be made to work, but I don't believe it can in the long run, or over a mixed population. I understand that in Russia many of the peasants are not yet "socialised": and if they were it would become a delicate matter to distribute the various kinds of occupations on a basis of equal wages. I don't think there is much danger of communism in the Western world: but the enormous production of rubbish (which I believe is the cause of the present trouble, because why should anyone buy rubbish, simply because it is offered for sale?) renders trade insecure: the demand can stop at any moment: and what can the producer do then?—The photo of the 3 kids is charming. But I'm afraid we shouldn't all look so nice if we adopted that costume.

To MRS. C. H. TOY

ROME, MARCH 12, 1932

Dear Mrs. Toy

You said in your last letter that you wished to make Oliver's [1] acquaintance. I am sending you his biography as far as his sixth birthday. The rest, though for the most part written, has not been revised or typed as yet. I have another copy of this part, but perhaps if it isn't too much trouble you might return these sheets when you have done with them, as I might like to show them to some one else. Any hints you can give me—short of burning it all up—will be most appreciated. I feel like a swimmer for the first time beyond his depth. And this part is so feminine—all about ladies and children—whereas most of the book is about young men, that your corrections would be particularly welcome. Of course, there is the whole first part presupposed, concerning the child's parents and their relations: but Oliver begins here: and as you asked for him, it is he that comes to make his bow. Have I put in too much psychology? I think not, when you remember that this is not supposed to be a novel but a memoir, so that description of the characters by the author is legitimate in itself, if it is not tedious or pedantic.

I have had—for me—a little excitement—an invitation to read

1 Oliver Alden, the hero of Santayana's novel *The Last Puritan*.

an address in the Domus Spinozana at the Hague in September, on the occasion of the 300th anniversary of Spinoza's birth. I couldn't refuse, especially as the invitation was couched in German in most flattering terms. It was signed by four persons. Brunschvicg (Paris) Gebhardt (Frankfurt) Oko (Cincinnati) and Carf (The Hague). Do you know who this Oko is? Not Japanese, I suppose. Can he be of Finnish origin? Anyhow, the idea of actually holding forth under the very roof which sheltered Spinoza as he wrote his Ethics, is very stimulating. I have already got my address half written. The subject given me was Philosophy and Religion; but that is a general heading for one whole group of lecturers—the other group being assigned to Physics and Metaphysics: so that I feel free to give my paper a special title—*Ultimate Religion*—and make it an integral part (with a few modifications) of the *Realm of Spirit*,[1] on which I have been doing a little work this winter, as well as on the *Realm of Truth*.

We have had a bad winter and it has given me one or two little jolts, but not serious enough to stop my work. On the contrary, although I have accomplished very little that is visible, I have been very assiduous, and covered reams and reams. But I am afraid the quality is rather mediocre, and perhaps I need a little change to refresh my wits.

I have just read Aldous Huxley's *Brave New World,* on top of Benda's [2] disparaging view of all worlds, old and new. There seems to be a general change of tone, among the modern school, from the optimism of our time. It is not our old pessimism, either, but a sort of horror of mechanism, which I don't feel, perhaps because I have always believed that the universe is mechanical, and that nevertheless the spirit can be, I won't say at home in it, but supported by it.

Yours sincerely

[1] The address was later included in *Obiter Scripta,* a volume of essays, and not in *The Realm of Spirit.*

[2] Julien Benda. See Letter. (Nov. 12, 1931).

TO MRS. C. H. TOY

HOTEL BRISTOL, ROME,
MAY 13, 1932

Dear Mrs. Toy,

Here are two beautiful letters of yours unanswered and unanswerable, because you touch on so many things that it would be beyond my mental agility to say anything apropos of all of them. Thank you for all your pleasant news and many-sided sympathy, and also for the prompt return of Baby Oliver. Before coming to him, let me say that I was rather alarmed to hear that your business man said discouraging things about the future; but I was reassured on reading that you were giving dinner parties and were ready to give more. So far, at least for me, the bark of this crisis has been worse than the bite. My account on Jan. 1st showed a drop of half the nominal value of my property (but made up by the inheritance from my sister Josephine) but the interest had hardly diminished at all, so that, for the moment at least, I am free from all anxiety. But the change of heart in my nephew,[1] and in many Americans that have turned up here, is astonishing. St. John the Baptist would not have to cry today in the wilderness. People are quite ready for repentance and a change of heart.

Your comments on Oliver & Co are none the less pleasant for being (I am well aware) biassed by kindness and tact: but I like to believe that my personages are alive: they are certainly living in my own imagination; so much so that I am a little at a loss to explain or justify them, because it simply is a fact, to my mind, that Irma said this or Mrs. Alden did that or Oliver felt in that way. The characters have grown up of themselves during these forty years (all of them aren't quite so old) and I don't know enough archaeology to account for their composition. When you say that Mrs. Alden is "impossible", I hope you mean that you don't *like* her. I don't *like* her myself: but you don't think she is improbable, do you? To me she seems elemental and rooted in nature like the

---

[1] George Sturgis.

hills: but this may be my illusion, because she may have incongruous sources in my experience. I can mention four or five persons that have sat for the portrait, and there may be more that have left their impress without my knowledge. I will send you later Part 1, in which her household and the circumstances of her marriage are described, chiefly in her own words, and also the whole history of her husband, whom you may not like so much on better acquaintance. It is indeed a great compliment to be told that Irma seems written by "Elizabeth". My experience of Germans is limited, and of novel-writing *nil*, whereas "Elizabeth" is an old hand in both respects. But I did have some thought of combining sympathy with satire in all my snap-shots, as "Elizabeth" does so well. And perhaps this is what makes you feel that at first Irma is "designing and ridiculous" and afterwards "humorous and intelligent". Now, whatever unlucky strokes I may have been guilty of in my sketch, the *real* Irma, I assure you, is *always* intelligent and ridiculous, but *never* designing or humorous. Her naïve and continual desire to find a lover and a husband may be humorous to us: it is the deepest sigh of earnestness in herself. Hopefulness is not intrigue. She never designs, but she is always ready to accept. So too with her position, good food, etc. This being so, I shall be particularly watchful in future revisions for any wrong notes that may have crept in, suggesting that she has any humour of her own, or is designing. She is as good as gold, but a "higher snob" (since you read Soliloquies in England) with a vengeance.

As to Oliver, he will develop very slowly, and not very much. There is no loud or obvious tragedy coming, only a general secret failure in the midst of success. But he is a wonderful noble boy, if only I am able to make the reader see it.

The year 1632 saw the birth of John Locke as well as of Spinoza, and I have been asked to read a paper in London in commemoration of Locke also. Being in for it, and my Spinoza lecture practically finished, I have accepted and expect to go to England in September, by the Hook of Holland–Harwich boat immediately from the Hague. Locke is a terrible come-down after Spinoza; but it is an easier and pleasanter theme. At the Royal Society of Literature (of which I have the honour to be a member, though I have never been at their place, 2 Bloomsbury Square, nor know even the name of any other member) the audience too will be easier and pleasanter to address. They will understand a little philosophic banter: because Locke, like Irma, is intelligent *and* ridiculous. This will be the comedy after the high tragedy of Spinoza.

Among the people who have been here this winter was Robert Herrick, who seemed rather a wreck, as I suppose we all are more or less, and who has now sent me his brother-in-law's translation of Dante.[1] Fletcher was a friend of mine, and a nice person: his preface too is nice: but the translation—! I have read the beginning, and the Francesca episode, and meant to read the Piccarda: but my courage gave out. It gives line for line: but ten English syllables are very much more than eleven Italian ones. The lines have to be horribly padded: and what can a man who is not a poet nor an Italian of the 14th century, nor a Catholic pad his lines with? Only pedestrian circumlocutions. And Dante is so simple, so familiar, so clear! His mind is so entirely on what he has to say! Only an inspired poet could translate him

Yours sincerely

To MRS. WENDELL T. BUSH

HOTEL BRISTOL, ROME
MAY 16, 1932

Dear Mrs. Bush

I hope you may have to return to Rome, and then we can discuss at length these perplexing matters. As to Henry Adams, how could he combine his Ruskinian admiration for "Gothic" things with his sceptical philosophy? As to Couchoud's book,[2] I read it with the greatest interest, devoured it, and felt more *reconstruction* going on in my mind than any book on this subject had ever caused before. I think he must be right *essentially;* I mean, in respect to everything that matters in Christianity. He sees it from the inside, in its true traditional imaginative growth. The New Testament is

---

[1] *The Divine Comedy*, translated by Jefferson Butler Fletcher.

[2] *Jésus, le Dieu fait homme*, by Paul Louis Couchoud.

a miscellaneous collection of Church tales, the sediment of early
Christian tradition. It is not the foundation of any living faith,
and never could be. The figure of Christ is just like that of the
Virgin Mary, a mythological figure. The dramatic, life-like, and
personal notes are just as frequent in St. John as in St. Mark: they
are the product of prolonged, intense, cumulative dramatization.
The Magnificat is no less genuine than the Sermon on the Mount,
which last is evidently not a verbatim report of a real "sermon" but
a disjointed collection of maxims, very like those of Hillel and the
revolutionary late Jews. All this, however, does not militate in my
mind against the existence of a historical Jesus, about whom we
know next to nothing. I believe in general in a dualism between
facts and the ideas of those facts in human heads: and nothing seems
more normal than that a religious Risen Christ should have been
identified with an earthly dead Jesus.

I have put aside the books and will send them—to America?—
if you don't turn up.

Yours sincerely

To HENRY WARD ABBOT

HOTEL BRISTOL ROME
JUNE 7, 1932

Dear Harry

I see that your seventy years leave you still full of vigorous indignation and a proselyting spirit. You won't allow America to re-
pent at leisure and you won't allow me not to be enthusiastic about
Poe. It was no doubt American sin—I mean worldliness, optimism,
and self-satisfaction—that made people disapprove of Poe: even
your "great poet" Edwin Markham seems to apologise for Poe for
not "whooping her up" with the crowd. I never disliked Poe for
that: on the contrary, that was the side that allied him to genuine
poets and brave minds. I remember that Frank Bullard once asked

me whether I preferred Poe's works or Lowell's works for a Christmas present, and seemed to be surprised when I said: Poe's. I felt there was something of the consecrated spirit about him, although very meagrely fed by tradition or learning or experience of the larger world: it was puerile love, puerile sorrow, and puerile love of beauty: yet these things were there; and I have always myself rather liked the *young* view of spiritual life, for being less entangled with shams and false compensations. But I could never stand Poe's versification: and as a prophet of romanticism what could he say to a person who fed, by day and by night, on Shelley and Leopardi and Alfred de Musset? Besides, I am myself romantic only north-north-west: all that grief seems rather an idle private indulgence. It is in steady comprehensive imagination, surveying the real world in its complexity, that the stuff is found for a true elevation of spirit: elevation away from, and against, all that medley, if you like, but raised to a real greatness by that total contrast and renunciation.

I gave Frank Bullard's present away again when I left Harvard: it is probably now making converts to Poe-worship at the Delphic Club: but not within reach of my hand, and, if it were I should probably prove deaf to the call of grace. It is increasingly hard for me to read poetry: I relish it only in snatches; as it comes in Shakespeare's plays, for instance. I have got a big edition of Shakespeare —for years I was without a copy—and am reading the whole through systematically. How wonderful! Yet how horribly impure, occasional, only half-lifted out of some vile plot and some ranting theatrical tradition. The best of it is that entrancing fusion of music in language with passion, colour, and homely saturation of every word in the humours of life. Just what Poe didn't and couldn't, have. But why send me Bliss Carman? Life is too short for that.

Yours sincerely

To MRS. C. H. TOY

VERSAILLES,
JULY 27, 1932

Dear Mrs. Toy

You have no idea with what reluctance I tore myself from my Roman diggings and undertook what now seems a great and troublesome adventure: for I don't know if I have told you that I am to go to England as well as Holland, and to read a paper on Locke before the (Bloomsbury) Royal Society of Literature. It is not only my elderly self that is changed: the good train from Rome to Paris has been taken off; the *rapide* that remains is as quick or quicker, being now largely electric, but the carriages are inferior, the dining-car occasional only, and altogether there is a feeling everywhere that the good old capitalistic days are over, and that the world is going native, that is, common. However, my trip so far has been easy and simple enough. Poor Strong had gone to stay with his daughter, who has just returned from America, for the summer, to her house at Saint Germain: but after a week he found the arrangement impossible and went home to Fiesole. When I arrived in Paris, he was gone. It had more than once occurred to me, in previous years, that Versailles would be a good place to live and work in in summer: and here was I with a free field, two lectures to prepare, and two months to spend somewhere before going to the Hague. So I looked up rooms in the swagger Trianon Palace Hotel: not very attractive; too "first class" for a person who feels old, shabby, and ugly. So I took rooms at this ——— ———, which matches such a battered personage perfectly. It was once an excellent hotel, and retains a certain air of faded gentility: reminds you of the Paris Opera House and the ballets of the Second Empire. I have been alone, or almost alone, in the place, but for the Sunday trippers and an occasional old-fashioned party for lunch; but I am comfortable, have done good work, and am training by walking vigorously. . . . Spinoza is finished and Locke well advanced.

My nephew George Sturgis, and other people who write to me from America, seem to be fundamentally alarmed, shocked, disconcerted by the CRISIS—such is the way my nephew says the word should be written. How wonderful if a first touch of adversity should convert the U. S., not only back to liquor, but back to God! I had once written a squib to that effect, inspired by Maritain (you know who Maritain is: a leading Thomistic Catholic critic) which of course was not to be published: but I am beginning to think that the idea (that Industrialism is diabolical) may have some truth in it. But the world seems to be so confused morally and politically, that one doesn't dare to form any opinion about it. What do you think, or at least feel to be the drift of things?

Yours sincerely

To MRS. C. H. TOY

7 PARK PLACE, ST. JAMES'S,
LONDON. SEPT. 23, 1932

Dear Mrs. Toy

You find me—or rather I find myself—once more in England after nine years' absence, and with strangely little emotion, pleasurable or otherwise. London is very much as it always was: a few Babylonian white buildings, and a little more motor traffic, is all that distinguishes it materially from what it was, even forty or fifty years ago. Morally and socially no doubt there has been a revolution; but I never knew London society, and now I don't know a single Londoner; so that I am not much troubled by the change. I mean, I don't know a single Londoner of those I see in the street: I might perhaps hunt up one or two old acquaintances; but I am little tempted to do so; I am sufficiently occupied with finishing my Locke lecture, reading various things that turn up, and walking in Hyde Park, which seems greener and grander than ever.

Your insistence on the designing nature of my poor Irma has given me a subject for many a nightly meditation: and while I know by creative intuition that she was *not* designing, I see very

well why she seems to be so in my unintentionally unfair account
of her little flirtation. Of course she was loving, sentimental, thirsting for romantic adventures; and my constitutional tendency to
be a little satirical made me dwell perhaps too openly on these
latent qualities in my little lady. You must remember that it is *I*
that tell the story of her affair with Oliver's young uncle; whereas
it is *she* that writes to her sister about the other matters: naturally
she doesn't bring out the absurd side of her character as much as
I do. However, you have convinced me that the scene in the tower
must be changed and elaborated, so as to show her psychology
(which I have clearly in my mind) less ambiguously and unsym-
pathetically. I am going to have her recite *"zum sehen geboren, zum
schauen bestellt"* (if that is correct: I am quoting from memory) and
actually lean, in her enthusiasm, rather too far out of the turret,
so that her cavalier is impelled chivalrously to snatch her from a
horrid death; and then a real dizziness and half faintness can very
naturally ensue—wholly unpremeditated, but not wholly unde-
sired. Will that do to restore the harmonious *honourable* sentimentality of my Fraulein?

   The *Domus Spinozana* at The Hague is very pleasing, with
an open door from the large room, occupying the whole ground
floor, into a small garden, and upstairs, under the sloping rafters
of the roof, the nook where the philosopher slept and died. They
have collected a few books and MS. belonging to him, but the
furniture is *rapportée*. The meetings were like all meetings and
international conferences, rather tiresome and futile. My own lecture was kindly received and apparently rather well understood
by the polyglot audience; and my eloquence transported at least
one, and the most distinguished, of my audience, Sir Frederick
Pollock, aged 92, into Nirvana, for (it being after dinner) he slept
peacefully through the whole. Prof. Edman of Columbia was my
only friend there: but I weathered the occasion, and the night
crossing from the Hook of Holland, better than might have been
expected.

Yours sincerely

To MRS. WENDELL T. BUSH

HOTEL BRISTOL, ROME
DEC. 16, 1932

Dear Mrs. Bush

Thank you very much for your good Christmas wishes, which I reciprocate, and also for your address, which has enabled me to send off this morning three books of yours which I ought to have returned long ago. The Couchoud [1] has made a great impression on me, and I have sent for others of the same series, to see what backing his views may really seem to have. I believe he is right in his religious psychology, that Christianity is an eschatological prophecy, not a personal morality corrupted into a theological system; but I am doubtful about the historical mixture of tradition, legend, & myth. Were it not that today being my 69th birthday, I have made a good resolution to write no more articles and give no more lectures, at least until all my projected work is done, I might be tempted to write something on Couchoud & Co: but I must abstain.

I myself have not seen the *Septimana Spinozana,* as the Hague volume is to be called. I have been waiting to receive a complimentary copy; but that may not enter into the Dutch way of doing business, so that now I have written ordering one: and heaven knows when I shall be allowed to reprint my article. The idea of publishing it together with the one on Locke has fallen through: on the other hand, the Royal Society of Literature (for whom the Locke was written) have been very kind and appreciative, and have asked for other papers of mine to join with it in a volume to appear under their auspices. I have fished out the best of what I had intended for "Symptoms"; the rest of "Symptoms" can be neglected; and in this way one item in my literary programme is actually executed without any further labour! I feel a great relief: but I am sorry to see the Spinoza floating hopelessly down stream, out of my range, in the international Noah's Ark of the *Septimana*

[1] See *Letter.* [May 16, 1932]

Spinozana. And yet, who knows: perhaps that Ark alone may survive the Deluge.

I am at work for the moment on the novel, with much amusement to myself, but little hope: it is too difficult and too complicated. When I tire of it, I shall take up The Realm of Truth, which ought to be soon brought to the boiling point.

Are you coming to Europe this winter or Spring?

Yours sincerely

To *LOGAN PEARSALL SMITH*

HOTEL BRISTOL, ROME
APRIL 12, 1933

Dear Smith

The end of your book on reading Shakespeare has set my mind going furiously and before the ferment dies down, I must send a wave radiating in your direction, by way of thanks. But first, putting all civility aside as unworthy of the occasion, let me confess that I don't like or agree with everything you say: you seem to me to over-disparage and to over-praise Shakespeare, and to talk of mysteries and problems where they don't exist. Of course no author, no child, no earthquake can be fully explained by general "laws", and an element of happy or unhappy chance, or conjunction of accidental circumstances, mingles with everything that we do or say. Shakespeare happened to have a great fluid imagination and an enormous eloquence or gift of storing and mating and pouring out words. These natural powers—which many a man has here and there—happened in his case to be set free, fed, and loosened by the circumstances of the age and by his special craft as an actor and playwright. Most other poets have been held down by tradition or religion or lack of opportunity to a single mode of expression, to one literary key. They were not allowed to mix poetry with prose, tragedy with comedy, love-making with politics, or edification with atheism. The top wave of the renaissance allowed Shakespeare to combine all these elements: and the wealth of Christendom and of paganism were at his disposal, without the restraints or limitations of either. Nevertheless his medium did limit him somewhat: he might have run over otherwise into the preserves of Rabelais, Cervantes, or Pietro Aretino. *Exuberance* seems to me to cover everything, the wealth of genius as well as the contempt for art; and in particular it covers the irrelevant elaboration of language and of characters which, to us, is one of Shakespeare's chief charms: those glimpses that he stops to give us of the back-waters and eddies and weeds of the stream of passion. He challenged and perhaps annoyed his public by doing so; but he just *could* manage it without being dismissed as a closet-tragedian; and these escapades of his imagination into the by-conscious now seem to us a proof of miraculous depth in him. I don't think they are that: but they are proofs of his knowingness and quick intuition. And this brings me back to your conclusion about his philosophy—that life is a dream. Yes, that is his philosophy: and when T. S. Eliot says that this philosophy (borrowed he thinks from Seneca) is an inferior one, compared with Dante's, I agree if you mean inferior morally and imaginatively: but it happens to be the true philosophy for the human passions, and for a man enduring, without supernaturally interpreting, the spectacle of the universe. It is a commonplace philosophy, the old old heathen philosophy of mankind. Shakespeare didn't create it. He felt it was true, and never thought of transcending it.

Yours sincerely

To THE MARCHESA IRIS ORIGO

[I am grateful to the Marchesa Origo for granting me permission to include the following passages from a remarkable letter she received on the sad occasion of the death of her little boy. As she says, "it reveals a side of Mr. Santayana's nature which was not often shown."]

[WRITTEN IN MAY 1933]

. . . . . . We have no claim to any of our possessions. We have no claim to exist; and as we have to die in the end, so we must resign ourselves to die piecemeal, which really happens when we lose somebody or something that was closely intertwined with our existence. It is like a physical wound; we may survive, but maimed and broken in that direction; dead there.

Not that we ever can, or ever do at heart, renounce our affections. Never that. We cannot exercise our full nature all at once in every direction; but the parts that are relatively in abeyance, their centre lying perhaps in the past or in the future, belong to us inalienably. We should not be ourselves if we cancelled them. I don't know how literally you may believe in another world, or whether the idea means very much to you. As you know, I am not myself a believer in the ordinary sense, yet my *feeling* on this subject is like that of believers, and not at all like that of my fellow-materialists. The reason is that I disagree utterly with that modern philosophy which regards *experience* as fundamental. Experience is a mere whiff or rumble, produced by enormously complex and ill-deciphered causes of experience; and in the other direction, experience is a mere peephole through which glimpses come down to us of eternal things. These are the only things that, in so far as we are spiritual beings, we can find or can love at all. All our affections, when clear and pure, and not claims to possession, transport us to another world; and the loss of contact, here or there, with those eternal beings is merely like closing a book which we keep at hand for another occasion. We know that book by heart. Its verses give life to life.

I don't mean that these abstract considerations ought to console us. Why wish to be consoled? On the contrary, I wish to mourn perpetually the absence of what I love or might love. Isn't that what religious people call the love of God?

To WILLIAM LYON PHELPS

CORTINA D'AMPEZZO
JULY 10, 1933

Dear Billy

Not Erasmus, Spinoza! But even that is not accurate. I went last September to the Hague, where they had a meeting in honour of the tercentenary of Spinoza's birth, and I read a paper which is only attached to Spinoza by way of the zenith: for, mind you, though physically every zenith is at a hopelessly different point from every other, spiritually the nearer anyone gets to his own zenith, the nearer he is to everybody else's. This paper is to appear in a polyglot volume entitled *Septimana Spinozana* which was to have been issued last November, but is still delayed. Perhaps it will appear by November next.

As I approach 70 (December next the venerable number will be completed) I feel that I may abandon the future more and more to Providence. I go on working, but without being at all confident that it will be possible, or would be best, for me to accomplish anything special. At present, I am crawlingly proceeding with my "novel": this is something nobody else could do, since it gives the *emotions* of my experiences, and not my thoughts or experiences themselves: whereas *The Realm of Truth* or *The Realm of Spirit* might perfectly well be described by some future writer better than I should do it. However, I am very well, and not worried by the crisis or the collapse of the dollar: it makes me much poorer on paper, but I had a broad margin to my budget, and as yet have no need of changing my way of living; and it is not impossible, if I should live ten years more, that I might finish my whole programme.

This place—where I have spent three previous summers—is really delightful: warm enough in the sun to make the system exude its waste substances, and cool enough at night to kill all mosquitoes and even flies. Besides the Dolomites are highly picturesque, the peasants also, and the people at this hotel very tolerable—since I don't have to speak to them. The trouble is that on

September 1st winter sets in, and I shall have to move to Venice or elsewhere until it is time to return to my Roman diggings.

Well: You at Great Yale are probably carried sky-high on the crest of twenty enthusiasms at least. Don't break your neck, and God bless you! Kindest regards—Come again to Rome: it is improving yearly more than if it were in America. You will be astonished.

Yours ever

To "A. E." (GEORGE WM. RUSSELL)

[I am indebted to Mr. Alan Denson, a young friend of Santayana, for having traced the following letter, and supplied me with a copy.]

SEPTEMBER 22, 1933

Dear Mr. Russell,

It is interesting to know that you have noticed the quotation from your poem "The Virgin Mother", in my *Realm of Matter*.[1] The devil notoriously quotes scripture for his own purposes, and you must forgive me if I used your words to point a moral which (as I now see) was not the one you intended. The immanence of "love" or potential "beauty" in the material world is, in one sense, a truism. When anything arises or happens we may say that there was a "mysterious" *tendency* in the conditions to produce just that

---

[1] In the Preface to *The Realm of Matter,* Santayana quoted the following lovely stanzas from "A.E.":

> "Who is that goddess to whom men should pray,
> But her from whom their hearts have turned away,
> Out of whose virgin being they were born,
> Whose mother-nature they have named with scorn,
> Calling her holy substance common clay. . . .
>
> Ah, when I think this earth on which I tread
> Hath borne these blossoms of the lovely dead,
> And makes the living heart I love to beat,
> I look with sudden awe beneath my feet—
> As you with erring reverence overhead."

thing. The God of Platonism and Christianity is simply a hypostasis of this tendency in nature towards the good, and is perhaps less "external" than we may think: if the tendency is a distinct power working in things, it is a part of nature. Perhaps this was exactly what you meant by saying that we should reverence earth and not heaven: the real motive force towards the beautiful is inside the world and not beyond.

The centre of my own interest is at a somewhat different point. I don't know, and I don't much care what the existing motive force is that makes for the beautiful: in any case it is very imperfectly successful. What I care for is the beautiful itself and the vision of the beautiful, in so far as they manage to exist, or to be suggested: and this frail, intermittent, but actual realization of the beautiful I call the spiritual sphere. All life is, intrinsically, a part of it; but horribly interrupted and perturbed.

Yours sincerely,

To STERLING P. LAMPRECHT

ROME, NOV. 15, 1933

Dear Mr. Lamprecht

Thank you very much for sending me your article,[1] and even more for troubling your head so much about my lucubrations. If you took them more lightly perhaps you would find them less aggravating; I don't mean that they haven't any serious intention, but that their serious intention would be intercepted if the form were not explicitly *poetical,* I mean, explicitly subject to the human perspective which nature has imposed on us, whether we accept it or not. A part of this poetic or human mist is the irony and the moral pathos without which any human consideration of such large issues would, I think, be pedantic.

[1] "Naturalism and Agnosticism in Santayana". *Journal of Philosophy,* Vol. XXX, No. 21. April 12, 1933.

For instance, the whole *Life of Reason* (as I explain in the Preface to the second edition) was written with an eye to describing experience, not the cosmos. It was inspired partly by Greek ethics and partly by modern psychology and critical philosophy. When I say that the ideas of sense are the true particulars, I mean, not in the universe, but in the mind only: and the cosmos (i.e. the *idea* of the cosmos) is a construction out of these, and in that sense a "fiction". But I never meant that this mental fiction had no physical object, which it described in human terms. I assumed that it had; and this you observe yourself, quite fairly. But you are also right in feeling that I was rather carried away, at that time, by a kind of humanism and like to degrade, or exalt, all things into the human notions of them, and the part they played, as counters, in the game of thought. It was a modern attitude which I hope I have outgrown —"*Schlecht und modern*", as Goethe says, or Mephistopheles.

So in the *Dialogues in Limbo,* you must allow me a little dramatic latitude. "Normal madness" is satirical: * it is a joke; but Democritus was the laughing philosopher. Moreover, my position is that of *The Stranger,* which Democritus disowns. (See pp. 84–88. Also in the *Realm of Matter,* the Preface and the passage against "Egyptian atoms"). Democritus, having thought he discovered "Reality", thought he must worship it. I am in that respect a disciple of his enemy Socrates, and worship only the beautiful and the good.

It would be useless for me to try to explain myself about naturalism vs. Scepticism: I should be only repeating what seem to you my ambiguities. But I will say one thing. By "given" I don't mean extant or met with, but possessed within the synthesis of apperception. Tables and chairs are not "given"; they are posited by animal faith. I am afraid this use of words was unfortunate and contrary to the inveterate practice of people nowadays. Perhaps you might catch my position if you asked yourself whether the minds of others (mine, for instance) were "given" to you or not. They are given dramatically to your social imagination, to your practical trust: but the *actual datum* in your own mind that *names* them is only an essence given to you as in a dream and probably not exemplified again in their innocent persons.

Yours sincerely

* I might have said "normal inspiration", = animal faith. [in text]

To MR. AND MRS. WENDELL T. BUSH

HOTEL BRISTOL, ROME
DEC. 16, 1933

Dear Mr. Bush and Mrs. Bush

Your very kind cablegram arrived punctually this morning and was almost the only exceptional event to mark the bitter sweet occasion of having fulfilled the days allotted to man. By reason of strength, or of equilibrium, we may all hope to reach fourscore, and not leave anything undone that we ought to have done.

In her recent very nice letter anent the little Locke book, Mrs. Bush said you, Mr. Bush, were not very well. I hope you are all right again. I wish I could have sent you my Spinoza lecture as well as the Locke, but the big book is too expensive for these days, and they have redistributed the type, so that no off-prints are available. However, the Dutch publisher is willing that after a year or two I should republish my paper in a book; and I may have two other essays concerning religion written by that time, to make up a volume, which you shall duly receive. I have two theological bees in my bonnet: one the perplexities of New Testament criticism, reawakened in my mind by the book of Couchoud [1] that Mrs. Bush lent me; and the other Bergson's remarkable (and unforseen) completion of his system, with almost a conversion to Catholicism! I suppose you have read his "Les deux Sources de la Religion et de la Morale". I don't agree with him any more than formerly, but now I *like* him better. I see him not as a shy German idealist and benighted vitalist, but as an isolated mystical intuitive mind, taking infinite pains to cut a good figure in the academic world and before the modern public, but secretly vowed to a private revelation. It is most interesting, pathetic, and worthy of admiration for his constancy & astuteness, and for the difficulty of the task accomplished. I have also read Loisy's criticism, with which I agree, except that his own position—a sort of Comtian positivism—seems prosaic and inadequate. Besides, I have gone over T. S. Eliot's Harvard lectures [2]—disappointing and ill-planned, but with some good things in them.

[1] *Jésus, le Dieu fait homme.*

[2] *The Use of Poetry and the Use of Criticism.*

I am waiting for the yearly account of my money-matters to see whether I can continue to live here. If not, I meditate moving to the Riviera, where it would be possible to stay all the year round and gather all my books once more about me. Many are at Strong's, and some at his daughter's house in Saint Germain. Strong, by the way, is very hard hit by the crisis—much worse than I—and is "taking boarders", though as yet only his two grandchildren and their nurses.

With best wishes for the New Years, always sincerely yours

To C. J. DUCASSE

ROME, APRIL 8, 1934

Dear Mr. Ducasse:

Your paper on "The attributes of material things" gives me the greatest pleasure, and I admire the clearness and simplicity with which you mark the right path through the labyrinth.

There remains an ambiguity, I think, about space and time, and you acknowledge it. The properties of a portion of *physical* space and time constitute a physical substance; but pictorial space and sentimental time have no properties, only qualities. They are essences.

I feel that there remains a difficulty also in regard to the "psychological" reality of given qualities. Nausea and green no doubt cannot occur except in feeling or (what I regard as the same thing) to intuition; but "four" can occur in the legs of a chair as well as in the mind of a man counting them. So that I think you can't stop at a psychological existent, but must end with an essence. Besides, the relation of the quality intuited to the intuition is not that of a predicate to a subject, but that of a "content" to a feeling. The feeling is not green. Yet we say the feeling is nausea; because here we are far more aware of the experience, or disturbance of life within us, than of the object, which is too fluid and unclassified to be easily named. So with pain. The quantity rather than the quality, the coming and going, rather than the "content," interest and absorb us; and therefore we name the intuition, the active feeling, and not that which it reveals.

No doubt you have convincing things to say on these points also; and I hope very much you will make a book of these articles, because otherwise they might not have the great and decisive influence which they deserve to have.

Yours sincerely,

To TWO BRYN MAWR STUDENTS
(in reply to a letter of inquiry from them)

ROME, DEC. 11, 1934

My dear Miss Jane & Miss Sylvia,

What? You don't understand "Materialism & Idealism in American Life"? [1] But it was written especially for a Young Ladies College—Bedford College in Regent's Park—and if not all in words of one syllable is surely all on one soft, sweet, clear, crystalline note. I know: because in order to determine what I may have meant by "moral freedom", I have had to re-read the lecture. You might at least have mentioned the page on which the peccant phrase was to be found: but I had to read almost the whole, since those words never appeared until next to the last page. You find "moral freedom" obscure, but you know perfectly well what "spiritual freedom" is: if I only had written "spiritual freedom", I should have saved you a lot of trouble. I am sorry: and by way of apology I will tell you what I gather from the context that I must have meant to say. Moral freedom is opposed to moral prejudice or constraint: it is the faculty of expressing in feeling and action the judgements of value which are prompted by your true nature, and not by custom or convention. A man is morally free when, in full possession

[1] Chap. VI of *Character and Opinion in the United States.*

of his living humanity, he judges the world, and judges other men, with uncompromising sincerity. Spiritual freedom, although you know better than I what it means, might perhaps be distinguished from moral freedom in this way: that a free *spirit* is something in a man that judges his own nature and his own impassioned judgements, and perceives their relativity. This perception does not contradict those moral judgements: it is not a rival conscience: it is rather a super-moral speculative or mystical insight that sees the human pathos in those feelings, and somehow transcends them.

Yours sincerely

To F. CHAMPION WARD

ROME, DEC. 14, 1934

Dear Mr. Ward

Your eulogy of me reads like an old-fashioned epitaph: strictly true to the facts but with no pretense to impartiality. It is very well expressed; and I am sending it to another friend who at this moment is writing an article about me, in case he should like to steal some of your thunder for his peroration. Would you mind?

As to the "subsistence" of essence, have I ever said that it subsists? If so, it was inadvertently. That is rather the neo-realists' word. In my vocabulary, if anything could be said to "subsist," or be an essence with a lien on existence and a certain obduracy against contradiction, it would be TRUTH. The compulsion that the triangle exercises on us in forcing us to admit that it has three angles, equal in all to two right angles, etc, is due to the definition and to the essence of Euclidean space, in which that triangle is inscribed. But this whole geometry would be an UNEXEMPLIFIED essence, and would not "subsist," if nature and experience had not led us to perceive and to study objects in which that essence is found, so that it is a part of the TRUTH about them.

Yours sincerely

To *SYLVIA H. BLISS*

ROME, JANUARY 19, 1935

My dear Miss Bliss

I should have thanked you sooner for "Sea Level" if I hadn't followed your injunction to read it by bits; after which I have reread it more or less as a whole, in search of your *philosophy*. You must have felt that I should sympathize with this, else you wouldn't have thought of sending me the book. Your perfect freedom from religious or mock-religious presumptions—and also from hostility to religion—your clear view of truth, and your sound naturalism do appeal to me very much. I have always felt, what you express in regard to trees especially, that our relation to the rest of nature is fraternal, and that the possession of consciousness or (if we possess it) of reason doesn't justify us in regarding plants, animals, or stars as unreal, or as made for our express benefit. And the sea, though you speak little of it, has always been a great object lesson to me, a monitor of the fundamental flux, of the loom of nature not being on the human scale. So far, if I don't misrepresent you, we agree. But I am ill conditioned to appreciate your knowledge and love of flowers and of the countryside generally; and I have been so immersed all my life in religious speculation, in literature, in history, and in travel; I have lived so exclusively in towns and universities, and amid political revolutions and wars, that your simple idyllic world, and your intense individualism, leave me rather with a sense of emptiness. And haven't you that sensation yourself? I don't know what trials you may have had to endure or what misfortunes; your individualism is wholly philosophical, it touches the ego in its transcendental capacity, and you tell us nothing of your own person; but your tone in speaking of death, of cities, and of the mediation of other minds between you and nature, seems to me overcharged with distaste and melancholy. Aren't men also a part of nature? And if we could really penetrate into the life of matter, shouldn't we find it everywhere essentially as wasteful, groping, and selftormented as is the life of mankind? And on this fundamental irrationality, human society builds so many charming things—music, for one, which you appreciate—but also material and moral splendours of every description. The refraction of truth in human philosophies, for instance, is no mere scandal: it composes a work of human art, and partakes of the force both of truth and of imagination. It seems to me a pity, therefore, to leave it out of one's field of interest.

Let me add that I appreciate the level dignity of your style and diction. You are doubtless aware that you often lapse into blank verse, and that, if you chose, you could print your book in that form with very little alteration. You have preferred a more modern arrangement, doubtless for good reasons; but you will deceive nobody into mistaking you for a real modern, like Mr. Ezra Pound, for instance, whose *Quia Pauper Amarvi* I had been reading immediately before receiving your book. But though your restrained voice may not attract attention so scandalously, I am sure that you will give more pleasure to those who do hear you, and will be more gratefully remembered.

Yours sincerely

To F. CHAMPION WARD

ROME, JAN. 26, 1935

Dear Mr. Ward,

Thank you for your letter and your first installment of my "life." Both require some reply: first, about this matter of "subsistence." You speak of the status of an essence "between" its exemplifications: but non-existents have no position: they have only eternal affinities: so that there is no distance, essentially, "between" one exemplification of an essence and another. What intervenes is the flux of existence in which, by hypothesis, that essence is absent. So that I should distinctly refuse to speak of it as "subsisting" during that interval.

Your account of my *vida y milagros* (as we say in Spanish)

is so largely composed of quotations from my own confessions that I can only admire your tact in selecting them, and particularly in using old verses to clarify later events. I haven't evolved, except as I was involved: and almost the only point at which you seem to misrepresent a little the truth of my history is in saying that I was "converted" to naturalism. No: it was not a conversion, but a decision. Both views had always been before me: I had hesitated or oscillated: but gradually it became impossible for me steadily to hold the Catholic position: the history and psychology of it, in the other picture, shone through; as if, through a too-thin back-drop at the theatre, I had seen the ropes and scaffolding of the stage, the scene-shifters hurrying about in their shirtsleeves, and the prima donna in her green-room, putting on the rouge. Still, though my judgement has hardened in maturity, I have by no means lost my taste for religious drama. Only yesterday I finished a lovely German book by Adolph Erman on Egyptian religion, laying it down with regret that I hadn't the learning requisite to write (entirely differently) on the same subject: because the author has no imagination, no religious feeling, and misses the immense persuasiveness and the immense tragedy of his subject.

A minor matter on which your emphasis is perhaps a little excessive is in my isolation in America. I was lieutenant colonel of the Boston Latin School regiment, I acted in the Institute and Hasty Pudding plays at Harvard, dressed as a leading lady and a ballet dancer, I was devoted (as a spectator) to football, and had for years, after I was an instructor, many close friends among the undergraduates. I also went a good deal into what was called "Boston society." So that my solitude (which was real) was only latent: I had a great many pleasant relations with the world: and, I ought to add, was always very fond of travel, and of life in cafes and restaurants, which I still frequent, as well as public gardens, with the nurses and children, and the military bands. You will discover this side of me more clearly when my novel appears, which is now finished, but may not be published at once for various reasons.

Another point. In my novel there is hardly a word about Spain: but if I ever write the autobiography I have in mind, Spain will come into its own in my life. It has always been a fundamental fact. That I have always retained my legal Spanish nationality has not been an accident or an affectation: it has been a symbol of the truth. Until the recent death of my sisters (who had returned to Spain)

I went almost every year to Avila, living *en famille* there. It was only officially, on my literary side, that Spain counted for little.

I mention these points because I think your account of me will be so sympathetic and penetrating that I want you not to miss any important fact.

Yours sincerely

To GEORGE STURGIS

HOTEL BRISTOL, ROME
FEB. 18TH 1935

Dear George

Yours of the 8th has just arrived, and I interrupt my revision of the novel at p. 400, (about half-way) to reply at once. I had rather expected to go to Paris this year, but one of my objects was to see Cory and get his opinion about some verbal matters in *The Last Puritan* about which my own judgement wavers. But he says he would rather come at once to Rome, and I am expecting him this week. That will make it unnecessary (as far as the novel is concerned) that I should make that journey: and I know no tempting place in or near Paris in which I could be comfortably settled for the summer. Even the old hotel I was at in Versailles is now shut up, so that I shall probably go to Venice and Cortina. However, nothing is settled; and if you can recommend some charming spot in or near Paris—or anywhere else—where I could have quiet and coolness and pleasant walks, I should be only too glad to go and meet you there. . . .

One effect of old age is that days and weeks seem to pass more quickly: there is hardly time to do anything, and evening and Sunday come round when you thought it was Wednesday or the early afternoon. I suppose the *tempo* of one's own blood-vessels, or whatever keeps time within us, has grown slower, and we glide over events as if they were nothing capable of leaving a mark be-

cause our brains are too soft to retain new impressions. It's not
at all an unpleasant condition, though a bit ignominious, like all
decay. A Mr. Keene, 79 years old, came to see me yesterday and
told stories by rote. He said he enjoyed his visit, and I believe him.
But he knows that I won't return it.

Yours aff^ly

To CORLISS LAMONT

ROME, MARCH 5, 1935

Dear Mr. Lamont:

Thank you very much for your book [1] and your letter. As far
as your argument is concerned, you know that you are preaching
to the converted. The subject of immortality, has long ceased to
be a living issue with me; and though I know that some people are
agonized about it, I am confirmed in my old impression that this
is a verbal or mythical obsession of the human mind, rather than
a literal belief. Everything, in myth and religion, must be understood with a difference, in a Pickwickian sense, if we are to understand it truly, and not to import an unnatural fanaticism into the
play of poetic fancy.

I have been particularly struck by your quotation from Key-
ser, on p.129. I suppose he has got this from Heidegger whom you
don't mention, but who, as you doubtless know, has made a great
deal of this notion of death as the totality of life, or as I should say,
as the *truth* of life, which is something eternal. With this insight
on the one hand, and the insight that life is movement, on the
other hand, I think a rather new and profound analysis might be
made of the notion of immortality. Orthodox heavens are peaceful: souls are not supposed to change and pass through new risks
and adventures: they merely possess, as in Dante, the truth of their
earthly careers and of their religious attainment. In other words,

[1] *The Illusion of Immortality.*

souls in heaven are mythical impersonations of the truth, or totality of those persons' earthly life. At the same time, this life and anything truly living, is something dramatic, groping, planning, excited, and exciting. It is dangerous; and Nietzsche needn't have told us to live perilously; it would have been enough to tell us *to live*. Put these two points together and you have a demonstration of the necessary transitiveness and finitude of any real life.

On hearing that you belonged to the Delphic Club, I took the catalogue of 1932, which I happen to have here, to see what class you were in, and incidentally I glanced over the early lists of names more familiar to me. Those are very pleasant memories: and they illustrate our philosophy of life: because it is what those young men were then, in the flush of youth, that is worth returning to and congratulating oneself upon, and seldom, perhaps never in the end, the later transformations which they may have undergone.

Yours sincerely

To GEORGE STURGIS

HOTEL BRISTOL, ROME
MAY 8, 1935

Dear George

My plans are still somewhat uncertain, but probably I shall go straight to Cortina about June 1st. The war-rumours seem to have died down, and perhaps it is reasonable to believe the Germans will not attack anybody until there is a good prospect of doing so with safety. Events in Austria or Russia or Poland, however, might at any moment precipitate a conflict: only that things will be so mixed that even if the armies held out (which is doubtful) the governments themselves would hardly have the constancy which they showed—most of them—in 1914–18. Anyhow, I am acting as if all would remain normal; and probably we should have timely warning before the Germans could get at us in Italy.

Cory has gone back to England, and the novel is being printed by Constable, who seems to have been favourably impressed by it. I am going to send the proofs, when they arrive, to New York, so that Scribner may reprint the book there, and secure the American copyright.

President Conant of Harvard, and the Tercentenary committee, have been writing to me in a somewhat queer way. First they asked me to come to Commencement *this* year, and get a degree of *Doctor of Letters*. (I mean, Litt.D. not Ll.D.) When I declined this honour, which I got 24 years ago from the U. of Wisconsin, they wrote asking me to come *next* year, read an essay at the Summer School, and get a degree, not Specified, together with 60 other distinguished Scholars—no politicians or even Presidents of Colleges being in the list. I have a feeling that they wanted to get me out of the way as inconspicuously as possible, without actually overlooking me altogether. But in any case, I should have declined, partly because I don't want to go to America at all, much less to an Academic congress, and partly because when my novel comes out there may be more or less offence taken at it, and it is better that nobody should be placed in the embarrassing position of countenancing naughtiness. All novels are naughtier now than they used to be: but how shocking that an ex-professor of philosophy at Harvard should write a novel at all, and call a spade a spade! At least they won't be seeing me, and finding they have unwittingly given me an honorary degree—almost of Divinity—at the very moment when I was unmasking my essential wickedness. With 3000 miles of salt water between us, I shall feel safer and less hypocritical.

I am afraid I shan't see you this time: but let me know if you really feel like flying to Venice about June 1st and I could stop there for a day or two on the way to Cortina.

Yours aff^{ly}

To MRS. WENDELL T. BUSH

HOTEL SAVOIA, CORTINA
JULY 5, 1935

Dear Mrs. Bush

You are right, you see, in supposing that, rather helplessly, I have come again to Cortina, but not to the Miramonti, partly because I didn't like the room they offered me, and partly because from the town I can vary the direction and length of my walks better than from that outlying starting-point. I was a bit tired of walking daily to the village and back, and also of the crowd of people. Here I am more as in a town, that is, more in my element.

I am reading Alain's *Les Dieux,* the most *obscure* French book I ever have come upon, ragged and perverse in places, but also full of wonderful insights. Besides, apart from his vulgar politics, I agree with him, and am encouraged to find so penetrating and spontaneous a thinker taking precisely my view of "Spirit". He says: "L'attribut de puissance, délégué à l'esprit pur dans une sorte d'emportement, doit être pris comme la partie honteuse de la religion de l'esprit". I must quote this in my book, *The Realm of Spirit,* which I am working on at present, being in the mood for it, although *The Realm of Truth* should be published first. But my mind isn't entirely clear for sheer philosophy, as the second proofs of the novel are about to reach me, and I shall have to go over those 723 pages once more. We are having some qualms about the hotels and inns (also personages) mentioned, all real ones, and the possible law-suits that the proprietors might bring for defaming them or their establishments: but I am careful to kill or remove all the persons, and not to say anything not flattering about the houses; so that I hope to escape prosecution. My weakness for real spots and their atmosphere makes me hate to give false names to places, or even to persons, when the true name is not positively out of the question. I hope people won't think it is impertinence: it is genuine love of truth.

If you don't feel up to going to Paris—which will be on your way home—I can hardly hope to see you here this year, or in

Venice—where there is, by the way, a Titian exhibition open. I expect to be at Danieli's in September and part of October, until I venture to return to Rome.

I hope Mr. Bush will find his cure efficacious, and that your summer will be otherwise pleasant for both of you.

Yours sincerely

To GEORGE STURGIS

VENICE, OCT. 3, 1935

Dear George

If you are as innocent as I am about the ways of the book-trade, you will be surprised to hear that between 35,000 and 40,000 copies of my novel have been sold before the book has appeared.

There seems to be a thing called the Book-of-the-Month Club, that performs this miracle every thirty days for one author or another. Not really so flattering, therefore, that *The Last Puritan* should have been one of the twelve (and not less than twelve) new books that *must* sell about 40,000 copies every year; but it is pleasant to get $5000 at once for the book; Scribner gets another $5,000; and there is likely to be a sale outside the circle of subscribers to the Book-of-the-Month; so that we are to be congratulated, so far, on the success of the book. But you must remember that the twelve apostles were chosen by Christ himself, and one of them was Judas; and though he got thirty pieces of silver, according to contract, it didn't do his reputation much good with posterity.

You may also wonder, as I did, how the committee of this club could choose my book before it was out: but the practice of publishers nowadays seems to be to send advanced proofs to the critics, so that reviews and notices may appear at the time of the publication, and my novel was in print (full of *errata*) in June last, when I read the first proofs here in Venice: and the New York critics received advanced copies at the same time. Hence these tears, or rather these smiles and these shekels.

The $5,000 haven't been paid yet, and I should be much obliged if you would send $1,000 again to Brown Shipley & Co. for my account. This will probably be the last extra draft that I shall have to ask for for some time, if the novel lives up to its present promises. By the way, it is not to appear in America before December or January, and they are going to reprint it. The English edition appears this month. I will send you a copy.

Yours aff^ly

To ELLEN SHAW BARLOW

HOTEL BRISTOL, ROME
OCTOBER 19, 1935

Dear "Cousin Nellie"

It was most kind of you to send me this message, which takes me back to the pleasantly foolish days when Bob [1] was a very young man and I thought myself only a little older. It is now 23 years since I left America and I have lost the thread of most of those affectionate friendships which I had there. I console myself with thinking that life would have divided us in any case in all that really matters, and that perhaps a complete break helps to preserve the memory of one's halcyon days purer than if it had been confused by gradual drifting apart or material impediments.

I don't know what I may have said that misrepresented my mother's relations with the Sturgis family. I am sure she had a real "culte" for them, especially for your mother and for "Uncle Russell" and "Uncle Robert". Their characters, their persons, and their way of living were what she thought absolutely right and superior to anything else to be found elsewhere. She especially despised, in comparison, Spanish ways and Spanish ideas. That is why I have never been able to make out why she ever married my father. But there were probably strands in her character and ex-

---

[1] The son of Ellen Shaw Barlow.

perience which I had no notion of, having known her only in her old age, when she was very silent and led a retired resigned and monotonous life. Family history, and even one's own past, are hard to decipher unless you have documents to go by. It is like deciphering the Roman Forum. There are the stones, perfectly plain; but they belong to different strata and it is impossible to piece anything out of them that shall correspond to what existed at any one time. The reason you say my mother gave for Susie's [1] not staying in the convent—that Susie liked meat and not vegetables— is most characteristic of my mother. She believed in dialectical materialism before anyone had heard of Karl Marx. And if we take that saying symbolically, I think it was most true, because religion with Susie was a social passion, not a spiritual one, and in her enthusiasms there wasn't very much peace. She was certainly not made to be a nun; but she was driven to make that experiment by dissatisfaction with her surroundings after the fun of first youth was gone.

I am writing separately to Bob, and will add nothing here, except to say "thank you" again for your kind letter.

Yours sincerely

To ROBERT SHAW BARLOW

HOTEL BRISTOL, ROME
OCTOBER 19, 1935

Dear Bob

It is indeed a pleasant surprise to hear from you and even more from your mother. I didn't even know that you were living together in Boston, my news of the family history, in spite of a constant correspondence with George Sturgis, being very scanty. I knew that he went often to the Bangs's and sometimes saw you there; but until I informed him of the fact, he seems not to have known that

[1] Santayana's half-sister Susana.

you and he were cousins. Boylston Beal is the only one of the old gang that I ever see nowadays, and he gives me melancholy accounts of the state of things in America, social, moral, and financial. I don't think I should care much for the new generation, in spite of my liking for mere youth: but it must be simple youth, not get-old-quick standardised immaturity. You will see in my novel —the English edition is out, but the American is not to appear until December or January—some sketches of what, as I now imagine it, youth was in your day; in your day rather than in my own, because, as you will see, my leading personages are not drawn from my own experience but rather from what I fancied to have been potential in my friends. Everybody who is in the know at all will recognise some of my originals. I could easily name several of our friends who have contributed something to my hero: but perhaps it will amuse you and Swelly Bangs to analyse the compound for yourselves. The ladies are also renderings of certain sides of people who have counted a good deal in my life; but the setting is so transformed that perhaps the likeness is rather an intention in me than a reality. "Rose", for instance, is a picture of what I imagine my mother to have been like when a young girl. I don't remember how much I said in that sketch of her life about her romantic adventures when all alone among the Indians in her tropical island: [1] but she had a wonderful coolness and courage, and a quiet disdain for what she didn't feel was quite up to the mark. For that reason she wasn't very affectionate to her children: we were poor stuff. . . .

I am tempted to send you and Bangs (since you discuss me) a little autobiography and a lay sermon of mine. They have appeared or will appear in books, but perhaps a pamphlet is less *rébarbatif.*

Yours ever

[1] See *Persons and Places,* Vol. I, Chapter 3, "My Mother".

To MRS. GEORGE STURGIS

Dear Rosamond

    . . . . I don't wonder that you feel some sympathy with Peter Alden: [1] he is an amiable type of failure; there were many such in my day. And thank you for being sorry for Oliver, instead of saying, like ——— ———, that Oliver is a mere idea. ——— says that, because he is a professional who doesn't need to read the books he reviews; and perhaps also because, in looking through the pages, he got an impression that Oliver was merely negative, just congealed. And when you say you pity him, and would like to blow him up with dynamite, so as to teach him to be more human, perhaps you express much the same feeling. But the negation in Oliver was double: he not only was austere to the natural man, but he was austere to all the conventions: to his mother, the Harvard philosophers, and even the Vicar's religion. And the dynamite was actually applied to him by Jim and Mario, and he failed to become human. Why was that? Just because he was tied up? But he wasn't tied up, intellectually: he was absolutely without deliberate prejudices. The real reason—and I am afraid I have failed to make this plain in the novel—was that he was a mystic, touched with a divine consecration, and *couldn't* give way to the world the flesh, or the devil. He ought to have been a saint. But here comes the deepest tragedy in his lot: that he lived in a spiritual vacuum. American breeding can be perfect in form, but it is woefully thin in substance; so that if a man is born a poet or a mystic in America he simply starves, because what social life offers and presses upon him is offensive to him, and there is nothing else. He evaporates, he peters out.—That is my intention, or rather perception, in Oliver. The trouble wasn't that he wouldn't be commonplace: there are plenty of people to be commonplace: the trouble was that *he couldn't be exceptional, and yet be positive.* There was no tradition worthy of him for him to join on to.

[1] A character in *The Last Puritan.*

Your friend Bernard Perry (who I suppose is a son of my old colleague at Harvard Professor R. B. Perry, and a nephew of Berenson) writes about me very correctly (as most people don't: see the dust-jacket of the American edition of *The Last Puritan,* all full of falsehoods) and it is evident that he has read what I say about myself in various places, already published. And he must have heard more or less frank criticism of me from his relations. He is very prudent, however, and leaves a certain impression of vagueness. Of course it is very hard to say the truth about a person still living, especially if one *knows* the truth: but I expect he is simply young and modest, and has not yet put his reading together into a single view.

I haven't yet received any other copy of the *Book of the Month* magazine, but someone did send me a cutting about my candidature for the American throne. Oliver would have served better.

Yours affectionately

P.S. I was much interested to hear that all your brothers belonged to the "Gashouse", and I have looked them up in the Delphic Club Catalogue, which I always receive and keep by me, to verify facts about my old friends. In the years 1891–1893 that club was absolutely my home, Howard Cushing, Julian Codman, the Potter brothers & Gordon Bell (not to speak of Boylston Beal and "Kid" Woodworth, the two elders who kept me in countenance there) made the place exceedingly congenial; we had a "Drunks Exercise Club" that took a walk and went to vespers every afternoon; and I became so attached to the place, that I kept going there off and on for some years after that, until 1896–7 when I spent the winter in England, and broke the intimacy of that connection. That second youth of mine was far pleasanter than my first youth, when I was myself an undergraduate; and the original of *Oliver & Mario* was to have been a story set in that club. But there was no possible plot, and the idea smouldered until the war suggested to me how it might be worked out.

To WILLIAM LYON PHELPS

HOTEL BRISTOL, ROME
FEBRUARY 16, 1936

Dear Billy

Your letter about *The Last Puritan* was one of the first that reached me, but I have put off thanking you for it until others began to come, so that I could have a certain background on which to place your judgement, other than my own necessarily internal or *a priori* view; because the hardest thing for an author, especially when he has lived as long as I have with his characters—45 years— is to conceive how they will seem to other people, when conveyed to them only by *words*. I have pictures, quite as distinct as memories; and my characters *speak to me,* I don't have to prompt them. This doesn't contradict the fact which you mention, and I point to in the *Epilogue,* that these characters speak my language, and are in some sense masks for my own spirit. On the contrary, that makes, or ought to make, them more living, since they are fetched from an actual life, and only dressed, as an actor on the stage, for their social parts. And I think you are partly wrong, like so many other critics, when you suggest that my characters are ghostly and not "living". Even the admitted literary character of their talk is not incompatible, as poetry is not incompatible in the drama, with individuality in tone and temper. Of course, I don't always succeed: yet I think, if you drop all preconceptions or clichés, you will find that there is a good deal of individuality in the way my characters talk, within the frame of what you might call my *metre.* It is my writing, but it is their sentiment. Only the book is very long, it can't leave distinct images if not allowed to settle. The great point is, as with poetry, to get the mind docile and free for suggestion, and then the dramatic spell will work. At least, that is what I can't help feeling, and what is confirmed by various witnesses. One notices Mrs. Darnley's special speech; another tells me he can *hear* Rose talk; and the author of Elizabeth and her German Garden at once recognized her late husband [1] in Jim: "Whose

---

[1] The 2nd Earl Russell, the elder brother of Bertrand Russell.

person and conversation", she writes, "are somehow curiously familiar". And surely Irma and Mrs. Alden are not echoes of myself.

However, that isn't the point that matters most in the book or in your letter. You say I don't love life and that faith is necessary. Very true: I don't love life unconditionally; but I enjoy the "mere living" (as Browning has it) when I am in good health, which is most of the time: and I enjoy the episodes, unless I am rudely prevented from doing so. If you have my *Dialogues in Limbo,* and will look at p.p. 156–161, you will find Socrates and me defining the matter exactly. It was Oliver, not I, who didn't love life, because he hadn't the animal Epicurean faculty of enjoying it in its arbitrariness and transiency. He was a spiritual man, incapacitated to be anything else, like Christ, who couldn't be a soldier or athlete or lover of women or father of a family (or, even, though I don't say so in the book, a good believing Christian). Now that is a tragic vocation, like the vocation of the poet; it demands sacrifice and devotion to a divine allegiance: but poor Oliver, ready for every sacrifice, had nothing to pin his allegiance to. He was what the rich young man in the Gospel would have been if he had been ready to sell his goods and give to the poor, but then had found no cross to take up and no Jesus to follow. Faith, as you say, is needed; but faith is an assurance inwardly prompted, springing from the irrepressible impulse to do, to fight, to triumph. Here is where the third sloppy wash in the family tea-pot is insufficient. And without robustness an imposed intellectual faith wouldn't do: it would only make a conventional person. You say you can't understand how I seem to hold my own in the world without faith, and almost without the world. It is quite simple. I have the Epicurean contentment, which was not far removed from asceticism; and besides I have a spiritual allegiance of my own that hardly requires faith, that is, only a humourous animal faith in nature and history, and no religious faith: and this common sense world suffices for *intellectual satisfaction,* partly in observing and understanding it, partly in dismissing it as, from the point of view of spirit, a transitory and local accident. Oliver hadn't this intellectual satisfaction, and he hadn't that Epicurean contentment. Hence the vacancy he faced when he had "overcome the world". *Basta.* Thank you a thousand times for your friendship.

To WILLIAM LYON PHELPS

HOTEL BRISTOL, ROME
MARCH 16, 1936

Dear Billy

Yes, of course, you may print my letter; [1] not that I remember what I wrote, because my memory disdains to record recent events, but I can trust you to leave out any indiscreet passages. For instance, you mustn't say who Jim Darnley is copied from, not only because it is too soon to pillory the dead, but because it is only the young and intimate Russell that is reproduced, not the elderly man with his politics and his matrimonial difficulties. His (third) wife [2] recognised him, because a lover is always young, but hardly anyone else now living would see the likeness.

There is something which I probably didn't say in my letter that I wish you would discuss someday in your "As I Like It" articles. An important element in the *tragedy* of Oliver (not in his personality, for he was no poet) is drawn from the fate of a whole string of Harvard poets in the 1880's and 1890's—Sanborn, Philip Savage, Hugh McCullough, Trumbull Stickney, and Cabot Lodge: also Moody, although he lived a little longer and made some impression, I believe, as a playwright. Now all those friends of mine, Stickney especially, of whom I was very fond, were visibly killed by the lack of air to breathe. People individually were kind and appreciative to them, as they were to me; but the system was deadly, and they hadn't any alternative tradition (as I had) to fall back upon: and of course, as I believe I said of Oliver in my letter, they hadn't the strength of a great intellectual hero who can stand alone.

I have been trying to think whether I have ever known any "good" people such as are not to be found in my novel. You will say "There's me and Anabel: [3] why didn't you put *us* into your book, to brighten it up a little?" Ah, you are not novelesque

[1] See previous letter to Phelps of February 16, 1936.

[2] The author of *Elizabeth and Her German Garden*.

[3] Mrs. Phelps.

enough: and I can't remember anybody so terribly good in Dickens
except the Cheerybell Brothers, and really, if I had put anyone
like that in they would have said I was "vicious", as they say I am
in depicting Mrs. Alden. But Irma was what I think good: she
wasn't sillier than we all are, except that we keep our silliness quiet.
And Oliver was very good: I don't think you like *good* people
really, only *sweet* people—like Anabel and you!

To ROBERT SHAW BARLOW

HOTEL BRISTOL, ROME
MARCH 29, 1936

Dear Bob

I have your two excellent letters, and feel as if our old acquaintance were renewed after forty years, without any loss of
sympathy. Your first letter especially, in which you describe your
mode of life, surprised and interested me, because that is not the
way in which I should have pictured you as living in your old age,
but rather the way I should have chosen for myself, if I had stayed
in Boston and been free to live there after my own fashion. A
bachelor apartment in a pleasant position, opening conveniently
into a club, and relations kept up naturally with young people, who
are agreeable anywhere, but in America, at least in my time, the
only people with whom one could establish frank and unprejudiced
communication. And now the young people seem to be better informed and better spoken than the average of our time. Of course
you and I and Swelly Bangs and a few others that you can easily
name had a little ballast, social and intellectual, to start with, and
if we were not altogether dragooned into the marching regiment,
we could preserve a little freedom and freshness of mind, even in
middle life; although for my part I feel that the last fifteen years
of my life in America were a dry season, a time of camping in the
desert, with very little manna falling from the sky. Besides, anywhere a man between 35 and 50 is, spiritually, under a cloud, as

I have made Jim explain in the novel. The only side of your life now that I should have arranged differently, if I had been the person concerned, would have been your professional work and your office hours. These I should have spent at home, as I do here, over my books and papers. But I think it was lucky that I got away and renewed my contacts with Spain and England. Italy, which I like even better, is only a stage setting. I came here too late to make friends: I didn't need or want society any longer: and the people I see are almost all travelling Americans, or Anglo-Americans living in Italy.

As to the novel, and the originals of the characters, you are really almost in a better position to judge than I am myself. I have lived so long with Oliver and Mario and the rest that they have an automatic existence within me. They do and say what they choose, and I merely take note, as in a dream. Naturally, this probably makes them all versions of myself: not only am I the substance of their being, like the author of a play, but I am also the actor who speaks their lines. Even in assuming the most different characters, something of the ventriloquist remains his own. You say Oliver is most like *me:* he was meant to be most unlike me, but only in his physical and moral character: in the quality of his *mind,* he is what I am or should have been in his place. This is true also of his father, of Jim, and of Jim's father: and it is even true of some of the women, such as Irma and Aunt Caroline. On the other hand, I think there is some exaggeration in the criticism made by some people that the characters are not living and have no individual way of speaking. They may not talk as people actually do: but they talk in their own way, generally, if not always: and if people opened the book in 100 years they wouldn't think the language not characteristic enough. And they would *understand* it.

Yours as always

To ROBERT SHAW BARLOW

HOTEL BRISTOL, ROME
MAY 3, 1936

Dear Bob

It is very nice of you to take so much interest in *The Last Puritan* and its fortunes. Apart from friendship, no doubt it is a curious phenomenon that the book should "take" with the public. You and Lonlie want to know how I feel on that point. Of course, I am gratified, and there's money in it, which I didn't expect or strictly need, but which it's pleasant to have, especially as my *earned* income seems more my own than the money in George Sturgis's hands; and I am going to regard it as income and not as capital, so that for a time I shall be very well off. At my age it makes less difference than it would have made formerly, and I hardly know what to do. I don't want to travel, which would have been my first thought when I was young, or to buy anything in the way of possessions, not even books, except such as I mean to read. However, I am thinking of going to Paris and taking a little suite in a hotel, such as I have here in Rome, so as to spend the summer comfortably and see if I can finish the *Realm of Truth,* which I am now working on.

My original feeling about *The Last Puritan* was that it was risky to publish it at all, during my life-time; but on the whole, at last, I overcame that apprehension. After all, I am out of the world, and it wouldn't matter much even if people abused me. But the dangerous sides of the book—and it has more than one such— seem to have been overlooked or timidly ignored by the critics. Perhaps in conversation some people discuss these matters, but their comments don't reach me. Granted, however, that the book went down and got a hearing, frankly I am not surprised that it is liked. Though it may become a little philosophical in places, it is written fluently, intelligibly, in pleasant English, and the characters (as one critic said) are "the very nicest people", that is, rich and refined, or at least cultivated; and the public not familiar with such circles likes to enter them. What Lonlie's friend says about being led to philosophize by an easy approach may also have had something to do with holding the attention of certain persons; but, hardly, I should say, of the public at large. However, you are in a better position to judge than I am. America and American books have changed a lot since I was there. Robert Dunn's *Horizon Fever,* for instance, which he sent me, is beyond me. I can hardly understand the language. Perhaps my old-fashioned long-winded prose may be a relief.

Yours ever

P.S. Which of my characters do you take to be Julia Robbins? Cousin Hannah or Letitia Lamb? Those of the characters that have originals at all, usually have more than one.

To MRS. THEODORE W. RICHARDS

ROME, MAY 18, 1936

Dear Mrs Richards

It is very pleasant to hear from you. This novel has caused old friends to rise again in various quarters. It is a *plébiscite* of interest which I didn't expect.

You ask about my childhood in Spain. A clever novelist might put in a good deal of melodrama between the lines of my childish experiences, showing what was happening in the minds of my elders. But I was unconscious of it at the time, and there were no conflicts or compulsions affecting me to my own knowledge. The relations between my father and mother were not unlike those of Peter Alden and his wife in my book, although the circumstances and the persons were entirely different. My mother, who had a little money, thought it her duty to bring up her three Sturgis children in Boston; but my father, who was over 50 and spoke no English, although he read it easily, couldn't think of living in America himself. It came to a friendly separation: and from the age of 5 to 8 I remained in Spain with him, after my mother and the girls had departed: my brother having been sent ahead two years earlier. My father and I lived in a large house in Avila, with an uncle and aunt and their daughter, Antonia. Antonia was married from the house: afterwards returned there, and died there in childbirth. In the confusion of that tragedy I saw and heard a good many things that made an impression, including the *green,* but perfectly-shaped body of the still-born child.[1]

My parents were not young when they were married and more like grandparents to me in many ways. The *warm* relation I had in the household, after my father took me, in despair, to Boston and left me there with my mother, was with my sister Susana Sturgis, who was twelve years older than I. It was from her that I learned about religion: also about architecture: because Johnny P.(Putnam) who was a beau of hers, was an architect. She forgot about art afterwards, and married an old lover—now a widower with six children—when she returned years afterwards to Spain. But the Ruskinian enthusiasm of Johnny P. stuck to me, and probably had some effect on my philosophy.

I could go on like this for pages. You can see from this sample that I had grounds for some childish cynicism in my early surroundings. But there were no troubles in my own life, except the troubles inseparable from being a spirit living in the flesh. I tried to describe them abstracted from my own person—in my Oliver.

Yours sincerely,

To THE CLASS OF 1886

[I am indebted to Mr. John M. Merriam, secretary of the Class of 1886 of Harvard College, for the following extract from a letter written on the occasion of the Class's 50th anniversary]

[ROME, 1936]

As to my inner or moral adventures during this half-century, they are in part recorded in my books, which, I believe, would

---

[1] See *Persons and Places,* Vol. I, Chapter VII "Early Memories."

fill all the spaces left vacant in the questionnaire by my non-existent children and grandchildren. Not living any longer in America or being a professor naturally had some influence on my mental tone; also the war of 1914–1918 when I remained in England, chiefly at Oxford. Nevertheless I think I have changed very little in opinion or temper. I was old when I was young, and I am young now that I am old. I have passed through no serious illnesses, emotions, or changes of heart. On the whole the world has seemed to me to move in the direction of light and reason, not that reason can ever govern human affairs, but that illusions and besetting passions may recede from the minds of men and allow reason to shine there. I think this is actually happening. What is thought and said in America now, for instance, especially since the crisis, seems to me far less benighted than what was thought and said when I lived there. People—especially the younger people —also write far better English. If I had the prophetic courage of a John the Baptist I might cry that the kingdom of heaven is at hand; by which I don't refer to a possible industrial recovery, or to a land flowing with milk and honey, but to a change of heart about just such matters and the beginning of an epoch in which spiritual things may again seem real and important. The modern world is loudly crying peccavi, but we know that this is not enough. There must be a real conversion or redirection of the affections. I think this may actually ensue, in the measure in which such revolutions are compatible with human nature.

To ROBERT SHAW BARLOW

PARIS, JUNE 22, 1936

Dear Bob

I have just finished Faulkner's "Sanctuary" and I think I have understood all the pornographic part, corn cob, etc., and the character of Popeye, which is like any villain in melodrama, just as Miss Reba and her establishment and her genteel friends entertained after the funeral; all this being very well done, so as to seem life-like, at least to the uninitiated. I found myself also absorbed in the story as a whole, without exactly following the thread of it, which it would have taken me a second reading to disentangle. But frankly I don't think it worth bothering about. Like all these recent writers, the author is too lazy and self-indulgent and throws off what comes to him in a sort of dream, expecting the devoted reader to run about after him, sniffing at all the droppings of his mind. I am not a psychological dog, and require my dog-biscuit to be clearly set down for me in a decent plate with proper ceremony. But Faulkner, apart from those competent melodramatic or comic bits, has a poetic vein that at times I liked extremely; in describing landscape or sheer images. This matter of images is very interesting, but confused. The image-without-thought poets often jump from the images supposed to appear to a particular observer, as in a dream, to images visible only to another observer, to the author in his omniscient capacity, as if they were the substance of the physical world common to all sane people. But there are no common images; there are only common objects of belief; and confusion in this matter of psychological analysis renders these modern writers bewildering, because they are themselves bewildered.

Faulkner's language I like well enough when it is frank dialect or unintended poetry; but I wish he wouldn't, in his own person, say "like" for "as", "like they do down South". And the trick of being brutally simple and rectilinear in describing what people do, or rather their bodily movements, becomes tiresome after a while; especially when these bodily movements have no great significance but again are mere images strung along because they happen to appear to the author's undirected fancy.

The absence of moral judgements or sentiments helps to produce this impression of conscious automata, wound up, and running round and round in their cages. I think there is biological truth in that view, but we have also a third, a vertical dimension. We can *think;* and it is in that dimension that experience becomes human.

It is very warm in Paris now, and my rooms too sunny, but if I stick it out, I hope to see Barley when he is here.

Yours ever

To ROBERT SHAW BARLOW

HOTEL BRISTOL, ROME
NOVEMBER 3, 1936

Dear Bob

I am glad to know that you are well again and going your usual rounds.

As to my letter about Faulkner's *Sanctuary*,[1] it is as well you didn't send it to any paper. I think the philosophical part at the end might be worth printing, but perhaps would bear a little amplifying and illustrating, which would turn it into a technical argument not interesting to the general public. The first part is more lively but not quite fair to Faulkner: his poetic side is not unintentional, and what I say about "droppings" would be more applicable to other people—e.g. Ezra Pound—than to him.

Yes, of course I am concerned about the war in Spain, and some of my connections there may be actually fighting—of course on the nationalistic side. I have no inside knowledge of the affair: but reflecting on it from a distance, I have a notion that it may be very important: a sort of turning-point in history, which in my thoughts I call *The Revolt of the Nations*. Since the triumph of Christianity, and again after the Reformation and the English, American and French revolutions, our part of the world has been governed by ideas, by theories, by universalistic sects like the Church, the Free Masons, the Free Trade Industrial Liberals, and last of all the Bolshies. Such influences are non-natural, non-biological; whereas the agricultural, military, and artistic life of nations is spontaneous, with ambitions that impose morality, but are not imposed by morality of any sort. Now isn't that perhaps what the world is returning to after two thousand years of hypnotization by medicine-men and prophets?

Spain has always been the most unfortunate of countries, and is now having a hard struggle to throw the Bolshies off, that had got hold of her always execrable government. But my friends write that the young people are unrecognisable in their energy and disci-

1 See previous *Letter*, [June 22, 1936].

pline, and that we shall soon see a new Spain as vigorous as in the Middle Ages. And of course Spain would not be alone in this transformation.

Yours ever

To ROSAMOND AND GEORGE STURGIS

HOTEL BRISTOL, ROME
DEC. 28, 1936

Dear Rosamond and George

Very beautiful double carnations, in profusion, came from you by radio, or however they come. It was very kind of you to send them besides the card signed by the boys as well. I am being treated very kindly by the world in my old age. Even an unknown friend I have in the Michigan State prison, called Wayne Joseph Husted, No35571, sent me a Christmas card. Years ago he honoured me with a psychological essay, really very good, on prison life, and since then we occasionally exchange civilities. I am now sending him *The Last Puritan*. I hope it won't be stopped by the authorities as dangerous to convict morals.

The reception of this book has been curious. I don't think many people really like it, yet it has had, as you know, a vast success. The other day I received a *Swedish* translation. The German version—with the nasty things I say about Germans and Goethe left out by agreement—announces that it is translated by two ladies, *aus dem Amerikanischen*. Fancy that, when I am so proud of my Received Standard English. But I gathered from what I could make out of the Swedish wrapper, and from other hints, that the interest taken in the novel by the Nordics is entirely scientific. Style, humour, etc, are beneath their notice: but they say the book is an important document on American life; and as America—I mean the U.S.—is important for them commercially and racially, they wish it to be studied in their country. Perhaps it will be quoted, as a warning, by the Nazi professors of sociology. This, like my convict friend, falls to me by divine grace, with no effort or merit on my part. We have uses we never intended.

I have had a touch of catarrh, very slight, as the injections my Italian doctor gives me seem to keep off the worst; I am now quite well and working with gusto, as I almost see my plans as to books completely carried out.—Here is an egotistical letter, all about trifles interesting only to myself: but the great questions like the war in Spain, and the Simpson affair, are too sad to write about.

Yours aff[ly]

To GEORGE STURGIS

HOTEL BRISTOL, ROME
MARCH 13, 1937.

Dear George

Much interested in the article about you in *The Chess Review*.[1] I had never heard, or properly taken in, the fact that you are a distinguished player. And as this article ends on a philosophical note, I am tempted to put a question that touches what I call the Realm of Essence, and the appeal it can make to the mind. Chess is a contest: but suppose we remove the motive of vanity or love of winning; you might satisfy that by seeing who can drink the other man under the table, rather than who can checkmate him upon it. And suppose we eliminate also any gambling or partisan interest in having one side win rather than the other, even if you are a mere onlooker. Now my question is this: How much of the fascination of chess comes from the excitement of carrying out a purpose under opposition: a suggestion or after-image of difficulties *in living?* And how much comes from the interest in *formal relations,* as in mathematics or stained-glass, or arabesques? This latter interest is what I call interest in essences: of course the interest itself, which we may feel, will be a form of life in us: but

[1] Vol. V. No. 4 (April 1937).

the *object* in which we are interested need not be living; and the point that touches my philosophy is whether the living interest in non-living things is normal in man, or is a mere eccentricity or illusion, in that nothing can really concern us except our own life.

If this is unintelligible, don't bother about it: or submit it to some other chess-player who likes speculation. . . .

Yours aff^{ly}

To MRS. C. H. TOY

HOTEL BRISTOL, ROME
MAY 24, 1937

Dear Mrs. Toy

Do you still feel that you are at heart a Virginian, or has Cambridge entirely won you over with its virtues and its blandishments? Not being quite sure of this, I feel some qualms in sending you two thick volumes about Poe,[1] not well written in any way and yet, as I find, most interesting. If you have read them— they come from "remainders" at Blackwell's in Oxford, sold at reduced prices, and often tempting—or if they don't please you you can always pass them on to some omnivorous friend. I am deep now in nothing but Americana, being still haunted with the idea of writing something about *The Old Mind of the New World*. I want to illustrate my thesis by some observations on Jonathan Edwards and Emerson—hard or stiff minds—and Poe and Hawthorne—soft minds. This book of Hervey Allen's will do to refresh my thoughts about Poe, and I am keeping the notes I made in reading him. I will get something of Hawthorne's to read this summer at Cortina; and I have procured an immense volume of Emerson's works, over 1000 pages, in which I have already reread *"English Traits"* and *"Fate"*. But this is too heavy for a traveller, and I will leave the tome here until the autumn.

[1] *Israfel: The Life and Times of Edgar Allan Poe* by Hervey Allen (1926).

Meantime, I have finished *The Realm of Truth,* which is in the press in England. It is a shortish book, about 200 pages, and perhaps more modern in its treatment of things than my previous *Realms.* It may possibly be better received than the others. But I don't know what Scribner will do in regard to the Triton Edition. This is too slight to make an entire XVth volume, and yet who knows when, if ever, the *Realm of Spirit* will be ready to keep it company?

I will see if I can find a better photograph of the *Fontana del Tritone.*[1] It ought to show the high jet of water rising from the shell, and the Barberini Palace in the background instead of those modern shops. My windows, by the way, are not seen in the view chosen; the Bristol is on the upper side of the square, the opposite side from the buildings visible in this photograph. And the whole Square, though modern, has more vistas and more space in it than this view suggests.

Cory has been here for two months, and a string of young American students has turned up; also some Professors. Now I am at peace again, until June 15th when I expect to leave for the Dolomites, Address: Hotel Savoy, Cortina D'Ampezzo. Thank you for kind letters and papers.

Yours sincerely

To *LOGAN PEARSALL SMITH*

HOTEL BRISTOL, ROME
JAN. 22, 1938

Dear Smith

I had heard of your autobiography and should have sent for the Atlantic and read it, if I hadn't expected to have it before long in the form of a book: but if the public clamours for more, you

---

[1] The lovely fountain by Bernini in the Piaza Barberini where Santayana lived for many years.

may have to keep the story going like Sherenazade (how is it spelled?) for a thousand and one issues. However, you might get out a first volume *Youth,* a second *Maturity,* and as much as may be of a third *Wisdom,* to be posthumous, as wisdom usually is.

I am reasonably well, having had no operations or serious illnesses in the past, and only a bronchial catarrh always knocking at the door, but seldom let in or kept long in full personal presence. I work every morning steadily for two or three hours on the last volume of *Realms of Being* or on *Dominations and Powers* (my political testament). They are my last works. If I should live to finish them, and the automatic habit of writing can't be stopped, I may compose an autobiography too. There are some fragments already: but I think story-telling is the form of expression that most improves with age, so that I have left that project for the end, if the end politely makes room for it.

Of course I shall be much honoured to be quoted in your Memoirs and the letter (which I had entirely forgotten) seems reasonable, if a little long. Don't hesitate to leave out any part that may seem superfluous. I think not mentioning my name may have a better effect—more mysterious—than if you mentioned it. But do as you like. Those in the know will at once see that it is mine—foreigner long resident, Harvard Lampoon, Harvard philosophical Faculty, and "genteel tradition".

Your letter is full of images, and that of the Berensons with the great-grandchild breaking like a ray of sunrise into the house is most attractive. We are doing very well in our old age, almost all of us. Strong is in Rome at this moment, happy and well in spite of his paralytic legs, and pleased by the new toy of a diminutive *closed* motor.

Saluti e auguri from your old friend

P.S. "La fille de Minos et de Pasiphaé" is the 36th line of *Phèdre.* Racine may have been struck by the euphony of it in the "Characters", and put it in. Prose has its magic, too. I don't deny that.

To MRS. C. H. TOY

HOTEL BRISTOL, ROME
MAY 6, 1938

Dear Mrs. Toy

Don't you remember that a long time ago you sent me a beautiful copy of Christopher Morley's *Powder of Sympathy*—only you called it *Power* of Sympathy, so I daresay you hadn't then read it with much attention? His talk about me is very pleasant; and I shouldn't venture to say that the rest of the sketches are not excellent, only I can't understand them. I mean that I don't feel the interest in the subjects or the treatment which the author expects his readers to feel. And I can't see the point of the jokes. This comes from what I was saying in my letter of the other day. I am not, as they say in Spanish, "in antecedents". The presuppositions fail in my case, because I have been too long away from America and America, at least on the surface, in matters of language and allusions, has changed too fast. It is almost so also with England. A friend—a German, a *protégé* of Westenholz [1]—has willy nilly compelled me to accept the gift of Tauchnitz editions of Somerset Maugham. I *could* read these, enticed by the familiarity he shows with Spain, and with Spanish-Americans, in whose moral complexion I feel a certain interest; but on the whole I felt the same wonder at anybody wishing to write such stories. They are not pleasing, they are not pertinent to one's real interests, they are not true: they are simply graphic or plausible, like a bit of a dream that one might drop into in an afternoon nap. Why record it? I suppose it is to make money, because writing stories is a profession, just as writing propaganda in the newspapers is. Are you aware that the world is now being systematically fed on partisan lies? And much more where the press is "free" than where it is controlled by the government. In Italy, for instance, the papers are monotonous and meagre, and of course partisan in sentiment; but on the whole the facts are reported responsibly, and there are no great excesses of mendacity. But a "free" press is financed by par-

1 Baron Albert von Westenholz.

ties or interests or fanatical individuals; and there is no limit to the ignorance or the malevolence which they can display.

Hitler has been making us a visit this week, I believe he leaves today for Florence, and home. Of course, I haven't seen him or the military review or even the illuminations. I don't change my daily routine for such trifles; but they have made a lot of the occasion. I like the Italian public very much. There is a free air about them, they are not flurried or pressed; but they keep order with a cheerful alacrity and understanding of the fix those in authority—poor fellows—so often find themselves in. I sympathize with that feeling. We nobodies are the real aristocrats. The bosses can hardly call their souls their own.

Yours sincerely

To LOGAN PEARSALL SMITH

HOTEL BRISTOL, ROME
OCT. 11, 1938

Dear Smith

No wonder your reminiscences [1] should have had a great success with the public; they are most interesting and humorous. The picture of Walt Whitman alone would suffice to justify the book, but for me, of course, there are many other points of interest. Only I wish you had been more specific, about Harvard and Oxford, for instance. Who were your real friends, and what were they like? What was their philosophy? Of course, you couldn't be frank about living or recently dead people, who may have loving families idealizing their memory. I hope, for the sake of posterity, that you may be writing a more detailed autobiography. You are a person exceptionally well placed and qualified to record the mental fashions of our times, and the relations then existing between "cultured" England and America.

[1] *Unforgotten Years.*

You may say that Henry James has done it once for all: but he, you, all Americans in print, are too gentle, too affectionate, too fulsome. The reality requires a satirist, merciless but just, as you might be if you chose.

At odd moments I have myself written down various reminiscences about my family and friends—*Persons and Places,* I thought of calling the collection, or *Fragments of Autobiography.* If I survive the writing of *The Realm of Spirit* I will devote the rest of my reprieve to that amusement. But I have not seen much of the polite world. Only an individual here and there really interested me, and the intellectual and fashionable Anglo-America that you have moved in has been out of my range, and not attractive to me. If I had had a little money when I was young I should have doubtless taken a house in England, like you; but I think I should have kept only to a few friends, and not felt, with them, any foreignness in myself at all. I have been a little surprised at your sense of your Americanism surviving after so many years, and at the exaggerated importance you give to other Europeanized Americans. Lapsley (who also keeps up a *culte* for his American connection) is more at home in England than you seem to be. Howard Sturgis (whom you don't mention; didn't you know him?) had more my relative feelings for America on one side and England on the other: only that, beneath his wit and humour, he was helplessly affectionate; whereas I should have kept bachelor's hall in quite another spirit, and probably migrated in the end to Italy, as I have actually done.

I have been reading Henry Adams's *Saint Michel,* etc. There is another perspective of the same world, but again fulsome, sugar-coated; beneath which manner one feels a most terrible bitterness and utter misfit with reality. My materialism, after all, is more buoyant.

Yours sincerely

To MRS. C. H. TOY

HOTEL BRISTOL, ROME
DEC. 6, 1938

Dear Mrs. Toy

The "Simple Prayer" can hardly be translated in two ways, but I have put it into the obvious English equivalent. Perhaps in the fifth line it would be better to say "faith" instead of "the Faith" although probably it was the latter that Saint Francis meant.

I am not sure of all the corrections (only 3) which I have made in the Italian, not having any other text at hand, and the original being naturally in archaic form. It is *ricevere* in Italian now, however, and it was always *eterna*.

It is a beautiful prayer, and truly evangelical. Galilee and Umbria have something in common. Writing about Spirit, as I am now, it strikes me as an example, on the side of sentiment, of living in the moment; because no hint is given about the objects or results of charity; all is the inward quality of the feeling. Just as it is purity of intention that fills the mind here, and banishes all selfish cares, so I think in intellectual moments it is purity of intuition that spiritualizes knowledge or belief. The truth of itself does not spiritualize the heart, but truth, or even error, are spiritualized when the heart is pure and the mind absorbed in intuition.

I have never seen Llewelyn Powys, but if you like his book I can send you another that tells something about his youth and family, and in which I have pasted a Walt Whitman-like photograph of him sitting amid the snows of Davos. He is consumptive. Miss Alyse Gregory, his wife (but still called *Miss*) was secretary to the *Dial* in the days of Scofield Thayer.—A happy new year!

Yours sincerely

SIMPLE PRAYER

Oh Lord, make me an instrument of thy peace:
Where there is hatred, may I bring love,
Where there is offence, may I bring forgiveness,

Where there is discord, may I bring union,
Where there is doubt, may I bring the faith,
Where there is error, may I bring the truth,
Where there is despair, may I bring hope,
Where there is sadness, may I bring joy,
Where there is darkness, may I bring light.

Grant, oh Master, that I may seek not so much
to be comforted, as to comfort,
to be understood, as to understand,
to be loved, as to love.
For it is thus: In giving, we receive,
in forgiving, we are forgiven,
in dying, we rise again to eternal life.

Saint Francis.

To MRS. C. H. TOY

HOTEL BRISTOL, ROME
DECEMBER 12, 1938

Dear Mrs. Toy

Your note of Nov. 25 is not like your usual letters, but sad, as if you were not well. I know you hate conventional inquiries or good wishes about health: they are *sous-entendu* among old friends. And your mood may have changed now, so that the old note might jar.

As to depositing the Cardoza book in the library [1]—in the Inferno, I suppose, with my old copies of Royce, etc—of course I am flattered and amused. Do as you think. In time the librarian himself will remove superfluous deposits to the cellar or the top shelves, and meantime some candidate for an A.M. or Ph.D may do "research" work by getting down the volume and copying a

---

[1] The Widener at Harvard, where the "Inferno" is a section of dubious repute.

pencil note of your humble servant's! How small and accidental the learned world seems when one catches it, like this, in its witches' kitchen!

I am reading a ponderous * *Anthology of American Literature* by Benèt & Pearson of Yale. It is called an Oxford Anthology, but it has nothing Oxonian about it, only it is published by the Oxford University Press in New York. It is modern, and therefore, to me, instructive, and it may actually lead me to reconcile myself with some authors that I could never stomach, Melville for instance. The recent poets at the end, however, still baffle me, and I don't know whether to blame my old age and prejudice, or to suspect that after all there is a lot of mystification and bluff about these geniuses without a background, a principle, or an audience. The book has short critical & biographical notices at the end, too favourable usually, in my opinion, except in the case of Longfellow, treated too much as if being *old-fashioned* were not a merely fashionable imputation. I appear, and am well treated. The anonymous critic says I perfectly represent the genteel tradition in my own person and writings. Is he right? I think Lewis Mumford came nearer the truth when he spoke of the "Pillage of Europe", except that in my case it was more the driftwood of Europe. I didn't go about buying museum pieces, but expressed, as soon as I became at all my own master, my *native* affinities to European things. Pity, when some right judgment is passed, that it shouldn't be accepted, but that fresh critics should feel obliged to think up something different and wrong. Van Wyck Brooks, for instance, is perfect on Longfellow. Why do these "Oxford" critics go back to commonplaces about him?

This will be too late for Christmas good wishes, let them be for the New Year.

Yours sincerely

* 1,700 pages in double columns [in text with asterisk. D.C.]

To MRS. C. H. TOY

HOTEL BRISTOL, ROME
DEC. 21, 1938

Dear Mrs. Toy

Certainly, I shall be glad to read Whitehead's new book,[1] and make marginal notes if anything occurs to me worth saying; but of course the innocent frankness of the thing is lost when you know beforehand that your comments are going to be seen, criticised, and perhaps repeated to the author. Besides, I know beforehand, from the review you enclose, what I shall think of the book in general. A view, which might be stated quite simply and philosophically, is put forth as *uplifting*. That is a trick of all Protestant philosophers, even of those rationalists that are Protestants only by tradition, not by belief. For instance, it is effusive in Walt Whitman; see "Message to India", included in my "Oxford" Anthology,[2] which I have been reading lately. It seems to an outsider annoying and hypocritical; but I am enough a friend of the family to feel that it is spontaneous, a sort of unattached affectionateness running over into things in general; and it does not prevent the sharpest analysis, e.g., in Berkeley or Fichte, or the most genuine speculative insight. So I expect to admire and agree with the sober parts of Whitehead, and not mind when he gets a little fuddled with spiritual drink.

I wonder if Mr. Toy ever mentioned to you an Oriental habit or practice called *Ketmân?* A French book on Persia that I have by me says it is very favourable to diversity of religious opinions, and toleration of them. It consists in never saying what you think, but if necessary saying anything else, that may serve to avoid disputes or ill-feeling; and it is recommended as giving a man a great superiority over his interlocutors. So my book says; although if the interlocutors are also addicted to *Ketmân*, it would seem to secure the same advantage all round. This of course is not at all the same thing as the uplift served up as sauce with one's opinions; but it

---

[1] *Modes of Thought.*
[2] See previous *Letter* [Dec. 12, 1938].

serves the same purpose. The Orientals probably practise it because they are very old-minded and know exactly what they think,
so that it is easy to avoid saying it; but our honest groping philosophers can't dissimulate, because their views are nebulous; they
are young-minded, and feel that what there is to discover must
surely be something splendid.

I think that perhaps, without knowing that the thing had a
name or was recommended by the wise men of the East, I may
have indulged in a little *Ketmân* in my earlier days. I was very
proper in *The Sense of Beauty*, and in many places in my other
books, although I had no thought of hiding my first principles,
only at most of being sympathetic and persuasive in my way of
putting things. My sonnet on faith [1] (no. 3) reproduced in this
same anthology is a case in point. It was suggested by a phrase in
the *Bacchae* of Euripides, τὸ σοφὸν οὐ σοφία, "Knowingness is not
wisdom", and was accordingly as sceptical as it is possible to be,
since it fell back on Bacchic instinct, or animal faith, because that
went with life, however completely it might fool us: although
really we were practising *Ketmân,* and lending ourselves to illusion on purpose, without in the least succumbing to it in our
hearts. That was what my sonnet grew out of: but it passes into the
religious calendars and anthologies as vindicating Christian faith,
or some faith very nearly Christian. My own Catholicism, which I
must have had in mind at the age of twenty, when I composed the
sonnet, was deeply tinctured with desperation. You had better hold
on to that, because otherwise there was nothing to hold on to.

I share your feeling about Pearsall Smith, but I don't believe
that he despises or avoids Americans, although he may have *said*
so. Sincerity is not his strong point, or rather, he has the sincerity
of the fancy: says anything that occurs to him and sounds well in
the ear, for the moment, and lets it go at that. But, as to his Americanism, I was struck by the rootedness and persistence of it in this
very book.[2] Terribly conscious of *not* being at home in England,
although he has lived there most of his life, and reverting to his
sisters and his family oddities with a sense of comfort and safety at
last. No doubt, he knows that reminiscences of America and Walt
Whitman are acceptable now to the English public; but they prove

---

[1] "O world, thou choosest not the better part, etc."

[2] *Unforgotten Years.*

that he is not inclined or hopeful to lose himself in the British
atmosphere, and forget that he is American. He is intensely so, only
of the expatriate tribe! If he were young now he would return and
live in Greenwich Village. England itself is no longer comfortable
or congenial to the would be aesthete of 1890.

Yours sincerely

To G. W. HOWGATE

HOTEL BRISTOL, ROME
FEB. 15, 1939

Dear Mr. Howgate,

Your book [1] about me is so appreciative—apart from the great
compliment of writing a book about me at all—that I wonder you
didn't send it to me, and am a bit afraid that perhaps you sent it,
and it went astray. This is one reason why I write, lest in that case
you should think I was somehow displeased and refused to thank
you. I am most highly pleased, and have to thank you not only for
the boost you are giving to my reputation, but much more for your
diligence and sympathy in reading everything, and doing such generous justice to everything I have written. I haven't read every page
of your long book: Narcissus himself couldn't look at his image
uninterruptedly without wishing to forget it; and your criticism
is too objective and steadily just to be exciting or to reserve surprises to the subject of it. As far as I have seen there are absolutely
no errors about matters of fact—none at least of your own. You
quote some one who says I learned English at the age of thirteen:
but as you indicate elsewhere, I was under nine when I began to
learn it, and at ten went to a common school with boys of my age,
and as far as I remember was not handicapped by the language.
You also quote a ridiculous invention of Miss Munsterberg's—or
rather, it must have been, her mother's—to the effect that I felt

---

[1] *George Santayana.* (University of Pennsylvania Press, 1938)

more at home at the Münsterberg's than at other Cambridge houses. I didn't go about in Cambridge society, but more in Boston, except for one or two friends; but the Munsterbergs took things sometimes into their own hands, and one had to go to their parties.

As to your interpretation and criticism of my philosophy, I have nothing to object. What you say is not what I should say: if it were, why should you say it? But it is all reasonable and natural. If I were to demur at anything it would be at the excessive attention you give to my poetry. I am no poet in the English sense; and the function of my verses is simply to betray the undercurrents of my mind in the formative period; or else, as in *Lucifer* (and some finished but unpublished plays of that period) to do fantastically what my novel has done realistically: study moral contrasts and possibilities. But as a whole, you are wonderfully intuitive and correct, and I don't see how I could have had a better interpreter.

Yours sincerely

To MRS. C. H. TOY

HOTEL BRISTOL, ROME
MARCH 5, 1939

Dear Mrs Toy

Yesterday, at last, I sent you back Whitehead's book,[1] covered with hasty notes. I liked him better than the tone of most of these might suggest. He is a dear old man, full of knowledge and originality; and I felt rather sorry for him (as for Russell, too) that he should have found it inevitable to give this kind of lectures, in this semi-flattering, semi-propagandist manner. Not that he abstained from being profound or obscure, in places; but that the whole is conceived as a sort of spiritual cocktail—concentrated stimulation —to promote conviviality of thought. But genuine thought is soli-

1 *Modes of Thought.*

tary, and as Emerson said, we "descend to meet". That is, in the direction of comforting opinions and the latest thing in science, gossip and not truth. We might ascend to meet, if we were in pursuit of repentance and not of self-congratulation.

As to Whitehead's general philosophy, there is one whole side of it which appeals to me, and in him is rather heroic. He has turned his back on British philosophy, Berkeley, Hume, Mill, and Russell, on "ideas" and "sense-data". He asserts (a great truth!) that they are superficial lights on a great dark ocean of existence. Our animal nature, and all nature, is at work beneath. They, the ideas, are like the bell-sounds heard coming from the engine-room when a steam-boat stops or goes full steam ahead. The passenger, the spirit, learns very little from them about the ship, the crew, or the voyage. Very well: we return to common sense, to naturalism, to materialism? Not at all! For there is another side of British philosophy that Whitehead sticks to, and that renders his naturalism, by a contradiction, subjective, literary, and nebulous. He is sure that "experience" equals "reality". The ideas, though superficial when clear, when confused are the very heart and substance of the universe. We are therefore everything and everywhere, although not so intensely as we are here and ourselves. And all other persons and things are in us, though less intensely than they are in their own places. A perverse way of saying, it seems to me, that things arouse ideas, or other effects, in one another, so that the ideas or effects of each may be in the rest, not the *parts* of each, diminuendo, in all the universe at once.

This denial of the difference between thought and its object also totally invalidates Whitehead's criticism of other philosophers, of Descartes, for instance. Not that Descartes' physics was adequate. No physics can be adequate. For the terms of a science are not parts of things, but only ideas of things; and just as one sense gives us one idea, say colour, and another sense another idea, say hot or cold, so one science may give us a classification into genera and species and another science a mechanism of a geometrical or atomic kind. These sciences may all be true; they will none of them be the whole or even a part of the material reality. They will be theories, just as our experience will be ideas or sensations. And both science and experience are only *languages* in which, for human purposes, nature may at times be described.

Whitehead has entirely missed the moral of the fable when

he complains that men of science may accept modern technique and yet hold on to ancient common sense in their beliefs. Of course. No harm in the modern technique as a *language:* but to suppose that Einstein or Bergson or even Whitehead himself, can "sweep away" the old world by inventing a new technique for calculating its movement, is to mistake ideas for things, words for objects, and "life" for matter.

I should have finished this little book sooner if I hadn't been absorbed in another, very much more instructive and exciting. It is by a Swedish Lutheran theologian named Nygren (New green?) and is entitled *Agapè and Eros,* in 3 vols, all to say what Oliver said in one page of his college thesis! Christian love, agapè, is unselfish, it rushes downwards to those in need. Eros, or aspiring love, is selfish and only wants satisfaction with good things. So that (though Newgreen doesn't say so) Martha was a Christian but Mary was not.

This is enormously instructive to me, although, in the person of Oliver, I knew it before. The book is very learned, fair, and clear (in a good English translation) and full of admirable quotations from St. Augustine, Luther, etc, which rejoice my heart. But good Nygren's theology limps, because if God is love and pours down upon sinners through good men, two things seem to follow; that God is *only* brotherly love of one man for another; and that the evil in the world must have existed before agapè (= God) could come down to mitigate it. So that both Manicheism and atheism are involved.

This is a very argumentative letter. Please excuse it. You brought it on yourself by sending me Whitehead's "babblings of green fields".

Yours sincerely

To WILLIAM LYON PHELPS

HOTEL BRISTOL, ROME
APRIL 16, 1939

Dear Billy

For two or three days I have been buried in your Autobiography.[1] It is an avalanche. All hasn't fallen on me, because knowing you and seeing the 1000 pages, I instantly decided to pick and choose. I would leave out everything about your childhood, your travels, and those of your friends whom I haven't known, and they are the greater number; but I would read (besides what you say about me, naturally) your account of your undergraduate days at Yale, your experiences at Harvard, and about those of your friends that I knew a little, so that I had something to back up or qualify what you described. Your impressions are truly *impressions,* effects produced on yourself; not that they are not perfectly fair and unbiased except by kindness and exuberant humanity, but that you don't pry, you don't analyze, you don't penetrate, you don't sum up. Take the case of Barrett Wendell. If I were to mention him in my autobiography (and I may yet write something of the kind, for my Realms of Being are almost finished) the first thing I should ask myself would be: How far was Wendell a fool and how far was he a martyr? That he was a mixture of both seems to me certain. But you make no such beginning. You describe his voice (why not his red beard and twirling watch-chain?) and mention the peculiar character of his learning and of his academic position. Externals, my dear friend; just what a casual stranger might report about him, and you knew him intimately and were truly fond of him, as we all were, who had any feeling. Now I ask again: *Why* did Barrett Wendell talk like that? It was not an attempt to be English. He was not an Anglo-maniac, as he himself said quite truly. Nobody in England then talked like that. How, then, did he fall into that strange habit? Now, I knew him only slightly, and have to make a hypothesis, but I should explain the matter to myself in

---

[1] *Autobiography With Letters.*

this way. Wendell loved New England, but the N.E. before the
Revolution. He would have wished to be a Cavalier, all courage
and elegance. His speech was a failure as a mark of elegance but it
was a success as a proof of courage. Anyhow, it was a profound constant protest against being like other people. He felt he belonged
to the London of Beau Brummel; and even in my day there lin-
gered in Boston a faint echo of those days, again not in their elegance but in their mannishness. "Rum and deco-rum!" he exclaimed once in an after-dinner speech: that was all we needed in
this world. A horrible pun, but an interesting mixture of reck-
lessness and propriety as an ideal of character. Then, saturated
with that pathos of distance, and being warm-hearted and affectionate, he was intensely sentimental, yet heroically kept his sentimentality in check, and put up with things as they were. That was
his martyrdom. And he married Mrs. Wendell.

But this may be all wrong, and I must come down to safer
ground, viz., what you say about me. It is all very kind and almost
true, but again quite external. Do you think the essential thing
about me is that I am "an atheist and a pessimist"? By the way,
you can't be accurate in your language; you report the second or
third edition of your stories as edited by your own memory. Lady
Ritchie, for instance, couldn't have spoken of being *on* a train;
and I, at the very most, might have said that I was *what people
would call* an atheist or a pessimist. In reality I have never been
either. Early Christians were called atheists and Buddhists are
called pessimists: that only means that they reject the *kind* of God
or the *kind* of happiness that the critic is accustomed to conceive.
But I believe in the reality of Truth, the denial of which by
Nietzsche, James, Dewey and a lot of Evangelicals and Idealists is,
according to Lutoslawski, genuine atheism. And I believe in the
possibility of happiness, if one cultivates intuition and outlives
the grosser passions, including optimism. But this play of dialectic
with concepts may seem to you forced. God and happiness seem
to you proper names for distinct facts. God either exists, or He
doesn't exist. A man is either happy or unhappy. But can you seriously maintain that? The idea of God has infinite shades: even in
the Hebrew tradition it is most ambiguous as an idea. It is only as
a verbal idol, as a formula in a ritual, that the object is distinct.
Would the God of Aristotle be God? Would the God of Royce be
God, although avowedly not a power? And how about Brahma, or

the God of Spinoza? These things are not so simple, if you stop to think a little.

By the way again, I have come upon a book by a Swedish Lutheran theologian, Nygren, on *Agape & Eros* which has interested and instructed me very much. It is fair and steady in its learning, but the moral of it (expressed in my words) is that Martha was a Christian but Mary was a Hellenistic Platonic egocentric minx. Is that your view?

I heartily agree that old age is, or may be as in my case, far happier than youth. Even physically pleasanter. I was never more entertained and less troubled than I am now.

Best thanks and best wishes from

To WILLIAM HALLER

ROME, MAY 21, 1939

Dear Mr. Haller

This long delay in thanking you for your book [1] comes from wishing to read it all before saying anything about it, and I have finished it today. At first I was a little frightened at your sending me a true account of the first Puritans, perhaps to rebuke me for my false account of the "last" one; but I was soon relieved. You study them all, up to Milton, with great deference and zeal; yet intentionally or unintentionally you don't leave a pleasant impression of their character or their ideas. Doubtless you are more attached than I am to the liberty of thought and faith into which you feel that the whole movement empties; but it does *empty* there; and what I had in mind was something that I imagined inspired that movement from the beginning and the *challenge* to every fact or precept, not by some uncriticised prejudice in oneself, but by *pure spirit*. The awful question whether one was damned or saved was a mere obsession; and the hatred of prelacy, etc., was positivistic; all that rigmarole was useless in business.

[1] *The Rise of Puritanism.*

Uprightness was not useless: be converted and you will soon be rich. But your comfortable sufficiently virtuous and absolutely self-satisfied positivist is not what the *spirit* can rest in: yet what else does reality offer us, when we have got rid of all foolish historical dogmas and obsessions? That was the problem for my last Puritan, to which he found no answer.

Severity in your real Puritans was nominally justified by the notion that we are on the brink of hell-fire; but this notion, unless taken as a symbol for the danger of real troubles, is gratuitous and insane. My well-educated little last Puritan had no such notion (as Emerson hadn't); it would not have shown true severity. Didn't the original Puritans, behind or within their Calvinistic theology, nurse true severity? And if they did, where would it have landed them? That was my problem.

Though I found your numerous early worthies a bit monotonous, I gathered a great many gems of pungent old English and a better picture than I had in my mind of that whole epoch. But was Milton such a prig? You speak of him in the highest terms, and then show him to have been a monument of conceit and artificiality. I have always felt that his strong point was his magnificent diction and cadences; but I didn't know that the substance beneath was so poor. Or is it poor only in my estimation, because I am not a Puritan?

How much I have been interested in your book would appear to you if you saw my comments on the margin: I often scribble them, sometimes in doggerel, on the books that I find "life-enhancing". For instance, there is this on your page 65:

> With learning Perkins head was crammed,
> Hell trembled when he shouted "Damned!"
> The godliest were on tenterhooks,
> And the shelves groaned beneath his books.

or on page 88:

> Don't let the flesh be without sin,
> Else spirit has no fight to win.

This I think shocking morality, but it is Calvinistic and Hegelian. *Spirit* is a witness, not a fighter. The fighter is the animal psyche.

Yours sincerely,

To WILLIAM LYON PHELPS

ROME, JUNE 1, 1939

Dear Billy

The postscript to your letter makes me forget all the things that I had meant to say in reply to the rest of it. Philosophically, we can't complain. The time has come for separation, and you and Annabel had had a long time of perfect union. The years that may remain, at our age, in any case involve the soft pedal, and however sad your material solitude may be at certain moments, in your thoughts you will not be alone, because you will always be conscious of what Annabel would have felt and said or done in the presence of whatever may be occurring. It is very hard to think of her except as a part of you: I have never known husband and wife who seemed so unanimous, except perhaps some very old couples, creatures of common habits. But with you it was not that; you were both lively and individual, with different minds, yet so harmonious, that as I say, you seemed treble and bass in the same piece of music. There is only one shadow that people might think they saw in your lives, the fact that you had no children; but the absence of this added bond, which in so many marriages is the only permanent and effective one, in one sense concentrates the affections, when they are genuine, and prevents them from being dispersed and perhaps disturbed by absorption in the young people, and plans for their future. Children are on a different plane, belong to a generation and way of feeling properly their own; there is seldom complete understanding between them and their parents, so that affection here suffers from some strain and uncertainty, all the more painful the greater the affection is. A childless marriage is sometimes more secure. Besides *Eros* and *Agape* it can include the third (and to me the most beautiful) bond of love, *Philia*. Friendship is not so warm as Eros and not so spiritual as Agape, but it is freer and more intellectual. It *chooses* in the friend the side with which it will sympathize, and it brings an unstipulated, independent contribution to that common interest. Now this intellectual partnership and give and take prevails more easily between two persons than in a family: a crowded home is not favourable to *friendship*. That is why friendship has to be sought outside. But I felt that between you and Annabel it existed and completed your lives in a different and subtler way. But perhaps my fancies are impertinent, and I ought only to assure you of my complete sympathy, not only in your loss, but in your eternal gain.

To *MATTHEW HOEHN, O.S.B.*

CORTINA D'AMPEZZO
AUGUST 10, 1939

Dear Father Hoehn,

I was christened in the Church and profess no other religion, so that from the point of view of the census-taker I am unmistakably a Catholic. My Protestant and Jewish critics also discover a good deal of Catholicism in my writings; but I have never been a practising Catholic, and my views in philosophy and history are incompatible with belief in any revelation. It would therefore be wholly misleading to classify me among "Catholic Authors".[1]

This is a sufficient answer to your inquiry, for the purpose of your book of biographies, in which I ought not to be included. Yet I may add, in case you are at all interested in my real relation to the Faith, that a well-grounded Catholic student might find my philosophy useful (like that of some of the ancients) in defending the moral, political and mystical doctrines of the Church. I think that all religious ideas are merely symbolical; but I think the same of the ideas of science and even of the senses: so that the way is cleared for faith, in deciding which set of symbols one will trust.

Sincerely yours

[1] Father Hoehn was at the time "gathering material" for his first book of *Catholic Authors*, and the above letter is Santayana's reply to certain definite questions he was asked. [D.C.]

To MRS. C. H. TOY

Dear Mrs. Toy

In a month it seems that you will be leaving Cambridge and that this may be the last letter I shall address to you there. It seems very strange, after so many years when you have been, whether I was there myself or not, the focus of all that was pleasant for me there. And for you, it must be both troublesome and sad—a sort of secondary mixed grief, as at a funeral, where one has to mind externals, under the public eye; whereas the pure grief came earlier, when the mind realized in solitude that a lifelong bond was snapped and a change had become inevitable. I hope the material side of this funeral will not tire and distress you too much. The moral part is less intrusive, and can be considered and disposed of at leisure.

Do you remember in Thomas Mann's *Magic Mountain* the old Mynherr Pepperkorn, who ended his speeches by crying: *Erledigt!* That word often occurs to me now-a-days, and expresses a great sense of relief. To *dispatch* something, to have it settled and done for, is a blessed consummation.

By a coincidence, I too am compelled to change my residence —not the town, but the house—because the Hotel Bristol is to be pulled down and rebuilt, the operations being expected to last two years. I expect to go about September 15 to the Grand Hotel— good but old-fashioned, and not one of those frequented by fashionable foreigners; but I may not remain there, and my address had better be % B. S. & Co in London, until I settle down in permanent quarters.

I have been having (for me) a great deal of company this summer. Cory has been here for six weeks, taking his meals with me, although living at another hotel; and an Italian admirer of my books, whom I call "Settembrini" (again after the *Magic Mountain*) walks with me every other afternoon. He is a professor of Italian in Berlin, but a sworn enemy of both governments, and a person of exactly Settembrini's mentality. How he takes to my writings is a mystery, but he does. This amount of society has not tired me as much as I might have expected, and has not interfered with my morning's work. There is to be a new edition of *Egotism in German Philosophy,* for which I have written a short new *Preface* and a long *Postscript.* The book is announced for October, and I will have a copy of the English edition sent you, as Scribner is often late with his publications. I am in the midst of the last chapter of the *Realm of Spirit:* it is difficult, partly on account of the accumulation of old versions that have to be compared and almost always rejected; but there is a good deal of substance concentrated in the book, and some new developments. It will have to do; and in any case it will be a great moment when here too I can say *Erledigt!*

The war-scare is not so much cultivated in Italy as in France and England, but foreigners have almost ceased to come here: not altogether a disadvantage for the lover of distinct *milieux,* but a woe for the hotel-keepers. Cortina, however, is crowded at this moment (the peak of the season) with Italians and transient Germans, and there is plenty of motoring, mountain-climbing, ladies in trousers, and good cheer.

My nephew's son, Robert Shaw Sturgis, named after my brother, has finished his school-days at St. Mark's but is too young to go to College, and is to be in Europe this winter learning languages. They talk of letting me see him in Rome, which would awaken in me a grand-fatherly emotion never yet experienced.

May you be content, if not happy, in your new home.

Yours sincerely

To MRS. C. H. TOY

HOTEL DANIELI, VENICE
OCT. 10, 1939

Dear Mrs. Toy

You probably had not received my letter from Cortina, addressed to Garden Street, Cambridge, when you last wrote, with the tragic feelings of a person condemned to exile. It is impossible for me to be sympathetic on that subject, since I am hardened to exile, and like it. If I had not always been an exile, I could never have had a good time. Now, in one sense, I am freshly an exile—from Rome, and I have never felt freer and more comfortable. I have a top corner room in the new part of this hotel, with a magnificent view of the long curved sea-front, the Basin of St. Mark, the Lagoons and the Lido; at one end are four grey destroyers drawn up in a row; at the other, the two training ships, three-masted and full-rigged, the *Cristoforo Colombo* and the *Amerigo Vespucci*—to remind me of America at its birth and christening, when it promised to be quite Latin. Yet if it had remained quite Latin, there would probably never have been this hotel for me to come to, and certainly I shouldn't have had the money to come to it, and to have my meals in the sunny corner of the great Venetian hall with its Gothic windows and marble columns, such as any millionaire in Chicago might have in his house. My friends (who are not very sympathetic) tell me Venice is *impossible* in winter, and tell me I shall soon be exiled again. Very likely: but the natives say it is quite habitable at all seasons, with dampness in the narrow canals and lanes, but splendid sunshine, most of the time, on this open sea-front. I am ready to go if necessary, and have picked my place of refuge, Riva at the head of the lake of Garda, where I could stay until it was time to return to Cortina; but I mean to remain here, and avoid all changes and journeys, if it can be managed. My doctor gives me injections against catarrh, and approves of my idea.

These are trivial matters, occupying the first place in one's animal mind, while the spirit ought to be exercised by great public and moral questions. But the questions of the day are of the same

kind, on a public scale, as the question of my exiles and my lodgings. There is no greatness about them, only habits, and whims,
and petulance, and Egotism. I take refuge in my philosophy, and
work away at my last chapter which seems to be recalcitrant, and
refuses to be completed and dismissed. But everything comes to
an end somehow, and when this chapter is done, and the whole
book [1] revised, I shall be free to amuse myself with politics and
reminiscences. Unfortunately, I have no books to read, and Venice
is not a learned place. However I have picked up, in the shop windows, a volume of Jacques Bainville, *Histoire de Deux Peuples,*
and a French translation of Nietzsche's *Gaia Scienza,* both admirable; and no doubt I shall find other things at a pinch. I also have
all my unpublished manuscripts (sent from Rome with my winter
clothes) to revise and correct—or burn—in view of not leaving too
much to the decision of my literary executor.

The other day, awaking from absorption in the newspaper,
whom should I see before me but Berenson! We had one good talk:
but the second (and last) already flagged and made me feel how
little sympathy there is at bottom between people who don't like
each other but like the same "subjects" or have similar professions.
These "subjects" become different objects to two minds that have
grown old and have grown apart in considering them. Berenson
surprised me by talking with juvenile enthusiasm about "art" (as
if we were still in the 1890's). There is an exhibition of Paolo
Veronese here, where he said he was spending day after day rapt
in wonder, and always finding fresh beauties in the pictures. I
haven't yet been to the exhibition (I mean to go tomorrow: I am
not *deliberately* wicked) but it is impossible for me now to regard
"art", any more than traditional religion, as a supreme interest in
itself. It is an illustration to history, and a positive joy when it
really reveals something beautiful in the material or in the spiritual world. But the social world, the world of convention, to
which the criticism of art belongs, has come to seem to me rather
a screen that keeps the material and the spiritual worlds out of
sight. This is because my philosophy is not humanistic or psychological, like that of most people nowadays, but combines old materialism with old Platonism: *babylonisch über einander getürm-
ten* systems, as Goethe said of the churches at Assisi. But this comes

[1] *The Realm of Spirit.*

of trying to penetrate and not merely to "experience" this world, and to penetrate it in every possible direction. I may be wrong, but I find great comfort in Nietzsche. He is not explicit, he is romantic but he *implies* my world of two or more storeys, if he does not draw its plan and elevation, as my architectural propensities lead me to do—without, I admit, any technical accuracy; because I am really a self-indulgent impressionist, like Nietzsche himself, and wish to sketch my buildings in perspective.

In order to keep up the game with B.B., however, I mentioned the constant pleasure I find in the light in Venice and in the aspects of the sky. "Yes", said he, "*they* were wonderful at catching those effects, due to the reflected light of the lagoon in the atmosphere. Paolo Veronese was supreme in rendering them". I thought of Titian and Tiepolo, but said nothing, because I don't really know or care who *painted* or who *saw* those harmonies most perfectly. Each probably saw a different effect, and painted it according to his own convention. What I care about is the harmonies themselves, which can't be had at second hand; they are strictly momentary and incommunicable; if you can get them out of a book or a picture, very well: but it would be an illusion to suppose that the *same* harmony had been felt by the poet or the painter. He had merely worked in a material, that could offer such harmonies eventually to the properly prepared mind; and his own interests—think of Shakespeare!—were probably much more mixed and hurried than those of a devout modern reader or connoisseur. It is lucky for B.B., in one sense, that he keeps the old flame alive; but I can't help feeling that it was lighted and is kept going by forced draft, by social and intellectual ambition, and by professional pedantry. If he were a real poet, would he turn away from the evening sky to see, by electric light, how Veronese painted it?

My last letter was sent soon before the outbreak of this second German war, expected to settle again what was supposed to be settled for ever by the first, and to settle it in exactly the same way. The mails, at first, were naturally at sixes and sevens and you may never have received that letter. But things are going more regularly now and I trust this will reach you and find you as content in your exile as I am in mine.

                    Yours sincerely

To *ARTHUR DAVISON FICKE*

HOTEL DANIELI, VENICE
DECEMBER 2, 1939

Dear Ficke

"Mrs. Morton of Mexico" arrived some time since, and has been filling various pleasant intervals, so quiet at this season, between sunset and dinner. You are a capital story-teller; have you really never written fiction before? I am ashamed to say that, since your book on Japanese Prints, written (morally at least) in the last century, I have seen nothing of yours, although I have heard of your activities, for instance in Llewellyn Powys' little book about his life in America. I am not a great reader of novels, and feel rather cheated when they move or harrow me, that is, when they are good, I suppose, from the professional point of view. But I enjoy the observation in them; and your book has given me vivid glimpses of Spanish America, about which I know very little. My family was in other days a colonial family, but in the Philippine Islands, and so long ago that the unrest of the present age had not yet penetrated to those idyllic regions, and both my father and my mother spoke of Manila and of the East generally as of a more human and natural world than the one we live in now.

By the way, in the flattering mention you make of me in your book, there is a slight and very natural error, which in spite of its littleness is strangely significant and shows how little the public really knows about its members. You speak of my half-Spanish *blood*. If you had said I was half-Spanish or half-American, it would have been true enough, because my dominant language and associations are American and I have lived little in Spain; but I am wholly Spanish in blood, and have always remained legally Spanish in nationality. My mother also lived little in Spain; but her blood was wholly Spanish, or, more specifically Catalonian, her father being José Borrás of Reus and her mother Teresa Carbonell of Las Palmas. But she married, in Manila, at the age of 22, George Sturgis of Boston, and promised him to bring their children up in America, in case of his death. This occurred in 1857; and she then moved to Boston where she stayed until 1861, when she went to Madrid, where she married my father. But later she returned to Boston; at first my father retained me in Spain, but in 1872 he decided to take me also to Boston and leave me with my mother and her Sturgis children. Still, our family life in Boston was wholly Spanish: I never spoke any other language at home; and you can't imagine what a completely false picture comes to the mind if you suggest that my mother was an American. Then, too, she and my sisters would have been Protestants, and my whole imaginative and moral background would have been different.

Excuse these details; but I have just finished my last philosophical book, and feel free to be reminiscent. With many thanks for your Mrs. Morton.

Sincerely yours

To MRS. C. H. TOY

HOTEL SAVOIA, CORTINA D'AMPEZZO
AUGUST 8TH 1940

Dear Mrs. Toy

Your good letters of June 27th and of July 10th are before me. I was particularly glad to receive the first (on July 25th) with the news of your complete recovery and pleasure in going to dinner-parties! Think how much younger you are than I, who have not had evening-clothes, not even a dinner-jacket, for more than ten years! Your other letter arrived today. They take about a month, unless they go by Air Mail, when with luck they come from Evanston, Illinois to Cortina in some ten days. You may wonder what correspondents I have in Evanston, Illinois. It is Professor Schilpp and his secretary, who are getting out a volume, second of a series entitled "Living Philosophers," the first being devoted to Dewey and this to me, by order of seniority. Croce is to follow, and then Brunschvicg and Bertie Russell. It is honourable company, and

my mind now is entirely devoted in the morning hours to answering
the criticisms that are to be contained in volume two. It is a good
long-range distraction from war-news and from the small uncer-
tainties about letters, money-drafts, and permitted places of residence that are involved in belligerency.

Since I came to Cortina, without any books, I have found
another distraction of an imaginative kind for the afternoon: it
is the complete works of Balzac in an excellent Italian version which
I get for 30 cents a volume in a book-stall under an arch in this
mountain town. I feel as I did in Oxford, where with all the books
of the world at hand, I found solace from war-news in Dickens.
Balzac is deeper in worldly knowledge, but never humorous or
moving, and he would not serve for much comfort if I were as
distressed now as I was in 1917. This picture of the world keeps
politics, finance, and human perversity in general well in the foreground, without any real allegiance to any ideal compensations
other than the artificial happy *dénouement* of some of the stories.
But he gives me just what I need now, clearness in judging men
and events. He is not cynical, he can even convert his villains on
occasion, but he has no illusions and no prejudices, and can see
the nobility or at least the humanity of all classes and parties. It
is a support to philosophy at this moment when the public mind
is subject to hysteria. I hope that events will soon bring us not only
material peace, but the peace that comes from understanding.

I hope I may be inspired to write the verses you ask for, but
poetry is even more remote from my habits than is a dinner-jacket.
You wouldn't want your little friends to laugh at me as an old
dotard, who thinks he can sing.

Yours sincerely

To MRS. C. H. TOY

GRAND HOTEL, ROME, MARCH 28, 1941

Dear Mrs. Toy:

. . . Thank you for yours of March 9 with extracts from Judge
Holmes and Sir Frederick Pollock about the *Life of Reason*. It is
sweet flattery after my Schilpp critics: but by chance, at the same
moment, I find the antidote in Montaigne; "Ils [Chrysippus and
Diogenes] disoient qu'il n'y avait point de plus dangereuse voluptez
. . . que celle qui nous vient de l'approbation d'autrui".[1] But that
was in 1905: what annoys me is that now people should still talk
about the *Life of Reason* as if it represented my whole philosophy,
or was the best part of it. That is because Dewey's disciples make it a
subject in their courses, and criticize it for not raising or not
solving the questions that they propose to their classes. It is not
me they are considering, but the convenience of having a readable
book to use as a stalking horse, their own books not being readable.
And another annoying thing is that they criticize my *concepts* and
the absence of *definitions* for them, as if I were talking about essences, when I am talking about history, psychology, and morals,
that is, about *things;* and a man who thinks concepts can be sub-
stituted for things, and that by defining concepts he sees things
truly is, to be frank, a fool. The more freedom and variety there
is in our terms, the more adequately we may hope to besiege the
reality of things, and to do justice to their influence upon us.

I hope there is no reason to fear that this letter of yours need
be the last. If correspondence between Italy & the U. S. becomes
impossible, it will also become impossible for me to get money, and
I shall have to leave for Switzerland or Spain. It would be a horrid
nuisance, but I am recovering my normal health and should be able
to manage.

Yours sincerely

[1] [They said that there was no more dangerous pleasure than that which comes
to us from the approval of others.]

To LAWRENCE SMITH BUTLER

PALAZZO DELLA FONTE, FIUGGI, ITALY

JULY 3, 1941

Dear Lawrence:

A long time ago, I think before this war began, I received a letter from you that was particularly welcome, because you promised to come that winter to see me, as well as Rome. I replied urging you to come; and have never heard from you again until now, when your letter of June 12 reaches me here. We have been unlucky, because most letters come through, in at most two or three weeks, sometimes sooner.

I am very well now, for my age (77) although I had a rather bad winter and am much less active than I used to be, taking short walks only, and rather liking days on which I have some excuse for not going out at all. The books I had planned to write are now finished and published, besides others that I never meant to write but that have been interpolated by pressure from outside. This does not mean that I am idle, for besides my autobiography (of which the proper title is *Persons & Places,* among which you will be included when I come to your period, but I am now at the year 1872, before you were born, and I may not live to reach 1895, when I made your acquaintance in mid Atlantic, (was it on board the Werra?) besides that, I say, I have a book of short reflections on politics and history, to be called *Dominations & Powers.* But these books are elastic and endless. My biography never can be finished, since I shall not be able to describe my own death; and the other also hangs fire, as there are always new wars and revolutions to give one fresh food for thought.

I see by your note-paper that you are a *bona fide* professional architect now, which sounds more serious than your lovemaking or even your music. I am glad you keep up all these humanistic interests. The great satisfactory thing about you as a friend (as I will say if I get to you in my Memoirs) has been that you are always the same. Most men—this is less true of the ladies—in America lose their youth and their liberty at 25: they are thereafter just what a German philosopher named Jaspers pretends that we all are: our situation personified. But you young men were such nice company in America because you were not your situation personified since as yet you had no situation: you were yourselves and you had *Lebensraum* about you: athletics, music, society, books: and the nice ones, like you, also religion, friendship, and family life. You have kept more of this freedom than other men of your time; and you would be as good company now as you were in 1898; whereas your contemporaries, almost all of them, would be, from my point of view, ciphers. Of course I know they might personify an important situation. But I don't want to talk to a situation. I want to talk to a man in that situation.

My situation at this moment is rather strange. I am rather well off, but threatened with starvation, because it seems that all credits belonging to foreigners, at least to Europeans, have been "frozen", and all my money is in America! I have enough on hand to last into the autumn, and I hope that by that time my nephew will have got a licence to send me funds as usual: otherwise, Goodbye.

Yours aff^{ly}

To *GEORGE STURGIS*

GRAND HOTEL, ROME, OCT, 12. 1941

Dear George

If my reply to your telegram asking for my whereabouts was a little vague, the reason was that I hadn't yet decided what to do, except that the proposed journey to Spain, on detailed inquiry, had rather upset me. I haven't the strength or endurance, nor the sharp ears, eyes, and wits that would have been needed to go alone, at my age, through those two nights in the train without sleeping-cars, those four customs houses, and that insecurity about money, since one is neither allowed to take Italian money out of Italy nor Spanish money into Spain. I consulted my doctor, and he agreed that I hadn't the health necessary for such a trial, nor for making the journey by air. As at the same time I can't stay in my present quarters at the Grand Hotel, because they are too dear, it occurred to me to move to the Blue Sisters' Nursing Home, where I knew that they receive persons not definitely ill, but old or delicate and requiring attendance. I went yesterday to see the place and interview the Superior. She showed me a very large pleasant room with a good bathroom, that I can have for 100 lire a day, including service as well as food, and as this is better and cheaper than anything I can get at this hotel, I am moving there in a day or two. The address (which I am telegraphing to you at once) is

Via Santo Stefano Rotondo, 6, Rome

The Sisters' official name is "Little Company of Mary", but it is not necessary to put this down. Of course they speak English, which makes it easier for me, and my doctor goes there constantly and approves of my decision. He has written to you about my state of health. I am well and can take good walks, but the catarrh is always knocking at the door and (as this decision shows) I feel much less capable of looking after myself than I was before last winter.

As to money matters, I still have 8000 lire, and am glad to know that you will be able to send me 250 dollars a month to Rome. I shall save on that, in view of the possibility of a total stoppage, although I am hopeful that it may not occur. If it does, you must appeal to head quarters either to let me have money in Italy or to obtain leave to reside in Switzerland, where I could go without trouble in my present state of health.

Yours aff^{ly}

To GEORGE STURGIS

6, VIA S. STEFANO ROTONDO, ROME
OCTOBER 17, 1941

Dear George

I have now been three days in this "Nursing Home", and feel as if I had miraculously been transported to Avila. This top of the Caelius [1] is like the old rustic ruinous Rome of a hundred years ago, and the house and the Sisters, all Irish, have the quality of provincial good people in Spain—the Sastres, for instance. It is a complete change from the international first class hotels that I have been living in of late. Morally, I like it better; I am interfered with more, because I am attended to more. I am surrounded by women: one old Irish priest, a patient, and my doctor Sabbatucci are the only *men* I have seen in this establishment. It is a nice place, with grounds; you come in through an old gate and a well-planted avenue; there is a church and several large buildings, and the old Santo Stefano Rotondo [2] is next door, overhanging the terrace. Food is also of a new type, not first class food, but in some ways better, and I have it in my room, as the *table d'hôte,* which I tried the first day, is dismal. What I most dread is the cold. Fuel is limited, and my present room has the sun only in the morning: but I can move to a sunnier room if I like, only I shouldn't then have my own bath-room.—As you may gather from all this, I am not ill, but I am *helpless;* too old and threatened by too many difficulties to look after myself successfully. The attendance I have here, although I should prefer not to need it, really is a safeguard, and it may become indispensable at any moment, if my catarrh, etc., returns.

Your telegram, addressed here, reached me on Oct. 15th. It is enough to put down the street and number, without the title of the house; especially as it is almost the only one in this old walled lane—again very like Avila . . .

Yours aff[ly]

[1] One of the seven hills of Rome.

[2] One of the oldest round churches in Italy.

To MRS. C. F. LAMA

VIA SANTO STEFANO ROTONDO, 6,
ROME, OCT. 10, 1944

Dear Madam

Several photographers have come here to take my picture—
something that never happened to me before, and I have had the
pleasure of seeing a great many young soldiers and airmen including a grandnephew of mine, who took me back to the days when I
lived in college. This is my reward for having finally written a book
or two fit for the public to read.

I don't know what photograph was reproduced in *Life,* but
since you were pleased to see it I infer that it corresponds to what
you think I ought to look like. That is not ever the case with me
now. I still think that the only true portrait of me was drawn in
the year 1896 by Andreas Andersen, by the firelight in my room in
the Harvard Yard; because like a true artist he caught the evidence
of several sides of my character. The instantaneous photographs
now in vogue are violent and good only when strung together
in a film, so that the eye may compose its own synthetic image out
of a lot of them, as it always does by nature. Andersen's drawing was
reproduced by Scribner in Vol. I of my collected works, and I dare
say it will appear in Vol. II of *Persons and Places* which covers those
same years.

With many thanks for your kind note

Yours sincerely

To LAWRENCE SMITH BUTLER

VIA SANTO STEFANO ROTONDO, 6,
ROME, DEC. 1. 1944

Dear Lawrence:

It is a great pleasure to receive your letter: both Mrs. Potter and Cory, who have written lately, mentioned you, knowing that I should be glad to hear that you were well and still leading the life of a young man about town. But you must be getting on, and much as I should like to see you, I shouldn't advise you to come to Italy until you hear that things have returned somewhat to the normal. In Rome, as you know, there has been little damage done to buildings: but the country has been thoroughly pillaged by the two friendly foreign armies that have passed over it; communications and victualling are difficult; and people have no work and no means of carrying on their trades. Food is scarce and bad, and the value of money and the price of everything are uncertain. We also lack coal, and electric light shines decently only every third day. Life would therefore not be comfortable or easy for a traveller. I myself have been lucky in being taken in by these Sisters. They have a nicely furnished house and nice English ideas of food and comfort, and we manage very well, in spite of all difficulties. Of late, too, I have received various presents, as well as many visits, from American army men, and am revelling in the lost luxuries of tea, marmalade, cheese, anchovies, shaving-cream, and even peanuts. I have been photographed and interviewed to exhaustion; but I am happy like a sky without clouds, and still at work with the pen.—In the second volume of *Persons & Places,* you are commemorated among "Americans in Europe"—I hope you won't be angry at the past tense: but I write of everything as if it were ancient history. Motto: *Veritas.*

Yours aff^{ly}

To (MRS.) *ASTA FLEMING WHITESIDE*

VIA SANTO STEFANO ROTONDO, 6
ROME, DEC. 8, 1944

Dear Mrs. Whiteside

Plato in one place compares the mind to an aviary: "The Arches", from which you send me your "Miracle Letter",[1] must be like that: a perpetual twitter of snatches of song. I am flattered and embarrassed to think that old and new chirpings of mine are audible there, among so much wit and wisdom that is out of my reach—out of my reach materially, because of difficult communications, and also intellectually, because your new world of letters bewilders me. However, I felt comparatively at home when I came to Mr. Cram,[2] although I find his words obscure. I liked his cream-green Perpendicular churches; and I respect his Catholic philosophy, but do not find its firm structure in his words as you quote them. I felt even more at home when I discovered that "Charlie" Walker, as we called him, is your "landlord". In the second volume of *Persons & Places* he will find a good many reminiscences of his Harvard friends. I am surprised and delighted to think that you can pick out bird-notes even out of this book, which I supposed and almost intended to be a humdrum chronicle of *faits divers* for some future antiquary to dig up to illustrate the low state of society in my time. You, of course, have changed that. Time has moved since the 1890's, which I feel to be my spiritual and chronological home. But you have the art of finding the beautiful in unexpected places, and to that I owe the pleasure of having received your letter, which for a moment has turned this monastic cell—I am living in the guest-house of the Little Company of Mary, or "Blue Sisters"—as I said, into a musical aviary.

With many thanks & best wishes

Yours sincerely

[1] Mrs. Whiteside writes: "The 'Miracle Letter' is some work I did during the War—a letter service for solace and inspiration in the spirit of Madonna. I interpreted that rôle for Max Reinhardt at Olympia, London and all the great European cities."

[2] Ralph Adams Cram, the American architect.

To THOMAS MUNRO

VIA SANTO STEFANO ROTONDO, 6
ROME, DEC. 10, 1944

My dear Munro:

Your letter came to me in the midst of an avalanche of Army visitors, most of them very young and raw, but characteristically looking for something they had heard of at home, or from home, very recently. Others came to photograph or to interview me, and some simply in search of a modest autograph. A few distinguished persons also honoured me, including Col. Poletti (who was our ruling authority) and Prof. T. V. Smith of Chicago, full of the only right way of governing the world. In this society, I put away your letter to be answered when the rear guard of war had begun to pass on. It has now thinned a good deal (like me on rations) and I return to the pleasant memories of you in Paris, and your enthusiasm for African figurines. *There* is a theme for your Society [1] to investigate philosophically and scientifically. I am glad you are approaching the vast subject of the arts from that side, rather than from that of precepts and taste. The philosophers have written a good deal of vague stuff about the beautiful, and the critics a good deal of accidental partisan stuff about right and wrong in art. If you will only discover why and when people develop such arts and such tastes you will be putting things on a sounder basis.

My seclusion here for three years, with few books and only meagre newspapers, has been good for my health and for my work. Besides *Persons & Places*, 3 volumes, of which the last will not be published for the present, I have written a theological book, [2] and am turning now, well instructed by two great wars and their effects, to my old *Dominations & Powers* which will, if I live, represent the wisdom of my old age. I have outlived most of my contemporaries,

---

1 Mr. Munro writes:
"The 'Society' mentioned is the American Society for Aesthetics, which I had recently helped to organize, and for which I had asked if Santayana had some advice or message."

2 *The Idea of Christ in the Gospels.*

all my family and early friends: but I have not lost them. On the contrary, reliving my life has been pleasanter than living it. In hopes of some day seeing you again.

Yours sincerely,

To MARTIN BIRNBAUM

VIA SANTO STEFANO ROTONDO, 6,
ROME, OCTOBER 12TH 1945

Dear Mr. Birnbaum

I have a clearer recollection of Grenville Winthrop's name than of his person, for although I remember his figure I think we never spoke to each other. He had gone from Harvard by the time that my relations with the undergraduate world were renewed; but his name often recurred in the talk of many of my young friends afterwards, as well as in Frank Bullard's, whom you mention. He moved just behind the scenes, when I watched the play, as an exemplary person that everybody knew and admired: and in later years I heard of him, no doubt at the Bullards', as a collector. But both he and I seem to have cared little for miscellaneous society, and our particular circles only touched at the circumference, in the persons of our common friends.

As to Sargent, I once made a voyage with him (by accident) from New York to Gibraltar, and then (by spontaneous agreement) we went together, in company with Dr. & Mrs. William White of Philadelphia, to Tangiers. I have a faded photograph of us four in a group, watching him sketching some picturesque corner of the town. Then, in 1893, the place was most primitive and he was chiefly interested in procuring genuine costumes for his Prophets in the decorations he was planning for the Boston Public Library. He was afterwards going to search in Spain for a characteristic image of the Mater Dolorosa, which he meant then to introduce into the same composition, but at the other end. I looked for it later, but could see nothing that corresponded to what, on board, he had explained to me was his project. We both felt the force of what might be called the impure wealth of Spanish art, passion in black velvet and seven gold daggers. I never saw Sargent after that trip, but always felt that I had a private cue to a certain side of his work.

I am glad to know that Grenville Winthrop bequeathed his collection to Harvard. That fact, which I had not heard of, explains perhaps the great expansion of the Fogg Art Museum—or is it no longer called the "Fogg"? For many years now I have had no true friend at Harvard, who could tell me about the changes there that really interested me. But Mr. Lowell's "Houses", to judge by the photographs, have been an architectural success.

Yours sincerely

To FRANCIS CLOUGH

ROME

NOVEMBER 4, 1945

Dear Mr. Clough:

Poetry of the reflective moralising kind practised by your namesake,[1] by you, and by me is out of fashion among poets, and those who like it like it only for the sentiment it expresses; but that might have been as well expressed in prose. For that reason I long ago gave up trying to versify. I was twenty when I wrote the sonnet [2] you mention. The one of yours that you enclose is recent, and I suspect you are not very young. Of course I sympathise, but—[sic. D. C.]

At the same time as your letter I have received a booklet by a young Argentinian, in Spanish and bad English, who is a poet but writes without meter or rhyme, and says he is full of "adoles-

1 Arthur Hugh Clough.

2 "As in the midst of battle there is room," etc.

cents" (sic) coursing through his body; that he kisses the barks of
old trees, as he used to kiss the stones, but ends by kissing warm
flesh.—Such is the poetry of today. *Morituri vos salutamus.*

Yours very truly

To CONRAD SLADE

VIA SANTO STEFANO ROTONDO; 6,
ROME, NOV. 4, 1945

My dear Slade,

You can't imagine what a pleasure it was to see your name on
the envelope, and then to read that all was unexpectedly well with
you, that your boy had recovered, and had taken you and his
mother to the Yosemite Valley in his own motor. This transforms
the picture I had of your later years. Perhaps it is pessimistic of me
to take the worst for granted, in order to be as happy as possible
no matter what happens. Everybody says I am so cheerful! And I
reply, "Why shouldn't I be. I have all I need." I am too old to
make plans for the future; but for your own sake I hope you will
find your way soon to the Old World. It is impoverished, but still
beautiful; and the ruins have included the ruin of some very ugly
things like La Troisieme Republique. I hope and believe that
La Quatrieme will be nobler and wiser.

Can't you send me at least a photo of your *good* pictures, and
better still of your statuettes? I want to see if your "Nordic" genius
has taken a consistent shape.

Another pleasant surprise, like receiving your letter, came
to me a while ago when Iris Cutting (Marchesa Origo) came unan-
nounced to see me. People, strangers, now flock to look at me as
if I were the oldest inhabitant of the village, and even leave me
little presents of marmalade or chocolate or books. Iris didn't (thank
God!) bring me anything but good news. I had supposed them to
be living in New York: but no. She and her husband had weathered

the war at his farm La Face near Chianciano, in central Tuscany; and they had had two little girls, of whom she showed me a photograph. I had said a word about her in my book, ending on a sad note, as in your case. Evidently I am a false prophet in matters of sentiment. I like to anticipate the worst, so as to be able to bear it if it comes.

Here, with the Sisters, I feel settled. They are reconciled to my seeming a bad Catholic, and look forward to my deathbed repentance. But I say to myself the words of Walt Whitman: "Words cannot express how much at peace I am about God and about death." So are you, no doubt. You were always "Nordic" in these matters, or perhaps Hellenic, like your old friend

To JOHN M. MERRIAM

VIA SANTO STEFANO ROTONDO, 6
ROME, NOVEMBER 15, 1945

My dear Merriam:

Senex ad senem de Senectute scribo; [1]

yet we are much older than Cicero ever was and also much more recent, so that we have a double chance of being wiser, having more experience of life, individual and collective. And the charm I find in old age—for I was never happier than I am now—comes of having learned to live in the moment, and thereby in eternity; and this means recovering a perpetual youth, since nothing can be fresher than each day as it dawns and changes. When we have no expectations, the actual is a continual free gift, but much more placidly accepted than it could be when we were children; for then the stage was full of trap doors and unimaginable transformations that kept us always alarmed, eager, and on the point of tears; whereas now we have wept our tears out, we know what can pop up of those trap doors, and what kind of shows those transformations can present; and we remember many of them with affection,

[1] An old man, I write to an old man about old age. Cf. *De Amicitia* I. 5.

and watch the new ones that come with interest and good will, but without false claims for our own future.

So much for the philosophy of old age. As for current events, state of health or decrepitude, etc., I have little to say. I seem to be perfectly well, but like the One Horse Shay, I am undoubtedly a little feeble all over, and less than an atom bomb, if it struck me, would probably reduce me to a little heap of dust. Meantime I continue to write more or less every day, and have weathered the little discomforts of war and muddled peace without serious trouble. The Sisters here look after me nicely, I have a pleasant corner room with extensive views over green country and mean to remain here for the rest of my days. As to society, I have never received so many visits as the American soldiers in Rome have made me. It has been very pleasant to see so many young faces and to autograph so many books, which is what they usually ask me to do. As to memories of 1886, I have written them out, and need not repeat them, but wish the survivors [1] a happy and peaceful sunset.

Yours sincerely

To *MARTIN BIRNBAUM*

VIA SANTO STEFANO ROTONDO, 6,
ROME, FEB. 4, 1946

Dear Mr. Birnbaum

I write to thank you very much for your reminiscences of Sargent, including those of Henry James and the plates of some of Sargent's paintings and drawings. I wish that you had gone more systematically into the problem of naturalistic *versus* excentric [sic] or symbolic painting. It is a subject about which my own mind is undecided. My sympathies are initially with classic tradition, and in that sense with Sargent's school; yet for that very reason I fear to be unjust to the excentric and abstract inspiration of persons

[1] Class-mates of '86 at Harvard.

perhaps better inspired. Two things you say surprise me a little: one that Sargent was enormous physically. I remember him as a little stout, but not tall: and I once made a voyage by chance in his company, and thereafter a trip to Tangier; so that I had for a fortnight at least constant occasions to go about with him; and being myself of very moderate stature I never felt that he was big. The other point is that he saw and painted "objectively", realistically, and not psychologically. Now, certainly he renders his model faithfully; but in the process, which must be selective and proper to the artist, I had always thought that, perhaps unawares he betrayed analytical and satirical powers of a high order, so that his portraits were strongly comic, not to say moral caricatures. But in thinking of what you say, and quote from him, on this subject, I begin to believe that I was wrong, that he may have been universally sympathetic and cordial, in the characteristically American manner, and that the satire that there might seem to be in his work was that of literal truth only: because we are all, *au fond,* caricatures of ourselves, and a good eye will see through our conventional disguises and labels. And this would explain what to some persons seems the "materialism" of Sargent's renderings; his interest in *objets d'art* for instance, rather than in the vegetable kingdom or in the life of non-sensuous reality at large. Crowding his house with pictures, and his memory with innumerable friends and innumerable anecdotes about them, shows a respect for the commonplace, a love of the world, that prevents the imagination from taking high flights or reflecting ultimate emotions. Is there, I wonder, any truth in such a suspicion?

Yours sincerely

To *MARGARET BATES*

VIA SANTO STEFANO ROTONDO, 6
ROMA, AUGUST 6, 1946

Dear Miss Bates:

You have done me a real favour in sending me your Doctor's Thesis on *Discreción* in Cervantes. I don't know when I have had so much pleasure in the savour of so much good Castilian speech and sentiment. Your method is discreet: you let the authorities speak for themselves, and amply prove, by the way, that you have superabundant learning to be, as they call it here, a *Dottoressa*.

If your study grows into a book, as it well might, you will have leisure to revise the errors that inevitably slip in (as I know only too well) when English printers and proof-readers deal with foreign languages. Sometimes, not being a philologist, I wondered whether a spelling was an error or an archaic form, particularly in the *concordancia* in gender and number when one word was in the subject and the other in the predicate. For instance, on p. 54, 7 and 8 lines from the bottom, shouldn't "gusto" be *justo* and "lo" *la?*

There is one general observation that occurs to me about *discreción*. It means *savoir vivre*, not *savoir régler le monde;* it is a question of tact and breeding, of knowing how to face a difficulty and making all right something that was in danger of going wrong. But wrong in *any* situation, on any occasion, for *any* purpose. It is therefore a virtue in form or method, not in substance or will. So on next to the last page, I feel that the question whether Don Quijote was *discreto* or not does not arise. He was singularly and brilliantly *discreto,* as Hamlet was, *on the hypothesis of his madness being sanity*. He kept his seriousness, explained his giants turning into windmills to rob him of his victory, and behaved always like a knight and a Christian, no matter how burlesque the occasion might be. I have often felt, for instance, when visiting English public schools, that breeding and education and sport of every kind were training in *how* to do, feel, speak etc., not at all in *what* you ought to do, think, or work for. That has to be the fruit of a second or a prior education in the world or in self-knowledge.

Excuse this moralising on my part: it is only a proof of the real interest I have felt in your book.

Yours sincerely

To *LAWRENCE SMITH BUTLER*

VIA SANTO STEFANO ROTONDO, 6
ROME, SEPT. 19. 1946

Dear Lawrence,

The parcel from you arrived this morning, full of just the right things. The jars of marmalade were safe, only a little had leaked out of one of them through a crack in the cover. I have not yet tasted the contents, but they look inviting, and please thank the lady who sent them; it will be a treat. The only objection is that I get used to luxuries, and the memory becomes a sort of temptation of Saint Antony when I find myself in the wilderness again without even the wild honey that St. John the Baptist allowed himself. Perhaps the same pious ladies supplied it. The Gospels don't tell us everything, but they do somewhere mention this charitable practice of good ladies in all ages and countries, in compliment to hermits. By the way, I have read a most charming story, written by St. Jerome about the visit of St. Antony to St. Paul the Hermit in the Thebaid: and I have found a photograph of a magnificent picture by Velazquez—his most beautiful one, I think; for his subjects don't often lend themselves to poetic treatment, which I have the vulgar taste to like in painting—representing the scene. I remember the original, with the most lovely landscape, a raven bringing a loaf from heaven, and a tame lion digging the grave for St. Paul, more than a hundred years old, to occupy when he has finished the sublime prayer which he is evidently saying. Look up this picture, and tell me if you don't like it. I have it in a book on Velazquez, which I will give you as a memento if you will come to see it and me.

Thank you especially for the black tie, which is splendid and will last me—if I live—for years. I feel very young and well, and buoyed up by the thought of perhaps finishing my book on Politics,[1] which will be more useful than any of mine hitherto, usefulness never having been a dominant trait in your affectionate old friend

To DAVID RUBIO, O.S.A.

VIA SANTO STEFANO ROTONDO, 6
ROMA, NOVEMBER 27, 1946

Dear Father Rubio:

It was very kind of you to send me your little book on *The Mystic Soul of Spain*. The soul of Spain, mystical and non-mystical is not at all understood among English-speaking people. It is well that an authoritative voice like yours should be raised to enlighten them, and I hope you will write other books developing the details more. For in a brief summary you can't do more than propose some generalities. Neither your "Spain" nor your "Mysticism" exist *in rerum natura*. They are essences. Now you probably know that I am a friend of essences and I would rather understand your ideal non-existent "Spain" and your ideal non-existent "mysticism" than understand the existing medley. But your American audience will think that you are a Don Quixote *mistaking* the facts rather than a contemplative spirit discerning ideal essences. I am afraid the real soul of Spain at present is rather disintegrated. Yet we are all capable of being disinterested and disillusioned. That is not enough, I quite agree, but it is the beginning of deliverance.

Yours sincerely,

[1] *Dominations and Powers.*

To MARTIN BIRNBAUM

VIA SANTO STEFANO ROTONDO, 6,
ROME, JAN. 22, 1947

Dear Mr. Birnbaum

Yesterday, almost exactly six months after the date of your letter of July 24th '46, I received your beautiful book on "Jacovleff and Other Artists". The parcel was weather-worn, but luckily so stoutly wrapped and sealed that no damage was done to the plates. You must have thought from my silence that the book was lost or that I had forgotten to thank you for it. But it was not that. Other parcels have taken as long, and I deliberately waited to answer your letter until I could announce the receipt of your interesting gift.

I have spent all yesterday evening and this morning over it, first looking through all the plates and then reading your text on Jacovleff, on Aubrey Beardsley and on Behmer. I will not venture to say anything about contemporary painting. I am incompetent to judge, having never been much thrown with painters or with connoisseurs, nor a frequenter of exhibitions, even when I lived in Paris. What you say about Jacovleff, and the variety of the plates reproducing his works, only fill me with wonder at the intensity and the confusion of artistic life in our day. I feel as if it were necessary to let the storm pass and the wreckage sink out of sight before we could survey the result and distinguish our veritable surviving treasures.

But there is a semi-philosophical point that kept coming into my head as I read what you say about Aubrey Beardsley and also about Behmer (whom I had never heard of!). You seem to be troubled about the impropriety actual and suggested of their compositions. Now I see that it would be shocking to exhibit an obscene drawing in Church or in a lady's drawing-room; but I do not see anything painful in an obscene drawing because it is obscene; if it is seen at a suitable time and place, and is not a bad composition in itself. Now I think in Aubrey Beardsley there often is bad taste, like bad taste in the mouth, because his lascivious figures are ugly and socially corrupt. The obscene should be merry and hilarious, as it is in Petronius: it belongs to comedy, not to sour or revolutionary morals. It is the mixture of corrupt sneers and hypocrisy with vice that is unpleasant to see, unless it is itself the subject of satire, as for instance in old English caricatures. But in Beardsley the charm of the design and the elegance of the costumes and of the *ballet* character of all the movement seem to *recommend* the vice represented: and *that* is immoral. But licentiousness is natural in its place, and the *fun* of impropriety is also not vicious; and I don't see why the books or pictures illustrating these things should be regrettable. The Arabian Nights, in Mardrus, seem to me *purely* delightful. Robert Bridges, who was a good friend of mine, used to deplore the sensuality in Shakespeare, and say he was the greatest of poets and dramatists, but not an artist. I think that some of the jokes in Shakespeare are out of place; for instance what Hamlet says to Ophelia in the play scene; but in a frank comedy, the same and much broader things would be excellent, as in Aristophanes: and the public would soon select itself that patronised such shows. But I am afraid I am a hopeless pagan. Aubrey Beardsley, converted to Catholicism, might beg to have his naughty drawings destroyed, and perhaps they were not all in themselves beautiful or comic: but I should not destroy anything aesthetically *good*. The beautiful is a part of the moral; and the truly moral is a part of the beautiful: only they must not be mixed wrong, any more than sweets and savouries.—Excuse my sermon and believe with heartfelt thanks

Yours sincerely

To LAWRENCE SMITH BUTLER

VIA SANTO STEFANO ROTONDO, 6
ROME, JULY 26, 1947

Dear Lawrence,

I am writing to thank you for the new box of good things to eat, American, Danish, and Swiss which apparently comes from Saint Gal; but there was no card or address of the sender brought here; they only asked the Sister at the office to sign a receipt. You see I am beautifully protected here from little interruptions and nuisances: they stop them at the outer door. But in this case I am left without your address in Switzerland, if you are there; and I am sorry of the delay in having to write to New York, because possibly you are thinking of coming to Italy later, and I should be so very glad to see you. Cory is coming from London (so he says) in September: if you could come then you would find him here, and it might be pleasanter for you, if you had few or no friends in town, as also for him, if you were both in Rome at the same time. But everything is unsettled, politically and touristically, and I oughtn't to urge you to come, if you are not assured by the people who know that everything would be all right.

It is not necessary to say that I am getting a little older every day; the trouble is that this involves getting deafer and stupider. However, second childhood, or as I prefer to think it, second adolescence, makes it easy for me to keep myself vastly entertained. My writing is slow, and I throw away most of what I compose on re-reading it and finding it very dull and commonplace. Something, nevertheless, passes muster, and my new (old) book, *"Dominations & Powers"*, grows slowly, like a big tree. What really keeps me awake is reading, and I find lovely things in plenty. There is Toynbee's "A Study of History", six thick volumes in small print already, and seven more to come; a very useful book for my work: and there is Ciano's *Diario,* most enlightening, and now I have received from Robert Lowell, who is at the American Embassy in Istanbul, his remarkable poems: *"Lord Weary's Castle".* It is hard for me to make it all out, and I find a lot of words that I have to look up in the dictionary, and don't always find there: but gradually I am learning to understand him, and it is worth the trouble, as most of the other cryptic poets have not seemed to me to be. He is very severe on Boston and on Convention: but he is no Communist or Atheist: on the contrary, evidently a Catholic, and a sort of Voice Crying in the Wilderness. Do you know anything about him? I have written to thank him for his book; but even if he replies, I expect he won't tell me much.

Thank you for the parcel. It was very kind of you.

Yours affectionately

To PHILIP RODDMAN

VIA SANTO STEFANO ROTONDO, 6
ROME, OCTOBER 27, 1947.

My dear Roddman

I have read almost the whole of *Les Temps Modernes*[1] not only with pleasure (it being for the most part in good French) but also with a sense of being instructed as to facts and feelings that are remote from me *by chance,* not at all because I have any hostility to them. It is only hostility in those alien quarters to what is more familiar to me that I should like to abolish, not affection on their part for their own ways or resentment at ill treatment which they may suffer. This was especially clear to me in the story or tract about the poor in Madrid. It is life-like and just to its own sentiments—not violently exaggerated; but of course this does not justify anticlericalism as a general policy. The roots and effects of clericalism must first be considered from its own side: since it is just as human as anything else in human society. Everything is bound to take up room and to shove other things aside in some measure: the question is to understand justly what hold each thing has normally in nature and in human nature, and how great is the ascension or flowering of life that it is capable of producing. On this ground I liked especially the conclusion that Merleau-Ponty comes to in his article, which I neglected at first, taking the title too literally. His position is, in principle, just that which I should take even if, *by chance,* we might have different preferences.

Sartre made a better impression on me in this long rambling article than in his plays; he seems to be less *bedevilled* (endiablado) here; but I feel that he is weak in his first principles, and that, among other things he does not understand America. The articles on Heidegger seem to be right in their technical criticisms; but the whole controversy rather dampens my interest in Existential-

---

[1] Mr. Roddman writes:
"I had visited Santayana in Rome during . . . 1947. Since he had expressed an interest in French periodicals, I sent him upon my return to Paris the latest issue of *Les Temps Modernes* . . ."

ism. Jaspers—whom I know only at second hand—with his cataclysm seems to be the most respectable philosophically of the whole lot. If a man wishes to take the universe for a feature in his autobiography, and as nothing else, Jaspers' analysis and his solution seem to be well justified. But why build philosophy on childish vanity?

Thank you very much for this review, also for your visits here, which stirred me up very pleasantly. If you come again, as I hope you will, attack me with objections, which may prove a help to both of us. You clear up the respective positions, without being rudely summoned to give them up.

Yours sincerely

To JOHN M. MERRIAM

VIA SANTO STEFANO ROTONDO, 6
ROME, JAN. 17, 1948

Dear Merriam

You ask me to write you, for your Class Luncheon, something about the political state of things in the world, and you tell me what the Marshall plan is. I know all about that and the views current here (I mean in Europe, not Rome or Italy) about it, whether it is prudent charity, to prevent Western Europe from being Russianised, or sheer enterprise, to secure larger markets and military outpost for American expansion abroad, now that the home lands have filled up. I don't know whether this second motive exists, consciously or unconsciously in any American circle, but if it does, my philosophy would at once dismiss it as a mere make-shift. For in a century or two (nothing for a philosopher) when Asia and Africa were filled up with men and industries up to the brim, the question would recur as pressingly as at present, and the *real problem,* not one of how to enlarge business but how to lead a rational life, would impose itself on the cosmopolitan government that we may suppose would then exist. Why should not this real question be put and answered now in each country and community, without looking for outlets or resources beyond its accidental borders?

As to what is likely to happen, I have no inside knowledge or divine revelation. I think the communist area, under Russian control, *may* be extended over continental Europe, perhaps without a great war, by the aggressiveness of the communist party everywhere and the apathy and disunion of conservative forces. If this process is resisted by force of arms, supported by America and England, there will be a great war; the character of it would be very like the Napoleonic wars, one side with its home strength beyond the risk of invasion and with undisputed command of the sea, and the other with determined unified leadership but an insecure possession of its conquests. The ultimate result, I think, would be the emancipation of the conquered countries, as it was after Napoleon; but passage under a far more destructive social revolution would leave the European (and Asiatic) countries in a condition radically different from what it was in the Golden Age of Queen Victoria.

The great change, however, might be in the other camp, where a *willing* union of the Americans and the British Commonwealth of Nations, with perhaps some clients beyond, would form what Toynbee, in his "Study of History", calls a "Universal State", not all-comprehensive but supervening over a crowd of small nations.

I don't think there is any cause for alarm about the future of mankind: but Europe may be knocked to pieces by the way.

Best wishes for the remaining fragments of '86

from

To MRS. GEORGE STURGIS

VIA SANTO STEFANO ROTONDO, 6,
ROME. FEB. 8, 1948

Dear Rosamond

Amory's book on *The Proper Bostonians* came long ago and I read it at once but for some reason haven't yet thanked you for it. In part it revived all my most youthful and tender feelings about things and people in old Boston; but on the other hand I felt that he treated them all in the wrong spirit, like a newspaper correspondent who is very well informed at second hand, and not scrupulous about not rounding out a story to please himself. For that reason I didn't read the part about old murdered Parkman. I was myself corrected by Morrison for trusting gossip on this subject; but I was writing a novel and not borrowing more from history, real or apocryphal, than I chose. And I gave George Parkman some traits of Mr. Thomas Wigglesworth, and a younger brother, Peter, to peter out.

This point about petering out I was interested to see confirmed by Amory; and he tells many things about the Great Merchants, as I called them, which I didn't know. For instance, that there was, and apparently still is, a Merchants' Row designed by Bulfinch by the water's edge at the foot of State Street. I have never seen it, and always regretted that there was no water front in Boston, to remind us that it was a seaport.

The other part that interested me most was the chapter about Harvard Clubs. It was naturally brought down to a date much later than my observations; yet on the whole it seemed true. There is a newspaper man's sort of error about the Gas House or Delphic Club of which I believe I am now the oldest living (honorary) member. He attributes its foundation to J. P. Morgan (who no doubt was the principle financial supporter of it) and to the year 1889: whereas its founder was my intimate friend Ward Thoron, in 1885 or 86. My other two best Boston friends, Herbert Lyman and Boylston Beal were also Charter members; but I myself was only elected later, when I was an instructor, in '90. It is of no importance as history to get such a trifle right; but it shows the love of turning a thing the wrong side out, if you are not in sympathy with it . . .

Yours aff^{ly}

To THOMAS N. MUNSON, S.J.

[I am indebted to Father Munson for supplying me with the background of this most interesting letter. He informs me that it expresses Santayana's reaction to a reading of an M.A. dissertation he sent him. "The thesis was written as a critical work. In my youth, I attempted, from a scholastic point of view, to trace the two basic trends which I found in Santayana's philosophy, his materialism and, as I termed it, his transcendentalism. What, I asked, were the ramifications in epistemology, psychology, theodicy, ethics, etc. Was the dichotomy a justifiable, consistent philosophy? I could not expect Mr. Santayana to be pleased; no doubt he was amused to see me happy in picturing the world in my own terms."]

VIA SANTO STEFANO ROTONDO, 6
ROME, MARCH 12, 1948

Dear Father Munson,

I have spent an interested day reading your thesis and being sorry to have been the cause of so much irritation in your study of my books. The latter parts of your paper are much nearer to the facts about my philosophy than the earlier, although even here you are a good deal misled or misinformed about me. I don't know who the interviewer was that said I *preferred to be called an aesthete:* it is an instance of the mendacity of interviewers. More important is the use you make of a sonnet [1] written when I was twenty as the "final" expression of my philosophy. And where do you suppose,

---

[1] The famous sonnet beginning "O world, thou choosest not the better part . . ." First published in *The Harvard Monthly*, April, 1886.

even then, I drew the inspiration that prompted me to write it? From the *Bacchae* of Euripides who says τὸ σοφὸν οὐ σοφία, which I translated, watering it a good deal in the second line [1] of the sonnet, building the rest round that sentiment. But it is true that I prefer the play of imagination round natural sentiments and natural scenes to any "explanation" of them. They all have natural causes, no doubt, but the interesting thing is what those scenes and sentiments are, and how they develop.

As to the technique of my philosophy, I find most of your exposition out of focus, and most of your criticism irrelevant. You don't understand my interests or my methods. If you had trace [sic] my works either chronologically or logically, you would have seen better how I came to disinter my system: because I did have to disinter it under the alien vocabulary and alien problems that were imposed upon me by my alien education. You are right in saying that from William James I got my strong sense of the "contingency" of all facts and of their primacy *in the order of discovery;* but he thought momentary feelings were the ontological basis of the universe, in the order of genesis and causation: and this I wholly rejected having always been a naturalist in belief (even when I was thinking speculatively on Catholic or on solipsistic lines): for it is possible to be interested in a play at the theatre, without forgetting that we are sitting in the stalls. When I describe a stage-setting, you say that I have *abandoned* my materialism. That is not true: I have turned my thoughts to something else, but this stage-setting, far from contradicting its sources in real life, gives real life its human form and reflective interpretation. You are absolutely just in saying that I care little for "explanations" (not often finding that they explain anything or make things clearer) for I like interpretations, because those express the tastes of the mind and its affections.

There are some odd assignments of influence, and odd omissions of it, in your account of my sources. For instance, Hodgson [2] I saw once at a meeting of the Aristotelian Society in London in 1887 [3] (long before "essence" had come within my horizon) never spoke with him, or read anything of his. Essences I gradually unearthed, like the rest of my personal grammar of thought, helped

---

[1] "It is not wisdom only to be wise . . ."

[2] Shadworth H. Hodgson.

[3] See *Letter* (May 21, 1887).

by various suggestions. One was the *idea clara et distincta Cartesii:* others the "infinite attribute" of thought, with its infinitude of modes (or instances) of Spinoza, and all the "possible worlds" of Leibniz; then Berkeley's "inert ideas"; except that he confused these with existing acts of apprehension, which are not ideas at all, but moments of spirit, or "intuitions" (not in the Bergsonian or feminine sense of this word, but in the Kantian). Capital of course were Platonic Ideas: especially an undeveloped suggestion in the first part of Plato's *Parmenides* about "ideas" of filth, rubbish, etc., which the moralistic young Socrates recoils from as not beautiful, making old Parmenides smile. That smile of Parmenides made me think. But the most exact anticipation of my "realm of essence" I found in a quotation from an Arabic philosopher whose name I have forgotten, in the *Life of Avicenna* by the Baron Carra des Veaux, a French Catholic of perhaps a hundred years ago. My ideas were also much sharpened in 1897 at the English Cambridge in talks with Bertrand Russell and G. E. Moore.

There are two points that I should like to clear up if possible in your criticism. The first is about the meaning of "knowledge". Are pure vision or hearing (in a dream) knowledge? Or must this datum be assigned as a predicate to a substantial object, and with this be "knowledge" (as in Berkeley) even if no such object exists? Or would this belief be then an illusion, and true only if there is an object on which the datum is projected? Or will this projection be still an illusion if the object has not, in itself, that character, although such an appearance may serve, conventionally, like a name, to mark the presence of that object and to induce in the observer the appropriate action in its presence?

I may not, in my earlier writings, always have avoided the use of the word "knowledge" for what I call "intuition of essence"; this is cognitive in intent, since the essence is an object which intuition may repeat, and memory may identify: but that object is ideal. Mathematics, or acquaintance with definitions and relations between them, is a teachable science and must certainly be called a sort of knowledge. Yet it is not knowledge of natural facts or their interaction in the world except when the mathematical calculations are found applicable to material facts in the heavens or in machinery: and it is in such cases that knowledge is *transcendent*, i.e. reveals an object other than the datum or definition or calculation concerned. Locke and others reasonably distinguished these as knowledge of fact and knowledge of ideas; but occasioned great confusion, since properly ideas themselves are the knowledge, or the terms of knowledge, in designating and recording facts. I can't help thinking that the distinction of essences from existentent [sic] things greatly clarifies this imbroglio.

The other point that I wish to make regards the psyche. You say that I can't define it, but that Aristotle explained it by saying it is the form of the body. He has a fuller and clearer description of it than that where he says that the psyche is the first entelechy (or functional perfection) of a natural organic body; and further he distinguishes the first entelechy for instance of the general's psyche when on the eve of battle he is asleep in his tent, from the second entelechy when in the morning he is mounted on his horse and giving orders in the midst of battle. The functional perfection, ready to act or acting, of a natural organic body is precisely what I take the psyche to be; so that if Aristotle is right your cavils about what you attribute to me on this subject fall to the ground. You say that the manifestations of the psyche are not "knowledge" of it. [sic] it is unknowable (or something of that kind). But the organic constitution and organic action of the body *are* the psyche. You know that I do not make it any more than Aristotle, an independent angelic soul that can quit the body or migrate from one species of animal to another, as Plato tells us in his myths.

I will send you back your thesis, on which I have marked two or three passages, as far as possible packed as it came.

Yours sincerely

P.S. I have forgotten to mention that what I quote from Leibniz about God choosing the best of possible worlds is not my opinion. I meant it as a reduction *ad absurdum*. You have not read Voltaire's *Candide?* Or Molière about *Cur opium facit dormire?* [1] It is a pity.

[1] [Why opium makes one sleep.]

To ERIC C. PARSONS

VIA SANTO STEFANO ROTONDO, 6
ROME, JULY 28, 1948

Dear Mr. Parsons,

I am much touched by your anxiety to help me—not out of my evil ways, as some benevolent persons are—but on the contrary in order to pay an imaginary debt. But fortune and the public and my many friends have always been so kind to me that I should have been amply repaid for any effort or sacrifice that I might have made to please or to correct them. But I have never made any efforts or sacrifices, so that according to old-fashioned morality I have deserved nothing. I have only been enjoying myself in a way which luckily has extended at moments to a few sympathetic spirits, of whom you are evidently one. That ideal sort of friendship is its ideal reward; and it becomes a positive satisfaction when it is discovered. So that I think it is I that owe you some real debt for telling me that you owe me an ideal one, for having been an unconscious partner to some of your pleasant thoughts.

Let me then thank you for your most friendly letter, and assure you that I have everything that I need materially, and all that at my age I can enjoy socially.—With best wishes and regards from

To MRS. GEORGE STURGIS

VIA SANTO STEFANO ROTONDO, 6,
ROME, SEPT. 23, 1948.

Dear Rosamond

It is a long time since I have written and owe you thanks for both the Camphor and the Vapex. They are both very useful. My laziness has had no definite cause, as I am well; but the whole Summer and Autumn have been unusually cool and cloudy, which perhaps has affected my catarrh, which has troubled me a little, especially at night, all through the season when by rights it ought to be in abeyance. However, I have managed to do a little writing and much reading, and have seen a stream of strangers who now insist on looking me up. The other day I even had an offer of marriage from a lady in California whom I knew in 1911. She tells me her husband is dead, that he died smiling, (at the change?), calls me George and says now is the time for us to put our heads together. I have replied, feigning not to understand, and congratulating her on being so happy with her painting and her friends and the eternal music of the Pacific Ocean. She may still write me another diplomatic note, as the allied ministers do to Molotov.

. . . They say now that it is wrong to save, that money should circulate, and that nobody should be allowed to have a large unearned income; so that if I don't spend the income I have and increase my capital, I am in danger of being black-balled and reduced by taxation to the semblance of democratic equality. But how am I, at my age, (unless I marry my California sweetheart) to spend all that money? I *might* go back to live in a hotel, as I did when you and George came to the Bristol; and then I could invite anyone I chose to come to visit me. But it is wiser for me to stay where I am, and perhaps I could make money circulate notwithstanding.

What are your views on this subject? Not being in Boston the *right* thing to do may not occur to me.

Yours affectionately

To PAUL ARTHUR SCHILPP

VIA SANTO STEFANO ROTONDO, 6,
ROME. OCTOBER 6, 1948

Dear Professor Schilpp,

I have not yet got over the pleasant surprise of suddenly seeing you in the flesh, and now you appear again in the spirit in your so-called "Lamentations on Christmas." [1] But they are not lamentations but explosions of wrath. One of the "Beatitudes" which you quote is "Blessed are they that mourn," so that if you were a really blessed Christian you would be mourning joyfully and full of expectations of soon being comforted, not by the "human Jesus," but by The Divine Christ coming with "more than twelve legions of angels" to put an end to this evil world. You seem to me very unregenerate in wanting to have no enemies to love, and no footpads to steal your coat, to whom you could give your trousers also. And you ought to expect tribulation and persecution (and you don't seem to be persecuted) so that you might be truly Jesus-like and not resist evil. You seem to me not to have understood that the "peace" that Christ is The Prince of is not the absence of wars in the world, but the absence of revolt in the soul to any temporary trial of martyrdom. You seem not to like to be martyred. Can it be because you have nothing to be martyred for? Christian peace is like that of St. Lawrence who said to his executioners, "Turn me over on the other side, for on this I am already roasted."

Yours sincerely,

[1] A rather undisciplined or ejaculatory type of *poem* that later, I believe, became the text of an "opertorio."

To PETER VIERECK

VIA SANTO STEFANO ROTONDO, 6,
ROME, OCTOBER 30, 1948

Dear Mr. Viereck

. . . . . Your new poems [1] show an extraordinary variety of observations and moods. I don't see how it is possible to digest and turn into poetry so many different impressions, even in the course of eight years: and I don't find "Terror" or "Decorum" emerging clearly as the burden of the whole. What struck me most was the vim with which you touch repeatedly on lust. Naturally that is a passion, suppressed by "Decorum", which peeps out in a military campaign. I remember some French book treating that point very frankly, but in a detached philosophical way; you, in the modern poetic manner treat it hotly, not at all as "recovered in tranquillity". I suppose nobody, except me has time for tranquillity now. Yesterday I spent most of the morning at the requiem mass sung by the choir of the English College and the priests of the Beda in the chapel of this house, at the funeral of an old Scottish priest (a convert) who lived here and often came to see me. It was tranquillity in view of life and death and of all things, for the service might have been Byzantine or Egyptian or pagan of the remotest times. But of course you have no time for such things in the modern experiment; for life has now become an experiment not the old old story that it used to be. Congratulations. It is what you were born to do and you will be great at it.

Yours sincerely

[1] *Terror and Decorum.*

To FRANCIS CLOUGH

VIA SANTO STEFANO ROTONDO, 6,
ROME, FEB. 11, 1949

Dear Mr. Clough

In recent times I have received a considerable number of volumes of recent American poetry, of which for many years I had completely lost the traces; and a few of them are like yours, in the versification and with the religio-cosmic questionings which we all had in the nineteenth century; but I am afraid we are destined, even if brand new, to seem nothing but back numbers. That does not remove the intrinsic interest which such verses possess; it only deprives them of public attention. A man would have to be a positive genius, with a vision of old truths and a great technical competence to seem a modern poet today if he were clear and rational. Most of those who honour me with thin copies of their cryptic visions are all for economy of exposition and concentrated pellets from which the miraculous intuition of the reader is expected to elicit vast cloudscapes of tumultuous but silent passion. We are not in that competition, and must be content with a few old-fashioned uncritical admirers. I long ago abandoned verse for prose, and I suppose you reserve your verses for private sympathy only. Your portrait,[1] unless the Italian love of violence misrepresents you, suggests hard usage and struggles. A novel, perhaps, would be the surest means of getting a hearing for such an experience.

Yours sincerely

1 *I, The Hymn,* a booklet of poems.

To *RICHARD C. LYON*

VIA SANTO STEFANO ROTONDO, 6,
ROME, JULY 11, 1949

Dear Dick

. . . . Although there are not many great French philosophers,
they all write good French; and why? Because they know how to
see and to judge the world. They are not so good in the heights and
the depths, because these can't be written about in good French,
and they don't talk inflated nonsense about those super- or infra-
human things, because the French language will not permit it.
Yet they do manage to say quite clearly what is intelligible about
the greatest subjects, for instance, Descartes about "Spirit", and
Pascal about "Existence" and its irrationality. There is a whole
class of clever French sophists, who reason well without first principles; Montaigne, Rousseau, Voltaire, etc; but what is far superior
in true understanding in human affairs is the wit and sentiment
of French poets like Lafontaine, Racine, Molière, and (in his short
comedies) Alfred de Musset. Let me know (if I am still alive) when
you begin to *enjoy* reading French, and I will send you these old
standbyes, or such as I can get hold of, to encourage you to think
and feel without *Angst,* but with good humour and just feeling.
And I forgot Leibniz, whom you ought to read someday, and
who wrote in French, though not a Frenchman, and his philosophy
is technically first rate, but absurd, because like Pascal, he was too
good a mathematician to be a man of the world. Descartes, also a
good mathematician, saved himself by stopping always at the edge
of the precipice. I think, nevertheless, that he was artificial in speculation in the hope of being exact: a false ambition in that sphere.

I am working harder than usual myself because I feel that my
book (Dom. & P'rs.) [1] is getting into shape at last and that I may
be able to finish it. My work is mainly revising, which I do on the
principles of a wise Frenchman, derided as a fool:

[1] *Dominations and Powers.*

"Ajoutez quelquefois et souvent effacez.
Add sometimes and often rub out.

With best wishes for the rest of the season from

To RICHARD C. LYON

VIA SANTO STEFANO ROTONDO, 6
ROME, AUGUST 1. 1949

Dear Dick,

. . . . . To begin with "existence", this word is used in French, and I daresay in Continental philosophy generally, for "life" as a career no less than as a momentary state of motion or consciousness in an animal. The Existentialists probably have in mind the history and continuity of a man's life rather than the pure, minimum, analytic *"constatation"* (another French term) of something going on. On such constatation what is caught existing is consciousness, not its object, which might be an essence only: but the fact that this essence is considered, reviewed, contrasted with something else, at least with its absence just before, introduces *existence* into the *fact* of observation or "consciousness". So that existence is a natural varying reality of being in time. Even in Berkeley's "Spirits" existence and consciousness would have to be in time, a *survey,* not an unchanging stare; for the latter would be sucked up into the realm of essence, without life or individuality through a continuous "existence". As to the proof of existence from consciousness, Descartes is perfect if you notice that by *"constatant"* thought he infers the existence not of the thought in its logical essence but of *himself* who thinks. If thought were not a process, a phase of natural life, its being would not involve existence either for it or for its object. (I worked this out in the new Preface to "Egotism in German Philosophy", 2nd edition, I believe this is included in the Triton edition).

On the dialetical or ideal (not biological) relation of life to death I think Heidegger is splendid. Hegelians are all historians at heart; history for them is the *truth* even of prehistory and futurity. Now a life is conditioned and bounded by the dates of its beginning and end, and by what happened in its day. Until a man dies, the picture is incomplete. (Hegelians forget that it is never correctly drawn afterwards). Death frames life in, completes its dramatic essence, and so "conditions" it: i.e. the truth about it. This has nothing to do with life insurance or reunion in heaven. It is pure "objective" or "conceptual" idealism.

As to *Angst* my quarrel with it is temperamental and you must not take it seriously. The reality is what Schopenhauer calls the Will, the Will to Live. It makes the child anxious to get the breast or the bottle, the lover his girl, the workman his Saturday night wages, and the invalid to get well. You can't help caring. But these natural cravings and fears are occasional, they can be modified or placated, you may "care" about something else, Latin poetry, for instance, which carries no *Angst* with it, though it is rich in interest and in *reassuring* knowledge of life. What I dislike about calling Will *Angst* is the suggestion that it is mysterious and non-natural. It is fundamental but can be appeased. It need not end in Collapse but may be transcended throughout by charity and reason.

The existentialists' reaction against inhuman philosophy and politics is healthy, but they do not seem healthy themselves. And egotism is not cured by becoming personal. It is simply made easier to practise. It is naturally prevalent and won't cause any wars or totalitarian tyrannies. *Meno male!*

To PETER VIERECK

VIA SANTO STEFANO ROTONDO, 6,
ROME, SEPTEMBER 8, 1949

Dear Viereck

You may not remember it, but after reading some years ago your first book [1] on the late war, without suspecting that you, the blond young man who had lent it to me, were the author, I told

[1] *Metapolitics.*

you on discovering your identity, that you would be a great man and a professor, and that then I hoped you would rewrite your book, which showed great industry in gathering information but not yet a sympathetic insight into the European mind. Now you have proved me a prophet,[1] as prophets usually are proved, by being partly right. You have now taken in fully the wisdom of Metternich, Disraeli, Burke, and (unknown to me) Melville and finally Winston Churchill. This list, and some incidental remarks in your text, make me doubt whether you ought not, another ten years hence, to write a third book. Of course you will; but will you have caught on to the European mind in its Continental forms? Metternich and Burke were philosophic statesmen, Disraeli and Churchill clear-headed politicians who could see the drift of things in their own day and from the British point of view, Disraeli humorously and Churchill passionately; only Melville, apparently was a pure universal philosopher, although until now I thought he smelt strongly of Martha's Vineyard or Nantucket: but I have not read his South Sea books; perhaps he restores the balance there.

Now as to your position, it seems to me quite well-informed and fair retrospectively, although the intrigues and the undercurrents of such a troubled time can hardly be unravelled yet by anybody: in *Der Monat* (which they kindly send me and which I read parts of with great pleasure) I have found very good things especially Crossman and Lüthy in Nos 8 & 10, on "Democratic Realism" and on "The Fourth French Republic". This last is new and penetrating. I recommend it if you want to know what I mean by "insight into the European mind." The author I believe is Swiss, but more French than German without the incurable French national egotism.

As to your outlook and "Conservative path to liberty" I should agree in the abstract heartily, for that which liberty sets free is the psyche, that is the *conserved,* largely *hereditary* demands and powers of a man or a society. If you are nothing liberty to go anywhere can't do you much good. Reform cannot begin by destroying yourself. The question is how much of yourself you can preserve and develop (for the psyche is a bundle of potentialities) without running up against destructive agencies. Can these be destroyed without hurting you much (that is the totalitarian solution) or

[1] *Conservatism Revisited; the Revolt against Revolt.*

must you fight to the death rather than yield an inch (this is the martyr's or hero's solution) or must you bargain for a compromise (this is the mercantile tradition, natural to England and America). I think the trouble with this is that it does not distinguish ends from means. Compromise is rational in regard to means, but dishonourable in regard to ends; unless indeed you can remodel your ends themselves and constantly become a new man or society to fit your changing surroundings. But this is martyrdom by inches to suit the timid. You should not demand it from everybody.

Yours sincerely

To MRS. DAVID LITTLE

VIA SANTO STEFANO ROTONDO, 6,
ROME. SEPTEMBER 23, 1949

Dear Rosamond

Two letters, a box of provisions, a magic bird's eye view of the Harvard Yard in two parts, and numbers of Life and Time full of innumerable coloured pictures of happiness, abundance, youth, travel, and laughter have transported me to a sort of dreamworld where everything is a merry-go-round. Is America really like that? No: I know it can't be. But you are having a splendid holiday after a good many years of comparative seclusion, and there is really a sort of youthful gaiety, as if everybody were dressed in brand new clothes and rushing from one "delightful" thing to another. Is this really so, or are people putting on a public smile as soon as they come in sight of anybody else, and do public prints reproduce the same appearance of joy as a professional duty?

I am perfectly happy myself in the absence of any gaiety or variety; but I feel that the world is very shaky indeed and morally lost and drifting among shams which it doesn't believe in, but can't give up. And I think most Europeans feel as if the end of the world were at hand. Even the late Mr. Whitehead, the mathematical philosopher who was for years professor at Harvard, but was an Englishman (I knew him in 1897 at Trinity College, Cambridge) one of whose books I happen to be reading is full of this feeling, although, writing in America, he veils it in a haze of cordiality and religious hope. He is an excellent philosopher in spots but there seems to me to be a contradiction between his physical science, which is straightforward, and his philosophical and moral reflections, which are all subjective: history, for instance, or the past, when he speaks of them, do not signify the "concrete" events but the feeling, memory, or imaginative view of them that people have taken or now take. The social world is a novel, like Balzac's: and the scientific world seems to disappear—However, he does recognise that this century, so far, has been catastrophic: which would seem to me to show that the philosophy of the nineteenth century was fatal sophistry; yet that is just the substitution of a novel for a science as the truer picture of the world.

Excuse me for running into these depths, or shallows; if you don't see what I mean, you might show this letter to your husband,[1] and give him my best regards and congratulations. I was surprised at seeing him looking so young, sturdy, and solid in his picture. He will perhaps tell you that I am all wrong, which may turn out true, because of America.

Yours affectionately

To RICHARD C. LYON

VIA SANTO STEFANO ROTONDO, 6,
ROME, NOV. 8, 1949

Dear Dick:

This, of November 2nd, is the most interesting letter you have written me, the richest in matter, and it would take more time and paper than I can fill up with writing letters at this moment to reply

[1] David Little, who had recently married the former Mrs. George Sturgis.

to all your suggestions. I admire your omnivorence and hope you are not overtaxing your strength with so much work and so much thinking at double quick marching time.

For one thing, at least in one subject, essence, you think you are in more trouble than you really are. I am sure that you can catch what Husserl called the pure phenomenon. Of course there is a lot of other things involved in its presence, so that looking about at once gives you existential subject and existential objects implied in its *presence here* to *you*. But when you play chess, and in deciding on your next move you trace the possible moves that your opponent might make in answer to each possible move of yours, your very intense (though not properly anxious or forced) perception of those various developments, though it *involves* you and the chessboard *existentially*, does not *contain* them *intrinsically*. That is all that is needed to distinguish pure essence in this case, the series of each possible move, response and further move, etc. Those are timeless and placeless series to positions in chess, with their essential relations according to the rules of the game, but not positions or relations in the existing world.

But the most interesting thing in your letter is what you say about love, which seems singularly mature for your age. But I think, in regard to marriage, that what you say does not preclude true love or true happiness in that relation. Love, in English, is a very wide term. What poets and philosophers, at least of the classic school, talk about is the *passion* of love, the madness, divine madness, of Plato. But attraction, confidence, mutual delight, and complete devotion to a chosen mate is not madness at all, it is a phase, a settlement, of the *sane* affections of one human being to another, where all sane possible bonds, physical, domestic, social, intellectual, and religious bind the two together for life—common material interests and children being strong material buttresses to such a complete union in after years. More than once, at friends' houses in England, or in hotels, I have found myself divided only by a frail closed door from the bed in which an elderly pair were exchanging confidential judgments and ideas; and I have been impressed by the *perfection* of friendship and sympathy in such a union. The only advantage—for me important—that the ideal friendship has over such a happy wedlock is liberty. Friends need not agree in *everything* or go *always* together, or have *no* comparable other friendship of the same intimacy. On the contrary, in friendship union is more about ideal things: and in that sense it is more ideal and less subject to trouble than marriage is. But I am not a lover of life; I prefer it at a distance, or in the distances pictured in it. When it is actually tumbling over itself I feel that it is spoiling its own treasures.

I too, by chance, have been just rereading the whole of Byron's Don Juan. Some parts bored me, the invectives especially: but as you say, he is witty and his rhymes sometimes surprisingly clever. But he did not respect himself or his art as much as they deserved.

To CORNEL LENGYEL

VIA SANTO STEFANO ROTONDO, 6,
ROME, DECEMBER 8, 1949

My dear Lengyel,

The heavy autumn rains, much wanted for public reasons, seem to be depressing to me now, in my last years, and have kept me from answering your letter to me (and to yourself): [sic] for this can't be an ordinary note of thanks.[1] You have invented, as far as I know, a new form of verse, the blank-verse sonnet; and from the beginning you have made it seem a natural and powerful instrument. The steady sure way in which you carry it through, without a hitch or any faltering in force or clearness, shows that it can be made to serve, as the traditional sonnet did in its day, almost any form of reflective or discursive poetry. In stripping the sonnet of its rhymes you have freed it from its chains and its too conventional music. It will be possible to write *modern* verse in that form. And where did you get your mastery of the single line in blank verse? You write these single lines, almost without a lapse in tone or quality, like Shakespeare in his early plays. And you avoid obsolete or affected language without falling into contemporary commonplaces or positive colloquialisms, as the "modern" school does. The horror, for instance, of passing in Ezra Pound, who *can* write good verse, into the most vulgar journalese, and the most insolent irrelevance does not threaten your readers. In one or two places you

[1] Mr. Lengyel had sent Santayana a copy of his sonnet sequence, *The Lookout's Letter*.

do use technical expressions, like "to contact", which surprise a man of the old school like me; but I think the *principle* of turning nouns into verbs or slang into good usage is good to keep language fresh; only particular instances may not be fortunate. On the other hand there is one *inexpert* quality in Shakespeare's earlier blank verse which you have retained, and that is, to compose long passages wholly of single lines. This came, I suppose, from having always formerly rhymed; but even in rhymed sonnets it was a great improvement to break the line occasionally in the middle with a full stop, and often to carry on the sentence into the next line; which was done by Racine and other poets in a way that broke somewhat the artificial monotony of their versification. Now you, in your blank-verse sonnets, ought not, I think, to neglect that improvement. You are still free to have a monumental single line stand up by itself, when it sums up a thought or contains a great truth in itself. But then the current should begin to flow again in a meandering flexible way, as the landscape and the lay of the land may require.

I indulge in these school-master reflections, because I have said enough in praise to let you feel how much I admire your performance, and what hopes and possibilities I see before you. The first "sonnet" about me is faultless, in form and in substance—much too exalted to represent my whole person, but true to what I should like to survive me of myself.

Yours sincerely

To CORLISS LAMONT

VIA SANTO STEFANO ROTONDO, 6,
ROME, JAN. 6, 1950

Dear Mr. Lamont

It is pleasant news that another professed philosopher has arisen in the younger generations of the "Gashouse," [1] and that

1 The *Delta Phi* Club of Harvard.

he is, on the whole, a man of my own persuasion. On opening your book and seeing its full title "Humanism as a Philosophy" I feared that this sort of agreement would not exist, as in my mind "Humanism" is a taste rather than a system, and those who make a system of it are obliged to explain away what is not human in the universe as a normal fiction; as Croce when one day he asked himself, "But where can the idea of nature come in?" and replied, "As a postulate of ethics." And in Europe humanism as a philosophy is rather identified with Auguste Comte and the British radicals (as you point out speaking of Bertrand Russell) who are *psychological socialists*, with the idea of nature absent, except as a social convention. On reading on in your book, however, I was soon relieved of that apprehension, and saw that you are as much a naturalist and materialist as I. I particularly like what you say of F. R. S. Schiller, who (like Dewey at first) wanted to annex me to the pragmatic heresy, and gave me some trouble in consequence.

You regret the later developments of my philosophy, and I notice that you quote only from my earlier "American" books. Let me assure you that Essence and Spirit in my sincere view are perfectly naturalistic categories. Material things and sensuous ideas have to have some form, which might be qualitatively identical in many instances, and therefore capable of logical and dialectical treatment in logic, grammar, mathematics, & aesthetics.

Without bothering you with technical arguments, let me suggest this natural status of immaterial forms and systems of relations in the case of music. Music accompanies savage life as well as that of some birds, being a spontaneous exercise of motions producing aerial but exciting sounds, with the art of making them, which is one of the useless but beloved effusions of vital energy in animals. And from the beginning this liberal accompaniment adds harmony and goodwill to dancing and war; and gradually it becomes in itself an object of attention, as in popular or love songs. In religion it also peeps out, although here it ordinarily remains a subservient element, inducing a mood and a means of unifying a crowd in feeling or action, rather than a separate art. Yet it is precisely as a separate art, not as an accompaniment to anything practical, that music is at its best, purest and most elaborate. And certainly the sensibility and gift of music is a *human* possession, although not descriptive of any *other* natural thing.

Apply this analogy to mathematics, logic, aesthetics, and religion, and you have the naturalistic status of ideal things in my philosophy.

"Humanism" has this moral defect in my opinion, that it seems to make all mankind an authority and a compulsory object of affection for every individual. I see no reason for that. The limits of the society that we find congenial and desirable is determined by our own condition, not by the extent of it in the world. This is doubtless the point in which I depart most from your view and from modern feeling generally. Democracy is very well when it is natural, not forced. But the natural virtue of each age, place, and person is what a good democracy would secure—not uniformity.

Yours sincerely

To CORLISS LAMONT

VIA SANTO STEFANO ROTONDO 6,
ROME, JANUARY 22, 1950

Dear Mr. Lamont

It is always a compliment to be quoted and I see nothing in the passage you cite from a letter of mine of 1935 [1] that I should wish to retract. And I should be glad if, when the new edition of *The Illusion of Immortality* comes out, you would send me a copy, where I might read your own reflections on the subject with which I foresee that I should generally sympathise. The Nicene Creed ends by asserting belief in "resurrectionem mortuorum et *vitam venturi saeculi.*" Translate *saeculum* by the word "age" rather than "world," insist on the temporality of life, and keep in mind that the resurrection of the dead means that of their bodies, without which the shrewd old Jews did not think immortality a *genuine* good, and you have the Illusion in question avoided, and the miraculous but naturalistic resurrection of the body in its place. Plato, and the delay in the second coming of Christ were ap-

[1] See *Letter* [March 5, 1935].

parently to blame for the *mythical* notion of the immortal soul to take root in Christian speculation.

Please present my compliments to Dr. Runes and tell him that I would much rather *not* see the proofs of my book,[1] as Mr. Cardiff will surely read them carefully, and my eyes are scarcely able to do the reading of indispensable stuff.

Yours sincerely

To GEORGE RAUH

VIA SANTO STEFANO ROTONDO, 6
ROME, JANUARY 31, 1950.

Dear Mr. Rauh:

Your splendid gift of White's Dante [2] arrived some time ago, but I have been kept by a bad turn in my health from reading much in it, and wanted to wait until I had examined at least a few well-known passages before saying anything about it. White's own short preface gave me the impression that he had not attempted to make more than a readable contemporary version, and that perhaps the use of Gustave Doré's Illustrations was not entirely the publishers' doing, but also looked to producing a popular gift book. Those Illustrations are dramatic and catch everyone's eye; and they add vastness to the perfectly definite dimensions of Dante's landscapes; but they are not in the spirit of the original, except in some figures in the Inferno—*not* those of Francesca and Paolo. White is clear in giving up the rhymes which are impossible at any length in English; but the way he jumps at once into blank verse seems to me hasty; especially as he does not free himself from the other terrible fetter of translating line for line, and not profiting

---

[1] *Atoms of Thought,* an anthology of excerpts from Santayana's works, edited by Ira D. Cardiff.

[2] Lawrence Grant White. Translation of the *Divine Comedy* into English Blank Verse. Illustrations by Gustave Doré. (Pantheon books, 1948)

by the chance that blank verse gives of breaking lines up and not *padding* them, as you have to do often in a line for line translation; since 73 syllables in English, or even 70 contain more words on the average than 11 Syllables in Italian. Then there is the grave difficulty of passing in English from the sublime to the homely, as is current in Romance languages. English has two vocabularies. It has occurred to me sometimes that a man with a full command of 16th Century English, like that of Shakespeare and the English Bible, might render Dante magnificently in verses, like those of the Psalms, each for a triplet in the original, in terse prose. Dante's language is simple, but learned, like Church Latin; and his poem is a procession of basses, altos, and sopranos three abreast, holding candles, but so arranged that the voices would link the trios to one another like the *Terrarima;* so if B stands for bass, A for alto, and S for soprano, as follows

B A B
A S A
S B S
B A B
etc.

and the language should be simple and good for any subject, yet a *sacred* language, not at all like loose common talk in the vernacular.

The translation is faithful and often literal, but it does not produce this *ritual* effect proper to the original, and of course gives no idea of the sweetness and limpidity of the Italian. However, White begins by making that sacrifice, and evidently hopes to attach the reader by assimilating himself to him in language, as far as possible, and no doubt he gains an important point in avoiding "poetical" words, now tabooed by the young poets. I am an old man, and have versified sometimes in the traditional English lingo; for that reason I can't help missing here, for instance, the *distinction* of Cary's blank verse, and even some phrases of Longfellow, neither of which White mentions in his preface. But let us be thankful for this devoted effort, without dreaming of any endless procession with candles, basses, altos, and sopranos.

With penicillin I have been pulled through my recent relapse and am hopeful of reaching the summer and the end of my new book. Best wishes to you and to Lawrence Butler from

To EZRA POUND

VIA SANTO STEFANO ROTONDO, 6
ROME, FEBRUARY 7, 1950

Dear Pound

Two messages from you are awaiting an answer. The first,[1] besides being a compliment to my materialism, or to the generative order of nature (as I call it in my new book,[2] now nearing completion) exemplified it in a cherry-stone able to produce cherries, after going a long way round, and facing a good many risks of perishing on the way. And it would be fussy to object to your word "intelligence" to describe that potentiality in the cherry-stone; somehow it possesses a capacity to develop other cherries under favourable circumstances, without getting anything vital wrong. That is "intelligence" of an unconscious [3] sort. I agree in respecting it.

The other message comes today with the observation that there has been no philosophy in the West, at least since Pythagoras, but only philo-epistemologia. That is true of English and even in part of German speculation, but not of the traditional philosophy which has never died out, in the Church and in many individuals. My friends Lucretius and Spinoza were not especially epistemologists but had theories of the measure of things, putting human "knowledge" in its place.

It was good of you to remember me. I have not been very well, but hope to last long enough to finish my book. Cory, who is now in Rome, is helping me *efficiently!*

Yours

1 Ezra Pound had written on December 22, 1949, conveying the "season's greeting" and his "respect for the kind of intelligence that enables the cherry-stone to make cherry; the grass seed to make grass."

2 *Dominations and Powers.*

3 Pound has since written to me asking "How the HELL does he [Santayana] KNOW it's 'unconscious'?" I can only reply that Santayana believed that "consciousness" was an intermittent "spiritual" dimension of highly organised nervous systems, such as human beings possess. He objected to spreading it over nature at large in the manner of the Idealists.

To CORLISS LAMONT

VIA SANTO STEFANO ROTONDO, 6
ROME. JUNE 8, 1950

Dear Mr. Lamont

Your book on Immortality [1] has made me think of what I thought of William James's Religious Experiences, that he had been on a slumming tour in the New Jerusalem. His New Jerusalem, and yours also, seem to me so very new! You dwell on ideas and sentiments that I never heard of and that hardly seem worth considering. It comes, perhaps, from the fact that among Protestants there is more theological independence than I am accustomed to, and they find arguments or proofs of their own, and what is more significant proofs or arguments for something different under the old name of "immortality." What you say about Resurrection is to the point: if Christians had reflected that *this* is the Christian doctrine—vitam venturi saeculi—and *not* immortality of the soul, except in theology to reconcile the Platonists. But immortality, logically, suggests pre-existence, and the Church could never accept that (*pace* Leibniz).

I wish you would write another book on the *Confusions about Immortality*. Besides Resurrection, which implies that the soul and body can live only together, and temporally, so that when recalled to life they ought not only to remain married, but after a long life, ought to die again, and so for ever. This would be like the Indian immortality, without a final Nirvana. The argument from the simplicity of the *transcendental ego* is good, I think, but does not touch the "soul," the psyche, or the person—and the crowning argument in the Phaedo about the number 3 being immortally odd (which you don't dwell on in your summary of the arguments there) is also good but tautological: Socrates conceived as existing can never be (conceived as) dead; but it has nothing to do with time. This play between time and eternity in the more intelligent discussions of the subject has always interested and exasperated me. You have noticed, I see, what I think about Dante's people in

[1] The new edition of Mr. Lamont's book *The Illusion of Immortality*.

Purgatory and Paradise (in Hell they are more repetitions or con-
tinuations of their life on earth) that they are only the truth or
the lesson of their existence in time, and evidently will never *do*
anything or *learn* anything new. They are living monuments to
themselves. But Dante could never have acknowledged that this
is all that salvation can be, or union with God, who is non-temporal,
because a material "other life" is required by the Jewish-Christian
doctrine of the resurrection of the flesh.

Has the belief in heaven been more often a longing *not* to
live, than to *live forever?* I almost think so. And you know the
verses of St. Theresa and St. John of the Cross: "Muero porque no
muero."

With best thanks for your book

Yours sincerely

To RICHARD C. LYON

VIA SANTO STEFANO ROTONDO, 6,
ROME, JUNE 18, 1950

Dear Dick:

It was a great pleasure to see your two thick envelopes even
before opening them, as they proved that the wire between us was
again, after I don't know how long, open to communications. I
have been, first, not very well during the winter, and, second, very
busy getting *Dominations and Powers* ready for the press. A part of
the MS is already in Scribner's hands, and the rest we (Cory and I)
expect to have ready early in the autumn, so that the book may
be expected to appear (and to reach *you*) in the Spring of 1951.
This is a great relief for me, as I have no "duty" hanging over me
after this is despatched, but can sing *Nunc dimittis* with a cheerful
voice. I am surprised (by the way) that you, who expected to be a
clergyman, should speak as you do about this *grave* subject of
"duty" and also of "sacrifice" as intrinsically evil; and I hope it

was not I that put these *dangerous* notions into your head. In a dago and a materialist they would not surprise but only *grieve:* but in you!

However, let us approach this subject in the respectable company of Milton; and although, as you suggest, speculation, even about "the good" is not his strong point, yet "moralism" oozes from his every syllable or organ-groan. I have never been a great reader of Milton and I may misjudge him: but I suspect that if I had read him more I should like him less, so that it is as well to give you only my superficial impressions. I don't at all agree with Ezra Pound in hating him. I used to know Lycidas by heart and to delight in saying it over—E.P. might say that this explains how bad my verses were, for that was just the misguided period of my life when I wrote them. But in Paradise Lost it is not the absence of a philosophy but the evident sub-presence of a sort of mummified Old Testament philosophy that fills his sails. I admit that he is sublime in his poses: but it is the sublimity of terror not of joy. And he doesn't understand at all the position of a real angel rebelling against a monarchical God. It would be the position of Berkeley rebelling against matter. He would not choose evil rather than good. That is only the nursery-maids "naughty" and "nice". He would be choosing the immediate, the obvious, the inescapable, the Schopenhauerian "the world is my idea", for faith of any sort, which is only an impulse to bet, to jump in the dark. I am very glad to see that at the end of your essay you suggest the question what Milton understood by "the good". He understood by it what the Calvinistic catechism calls good: the nursery-maid's "nice" translated into the cry of superstitious escape from terror. "Duty" also needs to be analysed etymologically. It means what is owed, what you are bound by contract to perform.

Yours

To RIMSA MICHEL

VIA SANTO STEFANO ROTONDO, 6,
ROME, JULY 8, 1950

Dear Mr. Michel

Your well typed Essay, in its flexible black leather binding, added to certain melancholy notes in your letter, made me feel at once that you were a young man of feeling, who liked to work like an artist: and I began to read with a little apprehension that you might be only that—or perhaps a sentimental lady: (your name not being decisive (for me) on that point) [1] and that you might really be impossibly mystical or poetical, like the theosophists. I have now finished reading the whole and find nothing of the sort, even at the end. You detach the meaning I give to "essence" clearly and soberly. In reading, for some thirty pages, I found only a faithful enough echo of *The Life of Reason,* as conceived in New York, and was uneasy only at what seemed an exclusive acquaintance with that and with my works in general, as if I were not a man but a text-book. This misgiving was corrected afterwards, as far as sympathy with my later writings is concerned. You not only know them all well but you are the only critic I have come upon who understands the character of the change that came over my manner. I have explained this, with a reference to my circumstances and uncongenial philosophic teachers, until I went to Germany, in the Preface or Introduction written for the one volume edition of *Realms of Being*

This leads me to the first jolt which I felt while so pleasantly conveyed in your carriage: your sharp objection to the word "Realm"—because it is not republican. Have you never heard that natural history, until the other day, divided nature into the Mineral, Vegetable and Animal Kingdoms? I didn't know that this word, like the word "essence" was taboo in America. I braved the inevitable prejudice in the case of "essence" because it is the only proper word for what I had in mind, and traditionally opposed to

[1] It is Miss Michel.

"existence", like "form" to "matter". But the reading that is now done, beyond "majors" in colleges, or at home, is very limited in proportion to what everybody was expected to know a hundred or even fifty years ago. "Culture" is collapsing into compendia and school-books, as at the beginning of the "dark ages". (You must consider that I am very old.)

It has been only in the middle of your essay, especially at p. 44, that I have come on what approaches a serious misunderstanding of my position. You speak of *matter needing the assistance of spirit,* as if it had to see where it was going before it started. My view, as you must be tired of reading in my pages, is that spirit is a result, not a cause, of material events.

The chief point that has arrested my attention in your interpretation is the relation, discussed at the end, of the good to the rational or moral. You understand perfectly how I get "beyond good and evil" not by abolishing or even modifying their common-sense reality, but by transcending them in view of their relativity. The last words of *Dominations & Powers,* the book—my last book—just finished, are these; "Comparison (of values) presupposes a chosen good, chosen by chance. The function of spirit is not to pronounce which good is the best but to understand each good as it is in itself, in its physical complexion and its moral essence."

The quality of your essay is so unusually good, and good in the higher insights, that I should like to know more of your "other failures" [1] and of the circumstances that can have occasioned them. Why should you be unhappy with so much capacity for discernment? And I should judge that it has not been material difficulties that have stood in your way.

Yours sincerely

[1] Miss Michel's essay had been rejected when submitted for a master's degree.

To *RICHARD C. LYON*

VIA SANTO STEFANO ROTONDO, 6,
ROME, JULY 28, 1950

Dear Dick

You end your long letter, just received, with a pleasing suggestion (as ladies used to do in postscripts) which I mustn't leave unnoticed. I didn't send you Cardiff's book [1] because I was disgusted with it and have not sent it to anybody, not even to Cory.[*] When he sent me half a dozen pages, I smelt a rat at once, but didn't wish to discourage him, because the project of a selection of maxims or thoughts or epigrams had always tempted my vanity, to show the water-lilies that might be picked in the stagnant pools of philosophy. But I told him that I felt that his selections, though good, were not diversified enough: too much commonplace rationalism (when I am not a rationalist) and not enough cynicism or scepticism or psychological malice: and I gave him a sample of what I wished he would include, what Mario says about our "having to change the truth a little in order to remember it." When the book arrived I saw that the old rascal had left that out! He also represented me as merely renovating Tom Paine, instead of Thomas Aquinas! Cheap and witless criticism of religion, without all the pages of sympathetic treatment of it, for instance in "The Idea of Christ in the Gospels!" I was furious: but in time, and on looking at other parts of the book, I have reconciled myself to it somewhat. But I am delighted to hear that you have had that project in mind, for some distant future entertainment. And you, who before you had seen me, chose that passage at the end of the Dialogue on *Normal Madness,* may be relied on not to miss the strong and really radical things. And that egregious Cardiff actually quotes the last few words, which seem, alone, a melodramatic piece of verbiage, when it is all the profound philosophy (not mere

[1] *Atoms of Thought.*

[*] Cory understands most of my philosophy very well: but he doesn't want to pledge himself to it, where English academic opinion disapproves; so that sometimes he allows himself unbecoming language.

physics) of Democritus when it comes after the picture of Alcibiades winning the chariot-race at Olympia and his dismay at thinking it all dissolved into atoms. Weep, my son, if you are human, but laugh also, if you are a man.

This might lead me back to the body of your letter and the question of the moral sense. But I don't feel like going into it. I read lately in the Times Literary Supplement a review of a Scottish philosopher who maintains the mysterious absoluteness of what is "right" as distinguished from what is naturally good. I have always wondered at the aura that hangs about the word "duty." It means only *owed*. If you have pledged yourself to pay something you are bound in honour to pay it—if you can. The propriety of this conduct is obvious; but the mystic awe that hangs about "you ought" is superstitious. Very glad you are deep in French. Tell me what you are reading.

Yours

To JOHN HALL WHEELOCK

VIA SANTO STEFANO ROTONDO, 6,
ROME. AUG. 30, 1950

Dear Mr. Wheelock

Many thanks for your letter about the sales of "Dialogues in Limbo". It clears up pleasantly the only point that interested me, which is that the new edition sold well for an old book of its kind. I receive occasional evidence that here and there someone is really impressed by it as not merely a *jeu d'esprit*.

I am enjoying, in spite of the great heat of this whole summer, the sense of *relief* from responsibility at having finished my last book; [1] and I am reading (besides the papers, for instruction) Droysen's old romantic standard book [2] on Alexander the Great. He is one of my favourite heroes, a *good* one, to balance a *bad* one

[1] *Dominations and Powers.*

[2] *Geschichte des Hellenismus,* by Johann Gustav Droysen.

like Alcibiades, and if I am fit a while longer I may write something about Alexander's attempt (and moral failure) to fuse East and West. Then there has been Christianity, Byzantium, and the Moors in Spain trying the same trick with no greater success.

This being an *unnecessary* letter with which to trouble you, I will add something else of no consequence that I always forget to tell you: That in a snap-shot of myself sitting by this window, one that we both liked, you took the white streak that crosses the background diagonally for Father Tiber, a sometimes formidable stream, while it is a new street opened up by Mussolini called Via Druso which runs from the Porta Metrona, at the foot of our hill, towards the Baths of Caracalla, where now in summer they have open-air operas. And the grand horizon in my landscape is made by the *inside* of the City Walls, going in a semicircle round the higher ground that forms the south west extension of old Rome and is now not thickly built, but prevalently green as if it were the open country. It is truly classical in being on the human scale, but all inside one corner of the city.

Cory is now revising *Book Third* the Rational Order of Society (imaginary) and I believe will send it to you before he comes to Rome in the middle of October, as well as Book Second, the Militant Order, divided into "Faction" and "Enterprise".

Yours sincerely

To RICHARD C. LYON

VIA SANTO STEFANO ROTONDO, 6
ROME. SEPTEMBER 5, 1950

Dear Dick

. . . I saw a review of Green's book [1] some time ago in the Times Literary Supplement, but didn't read it, because it was apparently not an elaborate review, and I felt I should not learn

[1] *The Mind of Proust*, by F. C. Green.

anything from it. Bergson is the prophet of duration creative, and Proust the poet of duration lost, but recoverable under the form of eternity. And there is a curious substitute for the latter in Bergson's *Mémoire*. *Matière et Mémoire* I think is the best of his books, original and explorative, not sophistical like the others; and I suppose you know that there he propounds the theory, repeated in *L'Évolution Créatrice,* that all the images formed during life remain unmodified for ever as if in coloured photographs, not in the nasty brain, of course, which is only an impediment to intuition, but in MEMORY: not in the recoveries of weak and confused images of the original image, but in that image itself still bright under the layers of other images that bury it for living people as they pass to creating other different images. Now this notion of *frozen* actuality of phenomena, is a sort of bungling phenomenalistic substitute for *the truth,* which contains the essences of all past and future existences and of their historic relations, as Proust and I conceive the truth to be. Bergson hated this truth, because it is an ideal panorama of the future as well as of the past; and he had a superstitious fear of the truth about the future *compelling* creative evolution to become what it wasn't *naturally* becoming.

When I have obtained Green's book I shall be ready to tell you what I think of his identification of Proust's time lost with Bergson's *durée* or budding time. Although I think Proust, in his last volume has exactly my notion of essence, he could not have got it from me of whom he probably never heard! The dates of our respective books might prove this. What are they?

I am sending my gentle push to the Committee on the Rhodes Scholarships today under a separate envelope.

                    Yours

To GEORGE RAUH

VIA S. STEFANO ROTONDO, 6
ROME. OCTOBER 12, 1950

Dear Mr Rauh,

I find to my cost and amusement that no reporter ever reports my own words but substitutes his own lingo for my scrupulously chosen phrases. I don't know what your particular interviewer attributed to me, but I certainly never said that the U.S. were "trying" to "impose" their form of government on anybody; and what the Russians *are* trying to impose is not only their *form* of government (communism, as for instance it exists under Tito's dictatorship) but their own government as it exists in Moscow and is exercised over the Satellites by the Commintern, that plans insurrections and police governments for other nations. The American system cannot be imposed in this way because it conceives "democracy" to mean government by the majority, and respects elections fairly carried on. I think this trust in majorities is a dangerous and unjust method where there are profoundly rooted and numerous minorities (such as the Irish were under the British); but my chief divergence from American views lies in that I am not a dogmatist in morals or politics and do not think that the same form of government can be good for everybody; except in those matters where everybody is subject to the same influence and has identical interests, as in the discipline of a ship in danger, or of a town when there is a contagious disease. But where the interests of people are moral and imaginative they ought to be free to govern themselves, as a poet should be free to write his own verses, however trashy they may seem to the pundits of his native back yard. I think the universal authority ought to manage only economic, hygienic, and maritime affairs, in which the benefit of each is a benefit for all; but never the affairs of the heart in anybody. Now the Americans and UNO's way of talking is doctrinaire, as if they were out to save souls and not to rationalize commerce. And the respect for majorities instead of for wisdom is out of place in any matter of ultimate importance. It is reasonable only for settling matters of procedure in a way that causes as little friction as possible: but it is not *right* essentially because it condemns an ideal to defeat because a majority of one does not understand its excellence. It cuts off all possibility of a liberal civilization. And it is contrary to what American principles have been in the past, except in a few fanatics like Jefferson who had been caught by the wind of the French Revolution. Americans at home are now liberal about religion and art: why not about the forms of government? I mean to send you or Lawrence Butler my new book on "Dominations and Powers", when it appears, where all this is threshed out naturalistically. Glad to know that Lawrence is well.

Yours sincerely

To CORLISS LAMONT

VIA SANTO STEFANO ROTONDO, 6.
ROME. DECEMBER 8, 1950

Dear Mr. Lamont

Besides your letter of Nov. 21st, I have one from Mr. Runes regarding a new preface or note to the coming edition of your "Humanism as a Philosophy" in which you quote and comment upon a letter of mine about the different quality of your naturalism and mine, and end by placing that difference, just as I should, in the difference between your *militancy* in ethics and politics and my lack of it. That this is what distinguishes (very naturally, if you consider our respective backgrounds and interests) will become even more evident to you if you read my forthcoming book on "Dominations and Powers" where I make "The Militant Order of Society" a special section of the whole work, in contrast to the "Generative" and the "Rational" order of it. And it is precisely this distinction that determines the nature of my "Fascism" (as it existed or exists, so far as it does so at all) and the "Fascism" which seems to you and to Joel Bradford positively immoral. Because you really agree with him and not with me about this; only that as you are not willing to think me a criminal you try to deny that I am a Fascist, even in the somewhat hesitating way in which Bradford seems to call me one. And I think that your defence of me is unconvincing, because you say I am a good fellow instead of proving, as you wish, that I can't be a Fascist.

Of course I was never a Fascist in the sense of belonging to that Italian party, or to any nationalistic or religious *party*. But considered, as it is for a naturalist, a product of the generative order of society, a nationalist or religious *institution* will probably have its good sides, and be better perhaps than the alternative that presents itself at some moment in some place. That is what I thought, and still think, Mussolini's dictatorship was for Italy in its home government. Compare with the disorderly socialism that preceded or the impotent party chaos that has followed it. If you had lived through it from beginning to end, as I have, you would admit this. But Mussolini personally was a bad man and Italy a half-baked political unit; and the *militant* foreign policy adopted by Fascism was ruinous in its artificiality and folly. But internally, Italy was until the foreign militancy and mad alliances were adopted, a stronger, happier, and more united country than it is or had ever been. Dictatorships are surgical operations, but some diseases require them, only the surgeon must be an expert, not an adventurer.

Let me in turn put this question to you: Can a Humanism that is a *complete* philosophy be naturalistic? Can *human* nature be the ruling force or universal moral criterion for the universe? Can the universe have any *moral* bias? Isn't morality the proper hygiene for a reasoning animal?

This brings me back to a point you raise at the end of your letter to me about the "eulogistic" use of the word "eternal" for certain special temporal states of reasoning creatures. But to attribute an everlasting existence to any state of mind would not be eulogistic: it would be nonsense, because a state of *mind* is a process of thought, a perception or a conception that has to be called up, rearticulated, and propounded. Now, the eternity of a truth, say of the perfection of some action, or the reality of some affection, is a quality of its form, not the length of its duration; and it is not the state of mind that is eternal but the truth which it discovers. There is no doubt a regrettable play of words in this matter when "eternal" is understood to mean everlasting or self-repeating for ever. That would be tedium in excelsis. But sympathy with ideal qualities rather than with variations in one's own condition, is the "life of reason;" the *human* side of animal life.

I had not meant to write such a long letter, but the subject is an old favourite of mine. Spinoza is the clearest philosopher on the "eternal": but Aristotle is quietly sound about it. Plato too often shows that his heart is in the right place but his political preoccupations make him lean more and more, as he grows old, to popularise his myths into dogmas.

Your zeal for converting people to your views is natural in America, where democracy perhaps meant at first to give unpopular interests their chance, such as the minor religious sects, for instance, slips easily into thirst for unanimity. I hope at least it will not lead America to attempt to impose one political system over the whole world. The same methods are needed where both the ends and the means at hand are similar, but not when both are not abroad what they are at home.

Yours sincerely

To JOHN HALL WHEELOCK

VIA SANTO STEFANO ROTONDO, 6,
ROME, JANUARY 30, 1951

Dear Mr. Wheelock

Cory and I, who habitually read the Times Literary Supplement, have been much interested of late in its articles on contemporary American poetry, especially in the leader in the number for January 19 on "American Poetry Today", which reviews John Ciardi's "Midcentury American Poets."

Would you do us the favour of asking your bookselling department to send me this book, and charge it to my account?

I am, and have been for some years, particularly interested in Robert Lowell's mind and work. He is now in Italy, and spent a week or more in Rome in the autumn, when I saw him almost every day. I think that he is a good deal like Rimbaud, or like what Rimbaud might have become if he had remained devoted to his poetic genius. There are dark and troubled depths in them both, with the same gift for lurid and mysterious images: but Lowell has had more tragic experiences and a more realistic background, strongly characterised. In these London articles he is highly spoken of, and although he is not a person about whose future we can be entirely confident, it may well turn out to be brilliant.

While writing this letter I receive yours of the 26th instant, for which many thanks. I was glad to see Dr. Chen and had some good talks with him, but my cell at times became rather crowded, and oriental peace of mind was not easy to maintain. As to the corrections in my text, I am happy to believe that there will be nothing overlooked that could give offence. Of course the academic specialists, whether historians or political philosophers—not to speak of philosophers pure and simple, will find much to criticise; but I am not troubled about that. It could not be otherwise.

Yours sincerely

To WARREN ALLEN SMITH

VIA SANTO STEFANO ROTONDO, 6,
ROME, FEBRUARY 9, 1951

Dear Mr. Smith

My philosophy would have had to be prophetic if it had contained views on what you call "Naturalistic Humanism",[1] which

---

[1] Mr. Smith had written to Santayana (February 4, 1951): "I am at a loss to know what your views on naturalistic humanism might be. Neither can the faculty at Columbia University help me. All agree that *The Genteel Tradition at Bay* discussed the moral adequacy of naturalistic humanism and attacked neo-humanism; also that in the tradition of naturalistic humanism were *Lucifer; Three Philosophical Poets;* and *The Unknowable.* However, all also agree that *The Idea of Christ in the Gospels* is along the lines of theistic humanism."

seems to be a product of strictly contemporary opinion. You tell me that it is "described in Ferm's *Religion in the Twentieth Century* and supported by John Dewey, Julian Huxley, Thomas Mann, Erich Fromm and numerous liberal religionists." And you add that you have "already received comments on it by Thomas Mann, Sinclair Lewis, John Dos Passos, Henry Hazlitt, Lewis Mumford, Joseph Wood Krutch and others in the literary world." If any one of these persons has given a clear definition of "Naturalistic Humanism," I wish you had quoted it for my benefit, but I am sure it cannot be the same in them all.

In my old-fashioned terminology, a Humanist means a person saturated by the humanities: Humanism is something cultural: an accomplishment, not a doctrine. This might be something like what you call "classical humanism." But unfortunately there is also a metaphysical or cosmological humanism or moralism which maintains that the world is governed by human interests and an alleged universal moral sense. This cosmic humanism for realists, who believe that knowledge has a prior and independent object which sense or thought signify, might be some religious orthodoxy, for idealists and phenomenalists an oracular destiny or dialectical evolution dominating the dream of life. This "humanism" is what I call egotism or moralism, and reject altogether.

Naturalism, on the contrary, is something to which I am so thoroughly wedded that I like to call it materialism, so as to prevent all confusion with *romantic* naturalism like Goethe's, for instance, or that of Bergson. Mine is the hard, non-humanistic naturalism of the Ionian philosophers, of Democritus, Lucretius, and Spinoza.

Those professors at Columbia who tell you that in my *Idea of Christ in the Gospels* I incline to theism have not read that book sympathetically. They forget that my naturalism is fundamental and includes man, his mind, and all his works, products of the generative order of Nature. Christ in the Gospels is a legendary figure. Spirit in him recognizes its dependence on the Father, and not monarchical government; i.e., the order of nature; and the animal will in man being thus devised, the spirit in man is freed and identified with that of the Father. My early *Lucifer,* which you mention, has the same doctrine.

Yours sincerely

To JOHN W. YOLTON

[Mr. Yolton writes: "I had sent Santayana a reprint (with a short letter) of my discussion of *The Last Puritan* which appeared in the April 1951 issue of *The Philosophical Review*. My discussion took issue with Vivas's interpretation of the relation between Spirit and Matter in Santayana's philosophy.[1] I also mentioned in my letter that I had been a student of Van Meter Ames, since I knew that Ames had had some acquaintance with Santayana many years ago."]

6, VIA DI SANTO STEFANO ROTONDO
ROME, JUNE 30, 1951

Dear Mr. Yolton

Your "Notes" on my *Last Puritan* are remarkably friendly and sympathetic, and it has given me much pleasure to read them. Residence in Oxford seems to have already given you a softness and caution which I hardly think Professor Van Meter Ames, though he means well, could have shown in his lectures. There is only one fundamental point in your account, and *a fortiori* in the position of the other critics whom you refer to, that I should wish to correct. It is not any of the judgements you may pass on me or on my personages in the novel, but the assumption you all seem to make that what matters is the judgements I make and the standards that I proclaim, and not merely the picture of the world and its inhabitants (including myself) that I present in my writings. Mr. Vivas, if he is a Jew, may proclaim a Decalogue; and every old lady of your acquaintance may tell you what is right or wrong in everyone else: that does not seem to me to be the function of a philosopher. In my books you may easily see betrayed, frankly or unawares, what are my own tastes or preferences, or the virtues or vices of my characters in *The Last Puritan,* or in *Dialogues in Limbo;* I have decided preferences amongst persons as amongst ideas and they are not always the current preferences. That is

---

[1] See the essay by Eliseo Vivas in *The Philosophy of George Santayana* in the *Library of Living Philosophers*, Volume II.

natural when you consider the unusual circumstances of my birth and early surroundings, and American education, to which I had to react or to succumb. The *rationale* of this will become obvious to you if you consider my convictions regarding the place and essence of mind in the world. The organising and directive force in living bodies is biological, not mental: I call it the psyche, in the sense given to this word in Aristotle's *De Anima*. When such a psyche reaches its full development, it generates a hypostatic light, sensation, emotion, or images, and the whole drift of passions and thoughts. To say that I *separate* mind from matter is therefore exquisitely contrary to the fact. Nor is it in any definite sense "happiness" that crowns this development: there is a sort of happiness in the fulfilment of any natural function; but usually there is much else at work as well in the psyche, and much sacrifice and renunciation is involved in any real moral peace. It may be society in general that is given up for a particular love, or *vice versa;* or it may be a general submission of everything definite in the routine of a busy life. I do not deny that for some psyches that last may be the least of evils; but I see no reason for thinking it the compulsory duty of everybody. And the desire to do good and improve the world is the active side of the natural tendency to establish an equilibrium between oneself and the world: it may serve you; you may serve it; perhaps both things can be realised at once, and then *tutti contenti.*

I should like nothing better than to be able to discuss with you the characters in *The Last Puritan*. I could tell you much about their origin, and you could show me better than I can discover for myself, how far I have succeeded in making them real persons for my reader. They are most real persons for me, even in the circumstance of retaining a hidden and problematic side. I have been told by various ladies that my women were "impossible"; one English critic, however, wrote that Irma was the "best" (morally?) person in the book, and several that Mrs. Alden was "the living picture" of an aunt or grandmother of theirs. That the first scene in the yacht between Oliver and Jim was the most "successful" was the judgement of a good critic; and the wife of a friend, who in his yacht had given me a model for *Jim,* wrote to me that when he appeared "his person and conversation were strangely familiar". A friend, the late Professor Lyon Phelps of Yale, however, regretted not to find a single *good* character in the book. I replied that that was only because I hadn't dared to put him and his wife into it.

You may gather from this unexpectedly long letter that I appreciate your interest in my novel and in my philosophy.

Yours sincerely

To HIRSCH L. GORDON

VIA SANTO STEFANO ROTONDO, 6,
ROME, JULY 2, 1951.

Dear Dr. Gordon

It was a happy thought on your part to send me your book on Caro,[1] which I have read through with special interest, as I have never come across any such vivid picture of what the life and mind of orthodox Jews has been until recent times in Europe and the Levant. It was evidently far more severe and studious, far less a life "in the world" than that of the secular Christian clergy was during the same ages. I feel clearly for the first time how little of the "merry" life of the Middle Ages and the Renaissance affected the Jewish population. Naturally, being a minority, they could not have preserved their moral and cultural heritage if they had mingled more with the Christian majority. And they did, as you know better than I, cut a great figure as merchants, bankers, and physicians; but they must have drawn the line sharply, as Shylock does in Shakespeare, against any festive or friendly association with Christians. With Moslems things naturally went on better for both parties: the two religions were similar and simple, the observances of both less public and noisy than the Catholic, and less pagan. Even a large and intellectually influential Jewish minority did not alarm a Moslem society. The philosophers, Averroes, Avicenna, Maimonides, and Spinoza, even if sometimes too pantheistic for the orthodox of either religion, were of the same school,

---

[1] *The Maggid of Caro*, (Pardes Publishing Co. N.Y.C.).

and they kept to the scientific realism of Aristotle, avoiding the mythical and political exuberance of Plato and the Christian Fathers. Your indignation at the persecution of the Jews is natural and just: but it has not been confined to Spain or to Catholic governments or to tragic times, somewhat like our own, such as the 16th and 17th centuries. Nationalities and Great Powers were then being consolidated, as now they are being challenged and perhaps dissolved; and the need, as well as the pride, of the rulers was to have a homogenous and united people to lead and to aggrandise. In Spain, just when a single monarchy had been established and the whole territory finally reconquered, this homogeneity was particularly requisite; and the expulsion of Moors and Jews not willing to be Spanish and Catholic was a *political* necessity. You mention once, but without indicating its political ground, that only Marranos, that is Jews who had pretended to be converted, so as not to have to migrate, were subject to the Inquisition. This was, and still is, a tribunal to judge any reported heresy or moral perversion arising *within* the Catholic fold; the accused being assumed to be pledged to support Christian faith and morals. The "people" are supposed to be unanimous, as in the present Communist countries; and torture was applied, as now in those countries, to extract confessions of guilt from the accused. Nobody was condemned who had not confessed sin, and fire, following on self-accusation, was calculated to burn the corruption away. I once read the verbatim reports of the trial of the Cenci family on the charge of having murdered their husband and father. The judge would say: "the Court knows," and would retail the crime as discovered or imagined by the agents of the "Holy Office": the prisoners all began by denying and all ended by confessing; and they were condemned to various punishments: the son to be branded with hot irons and then quartered; the wife and daughter to be beheaded, and the boy to be sent to the galleys for life. Horrible glimpses of hell, by which actual endless hell was avoided. There was a sort of rationality in this religious madness; and it is impossible not to be impressed by the overwhelming force of the moral tyranny asserted to rule the world.

As to Caro, you know how entirely I agree with you on the importance of his familiar Spirit's concession that all its words are but reflections of his own thoughts. A man's past or his native potentialities are the source of such visions, revelations, or strokes of genius as he may come to have. Did these not have their roots within, in his primal Will, they would not be illuminations but information, such as he might have found in the Encyclopaedia Brittanica. But does not the *religious* importance attributed to such phenomena disappear if they do not come from above? Do not they all become poetic fictions? This implication satisfies me and seems to me to make them interesting, instead of wretched delusions, as they would otherwise be: but I am a constitutional sceptic, and wish to believe in nothing except that which, in action, I find that I am assuming and verifying. Fictions, from those involved in sensation to those generated in play and in the liberal arts, seem to me the best of things and signs, when clear and beautiful, of a life being led in harmony with nature.

Best thanks for your book and best wishes from

To *JOHN W. YOLTON*

[I am indebted to Mr. Yolton for the following explanatory note: "I wrote . . . seeking clarification upon two main points: (1) his conception of philosophy and (2) how, if at all, we can deal philosophically with moral systems (such as Nazi Germany) which seem to endanger the whole of civilization. I interpreted Santayana on the first point as saying that philosophy as he conceived it was largely descriptive and that hence from this point of view criticisms which charged Santayana with being the advocate of a passive acceptance of matter were overlooking an important point. I urged, as regards the second point, that the imposition of some sort of moral ought upon all societies seemed to be required by the present world situation. In this, I was trying to escape Santayana's tolerance of each and every moral system, viewed internally."]

VIA SANTO STEFANO ROTONDO, 6
ROME, JULY 12, 1951

Dear Yolton,

Feeling that you are a sort of unofficial pupil of mine now, I wish to answer the chief question put in your letter, which I think can be done in a few words.

There can be, I should say, no morality where there is no *nature* determining the needs, demands, and innate aspirations of living creatures.

If such a creature were the only one of his race or in his circumstances, his good or his duties could be based only on his own idiosyncrasies.

If there are many, or a close sect, of similar creatures, the assurance with which each, if alone, would have distinguished his good or duty will be vastly intensified by the herd instinct confirming and solidifying that animal assurance. This is what happens to sects and nations of all sorts.

But in society, while natural virtues are sanctified by unanimity, they are rendered sad and embarrassed by contradiction, and *arguments* are sought for persuading oneself and others that one is right and others wrong.

But this is foolish. If each knows himself he knows what is good for him by *nature,* and he must ask others, as Socrates did, to say for themselves each whether his own heart has the same voice.

My new book is out in America and I will have a copy sent to you.

Yours sincerely

To ROBERT STURGIS

VIA SANTO STEFANO ROTONDO, 6,
ROME, AUG. 18, 1951.

Dear Bob

Your great letter of some time ago introduced me (as I wrote to your mother) to a new personage. Your three visits during the war had left an unsatisfactorily vague image of your mind in mine; my deafness and your reticence (added to the fact that my contacts with the Sturgis family and yours, though both intimate, had been in different branches of it and at different dates) made it impos-

sible for me to be sure of your character. You were very imposing
and attractive as a big boy; but what would you be as an architect
or philosopher? I remember laughing at that time and repeating
what the fox in Lafontaine says to the crow: *Si votre ramage se ra-
porte à votre plumage, Vous êtes le phénix des hôtes de ce bois;*
"ramage" in my version (which may be misspelled) meaning intellect, and *"plumage"* personal charm; but the *"bois"* stands only for
my brother's descendants, which hardly make a forest.

Now at last, and not because of any flattery on my part, you
have opened your mouth and splendidly removed all my uncer-
tainties. You are a firmly-knit man, and yet, happily for you, are a
man of your exact time and place. That is as it should be in a distinct and enterprising society. So long as the Niagara you swim
with flows steadily and victoriously, though you may have some
anxious moments, you will on the whole have a glorious experience, even if you are not a distinguished leader. And on this point
I was pleased to see very ancient wisdom sprouting unexpectedly
out of your modern discipline: that you wish to work in a small
city, where your objects and your taste will be that of your townspeople, and even of your workmen. I am expecting a book on small
medieval houses in Monmouthshire which I will send you if it does
not disappoint the expections [sic] that the review I saw of it
aroused. There is an instance of social unity creating and transforming a genuine local art; and this in the architecture of the
middle ages was as mutable as it can be in America. The only question that comes to my mind is whether American life is not too uni-
form to let even a small town be original in its transformations.
And your model for the City Hall though utterly different from
the City Hall in School Street that I think I remember, belongs to
a universally emerging type, however original the details may be.
I wish you joy in this and in other competitions. I suppose so large
a work will not easily be assigned to a young architect whose hand
has not already been tested elsewhere.

Congratulations to you and Chiquita on the advent of *Su-
sanna*. She comes at the right moment. Let me extend my love and
good wishes to her also.

To JOHN W. YOLTON

[I am indebted to Mr. Yolton for the following note:
    "In my letter of August 16th I replied to his of July 12th. He had sent me by then a copy of *Dominations and Powers* which I read before replying. In this letter of mine I tried to argue that the ideal which this book presented of an international government was more than just a description on Santayana's part. Moreover, I indicated that the ideal there presented was precisely the sort of ideal we needed to make sure that moral dominations of the stultifying sort do not triumph. I tried to argue that it seemed to me that Santayana did not really wish to commit himself to the wide tolerance of literally every moral society (even those who practice moral dominations); but that he wished and needed only to combat those narrowly moralizing persons and societies who fail to see the value in any other way of life but their own. A reading of *Dominations and Powers* had convinced me that the passivity so often associated with Santayana's moral outlook was not quite genuine or accurate."]

VIA S. STEFANO ROTONDO, 6
ROME, AUGUST 20, 1951

Dear Yolton

Your second letter shows me that you are probably older, and certainly more expert in dialectic, than I assumed when I rashly volunteered to tutor you. Your insights into the implications of my various views in natural science and in morals are individually clear; but why do you think they are incompatible? My book does not pretend to be a mere description, in physics or history; it is *philosophical;* that is, it selects and compares features in both directions, as they appear from a *cosmic* point of view. Now my cosmic point of view, from which I seem to myself to discover the origins and mutual relations of these chosen facts and judgements, is naturalistic. Description therefore *envelops* the sphere of preference scientifically, as preference, in each case, must envelop all the facts that it compares. You prefer my moral apprehensions to my scientific apprehension of morals in general, including my own morals; and so my naturalism seems to you to belittle all morality. It does, inevitably, belittle it in time and space; and in my personal opinion also in dynamic importance, since in my opinion all forces are inherently physical even when they carry ideal or passionate aims. But the prenatal history of morals, or all natural history, does not belittle *morally* any of its data. If you think so you are applying an economic criterion to vital facts whose value is intrinsic. It is because our modern world is obsessed with matter and trembling at its possible revolutions (attributed to moral magic) that it clings to that other cosmic point of view—proper to Judaism and to Platonism—that it is a moral aspiration or predestination that rules the world and that our efforts can accelerate that consummation.

This tradition is conventionally dominant everywhere, so that my book, if understood as well as you understand it, must be generally condemned by the professionals. I expect that; and should become suspicious of vague or incidental compliments from the dominant quarter. But is this still *dominant* assumption still *vital?* It is in America at this moment, for patriotic and optimistic reasons. But in Europe it is otherwise, and I hope to make even many Americans aware of the natural roots of all sorts of goods and the special conditions making each sort attainable.

I should be glad to answer special questions if you like, but I think you can easily answer them for yourself.

Yours sincerely

To JOHN HALL WHEELOCK

VIA SANTO STEFANO ROTONDO, 6,
ROME, AUG. 24, 1951

Dear Mr. Wheelock

I have no recollection of your previous letter about a somewhat condensed Life of Reason. The mere idea of having to revise those five little volumes would have imprinted itself indelibly on my mind. But if the task is committed to Cory or Edman [1] it would be not only agreeable to me (because I feel a little ashamed of some characteristics of that book, which would be removed or at least acknowledged to exist) but revision would be also an advantage to the book itself, which needs much pruning. As to the choice of surgeons, for cutting out the bad things, I should prefer Cory (if he could be brought to do the work seriously) and also because the royalties which you justly think of assigning to the reviser would then go to him by right of work done as well as for the somewhat insecure heritage of my royalties in general, which in the contrary case would have to go to the real collaborator.

Edman would be a more zealous and reliable reviser: but, alas! I fear that he would retain everything I should wish removed; although to do him justice I think he would retain the good passages also. He might make—by leaving out superfluities, repetitions, and blunders only (say 500 pages) while retaining all the pragmatisms, dogmatisms, and vulgarities that I should have expunged—make a better *historical* and *biographical document* of the condensed book, representing the tone and cockiness of the 1890's. Would this less select version not do better, as a publication, than an *expurgated* version by Cory and me—for if still alive I should want to help him, and consultations with him would be easy, as they would be difficult with Edman.

Edman in any case would be the man to complete the Selections, as you propose, which would be improved by representing the later phase of my interests.

Cory now intends to come to Rome in October. If you think it worth while to suggest the abridgement of the Life of Reason to him first, please let me know. Otherwise I will try not to speak of this subject to him, as I might be tempted to do. It would be better for you to sound him, and form a judgment as to his *working capacity* if you do not in any case prefer to ask Edman, who, I am afraid, is the safer man. But he *might* decline *two* revisions, and Cory *might* wake up to do something brilliant!

Yours sincerely

[1] Irwin Edman.

To JOHN W. YOLTON

[Mr. Yolton informs me: "Replying on August 24th to his of August 20th, I still tried to argue that implicit within his own pronouncements about moral societies, about the worth of each societal mode of life, was a stronger moral assertion than Santayana was apparently willing to admit. If we accept Santayana's statements about the worth of each cultural unity, and about the evil of moral dominations, it seemed to me that we are then committed to making a distinction between good and bad moral societies. That is, a moral system would be bad when it sought to impose itself upon others. Santayana's international ideal in *Dominations and Powers* presented itself to me precisely as what was required to realize his own humanistic sentiments."]

VIA SANTO STEFANO ROTONDO, 6
ROME, AUGUST 29TH 1951

Dear Yolton

During the last few days I have not been well, or I should have answered your letter of the 24th at once; for I am interested in your getting my point of view straight, as you are perfectly able to do, no matter how unfamiliar it may be to you.

A moral system, in my opinion, cannot be "bad", since it is the good as revealed to the Primal Will which that system expresses; that is, if it is the *genuine* morality of that person or society. Jewish religion and its off-shoots are not "bad" for being militant; they have to be militant because their "good" is partly material, such as prosperity, length of life, and personal immortality; and universal domination is a "good" in that system. If it were a spiritual system the question of universal *domination* would not arise for it, because spiritual goods, like correct grammar in one language, does not interfere with goodness in the different grammar of another language.

Militancy, in other words, is not implied in the inflexibility of a moral regimen. The inflexibility comes from the *truth* with which it expresses Primal Will at home; it becomes "bad" *for an-*

other phase of Primal Will, when it attempts to legislate for that other Will abroad.

The third "Book" in *Dominations and Powers* is concerned with *rationality* in government rather than with moral rightness in precepts or ideals. Moral rightness has its credentials in nature. All life, if not all existence, has an intrinsic *direction;* it therefore evokes phantoms of good and evil according as things (or words) seem to support or impede its own *élan.* There can be no question, no possibility, of abolishing moral allegiance: only, when it breaks down in part, to get it together again *rationally,* in its own interests.

If I seem to you to be condemning militancy or unification, it is only because, in my own heart, I love *things* that have grown perfect, and hate the *ideas* that sanction the ugly impulses that come to destroy those perfections. And there is an ultimate mystical aspiration (not personally strong in myself) that would really transcend good and evil. It would not make any type of existence dominant, but all, in their perfection, coexistent, as in the realm of truth. That all evils remain unexpunged there spoils this prospect for the moral man, with his vital specific standards. But it appeases the Primal Will, which bred all those goods and evils, by the lapse of Will itself, as in Buddhism and even in Schopenhauer. I have drawn a good deal from both.

Yours sincerely

P.S. You might compare the chapter on Chivalry in my book with all this. Also the motto from the Upanishads at the beginning of the *Realm of Spirit.*

To *LAWRENCE SMITH BUTLER*

VIA SANTO STEFANO ROTONDO, 6,
ROME. 28TH SEPTEMBER, 1951

Dear Lawrence

Your account of things seen and done in Rome is too much like an obituary notice of me, the Pope, St. Peter's, and life in general. Very kind and sweet of them to be so nice to you, and of you to be so nice to them. If you were naughty like me, (and you are much younger) you would "chuckle" more and make a little fun of it all. However if you are going to print your impressions of travel and your *observations about aged friends,* it is certainly better not to chuckle, but to be always duly sensitive, appreciative, and uplifted. You *are* so, for the moment: only there is another side of things round the corner which a satirical philosopher can't help being aware of, and chuckling in consequence. . . . .

I am glad the visit to the Pope made such a pleasant impression on you. I often wonder, when I see in the Osservatore Romano, the long list of persons and crowds of pilgrims that he has received, I wonder how he can stand it. Having to say affably, to hundreds of people in turn: "Have you been long in Rome? Only two days? But you had been in Rome before? No? Well, you must hope to come again, etc, etc", would make me resign the triple tiara and become a Trappist. This Pope is wonderful at the *job:* He must be a *Job.* (chuckle).

My chronic catarrh has ceased to be only bronchial and has become gastric as well. It spoils my appetite, and I shall die of hunger at a daily banquet, like Sancho Panza, only that the viands I can't eat were never tempting. I get on on weak tea and biscuits (as Cory calls my fare): but the tea has plenty of milk in it, and the biscuits include shortbread, sent to me from Limerick by Mother Ambrose, our former head here.

Your old friend

To RICHARD C. LYON

VIA SANTO STEFANO ROTONDO, 6,
ROME, NOV. 11, 1951

Dear Dick,

It is a relief, as well as a positive pleasure, to hear that you are happily settled in Clare College [1] and that England has not rubbed you the wrong way. Your early thoughts of becoming a clergyman may have prepared the soil somewhat for the seeds of Anglican culture to fall on favourable ground. It doesn't seem to surprise you, as it did Professor Northrop of Yale (with whom I have been having some correspondence) that people's minds should be aware of a historic past. Apropos of that I have read somewhere that past and future (and things remote generally) *must* be driven from a mind wholly absorbed in present events. It is a pity, because then they can hardly see those events justly. The wider background produces that serenity which you notice in English views. And I am glad that Clare pleases you architecturally. As to the change in your studies, I see a good side in it. Locke is not a great philosopher, but he had a great influence and cannot be overlooked. Observe in particular how he shifts the meaning of the word idea from a clear and distinct image of Descartes, or "given essence", to a passing perception. The false assumption that a passing perception *is* a clear and distinct unit of existence passes to Berkeley and Hume, and makes the verbal atomism of the present day possible in England. It has no hold elsewhere, as far as I know.

As to Leibniz and especially Spinoza for you next year, I don't think them at all out of place. On the contrary they are all the more necessary for you, as classics, on the highroad of speculation, in that you have no Latin and Greek. The English and German philosophy that we have become accustomed to is not normal. They are both, though differently, subjective, and therefore on a by-path in nature, the English being only literary psychology or autobiography and the German moralistic mythology. Leibniz's

[1] Cambridge University.

Theodicy is an intelligent abstract of Christian doctrine, exhibiting what it would be if it were essentially scientific, whereas it is essentially moralistic, so that its inspiration is missed, while its dogmas are harmonised as much as possible: Spinoza does much the same thing for the natural universe. He misplaces nothing, but draws it all in purely intellectual concepts. He is a great master.

There is a man at Oxford, named Yolton [1] who has written to me about some points to be cleared up in my views. He is to write the review of Dominations & Powers in "Mind". If you hear anything about him (he is an American) I should like to know it. Cory tells me that he belongs more or less to the verbal set. [2]

I hope you are making friends: it is a great help to acclimating oneself in a new country; and I send you a Xmas present to help you feel a little freer during your holidays. I have not been very well this year, but the changes are not important on the whole and I feel the relief of not having a book to finish.

Yours

To MRS. DAVID LITTLE

VIA SANTO STEFANO ROTONDO, 6,
ROME. 25 NOV. 1951,

Dear Rosamond

Christmas is approaching and I am writing to Mr. Wheelock of Scribner's asking him to send you my prosaic present, as on recent years he has been kind enough to do. Don't send me flowers, as they are rather wasted in my little room, which is crowded with books and tables and not meant as a stage setting for poetry and philosophical vistas, as ideally it should be. But many years ago I gave up all dreams of finding beautiful quarters and surroundings.

[1] Professor John W. Yolton of Princeton.

[2] [I don't recall having said this to Santayana, but if it is misleading, I apologise to Professor Yolton.]

They would prove more a burden and a tether than a stimulus to pleasant thoughts. Possessions, when I was younger were a nuisance for one who wanted to travel, and in time to return regularly to a fixed circle of chosen places, easily reached, as were Rome, Venice and Cortina; and now that I am in the last stage of my journey what I enjoy without qualification is to read, especially history. I have just finished (in three days, as if it were an exciting novel) a long book [1] by a man named Brandon on the destruction of Jerusalem in A.D.70, and its effect upon Christianity, which he thinks was decisive. And the excursuses in Toynbee, which I had skipped on first reading his six volumes, are better than his text, and almost inexhaustible. You travel all over the world and through all ages without leaving your den. This is what most of the critics of my "Dominations & Powers" evidently never do, for I notice that they are blind to everything except current events and current questions, as if they could have any true vision of such things if they were ignorant altogether of the world in which these things arise and pass away. Another, but perfectly normal difficulty that my critics have is that they don't know my philosophy, which is not an arbitrary "creation" of my fancy but simply the result or sediment left in my mind by living. For that reason I am compelled to imply and to illustrate it in all I say about anything; so that if they have a different philosophy or no philosophy laid up in their minds, of course they cannot see how what I say hangs together. A critic who has seen this is Oakeshott [2] in the London *Spectator*.

My health is naturally getting worse and worse along the old lines, and, by the way, I *should* like one or two more of those Benzedrex Inhalers that you mention. They help to check the flow of my catarrh at certain troublesome moments.

With love and Xmas wishes for all the family from

[1] *The Fall of Jerusalem,* by S. G. F. Brandon.
[2] Professor Michael Oakeshott.

To CORLISS LAMONT

VIA SANTO STEFANO RODONDO, 6.
ROME. 28 NOVEMBER, 1951

Dear Mr. Lamont,

I have not reread my "Three Philosophical Poets" for many years, perhaps never as a whole since its day, and I don't know what I would say about the book now. But there is one qualm, or sense of guilt, that has sometimes come over me regarding the treatment of the third poet, Goethe. Professor Norton, at Harvard, when he spoke to me, of course very gently, about it, once added: "But why did you choose Goethe for your third poet?" and the sadness of his voice warned me that I had done "very wrong." There was, he said, more and better philosophy in Shakespeare: "Poor ruined choirs where late the sweet birds sang." I have often tried to define Shakespeare's "philosophy," after noticing the strange absence of religion in him; but perhaps he might be set down for a Humanist or Naturalist of our sect, his ghosts and witches and Ariels being wise, sceptical inclusions of mad dreams actually visiting distracted minds. But as to Goethe I remember that I excused myself to Norton by saying that the sworn allegiance to Life, bring it what it may bring, was a romantic philosophy, justifying egotism which the Germans had really made into a philosophy. I never liked this "totalitarian" love of life of all sorts; but there it was pictured in Faust, also in Hegel and Nietzsche; and I had felt that I must try to do it justice.

I afterwards really tried to do it justice in "Egotism in German Philosophy," especially in the second edition with its epilogue; but when I wrote the "Three Philosophical Poets" I had not got to the bottom either of the animal courage or of the irrational obedience to impulse that romantic passion implies and lives out dramatically. I was therefore a bit embarrassed in presenting Goethe as a great spokesman for an inferior cause, not wishing to dishonour the great man that everybody at that time seemed to exalt. It was an embarrassment due to my still too foreign view of Goethe, taking him superficially, in order not to seem prejudiced against him. I remember my friend Strong saying, when we were talking about this, that Goethe's morality turned out altogether inferior to Dante's. I agreed; but I had not clearly perceived, or dared to assert, that it was so, when I wrote the book.

Is the American attitude to the world today the same as Faust's at the end of the second part, when he colonizes the Dutch or Flemish coast? I wonder. I should be sorry to think so.

Yours sincerely

To IRA D. CARDIFF

VIA SANTO STEFANO ROTONDO 6
ROME, DEC. 16, 1951

Dear Mr. Cardiff:

It was very kind and friendly of you to send me this cablegram with congratulations on my 88th birthday. In theory, I hardly think it deserves congratulations, at least not in the opinion of Ecclesiastes and other old fogeys with whom I should like to be numbered. But in my exceptional case the usual illusions of youth and disappointments and crotchets of old age have, I think, been reversed in a great measure. I was solitary and in opposition to my surroundings when I was a boy, and now I feel that the world and I, though both far from sound in body, understand one another and that it would be absurd to have expected and demanded that we should have been perfect. I am perfectly ready, however, and entirely willing to part company with the world, as it enormously is in regard to me; so that a sort of satisfaction in comic absurdity on our respective parts seems to reconcile us to have been and to be what we are and to part company. I am not in good health, but my uncomfortable moments are occasional only, and my general mood cheerful and filled with interesting public and literary events. Therefore I accept your congratulations with thanks, and corresponding good wishes.

To CORLISS LAMONT

VIA SANTO STEFANO ROTONDO. 6
ROME. DEC. 19, 1951

Dear Mr. Lamont

Your long cablegram [1] with its picture of your philosophic circle listening while you read my afterthoughts about Goethe's Faust and sending me their congratulation on being 88 years old, was very pleasant and unexpected. In general I should agree with Ecclesiastes and other old fogeys that living after eighty is not a blessing; but in my case I cannot complain of misery or decrepitude of a moral kind. My little ailments are physical and quite endurable, and I was less fortunate in my early youth than in my late old age. The world has grown steadily kindlier and more interesting to me (though less satisfied with itself) and my mind less *dépaysé* than it felt itself at first. I never expected to have much support from my contemporaries; but now that I have survived most of them I find ample sympathy, if not agreement from many quarters, and also much more to attract and absorb me in the history of the past. It is history rather than philosophy that I read now with satisfaction. It is often, if not always, tragic, but it is a rich and varied dramatic spectacle; and how should natural existence be anything else?

Yours sincerely,

[1] To George Santayana   Cable, Dec. 16, 1951
"By chance today read aloud your thoughtful letter about THREE PHILO-SOPHICAL POETS to a group of enlightened spirits, old and young. Then we discovered it was your 88th birthday and send this message of sincere greetings and warm congratulations, feeling it a high privilege to be in contact with one of the greatest minds in the philosophic Pantheon."

Corliss Lamont

To MRS. THEODORE W. RICHARDS

VIA SANTO STEFANO ROTONDO, 6
ROME, FEB. 7TH, 1952

Dear Mrs Richards:

You are much nearer in Cambridge now than I am to "happy snowflakes dancing" and even to my beautifully edited "Essays", which I had never heard of. My memory for current minor events is much worse than for incidents in my life in the 1890's, which seem to be, in retrospect, the vital period in it. Someone may have written to me for my consent to collect these "Essays" of which you tell me. I should naturally have consented; but I have forgotten the matter altogether. But not long ago a visitor brought me a copy of "The Sense of Beauty" to autograph, and I was dazzled by the size and elegance of my first-born little girl. This is not the case with all my progeny, some being very shabby and others buried; but I have had the satisfaction of seeing my favourite child, "Dialogues in Limbo" reappearing in its original type, with additions perfectly prepared to suit. And Scribner is planning an abridged edition of "The Life of Reason", in one volume, which will be made by my friend and occasional secretary, Mr Daniel Cory, and which I perhaps may not live to see.

Your name and your letter instantly turned my thoughts to Mrs Toy, who so often and so affectionately used to speak of you. Her letters in her later years, and what I heard about her, which was very little, left a rather sad impression, as if her health and spirits suffered in solitude from the absence of the duties and pleasures of her former life. This was not a matter on which I could speak sympathetically, solitude being for me a sort of liberty realized; but of course it could not have been so unless I had a private picture gallery of friends and places in my head, to be revisited always with increased pleasure.

It amuses me to read in the papers sometimes that I am now a recluse. It is accidentally a literal truth, because I seldom go about, on account of my bad sight and hearing, which makes crossing the city traffic dangerous; but I was never more conscious (or studious) of what goes on in the world, and there is nothing monastic about my daily life, in spite of living in a nursing home where the sisters are nuns. But I see only one of them, the housekeeper, often, and almost all my visitors bring the air of free (but now preoccupied) America with them.

Best wishes and thanks for your kind letter,

To *JOHN HALL WHEELOCK*

VIA SANTO STEFANO ROTONDO, 6,
ROME. 23RD FEBRUARY, 1952

Dear Mr. Wheelock

Some time ago I heard of Mr. Scribner's [1] death, and what you tell me gives me more reasons for regretting this loss to us all. I seem to have laid my social as well as philosophical eggs twenty or thirty years, systematically, before they were hatched. Those, like you and Mr. Scribner, who ventured to read and publish my "Sense of Beauty" [2] when I wrote it, have never seen me alive; I vanished into another sphere before I became distinguishable. And my books, when supposed to represent a new phase, regularly contain my discoveries of the previous decade or even century. By the way, Cory and I have both been surprised to find "The Life of Reason" so much like my latest views. The difficulty will be to choose the out-of-date passages. He is very much interested in the work and has already revised it all in a cursory way. I have stopped before the last volume, having fallen a victim of influenza on top of my double catarrh. But he will be able and happy to do everything himself. . . .

Yours sincerely

[1] Charles Scribner, III, the President of Charles Scribner's Sons.
[2] First published by Scribner's in 1896.

To RICHARD C. LYON

VIA SANTO STEFANO ROTONDO, 6,
ROME, MARCH 9TH 1952

Dear Dick

I was glad to have direct news of you after an interval that seemed the longer to me because I was ill and idle having caught the influenza from Sister Angela and Maria [1] and Dr. Sabbatucci who have been or are still down with it. But I am decidedly better now and counting on the Spring weather of which we have had some signs already. I have finished all that I mean to do about the revision and abridgement of *The Life of Reason*, leaving the rest to Cory, who is quite absorbed in it. I am therefore quite free to read and write as the spirit may move.

About Hume and your work in general at Cambridge I am too old to follow the new fashions that have set in lately in England, especially as it may be fifty years since I have opened a book of Berkeley or Hume, and they never seemed to me to belong, as the English think, to the main line of philosophy, but to a loop-line called subjectivism, and limited, in appeal, to the Protestant and romantic movements. What I hear of the present "logical realism" [2] from Cory (who is obliged by his fellowship to write an essay or two every year about it) seems to me to be a radical form of it "giving it away", and reducing it to verbal dialectics. Meantime I have a great esteem for both Berkeley and Hume in their personal dispositions and temper, each in a different way. I think you have read my paper on Berkeley: [3] but in regard to Hume I think I have written nothing. But as a man of the world and a historian he felt as I do, and was not subjective or negative at all. (I say "negative" rather than "sceptical" because he was a sceptic in official philosophy but a naturalist in his real convictions.) The quotations you make from him illustrate this: also a recent remark of Bertrand Russell in talk with Cory, that Hume had no right to use the word

---

1 A chamber-maid in the clinic.

2 Santayana must have meant "logical positivism."

3 "Bishop Berkeley." See *Triton Edition*, Vol. 7, p. 75–88.

"impression" for his fundamental facts, because that implies contact with an external agent. All "knowledge" does; dialectic and deduction only elaborate ideas: what the Germans now call "Problematik".

As to your holidays, you must trust your own impulse and the circumstances. When I travelled at your age I was always alone and bent on seeing Cathedrals; for that the north of France would be better than the south. And to drink in the spirit of a place you should be not only alone but not hurried. And a *real* friend, if a foreigner, is a better stimulus and revelation than any sight-seeing.

Send me postcards when you are actually travelling and gathering *"impressions"*.

To MRS. DAVID LITTLE

VIA SANTO STEFANO ROTONDO, 6,
ROME. MARCH 16, 1952

Dear Rosamond

The little parcel with its three little bundles of breakfast foods arrived safely the day before yesterday; but I wanted, before reporting progress to try at least two of them. They go equally well. The truth is that my palate is not sensitive and the conditions in this Irish-Italian establishment are not those of an American "cafeteria", such as the one in the little corner of the barbershop where, in my last years at Harvard I used to have a stand-up breakfast before going to my 11 o'clock lecture. All that, although I felt at the time that I was living in a railway station, now seems a sort of magic transformation scene, where things, if you knew how to take them, as I then did, all fitted perfectly together. I used to have lunch, after that lecture, either at the Faculty Club or at the Harvard Union, always at 12.30 (when the service began, and there were few people) tea in my rooms in Prescott Hall, and dinner at my Mother's with Josephina, my sister (for my Mother was then bedridden) or at some Italian restaurant in town, preferably the

Napoli, in the North End. Those impressions of my last years in Boston have somehow remained more vivid than my earlier, more social life.

. . . Work is definitely over: but I have several disciples or correspondents who keep me awake to the questions that they discuss now in philosophical schools, mostly verbal, as they seem to me: and my two daily papers give me the very interesting political news of these chaotic times. America takes the lead now with great courage, and we all hope for the best.

Yours affectionately

To RICHARD C. LYON

VIA SANTO STEFANO ROTONDO, 6
ROME, MARCH 16, 1952

Dear Dick

Don't worry about what I may have said about scepticism or about agreeing or disagreeing with me. In any case the distinction you make is evidently reasonable, although scepticism as a method, especially if only a temporary method, as in Descartes, is not a system of philosophy or morals whereas openness of mind and distrust of one's own opinion is a moral habit. Whether it involves, as you say, the *doctrine* that reality is unknowable depends on the definition given to "knowledge". *Certainty* about *transitive* beliefs is impossible; but awareness of a pain is not an opinion but a feeling not intrinsically asserting that something not a pain is hurting you; although animal instinct will lead you to look for what that possible cause may be; and examination may prove that it was a pebble; although this opinion, too, being transitive, may be wrong. You may find that it was "really" a hazel-nut or a button. Yet the "knowledge" so acquired, though intrinsically self-transcendent and therefore *perhaps* wrong, is scientifically reached and, if you trust memory and reason, is an approach to the reality: the pain *was really* caused by a small round hard object in your shoe.

I don't remember now what I wrote, in my letter, about Hume's scepticism; I think perhaps I ought to have been a historian rather than a philosopher talking about essences, for verbal logic doesn't hold my attention or respect, and I must turn to something imaginable. But I do believe in the incapacity of images or concepts to fathom or "explain" reality. Matter, or if you prefer, Wind, is not exhaustively representable in Spirit (which is an *original music* made by the Wind) but Spirit being secondary and an approximate index to the way the Wind is blowing in one place at a certain time, Spirit knows a lot about the ways of the Wind. The Hebrews were wise and prudent in speaking about the "ways" of the Lord, rather than of his nature.

The sketch I wrote about *The Wind and the Spirit* for Sir James Marchant's book on "What I Believe", which should have appeared about Xmas, 1950, has not yet turned up. But, when I made inquiries, they evidently thought I was impatient for my share of the profits, and sent me £20, saying the book would appear "shortly"—about a year ago. And I haven't a clean corrected copy of the text, nor the wit at present to rewrite it!

Best wishes for thesis from

To CHAUNCEY STILLMAN

VIA SANTO STEFANO ROTONDO, 6
ROME, MARCH 26, 1952

Dear Mr. Stillman

Your name, which was well known in the Harvard of the late 1890's (doubtless your father's) and the many others of my friends that you mention have naturally caused one of those frequent reversions of my memory to the circle that was at the "Gashouse" [1] during my second, and more agreeable, college life. I see, by refer-

---

[1] The Delta Phi Club of Harvard. See *The Middle Span*, Chap. V, "Younger Harvard Friends", for Santayana's inimitable explanation of the origin of the more popular name—"The Gashouse."

ring to the Delphic Club Catalogue that you were in the Class of
'29, and I wonder that I was so well remembered at the Club after
so many years. As to the inscription on my pewter mug I can explain it to myself after a little thought, because Boylston Beal, who
got it and had it engraved for me, was not so versed in Spanish her-
aldry as in English or even German. For some reason he seemed to
be less at home in Spain and even in France than in England and
Italy, and also in Germany, where we spent the winter of 1888 in
the same boarding-house. My full name in Spanish is sufficiently
absurd: *Jorge Agustín Nicolás Ruiz de Santayana y Borrás,* but
Boylston, in his zeal to miss nothing put in the "la" beside the "de"
and got them in the wrong place. I don't remember ever noticing
that the inscription was queer; probably I never read it as the mugs
were not often used. Let me apologize for accusing you for the joke,
if we say it must have been one.

Just now, while I am writing this letter, one of the Sisters has
come in bearing a huge parcel which turns out to be your present
of handkerchiefs, worthy of a royal bride. They are too superior
for my wardrobe, but at the same time very opportune, as catarrh
is my chief disease. I will use them and try to live up to that degree
of perfection. At least they will succeed in taking me back for a
moment to the pleasantest memories of my youth.

I have now given up all literary work and devote myself to
reading, especially history, which I ought to have done before writing philosophy, or at least moralizing about human life. And history is what the learned men of today are best able to write. They
are free (some of them) from moral or political preconceptions, and
scrupulous about the truth, which they can find in history, but
hardly in anything else.

Your kindness to me surprises me so much that I hardly know
what to say by way of thanks—

Yours sincerely

To ALAN DENSON

ROME. APRIL 20, 1952

Dear Mr. Denson

As to the letter addressed by me to "A.E." about Mother Nature,[1] I shall be gratified if you think it worth publishing in your book about him.

I have written too many books: "he writes, and writes and writes!" exclaimed the reviewer of my last one in The Times Literary Supplement. It is not strange if many of them are out of print.

That is not the case, however, with "Three Philosophical Poets" published by the Harvard University Press some forty years ago, since I get a yearly cheque from them for royalties. "Platonism & the Spiritual Life" was published by Constable, and doubtless he does not think it safe to make a reprint. They may have some stray copy at Scribner's in New York, and I am asking them, in that case, to send it to you, as well as a copy of the "Three Poets" which I am pleased to be able to add to your list and hope that your young friend will like the parts on Lucretius and Dante. The part on Goethe is not written with the same real enthusiasm.

Yours sincerely

To WINFRED OVERHOLSER, M.D.

VIA SANTO STEFANO ROTONDO, 6,

ROME, APRIL 20. 1952.

Dear Dr. Overholser

I shall be very glad to see you and Mrs. Overholser again, and hope you will carry out your project of another journey to Rome.

It is not a surprise to see my first sonnet, of 1884, raised to a

[1] See Letter [September 22, 1933]

sort of monument in a Unitarian temple. I was twenty years old and given to pious language; but the real inspiration of that sonnet was something that Unitarian respectability would not approve of. It was Dionysiac revels. The second line, of which the rest is merely a conventional development (with reference to Columbus, as inspired by "faith", really of the enterprising earthly kind) that caused it to be adopted for religious popular calendars and other innocent means of edification. That second line [1] was a loose translation of four words in a chorus in the Bacchae of Euripides: τὸ σοφὸν οὐ σοφία.[2] I often use this as a motto when giving someone my autograph. But the sonnet never expressed my own conclusions, and in the sequence of my early poems, published in 1894, I introduced it by two others as a starting point from which I had very willingly departed. But I am pleased to have done some good at least in my immaturity.

Yours sincerely

To JOHN W. YOLTON

VIA SANTO STEFANO ROTONDO, 6
ROME, APRIL 27, 1952

Dear Mr. Yolton

You were very good to send me the number of the Columbia Philosophical Journal [3] chiefly devoted to comments on my recent book, including your own article. I have at once read this, and most of the others, and my general impression is of the great difference in interest and taste that separates American feeling now from me, due doubtless to my advanced age and to the excited and absorbing sentiment that the political anxiety of the moment naturally pro-

---

[1] "It is not wisdom only to be wise . . ."

[2] Literally, *wisdom overmuch is not wisdom.*

[3] *The Journal of Philosophy* (March 27, 1952) contained various reviews of Santayana's book *Dominations and Powers*. One of the contributors was Mr. Yolton. See his article "The Psyche as Social Determinant".

duces in the United States. You are less affected (as I gathered long ago from your letters) than most of the others by this preoccupation, and yet I seem to see traces of it, not so much in what you say as in the omission of a point in my view of rational government which I regard as important: the idea of "moral societies". Individual psyches are surely the only seat of synthesis for political ideas; but these ideas are largely diffused and borrowed in their expression and especially in the emotion or allegiance that they inspire. Religion, especially, is traditional. In conceiving of a Scientific Universal Economy, with exclusive military control of trade, I expressly limited its field of action to those enterprises in which only economic interests and possibilities were concerned. Education, local government, religion, and laws regarding private property, marriage and divorce, as well as language and the arts, were to be in the control of "moral societies" possessed of specific territories. These would be governed in everything not economic, by their own constitutions and customs. Of course sentiment and habits would be social in these societies. Children would all be brought up to expect and normally to approve them; but any individuals rebelling against their tribe would be at liberty to migrate, and to join any more congenial society that would take them in, or remain in the proletariat, without membership in any "moral society". My view is that civilizations should be allowed to be different in different places, and the degree of uniformity or variety allowed in each would be a part, in each, of its constitutional character. It would by no means be expected that every person would lead a separate life. What I wish to prevent is the choking of human genius by social pressure.

Yours sincerely,

To JOHN W. YOLTON

[I am again indebted to Mr. Yolton for the following note:
"I replied to his of April 27th. Still seeking to come to grips with the problem of moral dominations, I raised the query: Can we

with philosophical justification allow to exist any and every sort of moral society, even those in which it is part of the accepted practice to prevent individual members from transferring out? I wondered whether we were not just as guilty of choking natural human genius by refusing to put an end to such moral militancy, as we would be by trying to impose our own way of life upon another?"]

VIA SANTO STEFANO ROTONDO, 6
ROME, MAY 2ND 1952

Dear Mr. Yolton

Argument has never been, in my opinion, a good method in philosophy, because I feel that real misunderstanding or difference in sentiment usually rests on hidden presuppositions or limitations that are irreconcilable, so that the superficial war of words irritates without leading to any agreement. Now in your difficulty with my way of putting things I suspect that there is less technical divergence between us than divergence in outlook upon the world. And I am a little surprised that you should attribute to official America today an ambition to *prevent* Russia from establishing labour-camps, etc. All that I should impute to American policy is that it *fears* the eventual spreading of Russian methods over the whole world. This is what the Russians mean to do, and gives a good reason for resisting, not for abolishing, them; which last, as far as I know, nobody intends. And it is what people intend or actually do that interests me, not what they think they or others ought to do. Therefore in my books, at least in the mature ones, I am not *recommending* a rational system of government but at most considering, somewhat playfully, what a *rational* system would be. And in considering this, I come upon the distinction between the needs and the demands of various human societies. The needs and the extent or possible means of satisfying them are known or discoverable by science. So medical science may prescribe *for all persons* the operations, cures, or diets that it discovers to conduce to health. And so, I say, economic science might discover how best territories may be exploited and manufactures produced, in so far as they are needed or prized. There should therefore be a rational universal control of trade, as of hygiene; and both involve safety for persons and their belongings. The police, communications and currency should be universal and international; and the limits of wages and profits in all economic matters should be equitably determined by economic science. There could therefore be no strikes, monopolies, labour-camps or capitalists, and a scientific communism would reign in most of the things that now cause conflicts in government and between nations. But the justification for this autocracy in the economic sphere would be that only [indecipherable word] the *force-majeure* of nature imposed on mankind in their ignorance; whereas, imposed by doctors of science, it would prevent all avoidable distress and unjust distribution of burdens.

With this foundation laid in justice and necessity all races, nations, religions, and liberal arts would be allowed to form "moral societies" having, like "Churches" among us now, their special traditions and hierarchies and educational institutions. Each would have an official centre, as the Catholic Church has the Vatican, but need not have any extensive territory. I am always thinking of the East where great empires have always existed, controlling in a military and economic way a great variety of peoples, and preserving a willing respect for their customs. It does not occur to me to say whether cruel institutions should be suppressed from outside if odious to other peoples. Violence, in any case, would be impossible, since that could be exercised, in the name of Nature, only by the rational universal economic authorities, and all the "moral societies" would be unarmed. They would not be able to prevent rebels within their society to leave it; nor would they be compelled to unite or compromise with any other moral society. They might mingle as Jews, Moslems and Christians mingle in the East when they have a good impartial government, such as Alexander planned to establish and the Romans and in a measure the Moslems have sometimes carried on.

I suspect that you naturally think of "moral" passions as guiding governments and instigating wars. You expect "ideologies" to inspire parties, and parties to govern peoples. All that seems to me an anomaly. And it is not the intellectual or ideal interests invoked that really carry on the battle, but the agents, the party leaders, who have political and vain ambitions. Mohammed was a trader before he decided to be a Prophet, dictated to by the Archangel Gabriel; and it is already notorious that in Russia the governing clique lives luxuriously and plans "dominations" like so many madmen. It is human: and the gullibility of great crowds when

preached to adroitly or fanatically enables the demagogues to carry
the crowd with them. There would be no "communists" among
factory hands if they knew their true friends.

I have nothing to do now, having decided that I must write
nothing more to be published, and I have run on in this letter out of
habit. Probably I have not said anything that will answer your objections, but I value your opinion and think you would be less
puzzled by me if you saw how different my *Weltanschauung* was
from that of modern politicians.

Yours sincerely

TO MRS. DAVID LITTLE

VIA SANTO STEFANO ROTONDO, 6,
ROME. JUNE 20, 1952

Dear Rosamond

I have been laid up by an accident for the last fortnight, which
came near costing me my life, but actually broke no bones and
seems now to have left no traces. I had gone one morning to renew
my passport at the Spanish Consulate, where I was served atten-
tively and quickly (I am becoming known in Spain) and had got
down almost to the bottom of the stairs when suddenly my head
swam or my foot slipped and I fell backwards on the (artificial)
marble steps. I saw that I had fallen, but in the effort to get up, lost
consciousness altogether. When I came to (it must have been some
minutes later) I was being carried by a lot of strange men into my
taxi. The chauffeur's round face and yellow rain-coat was all I
could recognize, peering at me through the opposite window. He
must have been fetched, since they are not allowed to wait in that
narrow ancient street: *Via Campo Marzio*. Four other men from
the Consulate, and the office boy outside, packed the taxi, and we
started on what seemed to me a strange and long way to this establishment. I was panting for breath, but hardly conscious of what
was going on.

Once lying on the couch in my room, where they had doubtless given me some strong injections, I felt at home and not in pain except in changing position or being pressed where I had been bruised, on the left shoulder and ribs, and on the back of my head, where the bruise as I was surprised to see had bled profusely over my collar and shirt. It was there, I began to understand, that the well-dressed man (probably the vice consul) who had been holding me up in the carriage, had been staunching the wound all the way from the consulate.

The Sisters told me, some days after, that the Spanish officials had said that they were in charge of everything, and I suppose went back to town in the same taxi and paid the chauffeur in full. They also telephoned later to learn how I was getting on. There is no doubt that they were most attentive, and yesterday I finally wrote a Spanish letter to the consul to make the best acknowledgements that I could think up. . . .

Yours affectionately

TO MRS. DAVID LITTLE

[ROME] JULY 22, 1952

Dear Rosamond

Your 4 parcels of rice-cereals arrived today, just when my supply was about to fail. Thank you very much.

You will perceive by this short letter that something else is beginning to fail me, namely my eyes, and reading is even harder than writing, so that it will be hard for me to do anything but compose old-fashioned verses.

It had already been enthusiasm for a poem [1] of Lorenzo de Me-

---

1 The poem in question was *Ambra*. Unfortunately Santayana did not live long enough (he died on September 26 of the year of this letter) to complete his English version of *Ambra* to his full satisfaction. One of his last remarks to me expressed his keen regret that he did not have time to polish the stanzas sufficiently for publication.

dici that had overtaxed my eyesight in making an alternative English version of it. At least I have something to balance my imprudence in 23 stanzas in *ottava* rima, making a complete partly original work: my last! For everyone tells me, that I am almost dead. It is more than tolerable in spite of the heat.

I must stop scrawling, although I have various other things that I should like to tell you.

Yours affectionately

INDEX

INDEX